Shoshana Alexander

In Praise of
Single Parents

*Mothers and Fathers
Embracing the Challenge*

HOUGHTON MIFFLIN COMPANY

Boston   New York

1994

Copyright © 1994 by Shoshana Alexander

All rights reserved

For information about permission to reproduce selections from
this book, write to Permissions, Houghton Mifflin Company,
215 Park Avenue South, New York, New York 10003.

Library of Congress Cataloging-in-Publication Data

Alexander, Shoshana.
In praise of single parents : mothers and fathers embracing the
challenge / Shoshana Alexander.
p. cm.
Includes bibliographical references.
ISBN 0-395-57436-6 (cl.)   ISBN 0-395-66991-X (pbk.)
1. Single parents — United States. I. Title.
HQ759.915.A44 1994
306.85'6'0973 — dc20   94-2063   CIP

Printed in the United States of America

AGM 10 9 8 7 6 5 4 3 2 1

Printed on recycled paper

Book design by Anne Chalmers

The poem in Chapter 11 is used with the author's permission.

To my son, Elias,
without whom this book could not have begun

To my mother, Carol Berry,
without whom it could not have been completed

To the friends who have sustained us,
especially Sypko Andreae

And to all single parents
and their children

Acknowledgments

No one can be a single parent, and likewise, no one can alone bring a book to completion. I am deeply grateful to the many whose participation and support over the past three and a half years have made both endeavors possible for me.

The single parents and their children who told their stories for this book have been my teachers and my inspiration. Whether directly included here or not, each has made a substantial contribution. In all but a couple of situations where composites are used, these stories are of real people — the majority identified by their own first names — openly sharing their lives.

It is impossible to adequately thank, or mention here, all those who have sustained me emotionally, intellectually, and practically during the course of this work. Sypko Andreae and Carolyn Shaffer have functioned like a duo of ministering angels. Carolyn often served as midwife to my spirit, generously offering her skill and time even in the midst of deadlines for her own book. Sypko has been friend, benefactor, dedicated assistant, and technical adviser, willingly helping with the entire range of support from taking care of Elias to supplying a computer and printer on lifetime loan.

Each chapter seemed to require a passage in my own life. I am deeply grateful to Ken Fox, Sharon Koukkari, Laurinda Gilmore, and Jill Breckenridge for their skill and their wise guidance in helping me to "turn myself inside out." Ken, Sharon, and Laurinda were generous of heart and time, and fearless in leading me toward where I had to go. Jill's insights into the writing process made it possible to continue to the end.

My family of friends at Harwood House in Oakland, California, nurtured me through long, often frantic months of being both rat and researcher. In particular, I thank Laurinda Gilmore, Sandia Siegel, Max Lan, Jasmine Parker, Wes and Rose Nisker, Ted Graves, Mike Reid, and David Graves. I am especially grateful to Laurinda, who taught me and an entire household that at the root of friendship and family is the courage to love with both honesty and heart. Special thanks to Will Smolak, John Steere, and Ted Aransky for joining her to subsidize my office space for several months, and to the Bodhi Brothers, Allan Cooper, and Oscar Valentinuzzi.

Many other friends enabled this work to continue. I am especially grateful to Virginia Mudd for her unwavering faith in the book and the inspiration of her caring, and to Gair and Rick Crutcher, godparents to Elias, for their genuine friendship and commitment to the truth. I also thank Tory Mudd and Maria Florio for hospitality and for getting us beyond the mountains; Janet King, Suzanne Harris, Cory Jackson, Faye Miller, Lois Meisch, Gayle Weber, Amy Fates, Gene and Sue Berry, and Frank and Lisa Berry for their kindness; Stephan Brown and Mary Anna Maloney for arranging our stay at Shenoa Retreat Center; and Ellen, Dennis, and Andy Wood and the staff at Shenoa for embracing us as family.

The members of my women writers' group listened and encouraged me to speak from the marrow. Barbara Austin expertly guided me through the process of structuring a chapter and dedicated many hours to this book. Jane Staw's incisive comments hit the core of each chapter, and her questions put my intellect in service to my heart. Helen Page's reflections and her generous ear carried me through a long winter. Nina Ham's insights as a psychologist deepened the material and moved me from ship to shore. Jane, Helen, and Nina, all single parents, deepened and clarified issues.

The idea for the book was conceived with Arlene Blum. Without her seminal contributions and encouragement, the book would not exist. Arlene also introduced me to her agent, Felicia Eth, who skillfully advised me in formulating a proposal and attentively chaperoned the book through the world of publishing.

I feel especially indebted to Ruth Hapgood, my first editor at Houghton Mifflin, for her profound understanding of the creative process and her unwavering support, which kept the book alive despite its many obstacles and missed deadlines. I am grateful to her for her insight in structuring the material and her sublime wisdom in leaving me alone to write it. Betsy Lerner took on the manuscript at the point when I was ready to respond to her energetic determination to complete it. I acknowledge with gratitude her substantial shaping of the manuscript, her enthusiastic support of it against the odds, and her careful shepherding of it through every detail of its production. I am also very grateful to Katarina Rice for her incisive final editing and for the warmth with which she delivered her alterations. In addition to her precision as copy editor, Katya attended to every sentence as if it were her own and dedicated many hours to clarifying and improving the text.

Numerous others played critical roles in bringing this project to fruition. Julie Lake, Siyanda, Barbara Gates, Mary Jean Haley, Linda Gunnerson, Nancy Bloom, DeLorez Houle, Carolyn North, and Abe Levitsky read various drafts of the manuscript and provided astute feedback and encouraging support. I would also like to express my gratitude to Christine Ciavarella, Richard Hruby, Eric Utne, John DePew, Joan Bergman, Nicole LaCore, Carly Newfeld at *Mothering* magazine, and Becky Saikia-Wilson for their generous help at various points; to Kristina Koukkari for stepping in to help organize the chaos; and to Vesta Copestakes for her way with words. Thanks also to the people of Minneapolis, in particular the staff of the Minneapolis Public Library and Information Center, the Southdale branch of the YMCA, and the Department of Human Services.

Finally, I am indebted to the many people who cared for Elias while I worked, especially Parvati Kumaraswami and Messod Azulay, who were all that a mother or a child could want. Special thanks to my own mother, Carol Berry, for giving me a living inheritance — she opened her home to us and provided well over a year of daily help of all kinds, including picking flowers for my desk. And I am deeply grateful to Elias for his forgiving love, for his honesty and wisdom, and for sharing his early years with a demanding muse. This book is for his world.

Contents

Prologue

Sometimes a person needs a story more
than food to stay alive.
                                  — Barry Lopez

I WAS THREE MONTHS pregnant and unexpectedly on my own.
The intimate pleasure of having a baby growing inside me was oddly
juxtaposed with the pain of a shattered dream. Two days before, my
baby's father had announced that our relationship was over for him
and asked me to move out of his house. We had often mused about
having a child together, but the sudden reality of an unplanned
pregnancy had shattered the underpinnings of our relationship.
Alone, I found myself facing the shelf of books on pregnancy, birth,
and parenting at the bookstore down the hill from what had been
home. I was looking for something that made sense to me.

My eye caught a title on single parenting, a thin volume amid the
multitude of parenting books. I flipped through the pages, not finding
myself in its focus on divorce and remarriage and fearing its predic-
tions of stress and overwhelming pressures. *Single parent*. I didn't
have a positive slot in my brain for the image of myself as a single
parent. Whenever I had thought about having a baby, I had imagined
doing it with a "daddy."

Though I had friends who were raising children alone, the label
"single parent" conjured up for me images of bedraggled and pov-
erty-stricken women with children in tattered clothes hanging on their
skirts. Women abandoned and betrayed by life. It wasn't quite like
that for my friends, although I could see it wasn't easy. But that was
them, not *me*. For me to be a single parent felt tantamount to wearing
the Scarlet Letter.

When I was in high school during the early sixties, the possibility of getting "knocked up" without being married was something we teased each other about. For some reason, "forty-two" was the code word we had assigned to that malady. Furtively scribbling it on the cover of someone's notebook or pegging some innocent with it under our breath as we changed classes could send us into spasms of laughter. We were nearly all virgins in a Catholic girls' school, deflecting our fears about the great forbidden and titillating attraction of sex. The possibility of "going all the way" was fearsome enough; but compounding the transgression by ending up "forty-two" was well beyond the limit.

By 1988 the number of American women giving birth outside of marriage exceeded one million. I was one of them and, ironically, I was forty-two years old. During the quarter-century between my high school days and my entry into motherhood, the number of American families headed by single parents grew to nearly a third of the total.[1] Yet as I stood alone and pregnant in that bookstore, the images of failure I still carried from decades before colored my response to the title on the paperback in my hands.

I put the book back on the shelf and chose something on pregnancy over thirty-five. "I am *not* a single parent," I declared to myself, like a two-year-old claiming omnipotence, and I momentarily soothed my specters by reaffirming that somehow daddy could make three. That was the only option I could imagine. Never mind that I was scarcely able to name a two-parent family that functioned in a way that felt attractive to me.

My belly would be nearly full-blown before I would see my way past fear and resistance to a positive dream of parenting on my own. As I would later recognize, I wasn't saying no that day in the bookstore to raising a child alone, but rather to my beliefs about what that meant. I didn't know then that what I considered a breakdown of family structure might potentially constitute a breakthrough into a new concept of family life. But I know now that at the moment when I first refused to fulfill my own stereotype of the single parent, this book was conceived, slipping into me as secretly as had the boy then growing in my body.

Single parents. Whether we got here by choice or by chance — through divorce or death, adoption or intentional conception or, like me, choosing what chance had delivered — we make up one of the major forms of family structure today. Indeed, our multitudes — over ten million women and men* — if joined with our more than sixteen and a half million children,[2] would stretch the distance roughly from Los Angeles to London. We are from all socioeconomic classes, from every ethnic group, every profession, every sexual orientation. Welfare recipients and film stars are single parents. Business executives and carpenters are single parents. Illegal immigrants and *Mayflower* descendants are single parents. Whoever we are, raising our children on our own may be both one of the most rewarding tasks of our lives and one of the hardest we ever undertake.

Most of us struggle alone to replicate a family structure that formerly depended upon at least two adults, often more, to raise children. The intrinsic need of every child to be loved, nourished, and nurtured hasn't changed, but the number of adults responsible for ensuring the fulfillment of those needs has diminished over time to add up to *one*. You. Me. Indeed, "double parent" might be a more fitting label.

There are now more than twice as many single parents as there were two decades ago. In 1975, as the fuse was being lit, social forecasts pronounced that "the breakdown of the American family is a collision course for our society."[3] In the final decade of the century, as we face massive social and economic dilemmas, a collision does seem to be upon us. But major changes in the family are more of a symptom of the crisis than a cause.

The breakdown is as much in the community that supported families as in the family itself. Our own parents by age fifteen would have been as likely to lose a parent through death as a child today is through divorce.[4] Loss and change, unexpected birth and death, are a part of family life in all cultures and at all times. But in cultures less fragmented than ours, the village, tribe, and extended family have cushioned these changes.

All industrialized nations have faced similar changes in families since World War II, yet nearly all others have put into place social

---

* These numbers count only those single parents who are considered head of household. They do not include those who share parenting while living separately, nor do they take into account others who are also parenting alone, such as the substantial number of single grandparents raising their grandchildren. While most in this book are the primary and often sole parent, some part-time single parents, including those who share care equally as co-parents, are also included.

policies — adequate parental leave, health-care benefits, housing and childcare subsidies for families — to ensure the welfare of children. In contrast, as Sylvia Ann Hewlett points out, the United States, while ranking second in per capita income, "does not even make it into the top ten on any significant indicator of child welfare."[5] We join with all parents in what one single mother I spoke with calls "an uphill battle all the way" to raise our children well.

As single parents, we inherit, in addition, a legacy of prejudice and fear, particularly those of us who have given birth "out of wedlock." As Jenny Teichman writes in her study on illegitimacy, "In the past, even the recent past — indeed, until about 1960 — the shame of being an unmarried mother was the worst possible shame a woman could suffer." Even beyond midcentury, she reports, "doctors refused anaesthetics to unmarried women in childbirth 'to teach them a lesson.'"[6] Roger Toogood, veteran director of a major adoption agency, recalls the convoluted coverups in the late 1950s to protect the reputations of unmarried mothers. "Social consequences were so great," he says, "that 95–97% of all unmarried pregnant women selected adoption as the best alternative for them and their child."[7] As Rickie Solinger points out, however, this route was not necessarily open to *black* unmarried mothers, whose babies were considered "products of pathology" long after that attitude had changed in regard to white babies and opened the way for their adoption.[8]

For all, in any case, the designation "illegitimate" still hung heavy over birth outside marriage. Less than fifty years ago, many states would have defined my own son by that status, announcing it on his birth certificate to indicate that he was not claimed, in name or inheritance, by a man.[9] The accompanying social attitudes, with their roots in the Middle Ages, would have held that as a "bastard" he was less entitled, less worthy, less "good" than his legitimate playmates. Even today, one unmarried mother I spoke with confided her fear that someday other children might wound her daughter with that label.

Other single-parent families as well were judged harshly against the "norm." Not even a quarter-century ago, if you divorced, your child would have been considered the "product of a broken home," and you the remnant of a failed marriage. An unmarried man or woman was discouraged from adopting through legal channels, considered unable to provide adequate parenting or perhaps suspected of "deviant" behavior as a homosexual. A widow or widower who did not remarry was to be pitied, perhaps avoided. In all cases, children in families with one parent were "different," singled out as living in what the sociology texts of the 1950s and '60s labeled a "pathological family structure."

"I'm so tired of my family being considered *substandard* or getting the feeling that there is something *wrong* with me when I say I'm a single parent," comments a social worker I talked with in a county welfare department. She is certainly not ignorant of the problems of raising children alone. But neither is she unaware of the advantages of the life she is now able to create for her young son, on her own. Social disapproval may be more subtle these days, but the label "single parent" still tends to be, for single mothers and fathers alike, more of a stigma than a commendation. Barbara Jo, a single parent and the owner of an espresso shop, related to me what happened when she was interviewed by a local paper for a feature article on her thriving business. When she identified herself as a single mother, the reporter paused and asked, "Are you really sure you want people to know that?"

As many of us know from experience — as both children and parents — the two-parent nuclear family model is not itself a guaranteed ideal. Many people no longer consider entering or sustaining marriage as the only choice "for the sake of the children." Radical changes during the last couple of decades have influenced attitudes as well as opened up options. Our families have been remolded by vast cultural shifts, including severe economic pressures, substantial changes in sex roles, the feminist movement, the lesbian and gay rights movement, the AIDS epidemic, the evolution of marriage from a social contract for the purpose of family into a shared commitment to personal fulfillment, the biological clock ticking for the baby boomers. In response, some of us have made choices for and about our children out of fear and some out of love. Amid all the uncertainty, one thing is sure: the family has changed.

We are fast headed away from the conventional two-parent model, with only 11 percent of U.S. families consisting of both biological parents living in the same home with their children.[10] Over half of all children born today will, for one reason or another, live in a single-parent family at some point in their lives.[11] In addition, for some, the single-parent family is an outright choice. It is time to acknowledge the changes in family structure and to consider how to make the families we do have work. This is what the single parents I spoke with are striving to do. It requires creativity and courage.

Changes in family structure are nothing new. As Stephanie Coontz points out in *The Way We Never Were: American Families and the Nostalgia Trap,* families in our nation have always been in flux.[12] Ever since our ancestors spilled out of holds and cabins onto Atlantic and Pacific shores, crossed borders that hadn't existed before, and walked long "trails of tears" away from their native lands, our families have made do, adjusted, found new ways.

One single father I spoke with, whose two children are now in college, considers the new role he played as a co-parent after divorce as falling squarely within the American tradition. "My own father has recollections of malnutrition and starvation in the old country that forced his family to move beyond the old way," Mordecai relates. "When they left Russia for America, they didn't know what they were moving toward. I see this as much the same for single parents today. We need to move beyond the old way, but we don't yet know what into. We are another stream of pioneers." Single parents are indeed pioneers, destined not for a place but for a quality of life for ourselves and our children based on our dreams of what family can be.

That's what I set out to do — to build a new dream. While the other mothers in my birth class leaned back into the arms of their husbands, I sat flanked by my friends Sypko and Carolyn. When my visions of what mothering would be gave way to nightmares as I faced it on my own, I determined to find ways to make it work. I set out to write the book I couldn't find, the one I wanted to read in the middle of the night when I was alone and terrified, a book that would reflect the sunrises as well as the sunsets of raising children alone, a book that might shed some light on where the new pioneers are settling.

With my toddler often by my side, I sought the real experts, single mothers and fathers who were creatively, enthusiastically committed to their challenging task. Some talked with tiny infants in their arms. Others had completed their childrearing years ago and proudly showed photographs and told anecdotes of their grown children. Some of the children, both young and grown, added their perspective.

Some of these single parents had deliberately chosen to raise a child alone, while others had had it thrust upon them. Among the more than one hundred single mothers and fathers in all parts of the country who shared their lives in depth, as well as numerous others I have met more casually, there was scarcely a story without some tragedy — and none without a great deal of joy.

Raising children alone is one of the most difficult tasks any human being might take on; many of us lead lives of quiet desperation. On the other hand, many of us find we've never been happier. Sometimes both are true at once. For most of us, the assessment is certain to change many times, and often within any given hour.

No matter what our individual stories may be, there are some basic questions and concerns we all share. We want to know how we can do the best job — indeed, if we can do the job at all. We want to know if we can give our children what they need. We want to know how we can give ourselves what we need. We want to know who else will love them, and who else will love us. What do we tell them about their other parent? How do we manage the double role of single parent? How will our children turn out? How will *we* make it through?

Whether we have entered the role of single parenting on the heels of tragedy or after extensive preparation, the job demands everything we've got, and it will make us into more than we ever dreamed. The triumphs and the challenges are daily entwined. We may relish the freedom to make decisions unimpeded by conflict with the other parent, yet at the same time feel the excruciating burden of having to make all the decisions alone. We might have hardly a waking moment to ourselves and yet feel deeply lonely. We may feel blessed to witness the beauty of a blossoming child and yet mourn the absence of a partner to share it with. This rigorous and nonstop journey reveals to us the best and the worst of who we are.

Some of my own fears about being a single parent have in fact come true. At times I have been that bedraggled and exhausted woman I feared becoming. I have learned how far over the edge, emotionally and financially, raising a child could lead me. But despite the terror and the exhaustion, I have found a life that could not have been imagined by that single woman who stood browsing for meaning in a bookstore.

I remember one morning when I had gone outside, still in my robe, to retrieve a baby bottle from the car. It was not yet light, and as I unlocked the car door I could feel every cell in my body sagging under the weight of sleep deprivation. Hearing a sound behind me, I turned. There, padding toward me, with a wide wad of night diaper nearly to his knees and a smile stretched to greet me like the sun, came Elias, eighteen months into his life as the child of a single parent. I never wanted to be this tired in mind or body, yet how could I have ever known what it would feel like to have my child in saggy pants come tripping toward me in the dawn?

As many I spoke with have revealed, parenting alone is not only an opportunity to break through our personal limitations, it is also the chance to go beyond a limited definition of family to discover that the so-called breakdown of the family can instead be a breakthrough into a more encompassing model of family life. Together, all of us are imagining new possibilities, and we have found some. Like any family, one headed by a single parent works best when it is held in the hands of a supportive community. It works best when we listen to our children and build our lives with them. It works best when we see that parenting alone is our mountain to climb, and that many are with us on our way up. This is our story.

CHAPTER 1

◆

By Chance or by Choice:
Becoming a Single Parent

> The future is not some place we are going to, but one we
> are creating. The paths are not to be found, but made, and
> the activity of making them changes both the maker and
> the destination.
>
> — John Schaar

RARELY IS THE AVENUE to parenting alone an easy one. We
arrive through heartbreak, through rage, through longing and love.
For most of us, raising children alone is less of a deliberate choice
than a response to circumstances. Either we haven't found the right
partner or, for any number of reasons, a partnership has not endured.
Sometimes, no matter what our plans for the future, death leaves us
on our own with children. We become single parents because we want
children or we already have them, and because doing it alone is the
way open to us. Whichever way we have begun, by chance or by
choice, we are on a challenging journey that leads deep into our
hearts, for to be a single parent requires an energetic act of love.

"I think one of the hardest parts about being a single parent was
the decision to become one," Angie remembers. Nineteen years ago,
Angie was a married parent with a baby daughter. Looking back, she
acknowledges that her final choice, to leave her marriage and raise
her daughter alone, was "one of the most profound reliefs I ever had
in my life." But her decision was preceded by a wrenching battle with
herself over what would be best for her daughter.

No matter what circumstances have led us to parent alone, no

matter how obvious or unfathomable the reasons, the common de-
nominator among the many single parents I spoke with is the intention to do the best we can for our children. That might mean challenging our own deepest beliefs and assumptions, as it did for Angie.
It might mean going against the standards of our culture. Often it
means facing irresolvable dilemmas in relation to our children's other
parent. More often than not, there is pain in the attempt to forge new
families.

By the time her daughter was six months old, Angie, worn down
by the emotional abuse of a frustrated and damaged man, "spent a
lot of time just crying." Marriage counseling wasn't helping, but still
Angie stayed. Although her husband was scarcely involved in his
daughter's life, "my belief had been that a child needs to have both
parents," says Angie. "I hadn't had any other experience growing up.
It was such a thorough conditioning that I felt there wasn't any other
way but to stay together."

Six more months of anguish brought Angie to the breaking point.
"Even if my belief was that a child should have two parents, I simply
couldn't see how I could manage it." She packed up her daughter and
boarded a train to the East Coast to visit some friends. "On the train
I met a young woman in her early twenties who had been raised by
her father alone. She had such an intact feeling about her for that age
that I realized, in one of those flash moments, that it *is* possible for
children to turn out whole and complete with only one parent. And
that was it." No longer willing to believe that a marriage made of
conflict, abuse, and frozen silence was beneficial to anyone, Angie
became a single mother.

During the two decades since Angie agonized over her decision,
divorce rates have exploded, births to unmarried women have more
than doubled, and the decision to raise a child alone has become an
outright choice, for some men as well as women. To explain, social
scientists cite causal factors such as economic pressures, changes in
social and sexual mores, the increasing independence of women. To
these, many single mothers and fathers I spoke with would add one
that lies closer to the heart. To look at how we have become single
parents is, in essence, to look at relationships between women and
men today and what those mean for our children.

The fact that more than 86 percent of single parents are women[1]
makes clear what we already know — women are, for the most part,

bearing the load of childrearing, both within marriages and outside of them. The same relentless wheel of "progress" that relegated women primarily to the home essentially isolated men from childrearing. And now, while mothers have entered the workplace in massive numbers, this has not been balanced by an equal number of fathers taking on the task of caring for children. Instead, the role of the emotionally absent father has further contracted into that of the outright invisible father, the walkaway daddy. While in some cases the father may have no choice, the fact remains that, no matter what the reason, the children are essentially abandoned to one parent. One survey revealed that 42 percent of children with a father who had left the marriage had not seen him in the past year.[2]

"There is such a crisis in this country of fatherless children," comments Denny, a part-time single father of two young boys.* "Something in me doesn't understand and sees almost as diabolical all of these men who are running around not raising their children. You travel around the world, and even in many of the poorest countries you see men walking down the road with their kids. I don't understand; I can't fathom what's going on here. In my view, the core issue of the men's movement is the emotional absence of fathers, and the core issue of the disintegration of the family is the physical absence of fathers. It seems like every problem goes back to it."

How far back would we need to go to find where the thread of fatherhood was snapped — or never spun? Perhaps too few of us, both men and women, grew up with a father who loved us with his presence, guided us into the world, and showed us that the arms of a man are safe. We neither know how to *have* fathers nor how to *be* fathers.

In all societies, fatherhood is a relationship far more shaped by culture than is motherhood, with its obvious definition arising from pregnancy and birth. In our own culture, many men have inherited a vacuum and are faced with healing their loss and forging the role anew or passing on the legacy of pain to their children. After his divorce, Denny had to decide what kind of father he wanted to be. "I knew it was going to be painful to see my kids twice a week and

---

* While the definition of the term has blurred edges, in this book single parents are those who, while not in partnership with the other parent of their children, lead individual lives significantly defined by their role as a parent.

then pull away again. And it's hard to miss out on all the wonderful little things that those who are there all the time get — like when they ride a bicycle for the first time, or when they come home from school with a great story. But I just figured, even if it was hard, I was going to do it."

With a fulfilling career and a wide circle of friends, Denny could easily have drowned his pain in distraction and drifted off into a new life. "There were a number of times over the years, particularly when I've been in a romantic relationship that's rocky, when I've come close to making some sort of adjustment in the time I have with my boys," Denny admits. "I'm sure a lot of men go through that kind of stuff. But now that the years have passed, I would never diminish my time with them, not for any reason — no more than the average mother would. I think men need to think that way about their children and do whatever we can to save our relationship with them. We need to really make a commitment — I think that is the key word in my definition of what it is to be masculine — make a commitment to our kids and say, 'I'm going to be here for you.'"

At the same time that a "crisis of fatherlessness" is happening, some men are making this other choice, *for* their children. Denny describes it as "almost a Jekyll-and-Hyde situation. While there seems to be a growth in bad dads — men skipping out on child support, men walking away from responsibilities — there is also this parallel growth in more involved fathers, good dads," he observes. "You see more men in the park with kids, more dads in the supermarket holding babies. I know a lot of other men who are not the distant way their own fathers were."

-Because roles are being reexamined, some men are making more conscious choices about childrearing. Because social values are changing, some men who *want* to raise children are able to make that choice. Perhaps one of the advantages of the "breakdown of the family" is, in fact, that fathers sharing custody learn how to parent their children. And there is an increasing number of full-time single fathers. Over the past decade the number has doubled. Currently almost 14 percent of all single-parent families are headed by a father.[3]

The story of how we become single parents is complex and sometimes tragic. Some parents who deeply long to raise their children lose them to the other. Some women, solely on the basis of "economic worth," lose children to less-than-adequate fathers.[4] Some men, judged incapable of parenting, lose them to less-than-capable mothers. Out of fear, vengeance, or ignorance, parents make their children a battleground. Because the assumption that women raise children still prevails, a woman who chooses not to is far more often the object of severe criticism than a man who does the same. Geoffrey Greif, co-author of *Mothers Without Custody,* reports that "while two-thirds of noncustodial mothers [in the research sample] had been treated negatively because of their parenting status, only one noncustodial father in sixteen had experienced similar negative reactions."[5]

To look at how we have become single parents is to consider issues vast and in many ways beyond our understanding or control. We carry deep-seated personal, familial, and cultural patterns that seem to have their own momentum. Men and women carry on a dynamic of mutual blame and fear that seems deeply entrenched. We are struggling to redefine not only who we are as women and as men but radically reassessing our roles as parents. Those of us who are parenting alone, not motivated by enmity for another but by concern for our children, are crossing those ancient barriers that have kept us in contention. In the maze of changes, it is the promise that we make to our children — that until they can care for themselves we will nurture, love, and protect them — that guides us as we, by chance or by choice, become single parents.

◆ TIL DEATH DO US PART

"I had postponed having children until I felt I was in a relationship that was secure and right and financially stable," Tracey begins. At thirty, two years into the marriage that seemed to fit the criteria, Tracey gave birth to a son. "I had wanted to wait until I had the whole thing in control," she says, laughing now, eight years later, after so much has changed.

Two thirds of all single parents were once married to the partner with whom they hoped and expected to raise a family. For the majority of them, it is separation and divorce that leaves them raising their families alone or as the primary remaining parent; for the rest, it is untimely death.[6]

With half of all first marriages and 60 percent of second marriages ending in divorce,[7] the bride and groom at any wedding might prepare as well for dissolution as for continuity. With half of all divorces involving children, "to have and to hold" takes on an additional meaning. Marrying in California, where the rate of divorce is higher than the national average, Tracey and Reid took their vows in good faith but aware of the odds. Their marriage agreement included the stipulation that if they were to divorce, they would share their children and "always fully support each other in having fair time with them."

From an office in their home, Tracey continued to run the highly successful herbal tea company she had launched a few years before she and Reid married. Raising her long-awaited son, Dillon, was also rewarding. But by the time Dillon was two, "it was clear that the marriage was falling apart," Tracey acknowledges. "There were lots of problems, but I thought I could force it to work because Reid and I both wanted the same thing — a family. We carried on for another two years after that; then we split up.

"That was an incredibly difficult decision for me. I came from a divorced family, and I had never intended to get a divorce myself. I didn't want to perpetrate on my own child what I'd had to go through. I remember that terrible quality of always being split, of going back and forth from one house to the other, from the East Coast, where my mother lived, to the West Coast, where my father resettled.

"But I also remember, before that time, my parents arguing and saying terrible things to me about each other. I was thirteen when they finally divorced, but it had been threatened and talked about for years. I remember many scenes as a child of crying and sobbing and trying to bring them back together. It was really horrific. It was a painful, tension-filled childhood that I lived — and all in the upper-middle-class ghetto that was home. Either way, it was the last thing I wanted to choose for Dillon's life or mine.

"At a certain point, though, I also realized that my own happiness was very important to my child. Reid and I were miserable together. It was clear that neither of us could survive living with the other. Like my father, he was an active alcoholic. And my pattern was to caretake — inappropriately — just like I did for my father when I was a child after the divorce. Once I had Dillon, I began to see what I was doing.

"When you have a child, you suddenly see relationships in a much different light than you saw them in before," Tracey continues. "You see whether the other parent is mature, able to take on responsibility, whether they are there for the child. I began to see Reid's needs for me as a child himself, and to see that I had been mothering him. Now I could say, 'Wait a minute. *This* is the child.' The strain of mothering him plus mothering our child eventually became unbearable.

"Finally, like my mother, I had to come to that same difficult decision — to leave the situation. But I remember how much courage it took getting that divorce. It wasn't that I was afraid to be on my own, but it went against everything I had wanted to create. It meant pulling apart the fabric of that family."

But Tracey was determined to honor her marriage agreement about sharing children. "In my mind, Reid and I were going to remain friends, have an open extended family, still be able to get together and do things with Dillon. I felt it was very important for our son that his parents maintain an active connection." Divorce didn't resolve the problems that had caused it, however, and amicably sharing custody has not been easy. "At least Reid has not just disappeared, and Dillon knows that his dad is there for him," Tracey says. "But at the same time, Reid's involvement also means a lot of conflict about different values, different lifestyles, and different standards for raising our son."

Some people find that divorce is the only way they can once again cooperate for the sake of their children. For others, forced to continue in each other's lives because of their offspring, the conflict goes on, draining for the parents, confusing for the children. Some single parents are relieved by the absence of the other parent after separation.

"In a lot of ways parenting was easier for me after my husband and I divorced," remarks Claudia, who raised three children alone after her twenty-year marriage ended. "I didn't have the conflicts to deal with anymore. I had more energy for the kids because I wasn't expending it on emotional survival. In many ways, parenting was not even that different for me when I was alone. I had really been doing it alone from the beginning. It wasn't like I had a strong support system and all of a sudden it was gone — except financially."

"The luckiest thing that ever happened to me in my entire life," says Kevin, who raised his two sons alone after his divorce, "is that my wife just volunteered our children to me and disappeared. She virtually left completely. I don't think the boys saw her more than twice a year for a couple of hours."

Their sons were four and six when Kevin and his wife separated.

"At first they stayed living with their mother, because that's what everybody did at that time," he relates. "I called her four or five weeks after our separation, crying and complaining that I had lost everything, and she literally suggested that I take the kids. I said, 'I'll be right over.' I'd had no concept that she hadn't wanted them. I basically moved in that very night and started the arduous task of being a single parent."

Now that his sons are grown, Kevin is fulfilling his longtime dream of writing and illustrating books for children to enhance their self-esteem. Raising his own children alone was a prime preparation for the job. "While their mother's leaving was a gift for me, I felt heartsick for their loss. I found out later that when she said good-bye to the boys, she told them she was going to the store and would be right back. And that was it. My heart just ached for them. So I just tried to love them as much as I could. Love them, love them, love them."

For the sole single parent, the benefits resulting from lack of conflict with an absentee parent nonetheless leave room in the heart for sorrow, especially when the question "Where is Mommy?" arises, or the far more frequently asked "Where is Daddy?"

"Whether it's death or abandonment, I think the experience must be the most complete rejection a child can ever have," Maxine reflects. It is eight years since the death of her husband, and she has built a new life, one intentionally centered around the well-being of her two daughters, now nine and eleven. "For an adult, someone who walks out might be more of a villain than someone who died, but for children, it's the same. They feel that if that parent had loved them, he or she would still be here. So I know that I've got to make sure that my girls are always absolutely certain of where I stand. My kids lost one parent, and they can't lose this one."

While many parenting alone feel this same intense commitment, Maxine thinks that there are some major differences between those who separate in life and those separated by death. "There is nothing in death that stops the love," she says. "If you separate or divorce, you may go through the hate and disappointment and anxiety, but unless the other person is cruel in a way no one could understand, eventually you can come out on the other side and see them as whole once more, and you can see them changing and growing. But with death, the person you loved so much is absolutely no more and that growing has stopped still.

"I know it affects the way I treat the children. I am very aware of their mortality. On a really deep level, I know they could die tomorrow. While I do have to prepare them for the future, that's not my main intent. I don't focus on 'Now I must teach them good table manners so that when they are eighteen . . .' It's more the feeling that *now* is what I know they have; I don't know what they have in the future. When I'm dealing with them I know the unexpected is possible, because it happened."

Maxine's husband had been out bicycling one day with their younger daughter, who was still a baby. In a mishap he fell in such a way as to protect her, but he hurt himself. The pain from the accident didn't go away. "By the time they diagnosed it, nearly three months later, it was clear that he had cancer all through his body," says Maxine. "He went downhill very quickly, especially after the chemotherapy. I asked the hospital what they could do there for him that I couldn't do at home. They said, 'Nothing.' So we took him home." He lived for two weeks more.

"The night he died, I went into the girls' room and lay there with them. Kitty, my older daughter, who was then three, woke up. I said to her, 'Your daddy is dead.' She looked at me and said, 'What are we three girls going to do now?'"

A marriage or a partnership may end, but the vows that we make to our children do not. Those of us who honor our commitment to them "til death do us part" are left to carry on, trying to love enough as single parents to make up for the loss.

◆ EXPECTING THE UNEXPECTED

For a family that began with two parents, the absence of one of them creates a vacuum and requires substantial adjustment. Increasingly, however, that absence — or its potential — is woven into the fabric of the family right from the beginning. Over the past two decades, the number of births to women outside of marriage has more than doubled, and currently 27 percent of all births are to unmarried women.[8] (Not all of these women are in fact single. Some have partners who may share parenting but are not acknowledged by census categories, as is the case for unmarried heterosexual or homosexual couples.)

While all ethnic groups have seen substantial increases in births outside marriage — whites, blacks, Hispanics, Asians, Native Americans — the noteworthy anomaly is in the steep rise of births to educated and professional never-married women. During the past decade, the percentage of these who gave birth has nearly tripled.[9] Sydney, a market research analyst and the single mother of a five-year-old son, is among them.

"I tend to have disastrous relationships with men, and I was in another that was definitely in the toilet," says Sydney. "It was a totally unexpected pregnancy. I had made two appointments for an abortion, but I was in such a mess about it. Even though I am vehemently pro-choice and had had an abortion once before, in my late twenties, I found it to be so emotionally wrenching that I was having a hard time facing it again.

"A nurse at the hospital represented the turning point for me. I was there to arrange something about the abortion, and I started crying. I told her, 'I'm pregnant with this guy who is an idiot, and I'm so unhappy.' She said, 'Wait a minute. Your issue isn't around the guy. Your issue is whether or not you can be a single mother. You could be madly in love with the father and still end up as a single mom when your child is two years old, or seven.' All of a sudden I thought, 'Yeah, I'm focusing on the wrong thing.'

"I spent another twenty-four hours thinking about it and decided, 'Yeah, I can be a single mom.' From the moment I made the decision, everything was fine. Of course I couldn't be happier I made that choice. I have not regretted it — not for a nanosecond."

The only thing she does regret is that her son's father wanted to be involved with his child but "in a completely and utterly negative way." Sydney explains, "He wasn't interested in Randall — he wanted power over *me*." Only after more than a year of traumatic episodes, including kidnappings and masterful double binds on the part of Randall's father, did the court-appointed mediator finally acknowledge the problem. Sydney and her son were granted permission to leave the state. Randall visits his dad once in a while now, but Sydney has no contact with him. "I'll never again be able to go back home to that town where all my friends live," she says. "But, you know, I have never badmouthed his dad to Randall. Considering what this man put me through, I deserve the saint-of-the-year award."

For Chun Hwa, a manicurist and the single mother of an eight-

month-old daughter, the unexpected was not pregnancy out of wedlock but being deserted by her husband before her baby's birth.
"Most Korean men are very responsible," she explains. "They are
really caring when it comes to children. But my husband . . . it was
so unusual."

For Asian women, choosing to parent alone constitutes a break
from tradition so radical that it can lead to being disowned by family
and friends. "After he left, when I told my friends who are Korean
that I was pregnant, they were completely against my keeping the
child," Chun Hwa relates. "They couldn't believe I would go ahead
and have her. How could I have a baby without the father! They
thought I was crazy. That cultural attitude is still there. The *idea* of
it is the major issue for them.

"I do feel on my own because of it, though. When I was pregnant,
my parents were very negative, and my sister who also lives in the
States was terrible. I was very lonely and depressed. I could almost
have gone crazy. Friends came by to see my baby after she was born,
and a couple of them did things to help, but it's very hard for me to
ask. I have some women friends who are Korean. They have children
and I have known them for ten years. I go and stay overnight there
sometimes. But these people live in Korean style in their home, so our
thinking is not the same. These women don't work, and they have no
idea that another world exists. They don't know what it takes to
work. Their husbands work.

"So I just take it one step at a time. I don't think about anything
except taking care of this child. I feel especially responsible because
she doesn't have a father. Every time I see a father loving his children,
I am just heartbroken. If only she had one who loves her as much as
I love her . . .

"I want to start a support group for Asian women who are single
parents," adds Chun Hwa. "We need that. Being a single parent is so
difficult for everyone. It's a very hard life, but also it has given me a
lot of joy having the baby. I just love her to pieces. That I want to
kill her father is beside the point! I am really glad I did it."

Chun Hwa had to face the unexpected alone and sort out her joys
from her disappointments. Too rarely do both parents face together
what an unexpected baby means for their lives. Chris, a microbiolo-
gist, had been married for thirteen years, and despite their attempts
the couple had not had children. Perhaps dashed hopes, when fertility

tests indicated that there were problems with Chris's reproductive system, contributed to the demise of her marriage. Whatever the cause, Chris, in her mid-thirties, felt ready to embark on a new life. When she met Ken, an environmentalist working for the state, it seemed a good match. Himself in the process of a divorce, Ken was sharing equally in the parenting of his eight-year-old daughter, and he adamantly did not want any more children — at least not at that point, and certainly not as a single father. Chris's medically pronounced infertility was a welcome fortress against the possibility. But as another single mother with a history similar to Chris's put it, "Human reproduction is such a mystery." Chris conceived a baby. "I, of course, was thrilled to death," she relates. "But here I was pregnant with a partner who didn't want to have a child after years with a husband who had.

"Ken assumed, since he had not been planning on becoming a father and since I knew he didn't want kids, that he wasn't going to take an equal share in raising our child," Chris continues. "I could respect his feelings, although I didn't agree. I felt we owed it to our baby and to each other to try to make it together as a couple." They did try, living together for a year after their daughter, Emily, was born. "We both put a lot of effort into it, went to counseling together from the moment I found out I was pregnant. But it was all work and no play. We tried, and the answer was no." Chris became Emily's primary parent, on her own. Ken agreed to help financially and to take his daughter one long weekend a month, but he found himself in an ethical dilemma that shook him to the core.

Despite birth control, infertility, and caution, life remains bent on sustaining itself. And when the unexpected happens, our lives are thrown into a chaos of questions about responsibility, freedom, choice. A woman's decision to be a mother makes a man a father. Both were present when life took its course. Where will both stand as life continues?

Some men stay, others flee. Some women are grateful if they are gone, others enraged. Some women want to parent their children alone, some fathers lament being considered "disposable daddies." In this quagmire, even assessing what is best for the children becomes a tangle of emotional and financial complexities.

"When Chris saw that little circle at the bottom of the pregnancy test," Ken explains, "it wasn't even a decision for her. She wasn't going to give up that child. But I felt very impotent and powerless.

Someone else was making a choice that has an incredible impact on my life. I would have been horribly guilt-ridden if I had had a child and her father was out there someplace with no interest in her."

And so a man who at one time in his life had aspired to the priesthood became a single parent twice. "Well, my baby-making days are over," Ken says with a wry smile. "I got a vasectomy." He fears his possibilities of relationship are also over. "Here's a guy who has a ten-year-old with one woman, an eighteen-month-old with another, and he's not married to either one. And he can't have any more kids. I'd be pretty damn leery if I were a woman.

"The issue is not about whether I love Emily and want to be her father; I do. The issue is about my not wanting to have another kid at all." Anticipating Emily's questions, Ken has written a letter to his daughter that is "tucked away for her to read someday, maybe when she's sixteen or so. It talks about what happened and why I had the reservations I had and how I hope she will understand. I wrote it down because I don't know for sure where Chris and Em will end up. But I hope I'm around to answer her questions when she has them."

Ken contributes several hundred dollars a month to his daughter's care and takes her for that long weekend and occasional evenings. He does far more than many fathers — and far less than Chris would like. And he worries about how his daughter will assess his choices someday.

This quandary reflects elements of the expectations and fears many of us who find ourselves unexpectedly pregnant encounter. The major difference here is the level of integrity Ken brings to the situation: he is facing the issue honestly and grappling with it. While he and Chris continue to struggle with their differences, both agree that Emily is a little person with a right to have her needs satisfied and her questions answered.

Differences in expectations are not only intensely personal, they may also be culturally influenced. Nicole, the single mother of an eight-year-old boy, pinpoints a general distinction between cultures when she comments, "My white girlfriend who's a single mom always has stars in her eyes about what's going to happen to her next — like getting married and riding off with some guy. She has always been looking for someone to take care of her. I think that black women don't necessarily look at that in the same way."

Nicole hastens to add, "I don't speak for all black people. It's a very diverse culture, and I come from different experiences from some." Nicole grew up in a very tight, middle-income, nuclear family on the East Coast. "My mom became a single mother when my daddy died. Up until then he had taken care of everything. He was a manager at the post office. After that she taught me a lot about how to make ends meet. But I think coming from that nuclear family might be sort of rare."

Being an African-American woman means that Nicole's chances and expectations of becoming a single parent are, for myriad reasons, much higher right from the start. For the half-century before World War II, marriage and family patterns among African-Americans and European Americans were virtually the same. After that point marriage and remarriage rates among blacks began to decline more rapidly than for whites. The trends are the same, however, and the fact that the number of births to unmarried women is now increasing more rapidly for whites than for blacks leads some researchers to suggest that "White family patterns are simply lagging behind those of Blacks."[10] As it stands today, two thirds of all single parents are white, and their families constitute 23 percent of the total number of white families. Sixty-three percent of black families are now headed by single parents.[11]

The subject is complex, of course, but ample research supports Nicole's assertions that particular sustained pressures on the black family contribute to the higher percentage. "Even at a young age, we had a lot of pressure. I remember my brothers getting beat up by the police. And I look around now and see that the African-American family is breaking down because there are no jobs, there's no money."

Unemployment rates for both men and women are at least twice as high for blacks. Wages are lower; for men the differential between whites and blacks is especially large. Mortality rates are significantly higher among black men.[12] There are only 77 marriageable black men for every 100 women, compared with 86 for whites and 104 for Hispanics, and interracial marriages are not sufficient to make up the difference.[13] These elements all contribute to the fact that an African-American woman is far more likely to end up as a single mother than a married one.

"I think you do develop this attitude that nobody is going to give you anything," says Nicole. In her mid-twenties Nicole took a transfer in her job as an electronics technician to her company's West

Coast branch. "I met a man and got involved, and ended up pregnant. When I called my mom to talk with her about it, the first thing she told me was, 'You know you're going to be *on your own with this.*'" Nicole delivers those last words in an intense whisper. "That's the first thing she told me. 'You realize that it's going to be all on you,' she said."

And it was. Despite attempts to make the relationship work with her son's father, it didn't. "He's got drug problems. I like who he is as a person, but he can't be there for anybody because he's not there for himself. He loves his son, but he's just not there."

Nicole pauses for a moment, contemplating. "Sure some African-American women are bitter about the fact that men are not playing a certain role in the lives of their children," she goes on, "but at the same time we understand why. The system has shot a lot of our black men to the curb. I can't hate my son's dad totally, because I know he's a good person. He even has some strong moral values. But he's gotten caught up in something that many other black men have.

"There is another difference I see as well. Black women are more likely to take the fathers back or not keep them from seeing their children on economic grounds. And while black men might initially deny their paternity, in the long run their children are valuable to them." Again, Nicole's personal observations are supported by a study that reveals that "poor African-American officially absent fathers actually had more contact with their children and gave them more informal support than did White, middle-class absent fathers."[14]

There are stresses on African-Americans that are hard for any white person to imagine — stresses that Marian Wright Edelman calls "this extra Black burden." She writes, "It is utterly exhausting being Black in America — physically, mentally, and emotionally. While many minority groups and women feel similar stress, there is no respite or escape from your badge of color . . . [and] the daily stress of nonstop racial mindfulness."[15]

One single father, Stephen, talks about feeling compelled to prove himself daily to overcompensate for projected stereotypes. "My ex-wife is white. I'm half-white, but I'm also half-black, so in most people's eyes I'm black. My own father left when I was an adolescent, and I know how easy it is for people to read that script. And I didn't feel like having that played back in my own son's life. I wanted to make it clear, to myself and to the world in some sense, that he was as much my child as my ex-wife's, and that I was not taking advantage of somebody, not finding somebody who would have my baby and then running away, like the movies and magazines and newspapers say."

Hallie, an African-American single mother with a fifteen-year-old daughter, says that being black in America adds "an additional element of concern to being a single parent. You can't send your kids out and not let them know the realities they're facing. I have to talk to my daughter in a way that makes her aware of that. I tell her, 'You are a black female and society is not going to lean over backwards for you.' It could tear her apart if I didn't tell her. So I talk to her about everything — drugs, sex, AIDS, racism — so that she's not going off into some rainbow land. I have to make it real for her, because I know the things she has to deal with. As a parent, there is always a part of you out there worrying about your kid. I worry more because she is a black female."

It takes tremendous faith in ourselves to counter what others may say or think about us and to carry on with determination. For one young woman, seventeen-year-old Dawanna, that challenge has become part of her motivating force. Two years ago, when she found herself pregnant, she was faced not only with the pressures of being an African-American teenager but with the ominous fact that 80 percent of all teenage mothers do not finish high school. "Everybody — family members, friends, kids in school who don't even know me — they said I was just too young to have my baby, that I wouldn't graduate, and all that. My parents wanted me to have an abortion. So did my daughter's grandparents on her father's side. People said I should give her up for adoption. They were giving me all these ideas I couldn't agree with. I wanted to keep her really badly."

Kyrsta is now two years old, and she and her mother are one of the success stories of single teen pregnancy. Dawanna's own determination was bolstered by the fact that the teenage father of her baby wanted to play an active role in parenting, a rare choice. Besides having sustained contact with his daughter, he took care of her for two months at his parents' home when Dawanna had trouble living with her own mother and had moved to a temporary shelter.

Another significant factor has been the excellent program for teenage parents available at Dawanna's high school.[16] She and the eighteen others enrolled in the program are picked up daily and brought to school, where daycare is provided for the babies while the parents attend classes. Besides their academic class load, these parents, including a couple of teen fathers, study child development, family living, and parenting skills; they get credit for working in the daycare center, participate in a support group, and have individual crisis counseling available to them.

"I just didn't want to become one of the statistics and drop out of school," Dawanna says. "I want my daughter to have a good life, and I know in order to do that, I am going to have to take my education as far as I can. That's what's kept me motivated.

"Another thing that's kept me motivated is people telling me what I can't do because I have a baby. They told me I couldn't play basketball for my school because I was a mother." In fact, Dawanna continued as co-captain of her team. But even more critical, she relates, is that "some people say, 'You're a mother. You won't graduate.' I just can't wait to see these people's faces when I get my diploma." With her determination, Dawanna may be on the way to joining a different statistic — the increasing number of professional women who are single parents.

◆ FOR THE LOVE OF A CHILD

Twenty years ago, almost half of all single mothers were teenagers like Dawanna. Today, the number of teen mothers has dropped to 30 percent of the total[17] as older women, including aging baby boomers, are joining the ranks of women giving birth outside of marriage — an increasing number by choice. An essential difference in the experience of these "single mothers by choice" is that from the outset they have separated having a child from having a relationship with the child's other parent. Many of them have prepared themselves psychologically, emotionally, and financially for their role before the fact — sometimes long before.

"Right before my fortieth birthday I broke up a relationship with a man and found myself in a grieving process that was far larger than the relationship deserved, and I couldn't figure out what I was grieving over," explains Cynthia, a therapist and the single mother of a nine-year-old daughter. As one of the first in the wave of single professional women to choose deliberately to birth and raise a child without a partner, Cynthia might well be considered a pioneer.

"One night I woke up from a dream," she remembers, "with the visual memory of some words, like the headliner of a movie, that said, 'Where is it written . . . ?' That's all there was." Cynthia turned that phrase over and over in her mind that day, and then suddenly it completed itself. "I realized that I ended that sentence with '. . . that you have to be married to have a child.'

"That was 1976, and nobody I knew at the time was deliberately having babies alone. I had never heard of that except for adoption." Cynthia's life went on, and her desire for a child got put on the back burner. It was four years later, during a silent meditation retreat, when, as she explains it, "there it was. The word BABY kept coming up in my mind over and over. Within a day or two after that, I went to see the movie *Kramer vs. Kramer,* and it threw me into such emotional pain I could hardly bear it. Later that evening, crying on the shoulder of a friend, I suddenly got it. 'I think I'm going to die if I don't have a child,' I told her."

Foreshadowing *The Big Chill,* Cynthia asked an old friend from college who was now married if he would consider donating sperm. He decided he felt okay about it, but his wife said absolutely no. "I really understand from her side," Cynthia comments. "This is a very loyal and loving man. If my daughter had been half his child, he would have been calling her, relating to her, being a father, even though I wasn't asking for that."

In the end she met an interesting man with good qualities who thought he would be moving out of town. "I asked to do this with him, told him he had no obligation financially nor to a particular role, although he would be welcome to visit." And that was it; Cynthia had her baby. "I'm a single mother by choice, which doesn't mean that I'm choosing not to be in a relationship with a man. It means that I was not in a relationship with a man and I chose to have a child. That's different."

For Sara that was an essential difference. She had been in a close and intimate relationship with a man for twelve years, and only near the end of it did they consider the possibility of having a baby. That dream ended along with the relationship, and Sara returned to school to complete her master's degree in social work. "I had never really thought of growing up and having kids. It wasn't something crucial for me," Sara explains. "I liked work and having a career. But the more I thought about it the more I realized that I didn't want to end up one day saying that I didn't have a kid because I got too old. I wanted to decide either to do it or not do it."

With that focus in mind, Sara sought counseling. "We covered lots of issues, such as why I wanted to have a child, what my images of motherhood were, how I would support myself financially. We paid a lot of attention to how I would get emotional and practical support — of the kind people think they are going to get with a mate but often don't. For me the very important issue we looked at was separating out having a relationship with a man and having a child. I knew that if I had my choice, I'd rather be in a relationship with the perfect man for me and raise a child in that context. But it wasn't in my style to go out seeking a partner and have the pressure of wondering whether I was going to have a baby with each person I went out with. The question about the importance of a father wasn't irrelevant, but given the reality of my life, the best option was to just go directly to having a child, and a relationship with a man would be a separate issue.

"Once I made that distinction, finding a man willing to get me pregnant was just not viable either. I don't like the complications. It is absolutely unpredictable how someone will feel creating a child." Sara chose donor insemination as the route for her. "But knowing that the identity of both parents can become a real issue for children, I absolutely wanted a donor who was open to revealing that one day. The sperm bank I went to had that option available. When my son turns eighteen, the identity of the donor can be released to him."

Still a cultural anomaly, donor insemination is an increasing choice for women wanting to bypass the social and legal complications of personal relationships. "Often it amazes people that I did it this way," Sara comments. "But it doesn't seem so amazing to me. I'm always more amazed at the people who do it other ways, like hanging in for terrible relationships."

The process of inseminating had its own challenges. "It was laborious, even ridiculous at times. It is the extreme total opposite of just sleeping with someone and getting pregnant. Every step of the way is so conscious. Actually it feels like a decision I made over a period of ten years, so a lot of the kinks were worked out internally. I realized that of all the decisions I have made in my life, this was one I would not be able to change." Sara gave birth to a baby boy who is, in essence, completely her own.

For Jane, adoption was the preferred avenue to becoming a parent. She was in a relationship with a woman who wanted to share parenting, but Jane was clearly *the* parent, and that continued when her partnership ended. "I had always known I wanted to be a mother, so once I was settled into medical school, I felt it was time to begin. I heard about a lawyer who had just started arranging a few adoptions to single parents, so I set up an appointment."

Jane considers herself "extremely lucky." The process of adopting as a single parent can be complex and frustrating and is actually prohibited in some states. Regulations vary, even by county. Some states require open adoption; others forbid it. Almost invariably, it is "special-needs" children who are available to single parents adopting within the United States — that is, children who are older or who have a disability. Also included in the special-needs group are biracial children. For Jane that was no liability. "Some of my relatives may not have been so supportive of me adopting children who are racially mixed. But I'm very good at ignoring those people who aren't supportive. I seek out those who are. When you operate in an alternative community, as I do as a lesbian, you're already good at knowing that it doesn't matter that there are a bunch of people out there who don't approve."

Because Jane had been an early childhood development educator before entering pediatrics, she got through the home study and approval procedure very quickly. "Within ten months of getting approved, I got Jordan. She was only five days old. I had requested a girl, because I think it's very hard to raise a nonsexist male."

Adoption can be a process of long expectation and sudden birth. Four and a half years later, when Jane was beginning a subspecialty pediatric fellowship, she made an appointment with the same lawyer to talk about adopting a second child. But before the day of the meeting she got a call from the lawyer; he had a baby girl whose placement had fallen through in court. "I had to make the decision within a couple of hours," remembers Jane. For someone planning to adopt, the choice of whether to be a parent (or whether to become a parent a second time) arises over and over as each document is filled out, as the home study is arranged, as policies for those adopting internationally change overnight, as court costs and travel fees mount, until that final choice when the long-anticipated call comes: *We have a baby available. Do you want her?* Alone, one says the final word that changes everything: *Yes.* When Jane brought baby Cameron home, Jordan said, "Now we've got a family!" That family would also come to include those in Jane's support group who helped care for her daughters as she met the taxing requirements of her fellowship.

Much as we like to have everything in control, when children come into the picture, that fantasy comes to its end. Sara's son was born with club feet and a dislocated hip, requiring a series of operations. Despite the unexpected trauma, Sara is very happy as a mother. "When you make the decision to have the child, the whole package comes with it, no matter what it is. Whatever Gabriel has to go through, I am there one hundred percent down the line. I have never felt that way about anything or any person before in my life. I have a very deep feeling that this is a unique relationship."

Like others who have chosen and prepared to be single parents, Sara can readily testify to its advantages. "I can make decisions myself about how to raise my son and what to do with my time. When it's nine o'clock and the baby is asleep, I can go to sleep too. I don't have to think, 'Well, I haven't seen my mate all week and how is he feeling and should we stay up and talk and what is happening in our relationship?' It's nice to be totally there for this child and not have a split allegiance. And I am never going to have to worry about split custody and all the kinds of horrors that so many of my friends have gone through.

"Sometimes it makes me sad that there isn't somebody here daily to share this incredible experience with. But I can't say that I feel *he* is missing anything right now. He gets lots of attention from my friends, both men and women, and my family and his babysitter, who he is crazy about. Not having a father has implications for later. But I'm not sure what that will be. It depends on him."

A few of us choose to become single parents; most of us find ourselves here by circumstance. Would any of us *recommend* having children alone? The answer of course varies, but Cynthia comments, "People call me up and ask that, because I'm a therapist. While I feel very clear that having my daughter was the best thing I've ever done, it's very hard work. Like being a ballet dancer, raising a child alone is as glorious as anything, but it's a huge life demand. There are lots of sacrifices. So what I say when people ask is, 'Don't do this unless you really have to. If you don't have to do it, I would *highly* recommend that you do not. But if you really must, then we have nothing more to discuss. Do it.'"

Women and men are not going to stop loving each other, babies planned and unplanned will continue being born, and parenting alone is here to stay as one of the ways in which we raise our children. No matter who we are — what gender, what color, what economic status — or how we got here, we all face some of the same issues. And in order to do the best for our children, we must embrace the task wholeheartedly. We must all become single parents by choice.

CHAPTER 2

◆

Victim or Victor:
Embracing the Challenge

That which does not kill me makes me
stronger.
— Friedrich Nietzsche

IT WAS DURING MY sixth month of pregnancy when a flu had
me so low that I'd been forced to stay in bed for days. My baby's
father had come over, ostensibly to bring me a good lunch, but what
he really brought was bad news. He had fallen deeply in love two
weeks before, he told me, and the woman was moving in with him.
A dark curtain started falling in my mind. Certainly the thread of our
relationship had stretched thinner and thinner since I had moved out
of his house three months earlier — but in my mind it hadn't yet
snapped. Until now.

As he assured me that he and his new friend were both looking
forward to caring for our baby, the curtain crashed. I didn't know if
I should understand his offer as an act of kindness or a horrifying
threat to my motherhood, but either way it signaled the end of
a dream. Stunned, I managed to squeak out something like I hoped
he'd be happy, and slid down a hole inside myself. When he said
good-bye and closed the door, I was finally, undeniably, on my own,
with child.

It is in moments like this — sudden and conclusive — that our lives
change. A heart attack takes Nan's young husband, leaving her to
raise their two babies alone. The mental illness that haunted Ezra's
wife claims her, and when the gavel falls, he has sole custody of their

child. Julian returns from work one evening and his wife is gone, leaving him alone with their three children. Patricia is slammed awake one morning by her husband's blows, packs her five-year-old daughter in the car, and drives away for good. I conceive a child in a time of shared love, and the father turns away.

This is not the way we wanted it to be. This is not right, we may protest. This can't be. We may well feel like helpless victims, injured and betrayed by life. We may well feel overwhelmed by grief at our tremendous losses — our mates, often our homes and financial stability, always our dreams.

But there are other moments as well that change our lives. These are inner moments, as profound and sweeping in their impact as those cataclysms of external change. These are the moments when an essential choice lies before us: we can continue to focus on what we have lost and perhaps yearn to replace it, or we can turn and embrace what we now have before us. At these points of choice, there may be no change in the outer circumstances of our lives — we remain single parents facing serious challenges — yet something very basic shifts within us. At those moments we stop seeing ourselves as victims and begin to create a new life for ourselves and our children.

Single parents who have deliberately chosen to raise children alone have often made this kind of choice months or even years before the child was in their arms. They too may have grieved the loss of a partner or the fact that they just couldn't find the right one to share parenting. But their focus is on creating a rewarding family life, not on mourning whatever they have lost.

Research indicates that those who chose parenthood and planned for it, within any family structure, are more satisfied, more effective in addressing problems, more willing to admit mistakes without feeling overwhelming guilt, and more open to changing their behavior when necessary.[1] On the other hand, those who feel there is no choice are more prone to guilt, depression, and panic, all of which contribute to severe stress. It is often the child who bears the brunt of it.

When Suzanne's husband left her on her own at twenty-eight with their eighteen-month-old daughter, Molly, she absolutely knew she didn't want to be a single parent. "I was both brokenhearted and shattered because I had thought this man would be with me all the rest of my life. I had a strong fear that I could not survive in the universe without a mate. The one thing I had always known I'd never be, other than someone who hit her child, was someone who was a single mother."

Now, twenty years later, Suzanne looks back at her life with the kind of perspective and honesty that years can bring. "Unfortunately for Molly, the history of her early life was Suzanne trying to get her own needs met and never fully admitting that she was a single parent who had to create her own family. I felt very guilty that Molly didn't have a father. But I kept falling in love with impossible choices of men who didn't want to be fathers. I wasn't a sex addict — I was nearly frigid. I just had a tremendous need for love and the idea of a partner. And really I was looking for someone to rescue both of us."

In the meantime Suzanne set out to survive. She registered for welfare, and a month after her husband's departure, she landed a contract for her first book as a photojournalist. "I was one of those people who was going to use welfare to get off it, and I did," she says. Working with a borrowed camera, often with Molly in tow, Suzanne threw herself into her project. "I was working to keep myself from collapsing with grief." On the surface, things seemed to be falling in place, but inside, Suzanne was falling apart.

"It was horrifying to find myself so over the edge all the time," she says now. "Most of the time I'd repress the tension, but then it would come out in sudden, volatile anger. One day when I had completed a chapter of the book, I set out to get it to the house of my editor in San Francisco. I was feeling shaky about my own abilities, very anxious about my deadline — and Molly wouldn't buckle her seat belt when we got in the car. Looking back now, I doubt if she actually could buckle it all by herself. But I went berserk. I *needed* her to get the buckle in, I needed it *now*, and I expected *her* to do it, because I really wanted her to be an adult. I didn't want to be a parent right then, and I sure didn't want to be doing it alone.

"I remember yelling at her all across the Golden Gate Bridge, 'I hate you, I hate you! I wish you were dead. I am not going to hit you, but I feel like hitting you.' On and on. I had barely enough presence of mind to tell her that I was just feeling those things but I didn't mean them.

"When we arrived, I leapt out of the car, ran up the steps of my editor's house, and thumped on the door." When she answered, all Suzanne could do was spit out, "You'd better get Molly because I'm going to kill her." She pushed her way past into the hallway, leaving her stunned editor with her mouth hanging open.

By the end of that first year a pattern was established that would continue for many years. "I suffered acute depressions where I couldn't function, couldn't get out of bed. If I did, I couldn't stop crying, I'd be terrified of dying, and worse, I'd lose all interest in Molly. People would say, 'Don't you want to stay alive for your daughter?' and I would say, 'No.' You can really get so low that your love of your child doesn't even pull you back again. And I really loved her. But this went on for years. I'd be present for her and then I'd drop out, either involved with another man or depressed again for weeks."

Suzanne felt trapped, and convinced that the only way out was to find a new partner. Yet her desperate and futile search only aggravated the situation. "I wasn't admitting that I was and might always be a single mother. I was still searching for an end to single motherhood. If I had faced the issue, I might have been able to sit down with a counselor and assess my living situation and address each of the problems: lack of money, unstable housing, my own psychological issues that made it difficult for me to be a twenty-four-hour-a-day mother. But I had such a need to look like a real competent mother that I just couldn't admit that I needed to talk to someone about how badly I was doing things, about my fears of being a mother alone, about my desire to abandon Molly in order to have my own needs met.

"I could not believe what was happening. I had been acknowledged as one of the most gifted nursery school teachers before Molly was born, and I couldn't give my own child what I had given to other people's children."

Suzanne eventually did remarry for a few years, but that didn't produce a partner who would be a father for Molly. Our connection with our children is unique, and single parents often report difficulty in finding someone able to match their own level of commitment. It can take years to let go of the fantasy and focus instead on what a new partner *can* give. But Suzanne knows now that resisting her role as a single parent only caused more anguish. "Now that Molly is in her twenties, she finally has a mother who knows what single parenting demands and is willing to do it on her own. But it would have been easier on both of us if I had been able to accept that from the start."

Those of us who, like Suzanne, entered single parenting in trauma or handicapped by surprise can't avoid the natural cycles of grief, pain, anger, and depression over our losses. Yet Suzanne's story makes it clear how important it is that we face our circumstances. Like those who deliberately choose to raise children on their own, we too can embrace our role as single parents and focus on creating our future. Making such a choice means starting from where we are rather than lamenting about where we want to be. It is a choice that frees us from the self-sabotage of victimhood. We may make this choice at any point — before conception or, like Suzanne, when our children are grown — and it is a choice we might find ourselves needing to make over and over as we meet the challenges of parenting alone.

◆ UP AGAINST THE WALL

I sat unmoving after the bedroom door closed behind him, listening for the creak that would signal the last step in the staircase, and then the click of the outside door as my baby's father walked off into his new life. My mind was melting with fever and I longed to curl up and forget everything. But the inexorable hunger of pregnancy prevailed, and I reached for that lunch he had left. As I choked down sweet-and-sour soup, I watched the scenes I had imagined crack and fall, like mirrors shattering under pressure. Baby didn't, after all, make three. Now I stood alone with my swelling belly. No man to fend off danger and intrusion as I proceeded into that vulnerable world of late pregnancy. No daddy to catch this newborn as he entered the world. No perfect family. No dreams.

I pressed into the wall behind the bed for support and reached for the phone, my usual antidote to panic. Call Amy. Call Anna. Lora. My mother. But I stopped midway through each number. The phone rang once at my mother's house before I hung up. What could any of them do about *this?* This was the end of the world.

That wall behind me felt like the only thing left to lean on. The help friends had been offering, the strength I'd been carving out in therapy — none of it existed in this moment. In this darkness, no one existed but me and a baby. Images of loneliness whizzed through my mind: a woman I once met, nursing her baby in a bare room off a hallway that smelled of urine; a scant-haired wisp of a girl from my childhood, in her mother's small apartment on a winter day, offering me her toys, begging me to stay. Phrases I had stored since childhood surfaced: "A woman is nothing without a man." "Every child needs a father." I could feel the bitterness tighten my chest. I would be a woman with a child, alone, poor, isolated. The jewel I had longed for would be born into a tarnished life.

Perhaps the friends who had suggested months before that I terminate the pregnancy had been right. Their words echoed in the darkness of my mind: "It's not fair for you or the baby." Not fair when a mother doesn't have a fat savings account; not fair when she doesn't own her own home; not fair without a husband and daddy. But I had wanted this child, I couldn't abort him. And now there was no turning back.

All wonder and delight over carrying a baby was expunged by fear in that moment. I believe I could have persisted in acting out a role of defeat. In that moment a choice lay before me: I could go along with the script of rejection and fear, or I could write a new one. I could fall as a victim, or I could rise through the challenges of an unknown future.

◆   MIRROR IMAGES

By the time Julian found himself backed up against that wall, he had already been in the role of a committed father and husband for some time. Julian had married his childhood sweetheart, Sylvia, and they had three children. It was for them that Julian had built his architectural firm, gaining prominence as one of the finest architects in Argentina. For them, he worked long hours to provide a stately home with servants and vacations on the Riviera. Following his father's lead, Julian and his family played an integral role in their city's Jewish community. Family was Julian's reason for living.

Then, one day when he returned home from work, Sylvia was gone. Not just out for the day, which was typical, but packed and gone. Julian automatically assumed responsibility for his three children: Marta, ten, Iva, eight, and Diego, six. "My pain over Sylvia was tremendous, but I kept my focus on the children. I attended to them minute by minute. What do they need? What must I do for them now? I was functioning. I was doing what I had to do."

Somehow Julian seemed to want to do *more* than he had to do. He relieved the hired help from all tasks directly related to the children and took them on himself. There was too much pain in looking back, too much fear in looking ahead. Just take the children to school, go to work, cook them dinner, put them to bed. But underneath it all, the questions burned: Why did she do this to us? Where has she gone? Will she come back?

For the first few days Julian told the children that their mother had gone to visit friends. After all, maybe she had. Just that previous weekend he and Sylvia had gone away together on the recommendation of their therapist. "After two days of beautiful intimacy, she had told me she was the happiest woman in the world to have a man like me by her side. And then the next week she disappeared.

"I appreciate life very much, but if there was ever a time when I felt I couldn't go on, that was it. My voice went completely; I could scarcely talk. I was functioning, but I was in such constant pain."

Less than a week after Sylvia left, ten-year-old Marta confronted her father. "'My mother's not coming home, is she?' Marta said to me. I had to finally admit to her — and to myself — that she wasn't."

It was the terrifying truth. For Julian, marriage was for life. As a young man he had seen his mother press her mouth to the lips of his dying father, prolonging the final moments of their fifty-six-year marriage. This image of union until death was set in Julian's memory. And now Sylvia was gone.

At times like this, darkness compounds darkness. Spiraling downward, the mind holds tenuously to the constructs we call normal life. Past and future collapse into a single moment of pain, followed by the next moment of pain. At such times, when we seem to have no choice in our lives, it takes tremendous effort to remember how much of life lies beyond.

"That night, after my talk with Marta, I lay on my bed in the dim light, feeling like my skin had been flayed from my body with Sylvia gone. The door opened and Marta walked toward me. She was wearing one of her mother's transparent nightgowns and very thin underwear. She had made up her face like Sylvia — lipstick, rouge, mascara. She sat down next to me and started to caress me."

Julian's eyes cloud with the memory of that moment. His voice strains with anguish over his daughter's innocent error of love. "What flooded my mind at that moment was this tremendous awareness that what my life was now about was caring for these children. I was no longer a husband with children, I was solely a father. And here was this beautiful kid trying to make it easier for me. Can you imagine

the damage that might have been done if I had not had that awareness, that clarity? If, because I was in such excruciating pain, I could
have let myself take her offer? But I knew at that moment exactly
what to do because of that awareness. I knew: This is my life now. I
am not going to harm them, not in any way.

"I sat up and took Marta in my arms. 'I want you to understand,'
I told her, 'the woman who left is my wife. You are not my wife, you
are my daughter, and I love you very much, as my daughter.' We
hugged, we cried. After a while she ran out of the room. About
twenty minutes later she came back. She had washed her face and put
on her pajamas. 'Can I cuddle with you, Papa?' It was my daughter
again. And I was her father.

"I absolutely had to make it clear, to them and to myself, that I
wasn't going to fail. This was my life now. I started from that hard
place of pain and moved into doing what was needed to function,
and then beyond that into . . . something else. The choice between
victim or victor? That's what saved my life."

Sylvia returned after six months, and a futile attempt to make the
marriage work again ended in divorce. In exchange for all of the
family's financial resources, Julian gained joint custody of the children. Diego chose to live with him, and the girls chose their mother.
"And so I became Diego's father," says Julian, defining in that phrase
the major role of his life for the next ten years. "From that point on,
I really chose not to be a victim. I had learned so much during those
first six months, handling all the needs of my children as well as the
pain and confusion inside. Sometimes, doing it all, I had thought,
'The only thing I haven't done yet is fly!'"

The choice between victim and victor. Although I wasn't aware of it,
that's what I was facing that afternoon in the fading light. I don't
know how long I sat there, pressed against that wall, with my heart
and mind and baby all churning inside me. But I still remember a
moment in that free-fall. My attention had been bouncing chaotically
from images of pain and loneliness to the physical particulars of the
moment — my spine pressing against the wall, my burning head, the
baby turning inside my womb, my back, that wall, my baby . . . and
suddenly the flood of memories shifted.

This wasn't the first time in my life I had felt lost and trapped. But
this time the stakes were higher — this time I had a baby. Then it

dawned on me: that was exactly the point. I was going to have a *baby!* The longing for a child, rooted so deep inside me, had finally blossomed. Was I now to consider my pregnancy a curse rather than a gift? Would I want my baby to have a mother who thought like that? The wall I was up against wasn't the end of the line; it was the beginning.

Suddenly I found myself laughing. There I was, encountering one of the greatest fears of my life, pregnant and alone. But how ironic. I was carrying within me the baby I had longed for. I could see quite clearly then that there were two ways I could walk away from that wall: defeated and bent on failure, or grateful and determined to triumph. I could describe to myself my entry into motherhood as either an experience of bad luck and broken dreams or one of love and adventure. Slowly in my mind some new pictures began forming: My friend Marguerite, who had chosen to have a baby on her own, proudly carrying her big tummy around on the streets of Santa Monica with no man's arm to lean on. The eyes of my cousin, baby Carl, as I rocked and sang to him through one magical night when I was fifteen years old. Cautiously some new words began to take shape in my mind: I can do this on my own. I will trust that there is a way. I will do this. I will be a single parent.

That first decision was only the beginning. It would be another two months before I would assume this task completely on my own, without the emotional or financial involvement of my baby's father. It would be years before I would see that some part of me knew, even then, that doing this alone was somehow best. But that day, propped up in bed and hitting bottom, I could have labeled myself a victim. Instead I chose to take on the assignment as a creative challenge. I became a single mother by choice.

◆ PHOENIX RISING

For Julian and for me, it was early on in our lives as single parents when we first determined to turn our roles into something more than the reflection of loss. Certainly our grief would entwine itself with our triumphs, but we could trust in the renewing cycle of life. For another single parent, Nan, it was different. The roots of her life followed her husband into death. Her little girls were living reminders of a fairy-tale marriage she had lost when he died.

Like Cinderella, Nan had caught sight of the prince before she was ready to join him. Her older brother's friend Ray had first held her in his arms when he taught her, at a gangly thirteen, how to swim. Five years later, a five-foot-ten-inch beauty greeted him on his return from medical school. Leaving behind her childhood as a tomboy, Nan's new image of herself as a woman was fulfilled in being the doctor's wife and the mother of his children. Then, when Nan was twenty-one, with a two-year-old and a baby, happily-ever-after was ended abruptly by Ray's heart attack.

Absolute and mysterious, death renders us helpless. It can take a long time before anything that feels like choice enlivens the barren task of just getting by. "When it's death that deprives you," says Nan, "victimhood comes out in spades." It would be years before she could even imagine the possibility of thriving or enjoying life as a single parent. Nan's identity was as a widow — who also had children — and death loomed larger than life.

At first life was only survival, hers and her children's. In a step to ensure their future, she enrolled in a sociology program that would lead to a doctorate. Nan wasn't destitute, but money and time were scarcer than she had ever known. "A nursery rhyme used to run through my mind over and over," recalls Nan. "Actually I had fused two different rhymes, and they became a daily theme.

> "Old Mother Hubbard lived in a shoe
> She had so many children she didn't know what to do.
> She went to the cupboard to get them some bread,
> But when she got there,
> the cupboard was bare . . ."

The fact that the shoe crawled with only one toddler and one baby didn't lessen Nan's feeling that she was at her absolute limit. "It was just me up against Ray's death and up against life alone with the girls. There was nowhere to turn. I simply had to do it all myself — physically, financially, emotionally. That rhyme would go through my head and I would fume, explode, rage. I have these children. I'm going to the cupboard, the cupboard is bare. Anger. A lot of anger. 'No, we can't go out to dinner. No, we can't do this or that. Shut up, I have to work. Go to sleep. Go play in your room, I have to study.' I'd wind just tighter and tighter and tighter into this deprived and depressed nonexistence. I was angry that I was left alone with this life and would be forever and ever. I was angry from trying to do too much, to be in school and raise two children alone.

"What do you do in such a situation? Kill. Kill somebody. Kill me? Kill them? I'd find myself wishing that the car would just crash into something and I'd be hurt so badly that I'd never come to again." This continued for several years. But then one day in a therapy session, Nan came face to face with a moment of choice. Hers was no moment of exhilaration but rather a paradoxical affirmation of her commitment to her children as their only parent. "I realized that if I wanted to kill myself," remembers Nan, "I would have to kill my daughters too. I couldn't leave them behind."

The bond between parents and children is a primal connection, deeper than the dictates of any culture, deeper than the formulas of morality. This recognition has in fact been codified in some cultures of the world. In parts of Japan, a mother must take the lives of her children as well if she chooses to take her own life. We are bound to one another, falling together and rising together. "It was that moment that at last married them and me into a common future," says Nan. Caught in the shadow of death, Nan had to take the hands of her children in that darkness. It would be years before she could hold them in a life that was anything more than survival.

"It was five or six years before I let go of being a widow and took off my wedding band," Nan relates. "It was eight or nine years before I actually started thinking we might get some pleasure out of our lives rather than just making it through." Grieving has its own rhythm. For some the process might take longer, for some shorter. Two years is considered an average length of time before memories have less emotional impact than current experiences, before one's identity is attached more to the present than the past.[2] Studies on divorce indicate a similar pattern of approximately two years for a new life to emerge after the breakup of a marriage.[3]

For many, some degree of sorrow will always remain. Years after Sylvia's final departure, grief still arises at times for Julian. "I've learned an enormous acceptance of this process and just how to allow the feelings to come and then dissipate again," he comments. "I've come to accept that this is just a part of who I am, and it's fine." Twenty-five years have passed since Ray's death, but Nan's eyes fill with tears as she remembers, "A very wise therapist told me once, 'You're not going to "get over" this. There's no such thing as "resolving" this loss.'" This reality is at the core of our victories — that in the midst of grief we act for the sake of others, our children.

For those bereft by death, abandonment, or unwanted divorce, grieving is an expected process. We mourn the end of the myth that baby makes three, the end of the myth that my spouse will be here for better and for worse, the end of the myth that someone will take care of me while I take care of the children.

All of us, whether we have become single parents by choice or by chance, face loss to some extent and must move through the grief that comes with it. A previous life has been dismantled, and a new one is not yet built. An image we held of who we are is dissolving. We face an extraordinary task of endurance throughout the years ahead, and in order to go on with our full strength and abilities, it is important that we grieve for what is gone. Grief unacknowledged and unresolved eats away a part of us and corrodes our vitality. In one way or another, grief will have its due.

Claudia was relieved when the dramas that ended her twenty-year marriage were over, and she set to her new life. "That first year I was working, taking classes, taking care of the kids and the garden, and fixing up things around the house. As part of that, I was redoing the closet in my bedroom. I had it all painted and had just about gotten all the new shelves up when the whole damn thing collapsed. I couldn't believe it. The shelves just fell off the wall, and I totally lost it." All the tears and anger Claudia had been storing came down with those shelves.

"The kids were all saying, 'What's wrong with Mom?' I finally said, 'Listen, you just have to leave me alone.' I took a hot bath, redid my makeup, and went down to the hardware store. By that point I could finally talk about what happened, and someone working there told me what I needed to do. So I went home and rebuilt my shelves.

"But that day was a turning point. I had been trying to be really controlled. The collapse of those shelves forced me to let out all that anger I was holding back: What had I done to deserve having to do this remodeling by myself! I should have help! I should be able to pay somebody to do it! Until that point I had been acting like everything was okay, and yes, I'm just fine, thank you. Well, all of a sudden I wasn't fine, and I allowed myself to let go. That day, I allowed myself to grieve."

Sometimes the feelings of sorrow and loss can get buried by the exigencies of the moment, or perhaps the delight over a new life. But the psyche is richly layered and complex. While Julian was in the kitchen with his children, learning how to bake cakes, while Nan was preparing for exams between loads of laundry, changing diapers, and shopping for groceries, while we are focusing on the details of our daily lives, our souls are diligently crossing the sands of Hades. When the rage and sorrow and depression surface, we need to respect their presence and be gentle with ourselves.

Grief is like a cocoon; in its deepest stages, it insulates us from the world. We may feel disconnected. We can't remember from one room to the next what we're doing. Our children call to us, and one percent of our mind answers. We're sure our circumstances will change — we'll reconcile or find a new partner. We cry whenever anyone asks us how we are. Everything makes us angry — our children, our bare cupboards, the unfamiliar details of our new lives. We can't wake up in the morning, can't get to sleep at night. There is scarcely a free space on the floor or countertops at home, but we have no energy to clear things up. At the same time that we need to pull the pieces of our lives together, we want to smash things apart.

This is grief. Shock, denial, pining, anger, depression. These stages don't necessarily happen sequentially; several can occur at the same time. For some, they might happen over the course of days; for others, like Nan, it might take years.[4] For myself, catapulted into motherhood and the consuming task of caring for an infant alone, it took over a year before I even actively recognized that I was grieving. Grieving takes time. Transition takes time. But the beauty of this process is that a transformation takes place, and when we're ready, we emerge from our cocoons.

"I decided to take the girls on a camping trip along the West Coast one summer," Nan recalls. "I had read something about the logging industry before we left, and there on the road we were actually passing a lot of logging trucks and mills. I began to notice that instead of worrying about whether I'd have to spend the trip screaming at them to shut up, I found myself telling them a few of the things I'd learned and wondering if they might get interested themselves."

As each logging truck rumbled by, Nan fanned the sparks of that possibility. "Maybe they'll start asking questions. Will they notice that next mill themselves?" In between, the fears would rise again. "I'd start thinking, 'Oh, they won't care. We'll just end up hassling, back to that old mode.'" But something else was growing in these moments. "I actually began thinking that we might get some pleasure out of this venture, rather than just doing it. I realized then that we were indeed going to survive, and since we were, we'd need to have some pleasure in our lives. We couldn't go on beating each other up in various ways. I realized we had to turn this around."

Nan, who once looked forward to a life as a doctor's wife and a full-time mother and in fact abjured the idea of herself as a career woman, eventually found fulfillment as the founder and head of an active social service organization. As a single mother she managed to redefine family life and discover some of the joys in it. "I look back now and see that not only was I willing to change tremendously but that the girls have benefited from seeing that happen to me. I may not have felt like a victor much of the time, but I certainly stopped being a victim. I often describe myself as a phoenix that arose from the ashes of my husband's death."

Each year as Nan and her girls celebrated Ray's birthday, it increasingly moved from being a remembrance of one they had lost into an affirmation of their life together as a family, existing because of him but not broken without him.

◆   CELEBRATING THE CHOICE

Many of us who are single parents have been thrust into these moments of choice. They are the beginning, the awakening. Sustaining a positive choice requires choosing it again and again. It may take years, as it did for Nan, before the small sparks of hope ignite a flame that can illuminate the darkness. But even in the midst of grieving what we have lost, we can — indeed we must — acknowledge and celebrate our small victories along the way.

At the urging of a friend, Julian and Diego got on a plane to San Francisco the day the divorce papers were signed. "I went in order to survive," Julian remembers, "but it was like stepping into a new world. I felt like Alice in Wonderland. I would never have opened up to what has become such a radically different and expanded life for me if Sylvia had given me even a little bit of herself — I would have been caught, because she meant so much to my life." After a week in San Francisco, Julian bought a huge card of the city and sent it to her. "On it I wrote simply, 'Thank you' — and I meant it."

To be grateful for the circumstances forced upon us is a triumphant act. In Julian's spirit it's easy to see that persistent impulse of life to renew itself no matter how enormous the obstacles. "My life had been totally changed — struggling with no money, being a single parent for this young child. I would cry sometimes at night wondering how I could go on. We used to have servants, and now I was renting a tiny place across town in a very different neighborhood. Diego and I were sleeping side by side in a one-room house.

"But life has given me this extraordinary gift — to be Diego's father. Waking up, the first thing on my mind, Diego, and the last thing on my mind before going to sleep, Diego. Oh, yes, there were times when I would have liked to wish him away, to have him just disappear. It was hard work, it was twenty-four hours a day, it was non-sleep. Yet with all the pain, with all the chaos and longing for it to be different, there was still this light. Diego."

So, too, has my son, Elias, become the greatest gift in my life, his presence forcing me to endure and grow to embrace new possibilities. I still remember how brightly the sun shone one July day a month before my due date. My friends Sypko and Carolyn had helped me to plan a gathering that would turn the traditional baby shower into a bona fide rite of passage into single motherhood. Smiling friends poured through the front door that afternoon. My huge, firm belly rose up and down as we danced to rhythms from around the world. Andean flutes, African marimbas, Turkish drums, Native American chants, a capella harmonies vibrated from the speakers. Four decades of independence were about to dissolve into an unknown future.

I was well aware of the absence of one person who was intimately connected to the unborn child whose presence we were acknowledging, but that loss was no longer the focus of my life. That morning, in preparation for this event, I had said my silent farewells. This gathering now was a chance to affirm that my baby and I resided in a loving and supportive community of friends. These people had all known me, many for years, as a friend, a co-worker, a fellow traveler. Now I was announcing to them that I was on the verge of a new identity.

When the music stopped, we gathered in the living room. A few friends had dressed me in white and hung a garland of daisies, roses, and bay leaves around my neck. "I am ready now to give birth to my child," I began. Suddenly the words I had prepared were surprisingly hard to say. They felt more real than I had imagined beforehand. "I let my old life go, this way of living I have known for so long. I am willing now to take this new life on. I am willing to be a single mother." Tears blurred the individual distinctions of all those faces shining back at me with such caring. One by one each person lit a small candle and, placing it on a tray in front of me, made a wish for my baby.

"May he be as strong as Hercules!" wished four-year-old Jason as he lit his candle.

Alice, a veteran of parenting a son on her own, stepped forward to light a match. "You'll not only be a mother, you'll learn something about what it is to be a father as well!"

The glowing circle of candlelight grew as each wish was spoken. Then gifts appeared — baby hand-me-downs, cards with gift certificates of meals and childcare, boxes with dollars hidden beneath tissues, checks peeking from envelopes.

Acknowledging my new life to and with those who were saying "Yes, we support you in this, you can do it" was another step in affirming that this was my choice and that I would do my best in it. Declaring one's status as a single parent in this way has a powerful effect. It lets others know that one is now in a role with different needs and a different lifestyle. Traditional rites of passage, marking the transition from one stage of life into another, have been considered a way to access a deep and empowering sense of the self as one sheds the old and is reborn into the new. Like the initiate returning from the forest, I was to be regarded now as fundamentally changed.

In our culture, baptisms, bar and bat mitzvahs, confirmations, weddings, and funerals are ways we recognize together deep shifts in the lives of our friends — and in how we regard them. Becoming a single parent is no less a profound change of identity and entry into a new life. Adoptive parents or those who conceived by choice may throw a party to celebrate their new family, but when marriage or partnership ends by divorce, separation, or death, many single parents slink off into their new role in hushed tones and whispers.

Yet it is possible to acknowledge, even celebrate, our new status in many different ways. When Tom and Linda divorced, they invited close friends to a ceremony in which they exchanged gratitudes and farewells. Everyone there, including their children, could experience the connections with others that still remained. The passage needn't be limited to this highly personal form, however. Mary Catherine, in the aftermath of divorce, took a public stance by bringing the story of her struggle with state-subsidized childcare to the press. She not only declared her identity as a single parent, she triumphed by starting a lobbying organization to call attention to the needs of many others in her circumstances.

Julian's thank-you card to his ex-wife, Nan's birthday parties for her deceased husband, my celebratory rite of passage — these are not the rites of victimhood, they are avenues to shared victory. Whether they are private acknowledgments or public announcements, some way of marking our intention to succeed in creating healthy families is essential to sustaining that intention.

Those moments of change, those turning points, when we first determine to create a rewarding life as single parents set the course. Sometimes the choice is not explicitly made or even formulated in words. Rather, it is a way of being, a set of actions in response to an urgent situation. But that the choice has been made is apparent, for an unknown strength sets in, an ability to persist despite ourselves. Boldly stepping forward on a path we embrace sends a tap root down to some boundless source.

"I learned so much as a single parent," Julian concludes. "Human beings are incredibly strong. The things I saw myself do. The things I see other single parents able to do. All of this is not in the nature of 'poor little me.'"

When being a victim is no longer an option, we are free to discover our own abilities, strengths, creative solutions. As one single mother, Michelle, puts it, "If they get past feeling like victims, single parents are the strongest people around. You have to be. Either you are a victim or you are very, very strong."

CHAPTER 3

Do Single Parents Try Harder?
Perfection and Guilt

Lo! With the ideal comes the actual —
Like two arrows meeting in midair.
— From a Zen sutra

"I MUST HAVE 'GOOD MOMMY' embossed in capital letters in gold across my chest, or maybe in my brain," begins Georgie. "I was going to be this really wonderful single parent who raised my children so that they knew about recycling and the rain forest, knew how to raise vegetables and bake bread, were socially conscious and spiritually aware. I was going to be the eternally present and eternally caring, concerned and engaged parent. I was going to prove that the good mommy could exist, and I was going to embody her.

"It's neither valid nor invalid to have those kinds of ideals," she adds. "It's just that I've had this onus hanging around my neck of 'I'm going to do this, and I'm going to be perfect at it.'"

Alone with two young children, Georgie found that she had to try harder and harder to catch up with her receding ideal. Eventually she would have to face giving up her lofty aspirations as a mother and consider sending her children to live with their father — or find a different way. We may set out on our journey determined to do the best we can as single parents, but our best may well fall short. The way we parent, the amount of time and opportunities we can give our children, the degree of attention — none may come close to our ideals. When we feel that our best is still not good enough, we can end up feeding the last drops of our vitality to the vortex of guilt.

The feeling of falling short is not peculiar to single parents; it seems to go hand in hand with parenting as it has come to be defined in our culture — a role stretching from playmate to provider. But parenting on our own almost guarantees that, given our limited time, money, and personal energy, we have to try a lot harder just to keep up. Drusilla, who has raised her two daughters as both a married and a single parent, says, "As a single parent you have to do not twice as much but *ten* times more. If you don't forgive yourself constantly, you can get to feeling very guilty."

Our ideals and values don't change just because we're parenting alone. We end up feeling guilty for not getting everything done, for taking time for ourselves, for working too many hours, for leaving our children too much with babysitters or alone. We feel guilty when we don't play with our children. We feel guilty when stress puts us on edge and turns us into monsters. And on top of all that, we feel guilty because our children might be missing something. "I constantly reproached myself for not being able to give my girls a mother," laments Alan, whose two daughters are now twelve and fifteen and have lived with their father for the past nine years. Helen, who raised her daughter alone, confesses, "I have no regrets about ending my marriage, but I have often had tremendous guilt feelings about not giving Pamela everything I could have if I had stayed married. I sometimes still do things for her out of guilt, and she's thirty-two years old."

While Alan and Helen feel guilt at not finding new partners, Hallie, who struggled for eight years in a new marriage to try to create a blended family, fears that she may have shifted too much of the focus away from her daughter during that time. "Lana even said to me recently, 'When you got together with Steve, you abandoned me.' I realize that's a little twisted because she wanted me totally to herself, but on another level it's true." Hallie explains, "It was much easier for me to be a lover than a parent. With parenting, I didn't know how to. It's one thing to withhold stuff, but when you don't even know what's missing, it's really painful. I feel like . . . I hate to say 'failed' . . . but I didn't know how to love her. I told her I was sorry, that I've made mistakes and nobody's perfect. She said okay, that was okay."

But sometimes our children also know how to turn the knife, and Lana at fifteen was no exception. "She says I'm not a real mother because I play conga drums. She thinks I carry on too much, because I laugh and I'm crazy." Waving a hand toward her elegantly shaped Afro, Hallie says, laughing, "She even says real mothers don't wear their hair cut like this. Her image of a mother is from TV, believe it or not!"

When we measure ourselves — or our children measure us — against an idealized image, we're bound to fall short. Feeling guilty, we may compensate and overcompensate, trying single-handedly to make up for what we think is missing. "I don't like that term 'broken family,'" says Jacki, who raised her daughter alone since conception, "because I think some families with fathers can be more broken than without a father — but because it was my decision to have my child as a single woman, I still felt guilt that maybe the situation I put her in was not the best, and so I felt I should do everything I could to make life good for her." Often this impulse can be a benefit to our children — we end up giving them a great deal. But guilt can also be a blind motivator.

Another single mother, Michelle, places guilt right up alongside money with what was hardest about single parenting for her in the beginning. "I felt I had done something to cause Melissa not to have a father, even by selecting him to marry in the first place. So for a long time after the marriage was over, I overcompensated by showering her with doting love. It wasn't just love, it was definitely doting. Because of that, I had a hard time disciplining her."

Giving in is a common atonement. Their daughter was three years old when Will and Sheila divorced and started sharing custody. "I found that I was letting Hilary get away with holy murder during the week she was with me, and Will was doing the same thing," Sheila reveals. "Neither of us wanted to be the bad guy, and both of us were trying to make up for our guilt. So we would give in to whatever she wanted."

We may overworry, overindulge, overbuy, trying to do the absolute best we can. "A friend of mine who is a single mother doesn't have very much money, can't afford a car, works long hours," Cheryl recounts. "But I notice that her daughter has a pretty new dress every Christmas and birthday party. On her birthday, she had the most beautiful cake from the most expensive bakery, and the perfect refreshments and decorations. I do the same thing for Sierra's birthdays — go all out." Cheryl laughs at how these efforts contrast with those of a family down the street. "That little boy has the ultimate yuppies as parents — they just sold their house for $750,000 — and they didn't even have a party for him on his birthday."

Some of that might be a matter of personal style, but Cheryl's point is clear. "I think we are just making sure our children have everything we can give them. If I can't give her another parent and, even though I have a desperate desire to do so, I probably can't give her a sibling, then I'll be sure to give her the best birthday party possible. But it's a high price for people like us who are struggling to make a living and take on all the roles."

♦ BETWEEN GRASP AND REACH

"Getting through the first couple of years was the hardest," Georgie said when we first talked. Her children were four and seven years old at the time, and she had been divorced for a little more than three years. "It was unpleasant most of the time. There was so much to grapple with, so much unformed and up to me to form. And I was wrestling with my own inner demons as well, sorting things out, learning to handle that it was all up to me. I would just sit down and weep sometimes, totally exhausted and overwhelmed. When I'd have a baby crying and a toddler in a full-blown tantrum, I was just sure one of us would die. I'd cry and wait for bedtime. And I'd be cursing Hugh and thinking, Why am I here doing all this by myself? He doesn't have to put up with the tantrums, he doesn't have to try to squeeze the money through to pay the rent and utilities. He's not up every night for a week with a child who has a fever and is vomiting. I've even had romances break up mainly because I have the kids, and he's getting remarried.

"Today, in fact, just about an hour ago, Hugh remarried. I'm fine about it now," Georgie hastened to add, "but over the last two weeks I went through a lot. I was afraid it would mean abandonment for the kids. But he has a strong relationship with them, and he has made it clear that they're major in his life. He flies up one weekend a month to be with them."

The divorce had been amicable. "We're still good friends," Georgie explained. "In fact, we married for friendship, because we got along so well. We knew each other from working side by side, ten- to twelve-hour days in a church program. We made a good team. But we didn't make a good married couple because we weren't in love, and eventually we both had to admit it. Because both of us came from broken families, and that had been so disruptive and unpleasant for us as children ourselves, we wanted to be very careful for the well-being of the kids."

They agreed that Georgie would continue as a full-time mother for Zoe, then a baby, and Jason, four, while taking classes part-time to build a career. "We both felt strongly that somebody needed to be primarily home raising them at this age. It was one of our values." To support that, Hugh sent $2,500 a month in alimony and child support — a whopping sum compared with what most custodial parents receive. But with a monthly rent of $1,200, Georgie still went "down to zero every month."

"But I make the sacrifice of keeping us in this house because it's a very safe neighborhood, ten other children live on the block, the local school is good and one mile away from here, and my mother lives nearby," explained Georgie. Even though suburban life was not Georgie's personal ideal, it fit the needs of her family. "Finding a niche for myself is very difficult, though. I'm the only single parent around."

Another advantage was that the size of the house enabled Georgie to set up a support system. For a while she rented two rooms to another single mother and her two children. When that didn't work out any longer, Georgie traded room and board for fifteen hours of live-in childcare a week, to cover her class time and to ease the load. When Hugh came up to visit the children, he stayed in the extra room for the weekend.

Georgie's mother was willing to help out and provide extras. "My mom bought about half the furniture and the washer and dryer, and she gives us a little every month. It would be just impossible to live like the woman who was my housemate. She worked full-time and had a huge daycare bill for her kids. She barely made enough to cover that and rent, and they had no family life at all. They all seemed miserable. That's the standard single-parent routine, which I think is abysmal. It's criminal that people have to do that."

Georgie certainly wasn't going to be that kind of single mother. And although the first years of adjustment had been very hard, she had developed what seemed to be a workable system. "It takes four adults to run this family," she told me. "Me full-time as mother, my ex giving us a large sum of money and being steady in the lives of the kids, my mom helping out, and the woman who lives with us and does childcare. And now that the kids are older, it's getting easier." Compared with her ex-housemate, Georgie considered herself "very lucky as a single parent."

A year later, however, when I talked to her again, Georgie didn't feel so lucky anymore. In fact, the exhaustion in her voice seemed buoyed up only by a sharp edge of frustration. "When I first talked with you," she began, "I felt we were a very comfortable, easy-moving cooperative family group. That has totally changed." Part of the change was that Jason, now eight, who had been diagnosed as "difficult" since infancy, had become a substantial challenge during the past year, and Georgie was worn down by his tantrums and defiance. "He seems to always need something that I'm not giving him, and I think that's a male role model."

Georgie was also worn down by her efforts "to do everything exactly right. I had been absolutely determined to do single parenting well and to be perfect at it. That included taking care of my ex-husband by making sure he stayed in touch with the children's development. I'd mail him their artwork every week, xerox their report cards, make sure the kids got on the phone to tell Daddy good night. Well, I've burned out. I'll flog a dead horse as good as the next guy, but what has come to light is that this isn't working and something has to change."

Something had already changed. Georgie was beginning to see that trying to develop a career was almost at odds with parenting alone. The support system that had enabled her to occasionally renew herself with breaks from her children and help her get through some of the hardest times had steadily eroded during the year. Her mother had returned to college and no longer had those free moments to help, the nanny had moved out and Georgie hadn't been able to afford another, and Hugh, feeling a need to establish his new marriage, had been spending less time with the children. Meanwhile, even as the load got heavier, Georgie's aspirations to be the good mommy had remained intact, and she seemed to regard her inability to carry on almost as a personal failure. "I'm feeling a lot of pain and frustration and sorrow at not seeing the family work. And I've had to let go of some really deep beliefs that I could do it on my own in the way I had in mind." Georgie had called Hugh and asked him to take the children. "All I said was, 'I can't do this anymore. I need help.'"

We expect a tremendous amount from ourselves. As single parents, we're at the end of the line in a shrinking family structure. Many roles that were once distributed among the members of an extended family and community have collapsed into one, and any parent, mother or father, taking on children alone may have to establish some solid priorities in order to avoid the guilt trap.

"I have always been a perfectionist," admits Tammy, a single mother who has spent her last two years undergoing the rigors of graduate school while raising her daughter, Mia, now five. Tammy says she is always "surprised when people mention what a good parent they think I am. I've had to learn to stop saying, 'You've got to be kidding,' and just say, 'Thanks, that's really good to hear.' That stems from my perfectionism.

"Every day feelings of guilt come up, and I have to struggle with them. It hits me most often at night after Mia is in bed. I start thinking, 'Oh, I could have spent more time with her today. I should have listened to her better. Physically I was there, but in my head I was thinking about all the things that need to get done. And I shouldn't have hurried her so fast at bedtime so I could have a break.' I go on like that a lot.

"When I look at it realistically, no, I couldn't have spent more time with her. And I probably did more than I should have anyway, because my dishes are still sitting over there in the sink. Being a parent is so much more important to me than having a clean house or having all of the laundry done. But to say that it's okay to let those things go is also really hard."

Now that she is graduating with her master's in social work, Tammy is looking for a job that will support her and her daughter. "So now I'm hauling Mia with me to the computer lab to type up cover letters. What kid wants to sit and be quiet for an hour or two? So I feel a lot of guilt about things that have to be."

For the majority of us, one of the things that has to be is earning a living, which means leaving our children for more hours than we might want. Knowing we have little choice doesn't necessarily assuage the feelings of guilt. For women especially, socialized to assume responsibility for children, these feelings can be particularly intense. For one mother, however, becoming single resolved them. "When I was married I always felt guilty when I was going to work, because I was leaving my kids. One thing divorce did was let me know what it feels like to be a man and go to work. You just have to go. There is no guilt about earning a living for your family."

A woman who adopted her ten-year-old daughter two years ago offers an additional supportive insight. "At my worst, I'm better than what this child has had," says Maggie. "And I think for people who have divorced, their kids are better off than they could be in a lot of circumstances. Sure you have to work, but I think that can be a really shining example to kids about their parent's dedication as well as how to pursue an area of interest. Even on the days when frankly I'm not wild about going into the office, I try to communicate to Tessa that I am, because I'd like her to learn that she can enjoy work. If you're saying, 'I'm sorry, dear, I *have* to go to work,' what is that saying to the child about what working is?"

But none of the explanations or reasons may cut through our feelings of guilt at times — and perhaps they shouldn't. A "Guilt Survey" of three thousand readers conducted by *Working Mother* magazine identified the three situations that "set off the most wrenching feelings: having a sick child, leaving a child who asks you to stay home, and not being at home when kids get out of school."[1] We *do* want to respond to our children's needs. Without the backup and support of another parent or partner, however, our ability to do so in these situations is severely limited. The feelings of guilt that arise can tear us apart inside.

◆ THE FACT AND THE FEELING

Often during his fourth year Elias pleaded with me not to make him go to school. "I'll play by myself. I'll be very quiet and not disturb you, I promise," he would beg. This was his first year of full-time childcare outside our home. Before that, sitters and other children had come to our house each day.

Whenever he balked, it caught me short. Seeking support and perspective, I'd call my friend Julie, who worked at the school. "What's wrong? What am I supposed to do? Is it right to force him against his wishes? It goes against the grain of my philosophy. Is it just me? Is it him? Is he trying to control me?"

Julie would just laugh in sympathy. She's a single mother too, but until her son was school-aged, she deliberately chose work, such as gardening, that could include him. "I watch the same thing go on with other parents," she assured me. "One child's father is a big, dignified man who is an airline pilot. Every morning, three days a week, he's down on his knees battling it out with his son. These children are going through feelings of separation, but Elias is not trying to maliciously manipulate you. You can't impute adult motives to them."

What she said may have been true, but it didn't change my feelings — especially on those days when I'd drop Elias off at school and he'd ask with trembling chin for one more hug. "I'm proud of you for being such a big boy," I'd say. "You'll have a wonderful time, and I'll see you later." All the right stuff. With my stomach tightening like a fist, I'd bolt, reciting to myself my litany of rights and reasons. I *have* to work. I even *want* to work. It fulfills a part of me that spending all day with my child, if I could, does not. I carried the evidence in mind: research shows that being involved in multiple roles enhances well-being, and that the children whose mothers enjoy their work are the happiest. Plus, I'd think to myself, Elias is in an enriching environment and learning how to socialize. And he's *four*. It's not like it would be if he were a *baby*.

In his earlier years, Elias would run off delighted when the caregiver and other children arrived, and I felt scarcely a pang about working. But remembering those days didn't ease the present moment. A passage from Liv Ullmann's autobiography haunted me most. An elegant and brilliant actress who raised her daughter as a single parent for many years, she laments that perhaps her success had been "achieved at the cost of something the two of us might have had together."[2]

I watched other children with their parents at these morning departures. Some cried at times, like Elias; others quite happily said good-bye and joined the group. Within the course of the year, the criers and the smilers sometimes traded roles. One little boy, Braun, usually quite happy to bid his father farewell, one day mysteriously clung to his neck; Scott had to hand him into the arms of a teacher in order to leave. I searched Scott's face for signs of distress as he headed toward the door, but he was smiling. Maybe he doesn't worry about the impact this might have on his child's life, I thought. Doesn't he consider, as I do, that this kind of trauma might turn our children into serial murderers when they grow up? How can he look so unruffled? Braun, appearing to me both determined and terrified, leaned out from the teacher's arms, reaching after his father. Scott turned and said lightly, with an encouraging lift of his eyebrows, "I'll see you when school is over." He blew a kiss and walked out the door.

I remained, a prisoner of internal conflict, feeling guilt at leaving my child and guilt at staying when I should be at work. I envied Scott's ability to so coolly get on with his day. He was a single parent too, and I decided to ask him why it seemed so easy for him to leave a crying child. Maybe it was a difference in style between men and women?

"I'm not willing to write it off as a gender difference," Scott told me. "When I first put Braun in childcare when he was two, it was much tougher for me to leave him crying than it is now when he is four and has matured more emotionally. Intellectually, I could tell myself then the reasons why it was necessary to leave him there, but I didn't have them all spelled out at a heart level. You don't like to see your child in pain, and that type of crying at separation is a form of pain."

After he and his wife separated, Scott managed to keep Braun, then one and a half, at home while he worked at his job as a freelance artist and cartoonist. "When we were married, my wife and I both worked intentionally during opposite hours. Our goal was to always have Braun be with one of his parents. And when we couldn't do that, his grandparents took care of him, until we moved too far away from them."

When Braun turned two, Scott realized that it was time for a change. "It was too much to parent him all day and try to get work done at the same time. It wasn't my ideal to put him into daycare at that age, but one of us had to work — and it wasn't going to be him!

"Still, there were a lot of feelings I had about becoming a single parent that fed into my attitude at the time about leaving him. I knew that the only reason I was bringing him to childcare was because my partner had left. If she were still there, we'd still be sharing care and he'd be at home and wouldn't have to go through that pain. So I went through that whole cycle of blame and guilt and hurt and pain at leaving him. It kind of churns you around inside."

Then how did he feel when Braun cried that day at school recently? Did it bother him? "No, it isn't hard for me to leave him like that now. It is a rare occurrence, and I know him well enough to know that it's kind of 'out of sight, out of mind.' When I leave, he'll move on to something else.

"I look objectively at what Braun's need is, and sometimes he has a need to be hugged, and other times I know that his need is just to get on with his life experiences. I don't try to rationalize or explain to him that Daddy has to go to work and make money and all that. I think the idea of going to work is too abstract for a child his age. What is really happening is at a feeling level. He's feeling loss and separation, and he wants to feel safe and secure. The most important thing for him to know is that he can turn around and go over to the toy kitchen and start playing. He's learning that. Braun is pretty adaptable, and he just got into focusing on his loss that day instead of focusing on what he was going to gain."

In the midst of doing all that we can for our children, we might lose sight of the fact that there is a difference between the *feeling* of guilt and the *fact* of being guilty. I'm not guilty for working but I do *feel* guilty when I don't spend enough time with my child. And sometimes what I feel is not guilt but rather a longing for things to be different. I wish I could sit down and teach Elias the alphabet, I wish I could be around to grab more of those rare and special moments when a particular value can be seeded in his heart, I wish I could simply hold him more before the holding time is over. But even if I had all those things, there would be others to long for as well.

When I *feel* guilty for the number of hours I work, I can try to figure out some way to change that. When I have felt guilty about leaving Elias in a childcare situation that I felt was not right for him, I have changed it. The feeling of guilt can, in fact, be a valuable motivation to change, a clue that something in our lives needs to be looked at.

◆ THE PROPER USES OF GUILT

"There had been a lot of stress before the breakup of my marriage, and then after it was also very stressful," relates Jeff, the single father of three young boys. "I had been having trouble blowing up at them, exploding, and shaking them. It was real bad. The counselor I was seeing said, 'Look, you have to recognize that you're this way, and just learn to live differently.' It was a hard thing to face."

Stress pushes us to our limit, the top blows off, and then we're full of guilt and remorse. What good does it do? Suzanne, who knows how short the fuse can get when you raise a child alone, eventually realized that feeling guilty in itself "was a completely useless response. It didn't help anybody for me to feel guilty. My father used to feel guilty after going on one of his violent binges, but it didn't help that he sobbed at the dinner table and told us he was sorry. That didn't stop him from doing it the next time."

Jeff did learn to stop, most of the time. "It's bad that I ever had that problem. It's not something I can erase — it's there. But what I have felt good about is learning to deal with it so that it's no longer a problem." Jeff worked with his counselor as well as attending meetings of Parents Anonymous and serving on the board. "One of the best things I learned there was that I didn't need to find the *perfect* solution. If something works, it's a solution, and it doesn't matter if it's perfect philosophically or not. So I learned to say to the kids things like, 'I'm feeling real angry and I'll be back in five minutes,' and I'd go for a walk. Or I told them that *they* could tell me to take a walk. I've learned to watch myself and know when I'm really tired and to say to them, 'Kids, we've got to eat early tonight. You should know that I've got to get to bed or have some time alone to relax.'

"One day about a year ago, I blew up again. It had been a long time, and I screamed and hollered at my twelve-year-old, Bobby. I just wouldn't let go. He started crying, and I realized that I had really lost it, and I left the house. When I got back, he had gone to visit a friend. There was a note from him saying, 'I don't like living with an abusive parent. When you yell and scream at me, it really hurts. So just quit.' I felt really awful about it again, but then I remembered how I used to do that all the time, and it had been so long that he had noticed it. And I felt good that he was able to write that to me. I thanked him later for the note and told him I'd been tired and that what I had done was really wrong, and that I'd do it differently next time. He said, 'Yeah, I know. Thanks.'"

Jeff had his feelings of guilt to thank for motivating him to seek help. But there is another feeling of guilt — a cruel, even misleading, self-torture that bores its way into our hearts, swallowing up all we have done and leaving only our deficiencies in the light.

Christine's voice is thick with tears as she remembers the years of raising her son alone in Australia. "I tried so hard to do everything I could for Nick as he was growing up," she begins. "At the time, to me doing a good job meant making sure he was provided for, that he was warm and comfortable. It meant teaching him to do all the things he should do, like getting to school on time and coming straight home.

"Oh, just look at me," she protests as the tears spill over. "I don't usually cry like this. It's just that I didn't know about giving him *emotional* support, about being loving and all those kinds of things."

It was twenty-two years ago that Christine, then herself just twenty, held her newborn son in her arms. "I remember thinking when he was born, 'What should I hope for him?' The word 'love' never . . . I just didn't know about it. I loved him but I didn't know that it was something you could work on or show. And — this just sounds so sad now — I thought what I could really hope for him was that he would become a good citizen. That was the highest I could imagine. I guess to me it meant that he would fit in and be comfortable and feel he had a place in the world, maybe feel as if he belonged some-where. I just didn't know anything else. I guess I never had those other things when I was growing up."

What Christine did have was an angry, violent father and a mother who "was extremely depressed. She just lay in bed crying a lot. So the treatment we were receiving wasn't mitigated at all by interven-tion on her part." When Christine's brief marriage ended and she returned home with her eight-week-old son, the only words her father spoke were in the form of a repeated question: "When are you leaving?" Christine didn't know. She didn't have anywhere to go.

"Then my aunt called up and asked if I wanted to live with them and work in their motel/restaurant as a waitress, and she would take care of Nick along with her own eight children. Of course I went. My uncle knew I was in desperate straits, though, and he had me working these Dickensian hours — seventy and eighty hours a week for twenty dollars. But my aunt was terrific, and Nick had a really nice time with her kids. It was better than it could have been. We were living in a huge house with them right on the beach. Otherwise we might have ended up in those terrible welfare buildings — fifty stories of ce-ment."

Compared with that time, the life Christine now leads must seem like heaven. When Nick was fourteen, Christine remarried. The morning she discovered that she and her new husband were pregnant, "I went in and woke Nick up and asked, 'Well, do you want a brother or a sister?' Nick was seventeen at the time and nothing in the world could possibly make him jump out of bed. But when he heard that, he leapt up and hugged me and ran all over. He was so excited." Nick got a sister, and a year later a brother.

Now twenty-two, Nick lives in Iowa, and his mother and her new family live in Wisconsin, where her husband is a graduate student at the state university. Their small apartment in the student housing area seems half given over to toys and child-sized furniture. Christine explains, "When I came to this country, I added an undergraduate degree in psychology to the teaching degree I got in Australia, and I intended to go on and do graduate work, but then my husband and I had these delightful interruptions to my study. What I want for my kids now is for them to feel loved every minute of their whole lives. I think it would have been a lovely thing to feel when you're young."

Christine dabs at her eyes again. "My husband is a very caring, thoughtful, reliable, respectful person — all of the things I had never known before in a man. He gave me a different sense of myself, and it opened up all this other stuff I didn't know about.

"But that's what made me recognize something about what Nick must have missed when he was little. After I realized that, I felt so horrible. I would wake up at night, at three or four in the morning, and stay up for hours feeling really bad about it, thinking, 'Oh, heavens, I didn't do this kind of thing or that kind of thing with Nick.'

"Yet despite me, he turned out great. He is just so nice, thoughtful, caring, sensitive. He seems to be emotionally really balanced. He's in a good, stable relationship with a very nice girl. I sometimes think, 'How could you turn out so fine?' Perfection and guilt. That's how you spell my name!"

When I asked if she had ever talked with Nick about her feelings of guilt, she answered no instantly, as if to banish the thought. "I've never brought it up. I'm so scared he'll say, 'I know. I missed that.' That's something I just don't think I could stand."

Several months after our talk, I received a letter from Christine. "It took me some time to pluck up the courage," she wrote, "but I did talk with Nick about the horrible guilt I felt that I may have emotionally neglected him. He denied ever having been neglected in *any* way! He was pretty convincing. I felt such enormous relief. Why did I torture myself for so long, I wonder?"

◆ TALK ABOUT REALISTIC EXPECTATIONS

"Being a single parent definitely made me more prone to questioning myself," says Angie. From the outset, she had decided to make her daughter, China, her life's priority, adjusting career and housing to fit the task. Yet Angie still found herself feeling inadequate. "I felt really vulnerable to other people's comments about my daughter or their assumptions about who she was and whether her behavior was appropriate." Until China was four, Angie worked as a midwife and took her daughter along when she was delivering babies or working with her clients. But when Angie enrolled in school for an education degree, China started daycare. That's when the trouble began.

"China was a fairly thoughtful child, and she spent a lot of time drawing and creating stories. She was introverted instead of outgoing and bubbly, which seemed to be what they were looking for in a well-adjusted child. They told me she was strong-willed and lived in a fantasy world, and they wanted to look at the kinds of things I did with her that might account for it. When I told them that we took lots of walks together, went to playgrounds, did drawing and painting and reading together, they said she should be having more contact with other children. She had a best friend next door and we had lived for a year with two other single mothers and their children, and she played with them just fine. But the teachers weren't seeing the behavior they wanted.

"It brought up a terrific amount of guilt in me that I wasn't being the perfect parent and that she wasn't turning out to be the perfect child. I felt that I had failed. I thought they as teachers had the authority, so for several months I went through agony, feeling I wasn't raising her to fit the norm. If I had had a partner, her other parent, or someone else closely concerned, I might have bounced my questions off them, or I would have had some support or confirmation that what I was doing was fine. I also might not have felt like I was the only one totally to blame."

In addition to her own fears of being at fault and the daycare teachers' rigid standards, there may have been something else Angie was up against: preconceptions about children of single parents. Another single mother, a lawyer and the mother of two, alerted me to this issue when we were discussing her children. "Wait until your son goes to school and they start asking you the questions," she warned me. "At the first school conference this year, the teacher sat me down and didn't want to talk about my son's grades, which were just fine. She wanted to know if he had any good male role models! She would never have thought to ask that question of the mothers in two-parent families, whose children might in fact be living with abusive fathers!"

Michael Stevenson, a psychologist at Ball State University, points out that the negative stereotypes commonly associated with children of single mothers are actually "based on unusual examples rather than the majority," and he holds that the greatest harm comes not from the absence of a father but from those erroneous assumptions.[3] One national survey showed that "children of single-parent households were not doing worse on IQ tests or achievement tests; yet they showed a tendency to be rated lower by their teachers on intellectual ability and performance."[4] Another study revealed that teachers of first-graders "tended to *believe* that children from single-parent households would do less well in school."[5]

Stephanie Coontz, author of *The Way We Never Were* and herself a single mother, relates a similar story. "My son tests in the ninety-seventh percentile of everything and is inordinately proud . . . of the fact that he never got his name on the board for bad behavior once in his entire elementary school history. At the end of one year, when I went in to say good-bye to his teacher, she said to me, 'I just want you to know that your child is the most together boy' — and I started to smile . . . 'of a one-parent family that I have ever met.' And my smile just kind of froze. I would like to know why that modifier was there."[6]

Expectation of negative behaviors or poor performance can be self-fulfilling prophecies in the classroom. And assumptions that we are ourselves less-than-adequate parents can doom us to unbearable guilt unless we step back and assess our individual situations clearly and honestly.

"It took me some time before I realized that I wasn't having difficulty with my daughter but with society," remarks Angie. "I finally looked and thought, 'Wait a minute. This person doesn't necessarily know more about China than I do. And besides, do I really want her to be what someone else wants her to be, or do I want her to be what I see is her potential?' I ended up knowing that there were qualities she had that I was nurturing, and I was laying a foundation for her to be able to choose and express her own values and personality. I had given over my trust in myself to let someone else define what was perfect or right or who she should be."

It took that affirmation of trust in herself and her parenting for Angie to stand against the assumptions that might have categorized her daughter as abnormal. The dynamics of our family life do differ from those of two-parent families. We expect our children to be more self-reliant perhaps, to take on more responsibility — or sometimes less, if we're overcompensating. They are full participants in our families, and often more like our friends than are the children of parents who are coupled.

If the children of single parents *do* differ from the norm, the differences may also be seen as positive. The sociologist Robert Weiss reported that children of single mothers "tend to be more mature, independent, self-disciplined and unusually self-assured."[7] That was in 1979, before "family values" became a political issue. (And it applied, of course, to *some* children of single mothers.) Other studies too have had positive reports. Preschoolers from single-parent families proved to be more imaginative than their counterparts from two-parent families.[8] Grade-school children of single parents scored significantly higher on tests of creative abilities.[9] Children raised by single parents, who are themselves fulfilling multiple roles, are less constrained by gender stereotypes in their play and behavior.[10]

Behavior that deviates from the norm can also be creative and inventive. In fact, meeting challenges and taking responsibility, if not overwhelming, can cultivate resilience, the prime index of mental and emotional health. That the structure of the single-parent family is not in itself a liability is clear. A study of schoolchildren in the Netherlands indicated that 24 percent of those with single mothers were just as successful as their counterparts in two-parent families, and — here's the clincher — 29 percent were *more* successful.[11]

The psychologist Nor Hall has found in her years of counseling single parents that "more than anything, I have discovered that empathy has meant supporting them against the criticisms of society that might say, 'You should not be so involved with your children, you should make stricter rules, you should get on with your own life.' I support the part of them that instinctually knows that it's all right to have their child sleeping with them in bed, or to have a different kind of relationship with their children than their neighbors might have. It's a deep understanding for the value of what they are trying to do that's most helpful to them — pointing out their courage and ability to know what they have to do, even if it's different from the norm, and encouraging them to trust that."[12]

Trusting our ability to do well in parenting and exonerating ourselves from unnecessary guilt results from assessing what we need to make our lives work well enough to approximate our ideals. A recent national study, conducted by the Search Institute, on risk and resilience in children of single-parent families has discerned specific assets that contribute to whether the children will thrive or whether they will become involved in alcohol abuse, cigarette smoking, antisocial behavior, early sexual activity, depression, and suicide. The thrivers have the assets we might assume: single parents who love and support them at home and outside the home, talk with them and advise them on social life and opportunities, set clear standards of conduct, monitor where they are and what they're doing, spend time with them at home, encourage them both to study and to be involved in school and community organizations. The thrivers care about other people's feelings, value helping people, and honor themselves.[13]

It's hard to give away our best hours at work and return, exhausted, to cuddle, encourage, teach values, help with homework, and seek fulfilling activities for our children. It's hard to be there for them. Still, those are the ways we try harder. "Guilt? — you bet," says Ed, speaking of how he has felt about the effect of divorce on the son he is raising as primary parent. "I used to think I had screwed up David's life. Now I know he'll be all right, but you bet I compensate for his loss. He's thirteen now, and I still call him every day if I'm on a business trip, whether he's with his mother, my brother, or staying with friends. I keep calling and calling. He always knows where I can be reached. He's got to know that somebody is there. A kid just has to feel secure. All the rest is fluff."

Feeling alone and isolated were among the greatest liabilities reported by children in single-parent families. It is no wonder that the researchers also note that a significant contributor to thriving is a high level of support systems surrounding the family: good schools, positive friends, supportive institutions. For the children who thrived, access to non-parent adults for advice and support was reported as almost equivalent in value to talking with their own parents.[14] In *Second Chances: Men, Women, and Children a Decade After Divorce,* Judith Wallerstein and Sandra Blakeslee point out dramatic disadvantages to children of divorce; but they also discovered that "only ten percent of the children had any adult speak to them sympathetically through the divorce process."[15] We can't do it all, and that is why the help and attitudes of all those who also care for our children are so important.

"David was in the second grade when his mother and I divorced and he began living with me," Ed continues. "Of course he went through his downs like any kid. He started having trouble in school, and his teacher called us in. During the course of our long meeting it came out that David was feeling a lot of shame and embarrassment about being from a family with divorced parents. He was thinking he was the lone ranger and the scum of the earth, and he didn't want any kid in his class to know what had happened to his parents. As we talked, the teacher began bringing in, 'Did you know that Janet isn't living with both her own parents? And do you know that Timmy and Cass and this one and that one . . .' — and she peeled off half of his class." While most of them were living with remarried parents, the key for David was that he wasn't the only one with divorced parents. "It turned out that the teacher herself came from a divorced family," Ed explains, "and she had a support group going for kids of divorce. David declined that, but by the end of the conversation he had a light go on. All of a sudden it wasn't a big issue for him anymore. You'd think this huge cloud would take a while to get through, but it was behind him in that instant. Once he knew that others in his class were in the same boat, he was one happy little clam.

"I don't pretend he's past everything, but he sure feels he's got enough of a grasp on it to coach other kids. I overheard him saying to a friend his age whose parents are now in the midst of a divorce, 'There are other kids in the class. Don't worry about it. I know it's tough, but you'll get used to it. And you'll still be able to see your dad.'"

For Georgie, moving beyond her feelings of failure lay in correctly assessing what she needed in order to live up to her ideals. The active support of others — "four adults to run this family" — was not incidental to her success but pivotal. When she let go of expecting herself to do everything, she was able to involve other adults again. Hugh began coming up to visit the children not once but twice or more a month and taking them for extended visits to his house. Georgie's mother, now aware of the need, again helped her out with money and time. "I closed the right door, so a lot of windows are opening," says Georgie. One window opened onto a welcome surprise. "I've just discovered other single mothers in my neighborhood as well. Two of them are sisters and they trade off care of their children, and we're getting to know each other."

Summing up their study of forty-seven thousand students from both single- and two-parent families, the researchers from the Search Institute report: "On the average, kids fare better in two-parent families. The key phrase is 'on the average.' But there is a sizable percentage of children in single-parent families who thrive and many in two-parent families who do not. Family structure, then, does not, in and of itself, explain child and adolescent well-being. What matters most — regardless of family structure — is what happens within the family."[16]

In the face of sweeping condemnations of single-parent families as the cause of society's ills,[17] we need the strength to honor what we *are* doing and the information to interpret misleading data. Children in single-parent families are, in general, somewhat more at risk of developing behaviors that are harmful to themselves and others, but other prominent social researchers also acknowledge that "while single-parent families may not be 'normative,' neither are they inherently bad. The evidence suggests that it is predominantly . . . poverty that creates disadvantage for their members."[18]

Poverty, not family structure, causes problems. Lack of adequate support from the other parent in the majority of single-parent families may be a contributor to crime and deviant behavior — but not single-parent families in themselves.

As one long-term study of over seventeen thousand British families revealed, many of the emotional and behavioral difficulties evident in children after divorce — and attributed by implication to single-parent families — were already there before the marriage ended. "Conflict hurts children," says Andrew Cherlin, a co-author of the study, "regardless of whether it leads to divorce."[19] We can't deny that children suffer when their parents separate, but we needn't add guilt to our burden by assuming that preserving the relationship would have prevented problems they may be experiencing. And many of us have seen the healing that happens when our children are spared the conflict. "Everybody who knows us commented on how happy Jed became after the divorce," Sharon says. "I don't feel guilty at taking him *out* of the marriage. I felt guilty keeping him in it!"

Sometimes we too quickly look for signs of pathology even in normal behavior, questioning whether anything less than perfect means difficulty stemming from living with one parent. Priscilla, the single mother of two young sons, has found that "it's important for single parents to be in touch with parents who are in what is considered 'normal' families in order to hear that our issues in raising our children are often the same. A two-year-old from a family with a father and a mother and sibling has the same behavior problems as mine does. If my two-year-old is fussy, it's not because I'm a single parent, it's not because I don't have a husband. It's because he's two years old!

"Being single parents is not the cause of a lot of problems," Priscilla adds. "It's just that we're people in the world today, and the entire planet is in crisis. No matter what our situation, we're encountering intense challenges."

The question to ask ourselves, then, is not, Is my family structure deficient? It is, rather, How are my children doing? What are they like? "I feel guilty about taking Mia along on my job search and having so much else to attend to, but she doesn't seem to be affected negatively by it," notes Tammy. "She is a great, healthy, normal kid with tons of self-esteem. I wish I had had half of that growing up. She is really wonderful. I think I beat myself a lot harder than I really need to about falling short. Times like sitting at that computer lab have actually brought us together. And at least she knows where I am, what I am doing, that I am busy and that she can be a part of it.

"When I start feeling guilty, I go back over the day and say, 'Wait a minute, you *were* there for her. Your mind might have been racing for ten minutes, but then you were right there, interacting. Sure I rushed her to the computer lab this summer, for the job search, and then to prepare my public testimony on post-secondary education for welfare mothers. But we also went on bike rides, we spent a lot of time just waking up and having breakfast together. I forget about patting myself on the back or looking at it in a positive light. Those are my reality checks, saying to myself, 'You are just looking at half of it.'"

It's likely that Tammy is in fact spending more time with her child than the average parent might. The writer and psychologist David Elkind notes that a survey found that "working mothers spend only an average of eleven minutes each weekday . . . and thirty minutes per day on weekends" in quality-time activities such as talking with their children, playing with them, and reading to them. The working fathers in the study spent eight minutes each weekday with their children and fourteen a day on weekends. The amount of time devoted to these activities by homemaker mothers was also surprising: thirty minutes weekdays and thirty-six on weekends.[20] As single parents, our efforts to compensate for perceived lack may result in our giving *more* than the average — and more than we may be crediting ourselves for.

When Angie's daughter, China, went away for the summer at age sixteen, she wrote back to her mother, "I don't think I could have had a better parent. Even though you were a single working parent, you gave me so much more love, patience, and creativity than other parents I have seen. It's staggering when I think of how many sacrifices you've made for me, how many times you've made me your first priority. Thank you."

Because of our efforts, our children may well surpass our hopes and dreams. Leah raised her four children in a small town in Idaho, along with a number of friends — many of them also in single-parent families — who had been a mutual support system. Observing now those young adults who grew up with one parent, Leah reports, "These kids have just turned out to be very special people doing remarkable things in the world. One way of looking at it," she conjectures, "is that we took our parenting role extremely seriously. Our children were the most important parts of our lives, and we were very conscious about how everything we did was affecting them.

"Yes, I did try harder as a single parent. When you realize you are *it,* you really work at parenting. Not that I am recommending doing it alone, but you do compensate for anything they might be missing. And when I look at the finished products, we have a lot to be proud of."

---◆---

CHAPTER 4

From the Bottom Up:
The Imperative to Grow

Life does not accommodate you, it shatters you. It is meant to, and it couldn't do better. Every seed destroys its container or else there would be no fruition.

— Florida Scott-Maxwell

MY FIRST YEAR AS a single parent turned out to be a drama of radical contrasts. On one hand, I felt like the first and only mother in the world, and the smiles of my child were the ultimate gift of the universe. Simply holding Elias next to me was heaven in a moment, and caring for him was an honor. The wonderful drunkenness of love! Whatever I might have grieved was buried beneath a mound of exigencies and forgotten in baby smiles. My work, when I resumed it, had enhanced meaning because it supported that chortling life being cared for in the next room. It was the longest period of continuous happiness I remembered in my life. People commented on how much I enjoyed my baby, and it was true. But underneath the life that arose from our love something grim and unattended was brooding.

The clock never stopped as I met one deadline after another in my work, struggled to find and maintain good, affordable childcare, contended with bouts of winter flu in myself and my baby, juggled financial demands I had never encountered before having a child, and woke at night, often several times, to feed, diaper, and comfort this tiny individual who directed my life with his perpetual presence. Days passed with literally no time for a shower. Normal life was a memory to which I remained linked by a fragile thread. During one of those quick checks new parents make to be sure their babies are breathing, the unspeakable escaped my mind before I could catch it: If he's not, I'll be able to sleep. No wonder sleep deprivation has been employed as an instrument of torture throughout time. A friend who was raising her daughter alone left a message on my answering machine: "Believe me, it gets easier." I rolled that line around in my mind with anticipation. It wasn't happening yet.

How could my life be so joyful and so extremely difficult at once? And then — suddenly, it seemed — everything went gray. For weeks I went through the motions of life, lightened only momentarily by baby love. I could remember what excitement felt like, but my body and mind were leaden. I could recall appreciating a beautiful sunset, but now everything looked two-dimensional. I remembered what it was like to cry, but my eyes were dry. I felt as if I were up against a wall again, but this time there was no sudden shock, no chaos of indecision. I was doing what I had chosen to do, I was doing in fact what I wanted to do, yet something was wrong. Recently I found a scrap of paper stuck in Elias's baby book from that time: "There must be a way out of this." I didn't want to stop parenting, and I wasn't looking for a partner. I needed someone to switch on a light.

No matter how well-informed or prepared we are, none of us can wholly anticipate what lies before us or imagine what it is like to face the double impact of being a parent and doing it alone. No parent can imagine, before the fact, the all-encompassing intensity of the bond we can form with our children. Who could foresee the wild swings of emotion when we raise them alone, with no partner to dilute the love or mitigate the stress? How could we anticipate the weight of knowing that, day after day, every move we make is intricately woven into the needs and desires of the children who depend on us for their lives?

At times, despite valiant determination to succeed, "I can do it" becomes "I thought I could, but now I'm not so sure." We set out for the end of the rainbow, and then one day we find ourselves at the end of our ropes. Even those who prepared themselves in every way for parenting alone sometimes find themselves scarcely bearing up under overwhelming stress.

All parents are forced to their limits, but for the single parent covering all bases alone, each need and demand is magnified. What might bring up stressful choices for a two-parent family can amount to full-blown crises for the single parent. All aspects of our existence are so precariously interrelated that, like a house of cards, the entire structure can tumble with the slightest change. We often have none of the safety nets that even the minimally functioning two-parent family might provide. If we live alone, there's no one else we can count on to give us a break in the evening or on the weekend, to stop by the grocery store on the way home, to turn to at midnight when we're in turmoil over a child. There is no one else to share the burden of errors and often no one else to supplement love stretched thin. If we are the only significant adult in our children's lives, there may be no one else to catch them when we let them down. And when we ourselves fall, we fall alone.

"I'm fascinated by what makes people finally change," muses Gwen, whose career in state politics before Michael's birth exposed her to both the private and public roller coaster. "In my experience it seems that most of the time you have to hit bottom before you do. You have to reach a crisis that becomes so intolerable that you simply have to bust out or something has to change."

Hitting bottom — slipping or plunging into rage, depression, pain, darkness — is not an unfamiliar ordeal to single parents. Our circumstances pave the way. Minor slips may happen daily, but the major falls are what bring us to the point where we say "I can't go on" or "I won't go on." When everything in our lives seems out of control, when the terror descends as we realize we are the only one holding up the house of cards, what then do we do, for ourselves and our children?

When things go wrong in our lives, it doesn't mean that *we* are wrong. At our darkest moments, perhaps we stand on the threshold of an essential and enlivening change, as we extend ourselves beyond what we assumed were our absolute limits. The frightening part of these dark times that compel change is that we have no idea of what is on the other side until we get there.

◆ SUPERPARENT DESCENDS

For Sophie the full impact of how alone she was in raising her son hit during fifteen outrageously prolonged seconds that literally shook the foundations of her life — the 1989 Oakland earthquake. We have all encountered a degree of that kind of terror, in the dark of the night when the canyon between our income and financial needs cannot be bridged, or when we watch each breath of a sick child with no one to share our fear. But it was when her home actually shook that a chink was made in the tight structure of Sophie's life. In time it would reveal a need that had been hidden and denied beneath her super-woman façade.

To all outer appearances Sophie had been doing just fine as a single mother. Clearly, she was no victim; it wasn't the way she approached anything in life. When she separated from her husband ten years earlier and found herself the single parent of a newborn, Sophie knew she could rely on deep reservoirs of strength. As a crisis-care nurse she had a good income, and she moved close to her parents for support when her son was a baby. With their help, she even had some weekends free to pursue her passion, painting. By the time Trevor was six, Sophie had moved back to the city and enrolled in a master's program in creative arts.

"I had a lot of pride in being a capable single parent. I was functioning as the breadwinner, and I had set up a nice home. I could keep the laundry moving, make sure I baked cookies in the evening so that it felt homey, wrestle with Trevor, sing songs with him. I was helping him grow through the emotional challenges of a ten-year-old. I was even making sure I had a little social life so that I stayed balanced myself.

"I was proud of how well-balanced Trevor was as well. He had great opportunities in the school I put him in. We traveled together on vacations. I was making a good life for him — better than a lot of two-parent families, in fact. He didn't have an alcoholic parent, he didn't have a mother who was depressed all the time. My work schedule let me be with Trevor when he needed it. I looked like the all-American woman who was doing above average for a single mother."

Sophie was strong. She knew the kind of strength that pushes past limits. When problems arose, Sophie knew how to fix them. Life was under control. And then the earthquake hit.

"During those fifteen seconds, our house was shaking so hard you could not stand. Miraculously, Trevor was standing next to me when it started, and we were five feet from the hallway. My instincts came up, and I threw him, this sixty-five-pound kid, between my legs and braced us with my arms between the two pillars of the hall doorway. There he was, screaming, me trying to keep him calm, all the while thinking this might be the moment we both die. And the shaking just wasn't ending. Any moment the house was going to cave in if it didn't quit. I was scared in a way I have never been before. And with me was my child, this kid I'm totally responsible for.

"What happened to me when those fifteen seconds ended was that I realized that everybody was scrambling now for their loved ones, but nobody was scrambling for me. I was alone. I was a *single* parent. What I wanted more than anything else in the world was to know that somebody else was going to be showing up, somebody whose first thought was to race over to make sure that everything was okay, to let me fall into their arms and cry. Because I was as scared as Trevor was. I realized because of those fifteen seconds how isolating the superwoman trip I had been on was. I had to admit that I wasn't doing this well all by myself."

During the year that followed, Sophie carried on in her usual way, but that crack in the façade continued to expand. "It began to feel like a clinical, sterile life I was leading," Sophie relates. "I knew that this wasn't what it was supposed to be about, but I couldn't seem to find the avenue out."

Over the course of a few late nights, Sophie planned a series of paintings about the creative spirit in women. "But when I set to it, I ended up painting the faces of men in crisis. They were at that point when you realize that everything you have been working for some-how isn't doing what you wanted it to do. I depicted it in the faces of men, because that's what I was seeing out there in the world — men dedicating their lives to trying to solve some problem, like the state of the environment or deteriorating social conditions — and standing back and admitting that it somehow was not working. And then over the course of a few weeks I found the same thing actually happening to me.

"Trevor started having trouble at school, and I plunged into a great fatigue. I think my reservoirs had been slowly draining out from trying to hold it all together for so long on my own, trying to resolve every problem for both of us — house, work, car, emotions. I felt exhausted because I absolutely needed a little time to paint but I was working full-time in a draining job in the emergency room." And Sophie could no longer deny the stark aloneness that she had recognized during the earthquake the year before.

"I started feeling like a potential suicide. It wasn't at all that I wanted to kill myself. Rather, I was so fatigued that I feared if there were a cliff in front of me, I wouldn't even have the energy to stop from going over it. I got really scared, because the truth was I didn't want to die. I loved my son, I loved life, I loved the dreams that were buried inside me. I just didn't know how to get to them anymore."

Sophie did in fact have a car accident. Maybe it was the fault of the other driver, or maybe Sophie was indeed too tired to get her foot to the brake in time. She walked away from the scene, but something inside had also stopped with the intensity of the impact. "For a couple of weeks I couldn't go to work. I could barely keep making meals for Trevor. Sometimes I just sat and stared at those paintings. There it was in those faces, the moment of meeting that absolute end when you don't know what the question is anymore, let alone the answer. There it was in me. This was no exhilarating moment of 'Ah! Now I know what to do! Here's what I can do to fix this.' No, it was the opposite. I didn't know what to do to fix Trevor. I didn't know what to do to fix myself. I didn't know the answer. I didn't know the question. I didn't even know what the issue was. For my usual way of thinking, that was total loss of control.

"Then I hit one of those nights when I just couldn't stop crying. I knew Trevor was distressed by hearing me, so I went into his room. He was sitting at his desk, his homework spread out in front of him. I sat down on the bed across from him, not sure what to say.

"He finally spoke first. 'Nobody loves me, Mom. I might as well die.'

"'What do you mean — nobody loves you?'

"'Well, even your life would be better without me,' he said.

"I was stunned. I never, ever complained to him. Never. But he knew of course that I have to leave my job early to pick him up at school and that sometimes I'm screaming at him because I'm late for work and he won't get dressed on time. He knows that he's making my life more complex. And you better believe these little kids take it personally. He loves me.

"That was it. I finally closed the doors inside and said to myself, 'I give up. I do not know how to go on.'" Sophie had always believed that she could figure out what to do. Now she knew that if she came up with an answer based on the way she'd been doing things, it would only perpetuate the old pattern of their life, which was not working.

"I could no longer be the director of my show. I felt utterly lost as a person and as a parent in being able to respond to my son's needs and my own needs. I was forced into that absolute silence where nothing is happening. All I could do was wait and trust that something else was going on that I had not yet begun to identify. And what I found out is that there you begin to hear new directions or new thoughts, because you're not filling up every moment with the old solutions."

Hitting bottom and letting go requires a breathtaking leap of faith. As single parents, as we make our way into unknown territory with few models to follow, it can also be a leap of discovery. As we build our bridges before us, we are bound to hit the limits of our knowledge. We are bound to feel totally helpless when we've tried everything we know of and we still don't find our lives working. Like Sophie, sometimes we have to stop and wait, peering into the fearsome darkness, listening intently to discover what might be bridging toward us from the other direction.

"I reached out and pulled Trevor over to me," Sophie continues. "'Trevor,' I said, 'this has nothing to do with you. There's just something not right, and I don't know what it is. I just don't know.' Supermom, the one who could fix anything, didn't have the answer. I just said in my heart, 'This kid needs something. I need something. Show us the way.'"

In these dark places, we may feel reassured by faith in a benevolent God or power in the universe, but whatever our refuge, we still face the unknown and only the possibility of something new. Caught alone and unknowing, with children who depend on us, can make the darkness seem so much deeper.

Sometimes in that place it is hard to reach out to others, to reveal ourselves. Inner voices may taunt, Who cares anyway? My own nonstop schedule during the first year of my child's life had left almost no time to stay in close touch with friends. I really didn't know who to turn to when the barren months unrolled. Like many of us, I had a hard time asking for help. To impose upon any of my housemates with so simple a request as "Would you hold the baby for ten minutes, please?" struck against something so ingrained that to push past it threatened to require more effort than the help could be worth.

Caught in the vise of internal and external stresses, I could no longer continue to merely endure from day to day. I hadn't been able to afford professional help, but now I couldn't afford not to. I made an appointment with a therapist who had also been a single mother, and arrived with a long scribbled list of the issues and problems: What am I doing wrong? What should I do? Why is it so hard? What can I do to change it? How can I get out of feeling so low, so overwhelmed, so empty?

The woman listened, nodded, understood. She lay me on her work table, massaged my back, held my head. Soon she was going to give me some clue. I knew it. The thick sheepskin under me seemed to cushion the fall. "This is the way it is," she said softly. Was that it? I wanted to run. What did she mean? "Each time your mind starts up again, I want you to say that to yourself: This is the way it is."

"But . . ."

"No. This is the way it is."

I hated it. What good was this going to do? But for days after that session, I forced myself to say it each time the chaos and questions nibbled away in my mind. Why is it like this? What can I do? *This is the way it is, Shoshana. This is the way it is.*

Gradually I began to see that this was no deadening song of submission but rather a way to ease the momentum of my resistance and allow life to pursue its ever-changing course. *This is the way it is.* In that brief pause, considered moment, the kaleidoscope turns and the pieces settle into a new pattern. We begin to discern a light moving toward us in the darkness.

◆   FACE TO FACE

Laurinda and her son, Eric, now a man of thirty, are sitting on the couch across from me. He is visiting from the East Coast, on vacation with his girlfriend. Mother and son both relax into the cushions, friends in each other's presence. "One of the things I like best about having Laurinda for my mother," Eric says, smiling, "is that she has shown me that it's possible to get through *anything.*" Laughing, they join each other to acknowledge the mixed nature of that blessing. Their story of "growing up together," as Laurinda phrases it, is not an easy one for either one of them, yet here they sit, gently inclining toward each other as they speak. Each has stretched an arm along the back of the couch toward the other, hands resting on each other's forearms. There the hands remain, sometimes patting, sometimes clutching, adding their own commentary to this tale.

Turning to Laurinda, Eric goes on, "What I mean is that ever since those two years when I went away to live with my father as a child, I have watched how your whole life has been about striving to become more real and truthful as a human being, no matter what you have had to face or how stuck you felt."

"And no one could have been more stuck than I was," Laurinda says, wiping her eyes as tears well up. "I was twenty-two going on two and a half when I married Eric's father, the first man I ever dated," she confesses. "And I was like someone ensconced in concrete." When Eric was a year old, Laurinda fled her marriage, taking him with her. In time she would discover that although she could leave the marriage and lay the blame for their difficulties on her husband, in her arms she carried away her undoing, that terrible gift of love that would ultimately force her to turn and face herself.

"I know now that the deep depression I was living in came from a profound loss of connection that started way back. When I left my marriage I was convinced I wasn't capable of loving anyone. I didn't even feel like I loved my child." Laurinda's hand tightens on Eric's arm for a moment.

"I didn't know what in the hell I had set up or what I was doing," she continues. "It was 1962 and nobody else I knew was divorced and had a child. I was working for the first time in my life. My husband and I had been living in England, so when I moved to Berkeley I had no close friends. Sometimes I was so desperate to get away from it all that I'd leave Eric asleep at night in his crib and go out to the movies by myself. I'd ask the old couple next door if they would listen for him, but a number of times I came home to find him sobbing alone. This was such a different life than I had ever imagined. I couldn't even think of what the possible repercussions might be of leaving him alone. I could only think of the moment and how to get away.

"And I was extremely erratic. On the one hand, I'd be warm and loving and sweet with him. We loved to wrestle and laugh. The woman upstairs used to tell me I was just like a kid, getting right in there and playing with him. But then I could suddenly turn cold and judgmental and angry. I had no room for error. I felt if I didn't have everything under control, it would all fall apart. So when he'd make a mistake, spill the milk, break something, I'd rage at him like he was worthless. I never abused him physically but I did verbally. I yelled at him a lot. He was the only person I was letting myself rage at," remembers Laurinda, "and he got a tremendous amount of it. It was all the rage that had built up over a lifetime."

Rage. I've found few single parents who haven't experienced it. Just dealing with the daily logistics of parenting alone can force us to the edge, let alone responding to the endless emotional needs of our children. And like mirrors they reflect back to us who we are. They do what we do rather than what we might want them to do. Their tears and demands remind us of our own unkissed wounds and ragged needs. No matter how intensely we vow to give them what we didn't get or never to do to them what was done to us, we find ourselves echoing the voices and actions of our own parents. Almost before we notice it, we may be shouting the hurtful phrases stored away in our own memories, or a hand may flash out to strike even though in more rational moments we disavow spanking. Our children, it seems, can exasperate us like nothing else can.

Of course we are good, well-intentioned people — but we each drag behind us, as Robert Bly puts it, a personal "shadow" stuffed into a long, invisible bag. We hope our children won't see it, but they walk right into it.[1] Someone spills the milk and suddenly all the hidden pain, self-doubt, and unresolved conflicts of our childhood reveal themselves. Our lack of confidence and feelings of powerlessness explode in a rage that far exceeds the crime. Wherever we are unconscious of our own pain, we inflict it on others. We see it reflected in the eyes of our children. "Don't be angry, Mom." "Please don't yell, Dad." No wonder children are fascinated by fairy tales — there the witch and ogre they might behold in their parents stand revealed. The fear in their eyes, of *us,* brings us face to face with ourselves.

"The potential for seeing my personal failings was more extreme with my son than in any other relationship in my life," Laurinda remembers. "It was horrifying to see what could come up, especially living alone, as we did, when there was no one else to deflect or reflect the emotional intensity. A child can't leave, is totally at your mercy. That leaves room for doing anything and getting away with it, short of killing them. You are your only moral guide."

Family life in any structure brings up the emotional intensity that comes with intimacy and interdependence. When our children are throwing tantrums, raging, rolling in the emotional upheaval that comes with the territory of growing, to be the only one fielding that energy is an exhausting task. Rage begets rage.

With no one else around to break the cycle, no one to relieve the pressure, who can remind us of limits? Who can hug and support us? Who was there to stop Suzanne and give her the break she desperately needed when she was holding Molly's shoulders down in the crib and screaming at her that she had to take a nap? Or when Diego, as a teenager, was countering everything Julian said until, trembling, Julian turned on him, who was there to say, "Let me try to talk with him"? Alone with our children, we confront some of our basest potential.

Of course Laurinda, like all of us, was doing the best she could. "I was going through so much in myself, wrestling with depression and rage. But in spite of everything, Eric kept on loving me. He was very affectionate. Cuddling him, holding him, carrying him, I was getting the loving touch I'd never gotten before in my life. He kept forgiving and accepting me, touching my heart in a way I had never allowed it to be touched I think since birth."

Laurinda turns to face Eric again. Their profiles are striking replicas. "I felt so much guilt over what I felt I was doing to you. But I couldn't tell anyone about how difficult it was for me to be a parent alone. I was ashamed, but I didn't know how to get out of it. You were the one person in the world I felt free to release those feelings with because you wouldn't leave me."

Then he did. Back from a summer visit to his father's house on the East Coast, five-year-old Eric had a new tactic. When Laurinda got angry with him, he would retort, "I want to go live with my father." One day Laurinda finally asked, "Is that what you really want?" Eric answered yes.

"Going to live with my father didn't mean to me *not* living with my mother," Eric the adult now explains. "It meant *adding* that on to living with her. As a kid I didn't understand the implications."

Laurinda wrote to her ex-husband and asked if he would take Eric for a while. "I didn't feel capable anymore, I felt if I had to go on, I would end up hating this kid. He agreed only if I would give up custody. I didn't know what else to do. Given how pushed to the edge I felt, I don't know what I might have done, to Eric, to me."

The new wife of Eric's father came to collect him, bearing the papers granting total custody. Laurinda signed the release, said goodbye, "and that was it. I closed the door and he was gone. I was numb. I didn't even cry. A few days later I had a remarkable and terrifying dream in which I was looking in a mirror. In it was the most frightening, ugly face I'd ever seen, worse than anything in the movies. I know now I was seeing the depth of my 'shadow,' which I had never faced. I told someone I knew at work about it, and she took me to a therapy group she was part of.

"It was the mid-sixties and all these experimental therapies were opening up. For the first time in my life it was okay to just allow all kinds of feelings to come up, rather than holding up that façade and then having it break in rage. I had thought all that anger was toward Eric, but it wasn't. He was no longer around to rage at and the rage was still there. And that's when I began to feel an incredible sorrow. I had given my son away. It actually felt like something had been ripped out of my heart. I thought, 'Oh my God, what have I done?' For the first time in my life I missed someone. I realized that I loved Eric — not the kind of obsessive love I knew from relationships with men. I loved *him,* the real article.

"I wanted to get him back. I was desperate to get him back. For two years I tried every way I could." Laurinda pauses for a moment. "Everything since those two years seems minor in comparison," she says emphatically. "I didn't know that anyone could mean so much to me."

Eric picks up the story. "I was dreadfully unhappy at my father's house. I loved my father, but he wasn't equipped to deal with the emotional turmoil that went on in me when I realized I was away from my mother. I cried myself to sleep at night, I hated going to bed because I knew the moment I closed my eyes I would get these horrendous images. And there was a lot of tension between him and his new wife over me. I felt like I was under one gigantic claustrophobic wet blanket."

Almost two years to the day after Laurinda had closed the door on her five-year-old son, she found herself waiting at the gate to his father's house on the other side of the country. She was there for the third and last day of her routine visiting rights. "They wouldn't let me come to the door, Eric couldn't stay the night or have breakfast or dinner with me. We could meet only from nine in the morning till five in the afternoon." That day Eric came running out with a note in his hand. "He had a big grin on his face. 'Mommy, Mommy, guess what?' he said.

"'You get to have dinner with me tonight?'

"'No, better than that.'

"'Can you stay all night with me?'

"'No, Mommy! When you go back to California, I get to go with you!'

"He handed me the letter. It said that they didn't want to talk to me, they had nothing to say, but if I still wanted him, he could go back to living with me. Eric and I went leaping in circles on the sidewalk, up and down. We called everyone that day. And the next day we went home.

"Now I felt thankful to be a single parent. It felt like a miracle that I had this second chance. And now I had room for Eric's feelings as well. When I got angry with him, I could say, 'I'm sorry, this is not really toward you. I got angry because of my mood or because I'm feeling tense or because I'm not taking care of these feelings somewhere else. And you got it because you're the one who's here.'" Now Laurinda had some tools. She could talk her feelings through with others. She had friends now. Eric was no longer the only one who touched or forgave her.

"It's unlikely that anything except a connection as deep as the one I had with my son could have broken me open to the fact that I have a heart. And I think it's unlikely that our bond would have been so deep if I hadn't been a single parent. As much as I hated being the only one who was there for him as he grew up, I know in the end that it saved me, it forced me to come alive."

These darkest pathways can bring the greatest gifts, not only to ourselves but even to our children. "Seeing my mother grow as a person has been extremely important to me," affirms Eric. "She let me see what it is to be human. And she gave me the role model that life is about growing."

"I saw that what made me grow as a single parent is also what made me grow as a human being," Laurinda adds. "This has not been just the story of raising my child, it has been my life story. This was what was making me grow up as my child was growing up. It's a myth that we're all grown up when we have children. Going through all that, learning how to be the best parent I could for Eric, showed me the way to my humanity, and to my humility."

Georgie, from her own experience of parenting alone, considers it to be equivalent to an intense spiritual discipline. "There is a concept, in the Japanese martial arts, of the *ukai* — the stone that sharpens the blade of a knife. It's an abrasive function, grinding away the rough edges and strengthening the sword. I think of single parenting as the *ukai*."

◆ TREASURES FROM THE DEPTHS

Our own stories may not be as dramatic as Laurinda's, but we are all brought face to face with ourselves raising our children alone. It is often through them and along with them that we carry back some of the greatest treasures of our lives. Opening our hearts, learning to let go and trust, we join our children in the mystery of life. Sometimes we have to hit bottom before we can learn to do that.

For many of us, single parenting pushes us over an edge we might otherwise never have come to, pushes us beyond limits we might otherwise have managed to maintain. But as we learn to ride the crises, we can begin to trust that we will survive each step in our growth. We learn to trust that life will sustain us just as we as parents sustain the lives of our children. This mystery is our ally. "Believe me," the poet Rilke unabashedly pronounces, "life is always in the right."[2]

"What I have learned by being a single parent," says Michelle, the mother of six-year-old Melissa, "is that there is always a solution." That hope was all she had to rely on when she abruptly found herself alone when Melissa was eighteen months old. In one of those astonishing maneuvers which produce single parents, Michelle's husband sold all of their joint property and moved in with another woman while Michelle and Melissa were visiting friends in another state. On her own at thirty-two and with no resources to fall back on, Michelle scrambled to pull her life together. Renting a cheap room in a house with another single parent and getting a job as a waitress seemed a good step. Crack houses and drug deals were part of her new neighborhood's economy, and Michelle's plan was to move when she had saved enough. Life had different plans.

One night she returned from work to find the front steps strewn with broken bottles and the place reeking of alcohol. In his mother's absence, the teenage boy who lived there had thrown a party. From the living room chair where he was sprawled, the boy grinned up at her with glazed eyes. "There I was, standing in the middle of that dark room, with Melissa in my arms," Michelle recalls. "I took a look at that boy and said, 'I'm out of here.'" She threw her three bags into the car, strapped Melissa in the car seat, and drove off. "I had no idea where I was going or what I would do."

Michelle spent the night on a friend's floor, and the next day she found an ad in the classified section of the local parents' newspaper: "Seeking live-in childcare for two young children, own child okay." Michelle called from a phone booth. The woman who answered became not only her employer but also her best friend. Michelle had found her springboard into a new life. "That's when I first really began to see that there is always help, there are always possibilities," Michelle says. "That is the key. If there is anything I would say to single parents, it is that in the darkest times there is *always* something there for you. Never think you are stuck."

I have often heard single parents talk about finding the right living situation, the right book, the right job, just at the point when they didn't know any longer where to turn. Not that the gem simply fell into their laps; they had to reach for it. They had to take a first step, or, like Michelle, make a courageous leap out of the pit. When the safety or health of our children is at risk, we can find ourselves propelled to action, fearless in situations that might once have paralyzed us. For some, the awakening happens in an instant; for others, it happens gradually, in the still moments when we can tune in to our hearts.

When Sophie sat with Trevor in his room, admitting her helplessness, the way opened up through the voice of her child. "We sat there for quite a while together. Just when my eyes would begin to dry, I'd start crying again. At one point Trevor put his arms around me and offered one of those astonishing bits of wisdom that I've just learned to accept from him. He said, 'Mom, the problem is that God didn't design it for one person to be everything. You're being my mother, you're being my father, you're being my best friend. You can't do all that. It's too much for one person. What we need is more people in our lives.'

"He was right. I had a lot of school friends and work friends. But they didn't come over and play with Trevor while I went grocery shopping, for instance. They didn't come over and cook dinner together. We needed people actively in our day-to-day lives. We're mammals. We're designed to be in herds and groups. That means we have extended families so that we're touched, we're felt, we're argued with, we're interacted with on multiple levels. That's the way we grow, that's the way we stay strong and healthy. I was denying that in myself as if that were a weakness. And I had to start recognizing that we had something to give to other people too. Family life is something some people are missing in their lives. It can be an opportunity for them to be around a child."

Trevor found a boys' choir. Sophie found a benefactor who wanted to invest in some products she was developing through her artwork. Together they began to open the borders of their family to reach out to others and bring others in. When Sophie stopped trying to do it all, that began to make room for others. The tight structure had faltered and fell, and slowly a new form was beginning to find shape.

"So asking the question 'What really is the answer for us?' opened up a whole world," says Sophie. "It took admitting that there must be something more gentle than the way I had been steamrolling it. Our whole life has changed. It's the best it's ever been."

I, too, needed to find my way to something more gentle. When I stopped the frenetic pace of my mind and grudgingly acknowledged that *this is the way it is,* I began to hear the hidden voices that were draining my energy. Voices of unresolved conflict and grief. Voices that said I had to do everything myself. I'd gotten into this; how could I bother anyone else by asking for help?

Unearthing some of the anger and sorrow I'd been carrying around led to my wasting less mental energy on worry and on wanting my life to be different. With a clearer mind, I was able to start addressing some of the issues that were making things harder than they had to be. I began to learn how to ask housemates to take care of Elias while I took a shower. I began to accept their offers of help as genuine rather than as niceties or statements of pity. The sunsets once again had depth and color. I could cry. I wasn't so brittle that I would shatter each time my baby cried. There were options again, and possibilities. I knew once more that my son and I were held in the arms of something vast and beyond us.

CHAPTER 5

＋

A Single Parent Is Also a Person:
Nurturing Ourselves

There are times when the needs of the care-giver are more
important than the needs of the child. We must consider
the care-giver's need for refueling — for care, nurturance,
support — to counteract the insidious myth that mothers
are an endless source of love and emotional sustenance.

— Jane Swigart

"ONE OF THE BIG things you deal with as a single parent is
'What about me?' versus 'What about them?'" comments Kevin, who
began raising his two boys alone when they were four and six years
old. "You feel like, 'I'm more than a single parent. I am still a human
being who needs this, this, and this. And how do I balance all of it?'"

On the desk in Kevin's studio is a framed photo of his two grown
sons, one blond and burly with an arm thrown around the other,
dark-haired and slight. Now that they are on their own, it's no longer
"them versus me" for Kevin. But he recalls, "My theory then was just
do what you think is best for all of you, not just for them. I refused
to live my life only for my children, but I probably leaned toward the
selfish side. I could have given up more for their sake. But that's all
hindsight. You just try to work out a balance as you go along."

When we're in the midst of it, the balance is elusive. Either we can't
give them enough or we're giving too much. But to run ourselves
ragged in self-sacrifice is not a gift of love. I was halfway through my
third year as a single parent before I began to understand that if I
didn't nurture myself, I couldn't possibly nurture my child. It wasn't

an epiphany of self-love but rather a rebellion of audacious voices rising up inside me.

I was in the kitchen preparing dinner, struggling as usual with the transition from work and worldly business to the domestic scene. I had held Elias in my lap for a few minutes, given him a snack, put a story I had taped on the cassette player so he would have at least a facsimile of my attention, loaded the washer, fed the cat, and made a couple of quick phone calls about childcare and play dates. By this time the tiredness had descended, and my legs felt so heavy that I welcomed the opportunity to stand still long enough to grate a carrot. Enter Elias, two and a half.

"Give me some apple juice."

"You already had some. No more before dinner."

"I want to eat right now."

"It's not quite ready."

"Watch me jump off this chair."

"I can't at this moment."

"Play with me. You said you would."

Before he produced another request, I retreated into a favorite fantasy. I knew better than to imagine that a husband or partner might alter this scene significantly. Rather, my mental refuge was in a dream of tribal life where at this time of day Elias would be off with his troop of buddies, trailing some teenage uncles on a mock hunt while I baked flatbread on an open fire and listened to crickets and distant voices. Instead he had only me at this moment, and I was not about to be fun.

"Stop," I said firmly in the midst of his next order.

He didn't.

"Please," I pleaded. "I can't right now."

No luck.

Sometimes there just aren't enough synapses firing to think of creative alternatives. I closed my eyes and set my jaw. I put down the half-grated carrot. A maelstrom of feelings and impulses crashed in me. Maybe I *should* play with him for a few minutes. After all, we're apart all day. When he's grown, I'll regret saying no. I'm not really giving him enough time. But then I'd be giving in. How can I maintain some kind of consistent discipline if I do that? It's not good for him if I don't set boundaries. But I don't want to be doing *any* of this right now. What is this? I feel like some kind of slave. I know I'm going to start screaming if he asks for something else.

He did. Something snapped. Suddenly I felt as if my body was being taken over by a powerful physical impulse while my brain collapsed into emptiness. All exhaustion swallowed up by this burst of adrenaline, I swept my son up into my arms and advanced out the door into the darkening night. Our march, measured by arcs of yellow streetlights, became an impassioned discourse on my selfhood as I poured out words that had been daring to invade my thoughts over the past few months.

"I am a person, not your servant," I began. "When you were a baby I tried to answer to all your needs, but as you grow you are learning to take care of yourself. And I need to take care of myself too. I love you and I will certainly meet your needs, but I can't respond to everything you want. I am me. I am a person too. I will stand by you as you discover your strength, but I cannot give myself up for your sake."

My proclamation felt like heresy. *I cannot give myself up for your sake.* It sounded like some devilish inversion of a biblical quote. How dare I refuse my child? The good mother is supposed to sacrifice herself. Isn't self-sacrifice ennobling? On top of that, as a woman I had been taught to put the needs of others before my own. Up to that point, I had been indeed the willing servant to my son. Those early years simply require it. Good parenting at any stage in fact calls for a high degree of self-sacrifice — and places us on a pathway parallel to that of saints and heroes.

But didn't saints dance to their deaths and painted warriors sing in the midst of torture? My own version of self-sacrifice was definitely not making me into any Mother Teresa. As I would later realize, the selflessness I was offering was a projection of my own misunderstanding, and there I held trapped in my arms one of its unwitting victims. After all, Elias hadn't asked me to forget to take care of myself. He was simply doing what he was programmed by nature to do at this point — get his own needs fulfilled.

The circles of light on the sidewalk were sharply defined by the time we set back. The warmth of the kitchen embraced us as we entered. I was still tired but now standing straighter. I had said it: I can't serve selflessly without also serving myself. My stand is not against my child but for myself. I also know that if I can truly stand by myself, I can honestly stand by him, without compulsion or resentment. I can't love myself less in order to love him more. Certainly in crisis I would risk my own life to save his, but to undermine my own needs daily for his sake is not the way of love.

Of course this declaration didn't immediately change my life, but it laid a foundation in my mind. I did the usual things that evening — dinner, laundry, dishes, bath, pajamas, stories — until I sank into bed, another day's mission complete. Things have to get done, and my new resolve didn't change my intention to provide Elias with what he needed for a happy and healthy childhood. Now the question was, How do I take myself into account as well?

We often give to our children what we don't give to ourselves. We comfort them, we treat them to activities that enliven them and give them joy, we look for opportunities to encourage their sense of themselves. We nurture them. But who nurtures the nurturer? This is one of the most basic and baffling quandaries of parenting alone. As many of us know, parenting *with* a partner doesn't guarantee that the need will be filled either, and sometimes it can actually increase the load. But when we are on our own, we are assured no periodic respite.

As single parents, how do we nurture ourselves when so much of our focus must, of necessity, be on nurturing our children? When the children legitimately deserve the sometimes minimal amount of time we might give them, how can we dare to put our own needs first? How can we even listen to hear what we might need when so much else is clamoring for attention? When a crisis arises in any other part of the system — a child gets sick, there's trouble at work, the furnace breaks in midwinter — our own personal needs are the first to give way. When we get sick ourselves, we often force ourselves to go on. As many single parents say, finding time for ourselves is one of the hardest aspects of parenting alone. However, not doing so is harder yet. Nurturing ourselves is not a luxury; if we don't give to ourselves, we simply cannot give to our children.

Cheryl recalls a phone conversation she had with her friend Catherine when they were both single mothers with newborns. Professionals in their late thirties, the two women had been accustomed to a lifestyle in which they could generally count on getting what they needed. Problems such as lack of sleep or desire to socialize could usually be solved with ease. Now, this late afternoon as they sat in their separate homes nursing their new babies, they were catching a few moments on the phone as their lifeline to support and comfort. "We were talking about how nursing and taking care of our babies was so exhausting. Suddenly we both realized that neither of *us* had eaten anything all day!" Virtually running on empty, Cheryl and Catherine had continued to nourish their children. No wonder if they felt tired or their supply of breast milk dropped.

Cheryl likes to point out that the nursing mother is a perfect metaphor for our role as providers. Without replenishing our reservoirs, we can't adequately give to our children. They will keep asking for what *they* need; they cannot, and should not, try to supply what *we* need. But sometimes we don't even know what we need or how to give it to ourselves, especially when anything we might do requires resources we may not have. Even to eat nutritiously to sustain our intense level of output each day requires money and information, time and energy. Other equally critical resources may also be scarce. The impulse to care for ourselves lovingly may be hidden under mountains of self-denial or self-deprecation. We may in fact be attempting to deliver to our children a kind of love we have not yet experienced ourselves.

Madeleine, a counselor and the mother of two school-aged boys, had that realization one night as she walked the floor with her first baby. "He was crying and crying," she remembers. "As I was carrying him around I began to feel incredibly upset myself. I started crying too. I ended up sobbing so hard I could hardly breathe. What I realized was that I was feeling totally jealous of this child because he was getting the kind of attention I had never gotten myself as a baby. And I was the one giving it to him."

As we all know, parenthood does not automatically uncap the springs of endless love. In fact, it can reveal — as it did for Madeleine — how deep are our own needs for love and attention. Just as our children reach to us for this, we may want to reach to others — family, partners, lovers, friends. Indeed, we must, but there are often major barriers, inside and outside ourselves, that we must overcome in order to admit this kind of nurturing into our lives.

And what about those times when no one else is there, as is so often the case for single parents? If we depend completely upon others to replenish us with love and care, we may end up not being nurtured at all. There are also cultural impediments to caring for ourselves well. We live in an individualistic, goal-oriented consumer society where we learn to achieve at all cost, often neglecting the natural rhythms of our physical and mental needs. We stay awake when we're tired, to get the job done. We wait until we're sick to take time off. We grab fast food on the run rather than stopping to replenish with vitamins and minerals in nourishing food. We repress our feelings so as not to rock the boat. As a culture we tend to push ourselves as if we're intent to get whatever we're trying to accomplish over with. The demands of single parenting only amplify that tendency.

The anthropologist Edward T. Hall points out that Americans tend to respond to *real* needs far more slowly than those in other cultures around the world. He writes, "In many countries people need less of what Americans would call urgency in order to discharge a tension. In the United States the need must be highly critical before people act." He illustrates his point with an example most of us have personally experienced: "The distribution of public toilets in America reflects our tendency to deny the existence of urgency even with normal physiological needs."[1]

Nurturing ourselves *is* an urgent need when we are single parents, not only in order to give to our children in a balanced way but also to protect them. If we aren't responding to our own needs in appropriate ways, we are likely to try to fulfill them through our children. If we aren't dreaming our own dreams, our children may not be free to dream theirs. If we aren't taking care of ourselves, they will feel compelled to take on the task.

It takes time to learn how to listen deeply to who we are and what we need. In moments outside the endless whirl of duty and action, we remember who we are. We are more than "single parents." We are individuals with lives that preceded our children's and lives that will go on after rearing them is complete. We have our own fulfillment and destiny, linked intimately now with our children's but also distinct from theirs.

We have chosen, in one way or another, to raise them alone. If we are to sustain our intention to succeed, we must also choose ourselves, listen to and nurture ourselves, or the entire system teeters, perhaps collapses. As single parents, we ourselves are the critical element, we are the only jugglers around.

◆ TO DO OR NOT TO DO . . .

A year after her marriage ended, when her youngest child was five and her oldest twelve, Leah packed up her four children and headed west, leaving behind the old memories and constraints of her life as a faculty wife in the East Coast college community where her ex-husband taught. Accustomed to being socially involved and determined to take care of herself as well as her children, Leah set out to become an active member of the Idaho town where they now settled. She got involved in the local art center, taking photography courses and painting. She joined a reading circle, formed a hiking group with some women friends, played tennis. She got up at five o'clock every day to go for a run and came back to meditate before making breakfast and lunches for the children. Then she got herself off to work as an art teacher in the local schools and ski instructor in the nearby resorts. She made a point of spending as much time with the kids as possible — breakfast together every morning, and Sunday was always family day. On top of it all, she dated. "It was like I was crazed. I didn't know how to sit still," says Leah.

Doing things that she enjoyed and that were good for her physically, emotionally, and spiritually had certainly looked like the right way to go. "But I don't think I knew what 'nurturing myself' really meant," Leah admits. "I was taking the lid off the stress with meditation and exercise, but I didn't really know what I was doing. What I did know how to do was add more stuff on, to run faster. The faster I ran, the less likely the balls were to come tumbling down on my head. I was just madly keeping everything moving."

While Leah's commitment to nurturing herself had begun to look like a frenetic attempt to establish a new identity now that she was on her own with her children, for another single parent, Jeff, a couple of years of parenting alone had seemed to leave him with scarcely a sense of identity at all. Immediately after his separation, Jeff had sought out a lot of support from friends and counseling as he struggled with the logistics of parenting his three sons alone and with the anger and grief over his inability to bridge the cultural gap between him and his ex-wife, an Alaskan Inuit woman. But eventually Jeff dropped the supports and settled into doing little else but getting to his job every day and coming home to the boys. They were young — two, four, and six years old — and needed a lot of care. It was a draining routine, and Jeff's job for the street department offered little by way of reward. With duty as his daily companion, Jeff slipped into chronic depression.

Seated in his living room, with books on philosophy and natural history stacked on shelves and tables all around him, Jeff explains, "I just didn't have any breaks. I was on call at my job and also here at home. I didn't go out on dates, didn't go off on my own at all. Sometimes I'd fall into this routine — and I still do occasionally — where life just seemed to be one chore after another. When I'd wake up, I didn't want to get out of bed because it felt like there was just going to be a long chain of things I had to do until night when I could go back to sleep."

After a few years of the grind, Jeff began to see that his heavy bouts of depression were affecting his boys. "I could see that they were starting to copy me. It was so irritating! They'd sit around on the couch and just mope and stare into space. Or they'd wander around the house aimlessly, just like I did."

Children do more than imitate our behavior; they replicate it at the deepest levels. Joseph Chilton Pearce, author of *The Magical Child,* points out that "the vast majority of all learning takes place beneath the conscious awareness of either the child or who the child is learning from. . . . Our children live in our emotional life, reflect it, pick it up. They become a perfect mirror of who we are. And what does it do to a parent? It enrages us. Nothing enrages a parent so rapidly as to see their failings reflected back to them in their children."[2] Jeff recalls that feeling. "I'd get so mad," he remembers. "'God darn,' I'd yell, 'get out of the house! Go play! *Do something!*'"

But Jeff himself didn't know what to do — not about himself, not about how he was affecting his sons. Eventually he returned to the counselor he had been seeing earlier. She suggested that he get out of the house himself.

"When I first started trying to take some time by myself, I would hire a babysitter or arrange a trade with another single parent," Jeff continues. "I would take off and go downtown to a restaurant or café — and then I would immediately feel depressed. I felt so selfish. I just hated it. I would sit there and feel miserable, but I knew it wasn't good to come back. I had to wait my time out. Sometimes I would walk around the streets just crying, feeling so sorry for myself. After a couple of times like that I gave up. It just felt like another chore to add to the list when I woke up in the morning.

"I tried to date now and then as well, but I didn't have the energy and openness to enjoy being out there. That's what happens — you lose touch with your own needs. So when I went out and said, 'I'm going to fulfill my needs now,' I found that everything was unplugged in me, nothing worked. I was totally wrecked and run down." When we start from that place, how can we hope to find real solutions to our very real needs?

◆ WHAT IS NURTURING?

When, like Leah and Jeff, we think of nurturing ourselves as just one more "should," it seems easier to shelve the plans. How do we break the vicious cycle? How can we guarantee that our efforts will in time replenish us? How do we get the relief we crave from our relentless responsibility as single parents? Anything that breaks the momentum of *doing* and allows us just to *be* for a few moments is probably pointing us in the right direction.

"Every Saturday and Sunday morning Christian and I go out for breakfast," Gabriele says, smiling at her four-year-old son. "That is actually the most nurturing thing I do in my life right now. During those five minutes after ordering and before the plate comes, I sit back and feel like a queen. I can stop and be with Christian, we can just sit and smile at each other, just sit and wait. People say, 'Why don't you put yourself on a budget?' But I'm not going to skimp on this. Whatever it takes, you have to nurture yourself. That's what I have learned. I need that."

Every night after Aaron is asleep, Billy enters the mythical land emerging from his wood sculptures. It's typically after midnight before he lays down the carving tools. Then he might play his guitar for a while before going to sleep. "I find that when I'm doing art or music, I am constantly balancing myself, and that allows me not to get fried," he explains.

Leaving Sierra with her housemate early in the morning before work, once a week Cheryl gets on her bike for a swift ride through the hills near her home. She might start out with a lengthy to-do list in her mind, but eventually the wind and cool air take over. Her body moving in tandem with the bike and the curve of the road become the focus. "It actually took until Sierra was over two years old before I started doing this one little thing for myself. I find now I absolutely can't get by without it."

It was usually eleven-thirty at night by the time Helga finished up a half-hour of slow yoga postures. "Even if it was late, I stayed up to do them because it sustained me. That was the way I created something to hold on to through all those times of turmoil. I relaxed my body so I could be friends with myself."

At five each morning Louise would sneak down the stairs on tiptoe, her three children still asleep. "I had to lay everything out the night before so they wouldn't hear me and get up too. I don't know why kids always do that." For one quiet hour, not on call, her mind not fragmented by requests and demands, Louise would sit in her kitchen, drinking tea and reading the morning newspaper. "This made such a difference in my life that one particularly stressful period of time when I had stopped getting up early to do it, I started to dream about sitting down with the paper and a cup of tea. That was my vision of peace as a single parent!"

"I am real anxious to get my kids into bed by nine o'clock," says Georgie. "My body seems to click in biologically and just know that this is my time for a bubble bath or to watch something on TV as long as I want or to read. When there is some emotional issue I'm dealing with, I make an appointment with myself to write in my journal after the kids are asleep. I become my own therapist. I'm almost ferocious about my inner life, and that I think is the key. That's how I listen to myself and take care of my needs."

Others talk about working in the garden, listening to music by candlelight, meditating in the early morning darkness. These are single parents with tight schedules on their jobs and in their professions, single parents dedicated to the home life of their families. These are their moments, with children, without children, late at night, early in the morning. Moments set aside to stop, to wait, to feel, to be; moments without a goal.

◆ THE EASY WAY

How do we begin? Often by doing nothing. By the time Angelina was four years old, Catherine was no longer struggling with trying to find the time to feed herself as well as a nursing baby. But four years of working as a freelance graphic artist and parenting alone had taken a toll that Catherine was not even aware of. When Angelina's father unexpectedly decided to spend a full day with his daughter every weekend, what happened to Catherine was just as unexpected.

Now, for the first time since Angelina's birth, Catherine had hours on end in which she could do anything she liked. But week after week, when she closed the door after seeing Angelina off with her father, "I would sit down with a book and start to read and end up falling asleep every time. Sometimes I was so tired I would sleep almost the whole day. I felt so guilty, like I should be doing something productive. I had to make a deal with myself that if I didn't want to do anything at all, it was okay. But that was really hard because most of the time I was used to moving at such a high speed."

Just as we would let a tired baby sleep, we have to allow ourselves to sleep all day or stare out the window or get nothing done. That may be exactly what we need. Putting on the brakes and sliding to a halt was difficult for Catherine, but it gave her what she required in order to go on in a more balanced way as a single parent. Eventually the need for sleep as nourishment gave way to other activities. Catherine's biggest struggle then became making sure that she wouldn't use more than half of her "free day" to finish up work from the week before.

To insist on our own needs as priority — over our income, our children, our lists of unfinished business — can seem impossible or foolhardy. But those who have taken the risk swear by it. Besides her morning tea-and-newspaper routine, Louise built another essential time of renewal into her day, right at the point of highest stress. The demands of her job as the director of a clinic for children with learning disabilities crashed headlong every afternoon into the perhaps even more stressful task of evening cook-counselor-referee-helper-mother for her three school-aged children.

"I think for me the hardest part of all in single parenting was coming home from work dead tired and the kids coming home with all of their emotional upheavals of the day," Louise remembers. "Maybe somebody had hurt them at school in some way, or the teacher had been rude to them and they were in tears. How could I find the emotional energy to give them what they needed when I could hardly see straight?"

Louise came up with an idea that really worked. "I set up a routine where at four in the afternoon I'd get home and get the kids all settled into something, and then I'd go into the bathroom and start running the water for a bath, really slowly. It would be loud enough to drown out the sounds of kids fighting but not the sounds of somebody really in trouble. I'd take a good book up with me and sometimes a glass of sherry, and I'd just sit and read with that soothing sound of running water. And then I'd have a bath."

Louise's time alone, listening to running water, sinking into that bath, provided her access to a still center. Outside the door of the bathroom, the world continued to spin. "When I first started doing this, my kids went crazy," she says, laughing. "They'd carry on: 'You can't do this!' 'I've got to talk to you.' 'When will dinner be ready?'" Louise went right on day after day, running that water slowly into the bathtub. "After a while they got to accept that this is what I did. For me it really made a difference. After that half-hour or so I was ready to go out and take on doing supper and handling homework and relating to all *their* needs."

Just as we tend to measure ourselves against some concept of the ideal parent, so might our children. "My kids would come back from someone's house saying '*Their* mom made apple pie for dessert,' as if to say 'Why don't you?'" Louise remembers. "I used to say to them all the time, 'I'm a person first and then a mother.' I'd tell them that it's in storybooks that Mother bakes apple pies and has an apron on and is always there. In storybooks Mother never cries and never gets sick. In storybooks Mothers are supermoms. I had to explain to them that I didn't have that capability. I was a person first, and sometimes I just didn't make it so well as a mom, and they would just have to accept that from me."

Acknowledging that we are individuals playing many roles, only one of them being a single parent, is valuable for both ourselves and our children. When we respect our needs and boundaries, they learn to respect them as well.

◆ DOING WHAT WE LOVE TO BE

It is not the nature of the activity that matters but whether it extricates us from the whirl and puts us back in touch with something in ourselves that is deeper or calmer. Leah's jam-packed days were not in fact nurturing. "I began to take a look at all those things I'd been doing," she comments, "and to see that they were activities that my mind and the trends of my era were saying I needed. Of course the physical exercise and athletics were good, as was the meditation — they released the stress. But I ended up finding out that what really nurtured me was one thing — simply making art."

One year Leah's mother gave her the money to spend a summer month in a little cottage on Cape Cod while the children were with their father. It was nearly seven years after her divorce, and her youngest child was now ten, the oldest seventeen. "That was the first extended period of time I'd had on my own, and it changed my life," says Leah. Released from the nonstop schedule, she found herself consistently longing to do one thing — paint — and it led her to a deep well of replenishment inside. Leah had stepped off the manic merry-go-round and found something that had been eluding her.

When she returned to her family after that month, she had a key to sanity that could sustain all of them. Even short periods of time painting renewed her. "I found I would even give up my free day skiing with my friends to stay in my studio." Leah's children sometimes challenged the time she took for herself. "'Okay,' I'd say to them, 'I love you *and* I also love me.'"

While the gift of that month alone awakened Leah to her needs, Jeff continued running the treadmill day after day until crisis drove its point home. "Eventually I really caved in and started having anxiety attacks," he recalls. "I went back to the counselor, and first she tried me on antidepressants. When I had problems with them, I finally saw I had to make a real change."

One of Jeff's first steps was dramatic. He threw out the television set, despite protests from his boys, who were still all under eleven. "I carried it out and dumped it into the trash. Literally. I've always felt depressed by TV myself, and I was tired of walking in and finding them in front of it. How can you raise a family when you have to compete with that? That has made a big difference for all of us. We talk more with each other. And some good playtime went in place of it for the kids."

In fact, recent research shows that although viewers are more relaxed while the set is on, they are less relaxed by the time they turn it off. People reported feeling more relaxed and in a better mood after reading a book than after watching television.[3] Jeff may have missed the "electronic babysitter," but the improved tone of his household justified his decision. The positive effect of any one nurturing activity begins to build momentum.

Eventually Jeff developed another replacement that gave them all a chance to relax together. "I noticed how tired out I felt when I was rounding them up for bed at eight o'clock. That was a low time for me. So I got a new deal going. Between seven and eight we all read to ourselves. They really enjoy it now too. Either we flop down on one of the beds together or a couple of us upstairs, the others downstairs. Then later, at bedtime, I read out loud to all of them."

These shifts expanded into other areas of Jeff's life. "I stopped working at my job, took out loans, and enrolled in college for teacher training. I just had to start doing work I really enjoyed and could get something back from. It was the counselor who first talked to me about what that kind of change might do, and I finally got it too — I had to change my self-concept."

Maybe Jeff had considered himself a failure because his marriage didn't work. Perhaps he felt he had to make something up to his boys for their not having a mother. Perhaps he imagined himself as someone who didn't get to enjoy his own life as an individual separate from his role as a single father and functionary. Learning how enlivening it was to give to himself what he was dedicated to giving to his children was the beginning of Jeff's shift in self-concept.

"School began to put me in touch with other interesting people, and I could get some real feedback on who I am as an adult. Now a lot has changed. I go on dates, I go to movies. I'm even starting to do some things just for myself."

Jeff had to persist in building that nurturing momentum, however. Old patterns, like old shoes, are often more comfortable. For Jeff, schoolwork threatened to take on the same tone of endless drudgery and duty. "I'd study and study and feel guilty for not doing enough studying. I tended not to take any breaks. Finally, the last couple of weekends, I figured it out. 'The hell with it,' I said. 'I'm taking off with the kids.' We went out camping and hunting for mushrooms. There is a whole subculture of Cambodians and Laotians around here who hunt mushrooms. Being in that campground with them and just letting go and being with my kids was great."

Soaking in the bath, reading, painting, or hunting mushrooms — each is a way of *doing* that supports the value of *being*. Doing what we love to do is essentially nourishing. Whether we are in motion or sitting still doing nothing, whatever helps us to feel connected to something greater than our practical, functioning identity is nourishing for everyone. "After my daughter, my second priority was meditating," Angie relates. "An hour of sitting gave me perspective. I'd be really mad at China about something, and it would wash away. I could keep finding a soft place of relating to her. If I hadn't had that as the foundation, our whole past together would have been really different."

Bringing these moments into our lives requires a commitment to ourselves equivalent to that which we give to our children. Acknowledging that there is a direct line of nourishment from us to them might encourage us to bypass any resistance founded in guilt. "What has made my life as a single parent extraordinarily joyful is that I am very disciplined in certain ways of taking care of myself, especially clearing through emotional blocks," says Madeleine. "I know that I am not going to succeed in being present in a positive way with my children unless I am in the best possible state I can be." Madeleine was firmly committed to participating in at least one session of co-counseling a week, "and more if I need it."

Convincing ourselves that what we do for our own good is also good for our children makes for guilt-free motivation. But because we are so rightfully dedicated to giving them enough of our limited time, it can be very hard to admit that it's also all right simply to enjoy ourselves without them sometimes.

◆ A SUCCESSFUL "ME" THING

"Knowing that not too many years from now it would be girls and cars and all that for David, I wanted to do something that would be great for us together," relates Ed, a regional sales manager for a major corporation. The five years that he had been raising his son alone had brought them closer than he might have imagined when he began, and now that David was almost thirteen, Ed knew their days as buddies would be fast slipping away.

The "something that would be great for us together" turned out to be an airplane. "From Chicago we can get to a lot of wonderful places," Ed explains. "We can fly to the Wisconsin Dells, go to Mackinac Island, visit the Air Force Museum in Dayton. In my mind, this was clearly an 'us' deal. And every chance we got, David and I flew off to some place together.

"At first it was terrific. But after six months I found that I'd be dragging David out to the airport to wash and wax the plane, and he'd be chasing butterflies instead. One Saturday afternoon, on a beautiful August day, I was out there all by myself while David was visiting his mother. I was feeling pretty bad, because what I had here was a failed 'us' thing. I had wanted to do something that *he* would like, something we both could enjoy, and it hadn't worked out that way.

"But that ended up being an important day for me. As I was scrubbing that little plane, all of a sudden I thought, 'To heck with him. I'm having a ball with this thing. I love sitting out here and doing this.' I realized that the plane was a successful 'me' thing, not a failed 'us' thing. After that, anything David wanted to do with me in the plane or around the plane was gravy, because in fact I was doing something that was a very positive thing for *me*."

As single parents we need some successful "me" things in our lives. Not only can we then give to ourselves without feeling resentment toward our children, but we also get out of their way of enjoying life. Particularly with David approaching his teen years, Ed's getting a life for himself was part of separating from his son in a healthy way. It is important for the sake of our children as well that we develop our own interests. However, personal fulfillment can so much imply something outside of parenting that we may miss the fact that our children themselves provide a deep nourishment. As Billy says, "Just being Aaron's father has been healing and nurturing for me. I get as much out of it as he does, if not more."

◆ IT'S A KID'S LIFE

One night as he listened to a single, childless friend express his longing to "get a life," Denny, who is raising two boys as a part-time single parent, realized something essential about his own. "This guy, pretty distraught, said to me, 'Do you have a life?' I said, 'Well, yeah. I've got a life . . . It's my kids.' As funny as this conversation sounds, it's really sad. This guy is in his late thirties, he's got a new Porsche, a dog, all the right things — but he doesn't have a life."

For Denny, raising his kids has meant a profound healing. "My own father died when I was five years old," he says. "But a really exciting thing has been happening over the past ten years with my kids. I do believe that when you're a father, you father yourself. I never got listened to by a father when I was six or seven. But now I am being listened to by a father, through my children. I am being loved, spent time with, played with. The father I never had is

now alive in me." By learning how to love ourselves as we love our children, by learning to receive their love, we give to ourselves through them.

Children are masters of the moment, and they cajole, plead, demand until we join them there. They give us an excuse to be zany, to be children again ourselves — and that in itself sometimes can help get us through the hardest times.

The first year of separation from her husband was terrifying and painful for Leah. She and her children hadn't yet made their move out west, and life was still crumbling rather than building. "I was going through a lot of doubts, wondering if I could handle this on my own, feeling rejected, and the kids were going through all of their pain." One of the children started having trouble at school, one started having bad nightmares, and the horizon looked bleak. "But we did something that proved to be important," says Leah. "Every night before dinner, we put on some music and we danced, every night for about a half-hour. That was great. It let out a lot of the stuff that would build up inside us."

As David Elkind points out in *The Hurried Child,* play relieves stress in children.[4] The same is true for adults. Our children invite us into that nondirected time in which there is no goal but to be in the creative present. Often I catch myself thinking of play as yet another thing I have to do for Elias. Indeed, when I am with him but wanting to get back to "important and interesting things," it is stressful. But when I can let go for a few minutes and just be with him in that open-ended dance, something happens that brings me back to a part of myself too easily lost in "adulthood."

Our children love us, and while expressions of their love may get overshadowed at certain points in their development, they are basically as concerned for our ease and happiness as we are for theirs. I have found that when I have been honest with Elias about my own needs, he could understand, even at age three. One typical evening as I was plowing through the normal routine of trying to do everything before I collapsed, I started lecturing him about how putting his toys away was part of being a family and that he should have his pajamas on by now and that I couldn't stand having to ask him to do it so many times.

"You're not doing very well with me tonight, Mom," he said, the corners of his mouth tightening to contain a smile.

The phrase was endearing, but I was not to be deterred. This was serious. "No, I'm not," I admitted, though I didn't appreciate being called out on impatience on top of everything else. "I'm just so tired, babe. And I feel like I'm the only one to get all these things done, and I just really want to lie down. Sometimes I need to relax too."

He looked at me for a moment, then headed over to get his pajamas on. A few minutes later he reappeared and made a serious announcement. "I'm going to give you a massage, Mom."

Children force us to be simple, to remember the moment and find our renewal there. Georgie comments, "Those mornings when I launch out of bed and into doing what needs to be done, the days don't seem to go as well. But when I just stop and sit quietly for a few minutes and focus back on what's really happening in my life — how much I love my children, what I feel is important to our lives, our connection to some order higher than our little dramas — it gets my priorities straight again and orients my day a little more."

While learning how to renew our resources is essential, there is another vital part of nurturing ourselves — being able to ask for and receive support from others. Where were Leah's children as she was painting on Cape Cod? Where was Sierra when Cheryl was out on that early morning bicycle ride? Where were Jeff's kids when he was taking a walk or out on a date? As we raise the children who will carry on our culture and society, we deserve help, but we may have many hurdles to get over before we might comfortably admit that.

◆ BLESSED ARE THOSE WHO RECEIVE

"When I first became a single mother with an infant, I found that it was so difficult to be always asking somebody to do something," Sophie remembers. As both a nurse and an accomplished artist, Sophie was accustomed to thinking of herself as self-reliant. But having a baby and separating from her husband had put a new and very difficult twist on life. "If I wanted to go grocery shopping and Trevor was asleep, I'd have to get somebody to step in. If I had him with me, maybe I'd have to ask somebody to hold him so I could rearrange my shopping cart to make him fit. It felt like I was always asking for something. I had a lot of pride and it was hard to do."

I heard a variation of that from most of the single parents I spoke with: "I don't accept anything I don't earn." "I wouldn't ask for anyone's help." Alan, raising his two daughters alone, encapsulates the basic attitude. "If I had been destitute, if there had been an emergency and I had to call a friend up and say, 'Life depends upon your coming over here for four hours,' I could have asked. But I couldn't just call someone up and say, 'I want to go out and ride my bike. Will you watch the kids?' Even though I was dying to be outdoors on a sunny day with adult company, I couldn't do it."

Even when we have an urgent need, it can be hard to ask. When Marina went into labor, she drove over to the house of a friend who planned to take her to the hospital. "I didn't ask her to come and pick me up. At that time I couldn't ask anybody to do that. I was very good at giving but I wasn't at receiving."

Certainly it can be easier to give — after all, the giver is in charge. It can feel as if we've lost control when we're on the receiving end. We feel vulnerable, in debt to the giver, in thrall to the whims of others, dependent. In a society that highly values independence, self-reliance, and individual success, asking has a bad name. "Nobody wants you when you're down and out" is a national anthem. Need scares people and makes them uncomfortable. "When Trevor was a baby," says Sophie, "my sense was that the strong person was valued. So if you were asking for things, it felt like there was a certain judgment of weakness: 'Uh-oh, there's a single mother. She's going to be needy.' And neediness was not considered a good thing. My self-esteem rested on being strong and together. That's what kept me from feeling free to ask for favors or help."

The prevalent attitude of "You asked for it, you handle it" is a sure impediment to our asking for help. Another single mother, Vera, admits that after the birth of her second child she was reluctant to ask others for anything, even when it had been offered. "I had a huge support system when I was pregnant. Women friends were saying, 'I'll be the father! I'll take care of the child. I'll babysit.' But after my son was born, they got busy and I got to feeling that I didn't want to burden anybody by asking. A major part of my self-image is, 'I've created this situation, and I have to take care of it.' I figure my friends didn't create this. And they're busy, they've got children, they've got their own lives. How can I ask them?" Zeroing in on the issue, Vera concludes, "You might even have a willing support system, but the question is: Are you going to use it?"

In the first year of Elias's life, asking for help made my heart pound, and I actually felt nauseated at times when I had to "put someone out" with a request. Even when the help was offered, accepting it sometimes made me cry, not just with gratitude but from the overwhelming frustration of conflicting emotions. I feared rejection. I feared losing friends if I appeared too needy. I feared how vulnerable I was and how much more vulnerable I felt when I declared need. To be held by the grace and goodwill of others felt precarious. If they let me down, where would I fall?

For Heidi, the worst-fear scenario actually happened when she moved to a new town with her year-old daughter, Sarah. "Until I found a place to live, I had arranged to stay with the only person I knew there. My life was a mess. I was completely freaked out about my boyfriend leaving, about where I was going to live, what kind of job I was going to get, who was going to take care of Sarah. Just a few days after we arrived, this friend got very mad at me and told me to get out of her house and never come back. I know it was basically a misunderstanding. She thought I didn't appreciate what she was doing for me."

Of course Heidi had been grateful, but she was also exhausted and shaken to the core. Expressing gratitude itself requires a state of graciousness, a reaching outward, that can feel impossible when we are already at the end of our reserves. Unless someone has walked this way as well, it can be very hard to understand — and witnessing this level of need might feel as overwhelming to a friend as watching a drowning person go under.

And, of course, giving does sometimes include a tacit expectation of reciprocity. As single parents we may feel we have little to give back, at least for the time being. So that means baldly asking — receiving without payment. It is a humbling gesture. But the truth is, as Sophie now puts it, "You're darn right we're needy! All human beings are! It takes more than one to do all the things it takes to raise a child. When you're doing it by yourself, you *do* have needs."

We need many others for both emotional and practical support, and the need is not just while we have infants. "Being a single parent doesn't stop because you've been one for four or five years or more," says Maxine, a widowed mother. "It goes on all the time, for twenty-four hours a day. There is never a point where someone can say, 'Oh, now I can treat this person as if they're just like a married parent.' You may get more used to dealing with the stress, but it's not as if the stress is absent."

Even small offers make a big difference. "Someone calling and saying, 'Can I come and play with the girls for an hour or take them on a walk?' really helps," suggests Maxine. "Or 'Can I bring a pizza over for everyone?' or 'Can I bring over some takeout after the kids are asleep, and you and I can visit?'"

Being able to ask for help and to accept it requires what might seem like a radical transformation. "I've stopped thinking about other people in a way that made me incapable of saying, 'I need help,'" says Madeleine. "I've stopped going through, 'Maybe that person doesn't want to . . . What if this or that . . .? What if they say no . . .? If they do, that's all right. I don't have trouble with that now, because I know I am valuable and that my children are valuable." Because Madeleine was able to honor herself and her children, she was able to ask without feeling that her world depended upon the response.

"But it took years of getting rid of my old emotional garbage and conditioning in order to feel this way," she acknowledges. "It takes enormous healing to understand something basic — all human beings want what I want. They want affection and joy in their lives. They want close friends. They want peace on earth. People want to be of assistance, they want to serve. And I just stick myself in the path of that."

Sometimes it simply takes practice to develop a new habit. One single mother found herself politely refusing when her child's father called to say he had decided to send some money. "I kept saying to him, 'You should think about this. Is this really what you want to do?'" Perhaps she feared attached strings, but that was a different issue. "I got off the phone and thought, 'We really need that money, and he was offering it. Why am I not taking it?' So I wrote down what I wanted to say, because it was so hard to just accept it. I practiced the phrase over and over, and then I called him back and said it to him exactly as I'd practiced, so that I wouldn't chicken out: 'If you want to give me this money, I want it.'"

I found out myself that I had to practice phrases such as "Why thank you, that would be great" or "Yes, I would like that, how nice" in response to offers. My custom since childhood had been to say some version of "Oh, no, you wouldn't want to do *that*." One of my housemates was especially relentless in refusing to let me get by with self-deprecations or apologies when I needed something. And when I wasn't paying attention to my own needs, she, who had also been a single mother, would ask another housemate to babysit and would usher me out the door — sometimes over my protests — and treat me to a movie.

In addition to overcoming personal issues around receiving, it takes a lot of effort to set up support systems. "I'm really good at reaching out to other people for support," says Jane. "If you want to have a good support system, you have to have the guts and drive to make it." Raising her two daughters while also going through her pediatric training meant that Jane needed a lot of help, but she was willing to reach for it. "I'm an initiator. I know plenty of single parents who don't have that kind of drive. But I do a lot of phone calling to ask people to get together and to organize support groups."

When Jane's first adopted daughter, Jordan, was three years old, Jane helped form a group called the Doulas — "a Hispanic term for a person who supports a family having a child," she explains. "We were a group of lesbians who all wanted to become mothers or were mothers. I had been wondering, since my relationship with the woman I had been living with was ending, how I would handle being on night call at the hospital. After a few meetings a couple of women came up to me and said they would be happy to help me out with childcare because they knew I had these tough hours. For almost a year they took my daughter every fourth night while I worked."

Besides babysitting, the group provided lots of practical support for its members. "We passed on clothes and baby equipment to each other. When one woman had her baby, we all got together and had a housecleaning party for her. When one of the women was stressed out from working and loss of sleep with her infant, several women created shifts for a while where somebody spent the night to feed the baby for her."

We need emotional support as much as practical support, and Jane found both in the Doulas as well as in another support group, a branch of the national association called Single Mothers by Choice. "In these groups I have met other people I could get together with when I've felt I need adult company with someone who also likes kids." Jane admits, however, that she is often the one reaching out. "I am much more likely to call up and say, 'Do you want to get together this week?' It just takes that kind of energy and persistence."

We can get so involved in the diurnal round that we forget to make time for the support we need. Gabriele found that even when she tried to start a support group, "nobody was willing to make the free time.

They'd say, 'We're busy that night,' 'I'm tired at night,' and so on.
For myself, it *was* hard to leave Christian in the evening after I'd been
away from him all day.

"When we finally did get a group going, I just forced myself to
make that time available. Most of the time I shove my problems
under the carpet and leave them there. I think people don't really
understand what I go through. I don't blame them. How can you
unless you've been through it yourself? The first few times I went to
that group, all they had to do was look at me and I'd cry. To find
others who do understand touches my inmost being.

"It also gave me perspective to go to the group. Even in my hardest
times, I have seen that there are people who have had it a lot harder.
That made me stop whining!"

Finding the right support group can require some exploration.
Because Gwen had chosen to have a child on her own, the groups she
first attended, made up primarily of divorced single parents, didn't
suit her needs. "Nearly everyone spent their time talking about how
sad or angry they were about their ex. I wanted to focus on the kids."
A local parenting group was closer to what Gwen was looking for.
"I'm more interested in parents — mothers *and* fathers — so I can
increase my opportunities of having relationships with other families." Gwen found, however, that the contact she made in group
meetings did not extend beyond that. Married parents tend to socialize with other couples, which can increase the isolation of parenting
alone.

For Chris finding a local chapter of Single Mothers by Choice
opened a new world. "When I walked into the first meeting, I couldn't
believe it. I had been so caught up in Ken's concerns about my having
Emily, and there everybody was so happy about having a kid. Imagine
that! Not having a partner wasn't a drawback or a disadvantage!"

Jeff, too, found that during the first two years after his marriage,
when he was feeling a lot of anger and anxiety, support groups were
a refuge. "It was sort of a weaning process for me," he says. "I went
to a men's group, to a Parents Anonymous group, I went to everything for a while." And, as for many of us, good friends were his
lifeline.

"When I was feeling sucked under and confused about how to deal
with getting systems going in the house or rehashing what had gone
on with my ex, I had a few women friends who were single mothers

that I could talk with. They were sympathetic and they'd point out positive ways of looking at the situation, so that I would usually end up feeling more positive about myself, even though the issues weren't resolved. And they'd offer another perspective about my ex-wife so that I could feel more sympathetic toward her as a human being rather than angry at her as someone who had abandoned me."

The fact that Jeff turned to his women friends for the nurturing and support he needed is significant. Single fathers tend to be more on their own, far less prone to asking for help, and, as Jeff points out, less accustomed to talking or listening in emotionally supportive ways. "My men friends haven't been quite the same in that way. They could relate to the battle with my wife, but generally how they related to me having children on my own was not in a way that did me any good."

The particular pressure on men to be independent seems to effectively isolate many single fathers. In one relatively small town I interviewed four men who were single fathers, and none knew of the others; one of them felt sure he was the only one around for miles. Another single father, Kevin, marveled that at a time when men raising children alone "was virtually unheard of, another single father had actually moved in right next door to us. It was comforting to know that another man was doing it, and we've become lifelong friends because of it, but I wouldn't say we were a support group. We didn't sit around and talk about being single parents or take care of each other's kids. It was just the fact that it was going on with another man at all that made the difference."

Like most men, Denny didn't try to find a support group when he became a single father. "They probably didn't exist," he says. Nor did he know of any other single fathers. Joining a men's group became his saving grace. "I think I'm really unusual because every time I meet men with kids, I don't hesitate to say, 'We should get together sometime with our kids.' If other men could just learn to do that . . ."

For another single father, Moshe, it was not a men's group or a parenting group that provided support but rather the Aquarian Minyan, a religious group that is part of the Jewish renewal movement. On Friday nights Moshe and his two children join others to celebrate shabbat. "It is a chance to sing and chant and pray, which gives me a spiritual grounding. And for me it is also a chance to be hugged and held by friends, accepted for who I am," says Moshe. "That kind of affection from other adults is often missing in the life of a single parent. So during these last years when there has been a lot of hardship, I have gained strength from celebrating shabbat and the holidays with my children and this loving community."

Many kinds of support systems, formal and informal, are available through community groups, churches, friends. Slowly a few businesses are beginning to support parents through classes, seminars, and other programs that encourage getting together to share common concerns. Support comes in opening our lives to others. Simply to be heard is nourishing. And to learn to receive graciously is a blessing that recognizes how intricately connected to one another we are. "We are here for a little space to learn to bear the beams of love," wrote the poet William Blake. As we reach out to others, we pass that lesson on to our children, along with the understanding that giving and receiving are not business deals.

"Because I didn't know what I could do for other people in return for their support and help," Michelle comments, "I just began to let people know that I would like to do something, and then I let go of the concern. In time I have come to know that we are always able to give back, if not to that person, then to another; if not at this time, then another time. If I let go, the circle of giving can flow."

CHAPTER 6

◆

Single Parent/Double Parent: Being One and Doing All

How can we know the dancer from the dance?

— William Butler Yeats

"I KNOW THAT IF I were still married and raising Aaron with his mother, I would end up playing the typical role of the father," Billy begins. He has been raising his son primarily on his own since Aaron was four, and his experience of parenting alone these past seven years has been considerably different from what went before. "If a woman were here, I would be the man. It's very hard to get out of that. And as a man I would be expected to play a certain role in parenting. But now as *the* parent, I expect to be all of it." As *the* parent, we fulfill functions of father as well as mother, packing two roles into one. And it changes us, profoundly.

"I realized," continues Billy, "that it wouldn't have to be overwhelming to both work and come home to do all the chores if the bathroom doesn't have to be sparkling clean and the rugs don't have to be sparkling vacuumed and if you don't mind eating sandwiches sometimes." Adjusting the homemaker standards might lighten the load for the breadwinner part of the role.

However, there is another, more critical challenge in this double role we have to play. Billy points out that what can also get polarized in the two-parent family is the way in which fathers and mothers relate to their children. "I found that when I was married, someone would always end up doing the disciplining and the other the nurturing, and we'd be at odds," he says. What happens when the mantle of both these roles falls on the shoulders of a sole parent? A simple shift in priorities does not ease the challenge. We may find that we are compelled as individuals to take on tasks for which we have not been prepared, and obliged to reach deep into ourselves to draw upon capacities we didn't know were there.

We've been talking in the kitchen of the tiny cottage where Billy and Aaron live together now. After the birth of their son, Billy and his wife had moved to this small West Coast town, seeking a healthier atmosphere in which to raise their child. When the marriage ended, Aaron lived half-time with each of them for a year, until his mother moved out of town.

"At first we were each going to have him for a year after that, but it didn't work out that way." Billy pauses. "How do you say nicely that his mom is a flake? She still moves around a lot, and Aaron ended up going to three different schools in one year when he was with her. The last time she had him, it was supposed to be for a long period of time, and then she broke up with her boyfriend and brought Aaron back after a couple of months. Since then he's been with me."

At thirty-two with an eleven-year-old son, Billy has been a father virtually all of his adult life, most of it on his own. The responsibility hasn't worn down a quality of playfulness. "It's a lot easier doing it alone," he says, laughing. "It's comfortable for us having our boys' clubhouse.

"My own dad left when I was twelve years old. That was in the sixties. He was teaching philosophy at a big university, and he took off with one of his students to be an artist in San Francisco. We were the first family we knew with divorced parents. My mom raised me and my ten brothers and sisters on her own after that. So when it came time for me to be doing it with just Aaron, I thought it was going to be easy. At first it was actually pretty hard, but we've worked it out."

Part of what helped was that Billy earns his living as a carpenter, working with a small group of friends who are builders. "My schedule could be real flexible when Aaron was younger. They didn't care if I worked the six hours while he was in school and then took the rest of the time off." Working at home would suit Billy even better. With a nod toward a burl of wood dominating the kitchen table in one corner, he adds, "Someday we'll live off my sculptings." Looking closer, I see, emerging from the natural formation of the wood, a mass of intricately carved snakes which make up the hair on the head of a beautiful woman.

"Medusa," says Billy. "I read a lot of Greek mythology the first year on my own with Aaron. Growing up in such a large family, I had never spent a single day by myself in my life, and I got married when I was eighteen. So I found it pretty difficult learning how to be alone like that. I read a lot in the evenings and spent time recording my dreams. It turned out to be one of the best things I've ever done for myself, learning how to be satisfied with my own company. After that, I started carving when Aaron goes to bed. I've spent every night for the past year working on this Medusa."

Medusa, I think to myself — an interesting protracted meditation for a single man raising his child on his own. Medusa, a mythical female presence so powerful that anyone who met her gaze was turned to stone. What had Billy met in himself during those long nights, those long years, as a single father?

Aaron comes in and asks us to take a look at the kittens he and Billy found abandoned under a hedge that morning. In a small box next to Aaron's bed, two kittens, eyes not yet open, are snuggled into a red plaid flannel shirt. Leaving Aaron hovering over the box, Billy and I head outside to resume our conversation.

Parked in the driveway is a second-hand, two-ton pickup truck. On the side of the garage, the blade from an eight-foot two-man saw, the metal disk of a circular saw, and the skull of a young buck with antlers are nailed up as a collage. Nearby, a mottled dartboard has a knife sunk into it a few inches off bull's-eye. Clearly this is "the boys' clubhouse."

"If I hadn't had Aaron, I would probably still be just backpacking around, maybe doing drugs, probably feeling unfulfilled like some of my brothers and sisters," Billy comments as we settle into a couple of chairs near the vegetable garden. "It's been really healing and nurturing for *me* — having him to come back to every day. I was there when he was born. I held him right away, and I've never stopped holding him. That connection is just locked in here." Billy lays his fist on his heart. "I don't understand how people miss that in their lives, how they just pass it by.

"It was difficult for a few years in the beginning when I felt like I needed to have someone else here to make the complete family picture. But as time went on I found that taking care of Aaron by myself began to fulfill a need in me to be nurturing. I feel now as if I have enough of the mothering capabilities that I don't need to go out and find a mom for him."

Aaron comes out with one of the tiny kittens, scrawny and meowing softly as it feels its way blindly across the boy's cradled arms. "Dad, I'd like to know if I can feed the kittens again."

"Sure, you can feed them any time you feel like trying. I'm sure they wouldn't mind. But if they're not hungry, don't push it."

"Well, do you think the formula is okay? Maybe we'd better get a different one."

"Yeah, we can do that later today."

Billy turns back to continue his conversation with me. "Nurturing is a mothering quality. To me that means doing things like letting Aaron's emotions flow, letting him express his feelings. When he comes home from school, we talk, he tells me how he feels about things. I also do other things I consider nurturing. I make sure I consciously show him that I care by reading to him at night, giving him hugs and kisses when he goes to bed, letting him crawl in with me if he has a bad dream. It's letting him know that I'm a stable presence and will always be there for him. I really think it helped being able to draw on what I saw my own mom do."

"Dad, watch," Aaron says, interrupting us as he smiles down at the kitten in his arms. "He wants to go to sleep."

"He likes it when he can sleep on your tummy or in your hands," says Billy, "because it feels warm and he can feel that it's something alive that likes him and is holding him, instead of just being in a box."

"See, Dad?"

"Um-hmm. He fell right to sleep."

Aaron turns back to the house with his tiny treasure. "I'm not sure how to explain it," says Billy. "It's not something I've put into words before. I didn't set out consciously to raise my child alone because I needed to become more nurturing in my life, but the more I do it, the more that becomes a part of who I am. Now it feels like it's something I couldn't do without.

"Maybe I could compare it to those kittens. I don't like pets. I don't like domesticated animals one bit. I like animals out in the woods and the wild. When Aaron brought these kittens home with us, I thought I'd take them to the pound and get rid of them even though I knew he'd be crying. But once I started feeding them with the bottle, it was like, 'Here we go. Two more without a mom — welcome to the boys' club.'

"'You're a rare breed,' my friends say to me. 'You're a rare breed.' But I believe that every individual has the capacity to be the father/mother, to be the nurturer/disciplinarian. If you believe you have the capabilities, you have them. That's what I found."

But believing is only half the game. Success springs from developing capabilities. Billy didn't just step into the role of full-time nurturer, fully formed and ready. Like that figure emerging from the textured wood on his kitchen table, the "mothering capabilities" were something he had to carve out of his own character. Although Billy's own mother to some degree had provided a model, his deep sense of *being* a nurturer was something he had to develop on his own, over time. The ways in which we are socialized as men and women can pose a challenge as we step into unfamiliar roles.

For Georgie, raising her two children alone has meant having to find the "fathering capabilities" in herself. In a division of assets reflecting the typical male/female stereotypes in our society, Georgie got the antique furniture when she divorced, and her ex-husband took the power tools. After nearly four years on her own, Georgie says, laughing, "This Christmas I'm asking for power tools!"

Flowers and herbs are scattered in pots and small plots around Georgie's big yard, where we are talking. The chocolate chips in the cookies piled on a platter before us still glisten with the heat of the oven. Georgie fills my cup from a porcelain pot of tea. "I've taken my job as a full-time mom really seriously. I'm intent on it," she says. "But I find that I've had to put a lot of time into trying to figure out how to be balanced as I work to build a career while also being a good mother. I walk the line between being the mommy at home and then going off to classes and lectures. I won't say it's exactly Jekyll and Hyde, but it's sure two different lifestyles. A lot of what we used to do as a family for playtime was based on 'When Daddy comes home, we'll do such and such.' With us now, it's 'When Mommy comes home' — and it's hard for me to remember to make that kind of family time instead of getting overwhelmed with all the 'mommy stuff' here, the cooking, cleaning, laundry . . .'"

The phone rings, and Georgie gets up to answer. It's seven-year-old Jason calling, as she instructed him to do when he left the house ten minutes before to visit a new boy on the block. I listen as she fires a series of questions through the receiver: Who is his teacher at school? Are his parents there now? Can I talk with them? After a brief pause, she tells someone on the other end of the line the exact time Jason should be home. No negotiation.

"I would have been one of those airy-fairy, sweet, nondisciplinarian, no-boundaries type of mothers if my son especially hadn't been such a bear to raise," Georgie comments when she returns. "He's what is considered a 'difficult child,' highly sensitive and overly reactive. He's been like that since birth. In order for him to feel healthy and secure, both physically and emotionally, he's needed tons of boundaries and I've had to learn how to set them myself. Really, though, both kids need it."

As if on cue, Zoe, four years old, comes flying out of the house and bounds across the yard. "I'm going to play in the school yard," she calls back.

As Zoe starts climbing the tree that branches over their fence onto the asphalt on the other side, Georgie catches her with her voice. "Zoe! We talked about that. You are not to go over there alone."

"But, Mom . . ."

"No."

Georgie turns back to me. "You know, one of the things I hate about single parenting is being in charge of all the discipline. Holding the boundaries. I would still prefer being the soft mother. I have learned how to be harsh out of necessity. It wasn't that I didn't do any disciplining before I got divorced. But now it's all on me."

Georgie goes inside to give Zoe a snack and set her up with paints and paper. I follow her in and look around as we continue talking. Pinned to the refrigerator with colorful magnets are a calendar for rotating chores, a chart with stars for good conduct, and a list of house rules. Among them: You get it out, you put it back. Help clean up messes friends make. No playing Saturday until rooms are clean.

On a nearby bulletin board, amid children's drawings and notes on index cards, are a verse from the Pueblo Indians, a quote from the Dalai Lama, and notices for therapy workshops. "I value trying to live in a way that doesn't rush things or try to control everything," Georgie comments, "but our lifestyle here is just not like the tribal village, so that value is always being challenged by what it means to take care of children in this kind of culture."

The door bangs open; it's Jason with his new friend. He stops, feet planted apart, eyes flashing. "Mom, we're going to ride around the block on our bikes."

"No, you are not. You went around the corner this morning without permission and your bike is still on time-out." Georgie turns back to me with a shadow of discomfort on her face. "Discipline was just something I had to learn how to do, like I have to feed them breakfast, like I have to get up at six A.M. It just goes with the territory."

◆ WHAT IS THE TERRITORY?

Parenting alone is a vast and in many ways uncharted territory. Certainly we can enumerate the challenges we face daily in fulfilling our role as double parents — challenges to our bodies, minds, and hearts. But there is another challenge we face that is not so overt. That is the one that arises to our sense of self when we must take on behaviors and ways of relating that we may have learned were in the domain of the opposite sex. What happens to a man when he must function as a mother? What happens to a woman when she must fulfill some of the roles of a father? Billy's and Georgie's stories focus on nurturing and discipline as aspects of those roles, but these functions are only part of what being a double parent entails.

Gender is one of the most basic ways in which we define who we are, and the basis for defining roles in any society. By the time we are two years old, we're savvy to the fact that there are boys and girls in the world, and in most cases we know exactly which we are.[1] When we cross certain thresholds with first menstruation or first ejaculation, we step more deeply into a sense of identity as a woman or a man. As we continue to mature, our sense of self is increasingly directed by our culture into distinct gender roles. When we become *the* parent, however, we may find ourselves compelled to do things that call upon unfamiliar parts of ourselves. This can be especially true for parents raising children of the opposite sex.

"Having a son, I'm particularly aware that I'm trying to fill in for what a father or other male might do," says Sophie. We are sitting on the couch in the bedroom of her Oakland apartment, having retreated here from the labyrinth of Lego space stations that ten-year-old Trevor and a friend are building across the living room floor. The wall above the couch in Sophie's room is dominated by one of her paintings — a nude woman with fiery red hair and massive thighs reclining luxuriously.

"I was brought up as a female, not just in my family but following the prototypes of the whole culture. That meant I never much wanted to play with erector sets or take an alarm clock apart to see what was inside. But Trevor did, and not wanting to stop his growth, I started joining him. He asked questions in a way too that I didn't remember doing as a girl growing up. And he needed lots of physical activity. I'd come home from work and want to find a moment to relax, but his way to come down from the day was to start to wrestle. So I'd get into it. Okay, this is what a father would do, so I'd wrestle. If there was something he was afraid of, I would take his hand and say, 'Let's go see how we can do that. That tree is too scary to climb? I'll climb it with you.' If I had been with a husband, I might have said, 'Honey, take him up in the tree.' Being the only one there for a boy, I had to grow up as a boy myself."

When he first took on responsibility for his two daughters, six and three years old, Alan remembers feeling "adrift in a world of women raising kids." Their mother, ten years younger than Alan, had begun to discover that her own values ran contrary to her life as the wife of a successful Manhattan lawyer. Eventually, having found a partner who shared her desire to live more simply, she moved to a plot of land hundreds of miles from any major urban center. And Alan entered an unknown world.

"I found I was always dealing with women. I'd go to the pediatrician's office, and there would be all women in the waiting room. At parents' night at preschool, it seemed to be all women. Some of this is changing now, but this was ten years ago. I'd go to a parent event, like Thanksgiving at school, and there would be one hundred women and myself. And they all seemed to have an easy relationship with each other, based on a women's world or something that didn't extend to me. I felt like I was either an object of pity or else a little bit scary. 'Who is this guy? Can we trust him?'

"My image of myself for the first few years was like someone on the deck of a ship in a storm, or on the prow of a boat peering into the gloom, trying to find out which way to go," Alan remembers. "I just held on. I felt I had no models and no support system. The idea that a man could end up with kids, especially two girls, was absolutely unheard of by anyone I knew. I felt a lot of pressure that I shouldn't be in this role. Everybody told me, 'Get married as quickly as you can find a woman to move in.' I couldn't help but feel a lack of self-esteem or confidence. I felt like I was doing a lot of things wrong."

One of the places where Alan felt like he was doing things wrong was in the "women's world." "I had to take the girls shopping to get clothes when they were little, and I'd end up having to pick out dresses for them. I knew nothing about clothing or what they should be wearing, what kind of 'fashion statement' they might want to make. Even the process was foreign. My four-year-old daughter would end up going into the dressing room alone because I couldn't go in there — the whole section is for women! Or my older girl would lay her lingerie on the countertop and I'd stand nearby to write out the check. It was just a whole other world I wasn't familiar with. It sounds trivial as a problem, and I feel ashamed to complain because I had it so much better than others, at least financially, but if you're feeling already like you're not sure what you're doing, it sure doesn't help to be in such a foreign world."

It wasn't just outside his home where Alan felt ill at ease in his new role. "I was so aware too that mothers relate to daughters in a certain way that I couldn't. A mother might sit and brush their hair for hours or they could snuggle up and watch TV together. But that just wasn't natural to me. I was raised to be pretty standoffish. Gradually I had to learn how to be more affectionate. If they were crying, I knew I had to hug them more than might feel natural to me. And I also tried to do other 'motherly' things for them. Although I couldn't show them how to bake, we would read the cookbooks together — the things a mother normally might do with a kid."

Of course, what mothers and fathers "normally do" is not pre-ordained, but culturally defined stereotypes are pervasive. While it might be especially uncomfortable or challenging to face the unfamiliar worlds of opposite-sex children, *all* of us as single parents find ourselves forced to take on some of the roles the missing parent might have filled. Because the roles of mother and father have been so equated with biological functions and gender, we almost automatically define mothering in terms that are considered feminine and fathering in traditionally masculine terms. Mothering suggests diffuse awareness, inclusiveness, relatedness, and nurturing warmth. Fathering suggests focused awareness, strategizing, the ability to set limits, the tendency to prefer function over process, and the distance that fosters independence. The "mother," the feminine, offers presence and embrace; the "father," the masculine, models action and discipline. Of course such an absolute division of labor doesn't exist, but the schema delineates the spectrum of qualities and behaviors we have come to consider necessary for adequate parenting.

As we ourselves attempt to span the spectrum, as we become both nurturers and disciplinarians, as we hold our children close and push them toward independence, as we climb trees and brush hair, something in us undergoes a profound change. We find that we are not just *playing out* roles. We begin to become what we do.

From the androgynous gods of Mesopotamia to the anima and animus of Carl Jung, the spectrum of masculine and feminine qualities in each of us has been affirmed throughout history. Even Freud concluded that "all human individuals . . . combine in themselves both masculine and feminine characteristics."[2] More than merely psychological constructs, these aspects are firmly rooted in our physiological makeup as well. Every individual produces both male and female hormones. "What differentiates 'males' and 'females' is not the kind of hormone," researchers point out, "but the relative amounts of each hormone,"[3] so that "the difference between 'males' and 'females' is really one of degree," and "aside from a few biologically based limitations . . . people can enact the same behaviors."[4] Extensive research has concluded that there is little evidence to indicate that the biological sex of individuals directly correlates with characteristics (such as assertiveness or empathy) or ability to perform roles.[5]

The sociologist Barbara Risman points out that the circumstances individuals are placed in invariably affect how masculine or feminine their behavior is. Women in the same career positions as men exhibit identical tendencies and abilities. Likewise, men who are the primary and continuous caretakers of their children provide mothering that in many ways "is nearly indistinguishable from the behavior of women in the same situation." On Risman's tests, in fact, single fathers turned out to have scores indicating levels of femininity identical to those of married working mothers.[6]

Despite the boundaries of conditioning, we as single parents reach beyond them. Does this mean that single fathers become more feminine when they *do* "mothering"? Do single mothers become more masculine when they *do* "fathering"? Maybe. Like Joan of Arc, who donned the garb and identity of a man in order to fulfill her mission, single parents are called upon to "cross-dress" psychologically in order to provide the full spectrum of services children need in a family.

◆ GRAPPLING WITH OUR OTHER HALF

"Definitely over time I have become more masculine," reflects Sophie. "And that has had both good and bad consequences to it.

"Trying to get everything done in a day, to be at all the PTA meetings and to work at the same time, I know I get that look on my face of being very purposeful, which *looks* more masculine. To me it *feels* more masculine. When I walk across a room, it's with purpose, both at home and in public. I don't want anybody to stop me and say, 'Oh, how are you?' I just want to keep going, stay focused, stay organized." Sophie found that not only did this behavior change her own sense of herself as a woman, it also ended up affecting her relationships with others, especially men.

We may at times feel as if we are flailing about in an ocean of immediate demands, trying out different behaviors to make our lives as single parents work. It may be with pain and resentment that we attempt to fill the shoes of the absent parent. It may be with confusion and frustration that we enter unfamiliar territory and collide with cultural mores. Taking on a new role can also mean leaving something of an old one behind us.

"I have felt heartsick sometimes," says Sophie, "when I've had to move into that more functional 'male' role. The feminine part of me wants to spend time with my child talking about his feelings and explaining things, figuring out what's going on and its relationship to everything else in our lives. But I'm forced to drop that at times and say to him, 'We're doing it this way because this is the way it is. We can't talk forever about how it might be. We just have to get the dang thing done.' I have to get into that real action mode. As a mother, then, I feel as if I've ended up missing a valuable moment with my child."

While it is sometimes uncomfortable for a mother to be in that more assertive, goal-oriented mode we have come to call "male," it can be just as uncomfortable for a man to engage the female aspect of himself as a single father.

"This sounds goofy," says Ed, "but I needed to become more

female when I became the primary parent for my eight-year-old son."
Briefcase at his side, Ed is on his way back to Chicago after a business
trip. We are talking in the Minneapolis/St. Paul airport, and although
we chose an area to sit in that seemed out of the way, suddenly a
door has opened and a stream of people leaving a plane fills the room.
Ed lowers his voice. For a man to "become more female" must
certainly have been taboo in the Dutch community in Michigan where
Ed was raised.

Because Ed's job didn't demand the same level of travel as his
wife's, he ended up as the primary parent when they divorced. "The
circumstances of our separating were typical of a lot of people — we
just grew apart," explains Ed. "I'm not sure that she would agree
with me, but my orientation is probably much more what people in
the past would have thought of as the woman's role. I wanted to be
at home with David, and my work allowed that."

David sees his mother, who lives in a different city, on some weekends and during the summer, but Ed feels he needs to provide "mothering" for his son when he has him, and he has worked hard at it.
"Probably the toughest part of the adjustment for me into being a
single parent was to develop ways to give my son some of the things
that are considered feminine," he says. "I'm kind of a cold Capricorn
— don't touch me in public, don't even think of a kiss on the cheek.
So I had to teach myself. It just wasn't the most natural thing for me.
I'd be standing next to David and have to tell myself, 'For crying out
loud, touch him! Put your arm around him.' When he'd walk past in
the house, I'd have to remember, 'Oh, yeah, brush him on the shoulder.' It was a training in how to become soft — not that men aren't
soft, but softer. And it took a conscious effort for me.

"The way I really learned this affection angle," Ed remembers,
"was when I vowed that I would never be the first one to break an
embrace with David — and I never have." Ed would find himself in
broad daylight, standing on a street corner, his son's head pressed
against his stomach, their arms wrapped around each other. "Sometimes the embrace was almost embarrassingly long. I would hear the
bus for school coming down the street, and I'd think, 'Okay, I'll drive
him to school in the car then.' But I would hold him until he broke
away, when *he* was finished."

Getting past the discomfort of that public display of affection, a
discomfort so common in men of Ed's generation, is a start. He

knows he still has a way to go. "David's mother is much better at handling emotions and helping him work through what is on his mind. I get to talking with him as if he's an adult and forget that there's the emotional side that is a child. Then *boom!* — suddenly he needs emotional support, and I've got to struggle to make that rapid transition with him. Eventually the two ways will merge in me, but now there's still a gap."

◆ THE BALANCING ACT

Getting to know our other half over time — how it feels to be more masculine or feminine, what actions and words accompany those modes — can be exciting and enriching. However, striking a new balance can be as difficult as creating harmony in any relationship.

To become more masculine, as Sophie calls it, or more female, as Ed puts it, is to step beyond the personal and cultural definitions of what it means to be a woman or a man as we create the role of the mother/father parent. I remember pausing on the steps as I ran out to work one morning when Elias was still a baby, suddenly realizing that I didn't have a sense of myself as either feminine or masculine. Whatever way I had formerly known myself as a woman seemed to be gone. When I had eased out of the rocking chair that morning after nursing Elias, it was as if I had to clamp a shield down over the breasts beneath still filled with milk in order to stride out into the world. The part of me that wanted to relax and nurture had no place in the thrust to accomplish a day's work. I found myself suspended somewhere between, something neither female nor male. In a way, it was almost a welcome feeling of liberation, but it was also disconcerting. Stopping there at the top of the stairs, I began to see that any number of capacities were open to me, and as a single parent I'd have to embrace a broad spectrum of them whether I wanted to or not.

"There are two times when I feel my best," says Sophie. "One is when my heart, my affection, my softness, is wide open. I'm sitting next to Trevor and he's leaning into me while he reads. Or we're talking about something and I'm rubbing his back. I would consider that an extremely feminine maneuver and I feel really good in those moments.

"I also feel really good at those times when we're exploring something, or we're having a really strong intellectual discussion. When

we're researching the origins of a particular object, or fixing something, doing a task together — that's when we're in what I would call
the ultimate masculine mode. The world feels right then too.

"But all those other moments in between, which is the majority of
the time, I feel a sense of tension in terms of the balance of male/fe-
male, mother/father. Should I be sitting down with him more? Should
I be arguing more? Should I be more strict? Should I be more soft? I
have all these niggly little questions which wander around constantly
like little demons inside me. But in one extreme or the other, I feel
quiet and really strong. I feel strong in my femininity and strong in
my masculinity. In between I'm doing the balancing act."

The balancing act. Does my child need mothering now or fathering? Even if I know, how do I span the gap that Ed talks about? We
can never take the place of a parent of the opposite sex and, especially
as our children mature, we need to put them in touch with same-sex
role models. However, on a daily basis, we alone are confronted with
the absence and how to fill it.

Jane Anne, whose son is now a teenager, remembers how she could
barely watch Jonah at bat for fear of seeing him fail. Meanwhile, the
fathers of the other players on her son's team would be unabashedly
priming their sons from the sidelines: "Shape up, kid!" "Hang in
there."

"It's not that I wanted to adopt their approach, but it made me
aware of how my own fears for Jonah were out of balance. I wasn't
sure how to change that, but I thought, 'I need to watch these guys.
There's something here to learn.'" We can indeed learn from each
other — for the good of our children and because it can actually
make our parenting easier.

◆ LEARNING FROM OUR DIFFERENCES

"I was at my high school reunion picnic," Sophie remembers, "and
my cute little three-year-old was running around in his cute little
outfit. I was sitting at a table eating with friends, and suddenly Trevor
fell down a little distance away. He was lying on his back crying,
'Mommy! Mommy!' Now, up to this point in time, Trevor's life
had been almost exclusively governed by me and my responses. I
jump up, of course, to go over and help him. Suddenly this big arm
stretches across the picnic table and stops me. It's the high school

basketball champion, Jake. He says, 'Don't do it.' 'What do you mean?' I toss back at him on my way to the rescue. 'Trevor's *hurt.*'

"For me my child being hurt meant the automatic response of running over and kneeling by his side, touching him, saying, 'Are you okay? Are you hurt, honey?' It meant being very supportive and encouraging. I watch Jake head out in front of me. He says, 'Just watch. This is the difference between how a woman would handle it and how a man would handle it.' Jake bends over Trevor, doesn't touch him, doesn't kneel by his side. In other words, *he maintains his separate self.* He says, 'Hey, any blood? Let me see your hands. Any blood there? No blood. Let me see your back. No blood there. You're okay.' He pulls Trevor up off the ground. 'Gimme five,' he says. They slap hands and walk off.

"I tell you, my life changed!" says Sophie. "I realized I was teaching my child to be picky about little things. I had been taught to be the nurturing caretaker. When someone was hurt, I wanted to make them feel better — because it made *me* feel better. I even notice it with my own mother. I call home, still being her little girl even though I'm in my thirties, and I'm crying because I'm lonely, Trevor's not doing well, my job is not going well, my car is broken. She's right there. She'll even bake me a cake, come over and take me out to lunch. If I complain to my father, his response is just to be very quiet. He tends to respond more when he's supporting my triumphs. I get strokes from my mother when I'm hurt.

"Well, what I'm learning, and what Jake set off in me, is that there is a time when being nurturing and protective is not healthy. It doesn't allow the child the space to develop their own inner strength. And it's not necessarily meeting the child's needs as much as the mother's need to be wanted and loving and important."

We grow up learning what makes us feel wanted and needed — and in many ways that's different for girls and boys. Right from the outset, biological differences are intensified by differences in treatment. Girls are cuddled more by their parents than boys are, mothers encourage more independence in their sons than in their daughters. A little girl, sporting a doll like an essential accessory to her wardrobe, will tell you that she wants to grow up to be a mother. How many little boys tell you they want to grow up to be fathers? Relating to children is not generally cultivated as a primary identity in boys, whereas doing something active, out in the world, is. The double role we play as single parents challenges these tendencies that have been encouraged in us since childhood.

In a study of households where mothers and fathers share parenting, the psychologist Diane Ehrensaft noted some crucial differences between the parents in their childrearing behavior. "A woman has a terrible time disengaging herself from her child," she writes, "not just because she thinks she 'ought to' do something for the child but, more deeply, because she has trouble not 'being' a mother. . . . For women, mothering is a form of existence, a way of being. For men, mothering is a set of activities they are doing, defining a relationship in which they are involved but which does not reside at the very core of their being. . . . Father is much clearer than mother as to where he stops and where baby starts. He is so aware of this that he grows agitated when his child's needs encroach on his. How different this is from the experience of mothers, who have a hard time even sorting out their own needs from their children's."[7]

Men do in general have the ability to categorize their activities more easily. Interestingly, this may be due not only to conditioning but also to a difference between men and women in brain structure and function. The same difference that provides women easier access to verbalizing their feelings gives men increased ability to compartmentalize responses, to put aside feelings and turn their focus toward the task at hand.[8]

Ehrensaft's work illustrates how these tendencies get amplified and expressed in parenting roles we have been conditioned to think of as "natural" for mothers or fathers. We carry these attitudes and tendencies into single parenting as well, where there is no other half to provide a counterpoint. We may be overly involved as mothers and too detached as fathers, and our children have no recourse.

Kevin, who began raising his two sons alone when they were toddlers, arrived at his task from a conventional marriage, and it didn't occur to him to learn how to parent differently once he was on his own with his children. "I never got down on my hands and knees and played games with my boys. I never even considered it at the time," Kevin admits. "If they wanted to throw a football around, fine, but I wasn't going to play Uncle Wiggily. I wanted the separation. 'Go do children's things while Dad is doing adult things.' That was part of my discipline with them, but now I regret some of that.

"I think single fathers need to be aware of the fact that we are prone to being male and doing male things and feeling male ways. Sometimes we have to fight our own deep tendencies to be out there as 'hunters' or to be just disciplinarians in order to remember that our children have real live needs, here and now, and we've got one chance to fill them.

"You see," says Kevin, with a certainty born of hindsight, "I think it's important for men to take note of how women play with their children — how they get down in the grass, for instance, and look for bugs together. And if you can do it, do it.

"As fathers we need to pay attention to the fact that in spite of how we feel or what we think, our children need unconditional love and attention. Women seem to have a way of making their kids feel like the center of the universe in a way that men just don't seem to do. I actually thought in the beginning that men made better parents than women because I thought every mother I knew spoiled her kids rotten. But there's a lot to be said for unconditional love. It builds self-esteem. Everything that anybody I know has wrong with them comes from lack of that."

Kevin's work now is an attempt to remedy that lack. The books he writes and illustrates for children are specifically intended to cultivate self-esteem and provide images of how it might feel to be loved unconditionally.

"But I think men's love is quite conditional," Kevin goes on. "And the condition is this: Everybody has rights, and we all respect them. A lot of mothers, on the other hand, are quite willing to give up their rights for a period of time on behalf of their children — at least that has been my observation."

This difference between mothers and fathers in their parenting habits is something I noticed as well. While many of the women I spoke with made their lives revolve around their children, many of the men drew their children into their *own* lives. As Ehrensaft points out, women seem to collapse themselves into their role as mothers more than men do. "Women 'are' mothers while men 'do' mothering," she writes.[9]

All of these distinctions are general *tendencies,* not absolutes; environment and experiences influence how they will be expressed. So does individual choice. "The way I see it," says Kevin, "is that regardless of how you feel or think, you have a job to perform. As a single parent, you've basically chosen to be the sole source of love and affection and nourishment and nurturing for your kids. You've got to step up to the challenge of that role just as you would if you were given a promotion at work. You don't really know how to do the job, but you bust your ass to do it. That's what you have to do to be a decent father, to be a decent parent. You may not like what you have to do, but by God, it has to be done and nobody else is going to do it but you."

No matter what abilities and behaviors we might develop through parenting alone, however, we will never take the place of the other parent. A single mother will never fill the shoes of a father; she will "do fathering" according to her individual abilities. A single father will never fill the shoes of a mother; he will "do mothering" in his own unique way. As Robert Bly so aptly puts it, "Geneticists have discovered recently that the genetic difference in DNA between men and women amounts to just over three percent. That isn't much. However, the difference exists in every cell of the body."[10]

◆   LEARNING TO BE DIFFERENT

Max, one of my housemates, had invited Elias to the annual children's day held by his men's group. I was delighted. My son would have an opportunity to drum and dance with the guys and explore his young masculinity in one of the typical settings of the men's movement. Glad to have the time to get some work done at the library, I carefully packed everything Max might need to take along to care for a two-year-old. Next to the stroller I put a bag with a change of clothes, fresh diapers and rubber pants, a plastic bag for wet diapers, a cloth for wiping up, a lunch, a bottle of juice, and a snack. On it I pinned a big note reminding Max what time Elias would take a nap and that he was used to sleeping in the stroller. Max had been a single father; I was confident everything would be fine.

When I returned in the late afternoon, Max and Elias were no-where around, and there in the hallway sat the stroller, the note, and the bag, untouched. My first thought was, "Oh, they must not have gone," for to me going away with Elias simply meant having all those things along. But they were indeed gone. Two hours later, when I was about to start really worrying, Max and Elias came laughing through the door drenched in camaraderie. A big bulge at the bottom of one of Elias's pant legs indicated the location of his soaked diaper. My son had drummed and danced, had feasted on the potluck lunch the men had brought, slept against Max's arm on the train home, hadn't asked for a bottle or a snack, and had gone into stitches along with Max over that dangling diaper as they walked back the half-mile from the train station. Six hours with no props and he was fine. "Hi, Mama, can I have a bottle?" was his only gesture of recognition.

In that instant, my convictions about what constitutes proper care underwent renovation. I had fully assumed that Max would replicate my method of care, down to the diaper bag. He of course had his own experience of what worked. He took Elias into his world in a casual and more detached way. He mothered like a man. What began to dawn on me was that I was also "fathering" like a woman. And not only was that all right, it was the only thing I *could* do.

"I had to finally realize," comments Sophie, "that this is not a good notion, to try to be the mother and the father. And, in fact, I'm not. I am not a father. I am a parent and a mother. To pretend I'm a father is narcissistic, egotistical, and totally crazy. It would lead Trevor astray and definitely ruin me."

By the time Trevor was nine, he was clearly no longer "androgynous in his needs," as Sophie had described his early years. Wanting to support his burgeoning manhood, Sophie set out for a trip with Trevor across the country, their destination the dismantling of a B-56 fighter bomber from World War II. It was the exact model in which Sophie's father, Trevor's grandfather, had won his claim to a Congressional Medal of Honor, and Grandpa was going to be there for the event. Sophie wanted Trevor to have this opportunity "not only to bond with the history of my dad, but also to witness the dismantling of an instrument of war. I wanted for us to hear Dad's story and to try to feel what he had experienced during those ten hours when he and all those men in a disabled three-story plane above the ocean had faced their common death."

Their day began with following Grandpa through the plane, trying out the seats and passageways he had known as a young man, pressing through the hole onto the wing as Grandpa had done at twenty thousand feet to fix the broken landing gear. "I started wondering," says Sophie, "how a man could live in this world. This is what my father had done supporting his family. It was a very unreal world for me."

By the time they came upon "the tunnel," Grandpa had gone off on some mission to another part of the plane. This narrow tunnel, about forty yards long, was the only mode of passage from the front to the back of an airborne B-56. There was a platform conveyance to lie on, like a surfboard on wheels. The rope pulley that the men had used to move themselves along, hand over hand, had long since broken.

"Trevor announced that he wanted to go through that space — with me," Sophie continues. "Everything in me contracted. If I said no, I was denying him the experience of something in his male heritage; if I said yes, I was not honoring my own terror. I finally convinced myself: Okay, I will experience what my dad did.

"The only way we could do it together was with Trevor lying on my stomach. He couldn't even lift his head. I had to push with my arms against the metal sides. The wheels of the cart were rusty, and it felt like the tunnel would never end. I kept imagining the plane rumbling along at twenty thousand feet and being in this tiny tube with bombs stored on either side. By the time I got out of there, I'd had it as a father. Trevor needed a man to do these things with him.

"Later, as I sat on the lawn with my dad and my son, looking up at that B-56 and reflecting on the day's experience, the sense deepened in me that this was not my world. There is a male psyche, a way of thinking, of interacting, a way of courage and fear, that is foreign to me as a female. I realized that it was an awesome world to me, one that would forever be a mystery, just as I'm sure birth and menstruation are for a man. I could feel that fundamental difference in the way we walk through our world, not as one being more sensitive than the other or anything like that, just different — in ways that are exciting as well as threatening to each other. I saw that there are some worlds my son must go into where I cannot go, and worlds I am in that no matter how sensitive or philosophical or nurturing he may be, he will never perceive in the same manner."

While Sophie clearly could manage some aspects of "fathering," she struck her limit in the B-56 bomber. As single mothers and fathers, we can fulfill our double role to a degree. But we may have to admit, particularly as our children grow older, that we can't do it all and that, even if we play the same roles, we do them differently.

"I feel I'm every bit as loving and nurturing as any mother could be, but it took a couple of years to develop my own rhythm and way of doing this," Denny explains. After seven years of sharing custody of his two boys, he reflects back on the evolution of his role. "Parenting is done so much by women that a man can't quickly get the feel for it. So at first I fell into the trap of trying to be a mom in order to do this job right. Or I'd try to follow the routines as if it were their mother's house. Well, now I know I can't be a mom. I am with my boys the way that feels right for me. And I feel very competent and responsible in that. I can't create an artificial, pretend life here for my kids — 'This is just like home except Mom's not here.' No, this is me, this is Dad's world.

"I don't think a single father should worry about being a mother. I think he should just be a father. And if you are a father, and a good one, I think there's enough nurturing inside that you don't have to worry about it."

Learning to play the double role of single parents entails reassessing our identity as mothers, as fathers, as parents, and as individuals. It means journeying into unfamiliar territory and returning to ourselves changed. I am beginning to see that as I learn to be gentle and firm, strong and soft, detached and involved, I am tracing a path of wisdom not just as a single parent but as a human being, and I'm practicing it in the particulars of daily life in the mother/father role.

◆ PASSING THE TORCH

Our children seem to have little trouble recognizing our double role and the fact that it can make us "different" in some very positive ways. "You're more like a boy than my friends' moms!" a ten-year-old proudly tells his mother. Elias, when he was nearly three and obsessed with trains, came up with his own acknowledgment.

"You have lots of engines inside you," he said to me as we walked hand in hand along the sidewalk one day.

"Oh?"

"One of them makes you move. Another one makes you into a mother. A different one makes you into a father."

The mother/father parent may indeed be "a rare breed," and yet I saw evidence of it over and over in the homes of the single parents I visited. Hanging on the kitchen wall in one home is a plaque with MOTHER written on it in small multicolored seashells. Noe, who is raising his son alone, explains, "They often do projects at school for Mother's Day, and Oliver gives me the stuff. He tells me, 'You're like my dad *and* my mom.'"

Mary laughed when she showed me the card her teenage daughter had given her for Mother's Day. The fact that a major national card company had produced it indicates how much the mother/father role is being recognized in our culture. On the front of the card under "To My Single Mom" is a litany of praise: You're great, we have a lot of fun, you're always there . . . I love you madly. Topping off the eulogy is testimony to that dual role: "And to me you are quite dadly."

This unique role we play in the single-parent family not only changes our sense of ourselves, it also begins to break down limiting stereotypes, and it models different options for our children. Back in Billy's yard, as we are finishing up our interview, Aaron, looking worried, appears again with a kitten. "Can we get better nipples, Dad? I think he might have gotten too much, because he started gurgling."

"Let me see him." Billy checks the kitty, who's now meowing again. "Yeah, he's okay. And we'll try some other nipples. But later, Aaron, later."

When Aaron leaves, Billy says to me, "I want to make sure he gets that kind of experience. I don't want him to think that being a man means going to bars and drinking beer. I know that if a boy has constant access to a man who is being nurturing, he will understand that a man can be that way. And he seems real balanced. He's got those nurturing qualities, and when I watch him at school, he's also got leadership qualities. He's out there getting kids to start games and make up fantasies.

"As I see it," Billy goes on, "one of the roots of the problem is that people are brought up as men and women instead of human beings. I'm trying to teach him to be a human being."

Children growing up with a mother who is competent in the world and comfortable with her sense of power, or with a father who isn't afraid to hold and listen, who knows how to cook and keep house, will certainly have a different set of expectations of themselves and others. The limited research that has been done on the subject in fact reveals that children from families headed by single mothers tended to be "less sex-typed in their behavior" than those from two-parent families. The researchers explain: "Daily interaction with a mother who is required to adopt a wide variety of behaviors may contribute to the greater flexibility of children from single-parent families."[11]

Likewise for those from families headed by single fathers. "One of the things my two sons will have noticed," says Duane, a burly man who relishes breaking the stereotype, "is that I iron, I vacuum, I scrub floors, I dust, I cook. I didn't grow up like that, but they see that men can do this. They scrub floors too, they both know how to cook and how to sew."

At a time when the role of father is searching for definition, the children in these families are perceiving one they can readily grasp. Pleased by the compliment, Scott reports that his five-year-old son, Braun, tells him, "When I grow up, I want to be an architect and a dad."

Just as being released from stereotyped roles might give our children a head start on being balanced human beings, we too in our double roles have this opportunity to break out of an often unconscious prison. Perhaps as we learn to take on behaviors and qualities of the opposite sex, we might begin to cross some of those barriers of contention between men and women in our society. As men experience how taxing it can be to never have a break from children, as women learn more about the depersonalizing pressures men encounter in the workplace, we might not only begin to understand the world the other lives in, we can also begin to do something about changing these contexts in ways that can benefit all children and families.

CHAPTER 7

◆

Walking the Bottom Line:
Finances and Treasures

Where your treasure lies,
there also lies your heart.
— Luke 12:34

HALFWAY THROUGH WRITING this book, I sent a letter to a friend to ask for some advice. Not only a writer but also an astute businessman, he had the perfect combination of talents to address my concern — financial survival while completing a manuscript. An issue familiar to many writers, it had become grossly amplified for me by the fact that I had sole responsibility for my child. I was hoping my friend might give me some clues on how to survive the financial precipice of my present without squandering our future. The advance on my book had run out, the manuscript was far from finished, and loans and credit cards looked like my only option if I was to continue writing.

Certainly as a single person without a child I had sometimes lived on the edge. Money had not been the foremost value in my life. Choice had. My generation had encouraged it. If minimal pay meant doing interesting work with a nonprofit organization, or if spending savings meant the opportunity to explore the world, that's what I chose. There were times when I scraped the bottom too clean and scared myself, but I could always scramble back up. My brilliant and talented childhood friend Lynn, who had followed a similar path, used to laugh when people wondered why she wasn't rich and successful in society's terms. "Because I do what I *want* to do!" she always replied.

She went on to get her Ph.D. later in life. I had a baby. From that point on, what I might have once referred to as financial concerns became paralyzing terrors. Not only did I have more bills and less time to work, my priorities had shifted dramatically. Now the most urgent task of my life was to ensure the life of another. Matters of when I worked, how I worked, whether I worked, how much I earned, and how much I would need to earn were all dictated by the existence and the needs of my child. How would I be able to care for him with my presence as well as with my paycheck? Could I earn enough to cover childcare costs? Would I be able to give my work the time it required? Could I manage without going into debt? If I did, how would I get out with one hand tied to a child and only one to earn a living?

There were nights when I had to strike deals with my mind to let me sleep. *If you stop thinking about this right now, you can go over it as much as you like tomorrow.* Still I remember the digits glowing in the dark: 1:30. 2:30. 3:30. Sleep would come, weaving the loose ends of anxiety into dreams. *I am hanging from a cliff by one hand. From the other, Elias is suspended over the dark abyss.* The worst part was that it wasn't just a frightening dream I could wake from, it was a frightening reality I woke to. The full weight of raising my child alone seemed to rest right in that bulging folder of bills on my desk. Childcare, doctor, diaper service, all the major and minor and unexpected necessities and incidentals I had never had to add to my food-clothing-and-shelter basics when I was a single woman.

I grew up in an era when freedom meant you could change your mind about most things. Quick purchases were easily undone by quick returns. But I don't have a receipt on this child; we're in this for good. Yet should something so natural and wondrous as raising a child demand a ransom so high that the struggle to support him turns him into a liability? Should earning a living be more important than raising my child in the best way I know how? Does raising a child mean that I become a drone, ensuring survival but forgoing all options for fulfillment except parenthood?

For the majority of single parents, perhaps no issue is as pervasive in its impact on our lives as that of how we financially survive and care for our children. In an economy in which the majority of families are supported by two incomes, we can be hard-pressed to support ours on one.

Catherine, raising her daughter alone, works steadily from nine to five and just as steadily slips into debt, paying for medical insurance and childcare with a credit card year after year. Peggy's job cleaning houses doesn't bring in enough to support her two children and pay off the debts she was left with when her marriage ended; she gets a job at Payless in the evenings, cleans a furniture store Saturday nights, and sees her children when she can. Exhausted by working a full-time job and caring for two young children, Moshe is no longer as productive at work; when his company needs to lay people off, he is the first to go. Meg's husband drops her and their two small children at the welfare office on his way out of the country to join a lover, and she confronts the reality of sudden and complete poverty. Nicole is told she must travel out of town as part of her job — impossible with a baby, and the ax falls.

Even those with satisfying and secure careers and substantial paychecks can be brought up short by the fact that children cannot simply be shelved for ten hours or more a day, then fed and bedded down for the evening like pets. Those on a career track find themselves racing in the same loop with career couples, with people whose spouses provide support systems, and with single women and men — colleagues who can work overtime, who are more free to travel, and who take sick leave only when they are sick themselves.

The financial tightrope most of us walk not only may cause us sleepless nights but also may seed the same anxiety in our children. "My daughter Hilary still has a poor person's mentality," says Sheila, who had to file for bankruptcy after her divorce. Now remarried and a tenured professor at a state college, Sheila has a very different financial picture from the one she had as a graduate student raising a child alone. "Somehow we always made it. But Hilary still has this fear. 'You know why I'm neurotic about money?' she says to me. 'Because you always were. You never had any money. That's why I always worry about it.' I say to her, 'Hilary, there are two kinds of people who don't worry about money. Fools and the very rich.'"

"People say money can't buy everything," begins Ann, who raised her three girls alone after her husband's death. "But I would say most of the problems I had raising my girls were centered around money — not having enough. I was always in debt. Oh God, Golden Finance! Every December I'd borrow $300, which I think was the limit from Golden. It was a horrible thing to do — their interest rates were incredible. But I'd get the girls new clothes and Christmas gifts. It would take me all year to pay it back. Maybe by October I'd send in the last payment, and then borrow another $300 in December."

The difference between those who say "Single parenting really works!" and those who feel overwhelmed by the challenges is often money. When we're breaking open our children's piggybanks just to get by, we're probably having a hard time fulfilling their other needs as well. "Single parenting has been happy and deeply rewarding for me," Madeleine says. She is the ideal mother — strong, playful, at ease with her two boys, creative. She loves parenting. This is due partly to the tremendous amount of personal psychological healing she has done. But by her own admission, it is due in large part to her income, an income that allows her to make her children the priority in her life and to work at a job she likes when she likes.

"I have had nearly $30,000 a year coming in without me moving a finger. I have an inheritance of $17,500 a year, plus the father of my first son contributes $1,000 a month. It's still not enough to raise two kids on in our town, so we live with my mother. But it's a whole different ballgame for me than for someone who doesn't have money coming in like this. I can work part-time as a counselor and bring in $400 or so a month without worrying whether we can survive, *and* I have time for my boys."

Ideally, work is our way of participating in society, of making a contribution, of unfolding our potential in the way we wish to see our children unfold theirs. Yet so many of us find ourselves forced by supporting them to do whatever we can to get by, perhaps passing that legacy on to our children as well. Staying alive is more than making ends meet. It is about the dreams and visions each of us brings to life. Some of us run the tightrope between work we love and children we adore, but all of us juggle our need to dream as well as survive and our need to ensure the same for our children.

My friend did write back. Delighted, I tore open the letter. The crux of his advice leapt out from the page: Get a job and write your book in the early morning hours and late at night. His suggestion was reasonable enough. For months I had tried essentially that: I had done work that produced income for part of the day and worked on the book when I could. But I had fallen far behind my deadlines. There was no way around the fact that raising a child was having an enormous impact on my ability to control my time. There was no denying that part of my psyche was interwoven with his, deeply aligned with a way of being that had no concept of deadlines and goals.

I already did work during my late night hours — washing dishes and laundry, paying bills, cleaning house, and the other requirements of homemaking. My early morning hours were spent with an early riser, getting his breakfast and preparing him for the day ahead. With the help of friends I could sometimes squeeze a few hours out of an evening or a weekend for "the book," but I could not count on anyone else to be there for my child. And nothing about him was predictable — his health, his childcare, the state in which I might find a room he had entered. Perhaps there were some author-mothers who could manage the kind of schedule my friend had suggested, but I could not. The letter had brought into focus a major difference between my life and his. He was married; his wife took care of the children, cooked meals, and cared for the house.

I knew I wasn't going to complete the book in the early morning and late night hours. Yet I knew it would be written and that I would do my utmost to sustain my values about how to raise my child at the same time. I also knew I had reached a moment of truth that would mark a fundamental shift in my concept of finances and how I judged my own worth.

Our standards of self-esteem have been distorted by attitudes and policies which have valued production over the welfare of children. But true success, in our individual lives and that of our nation, depends on something far less tangible than numbers. The single parents in this chapter lead lives of widely varying circumstances, yet there are aspects of their fears and triumphs that we all share as we walk the bottom line.

◆ DOWNWARD MOBILITY

"Plop me down anywhere in the world and I can make it work!" That's how Catherine described the way she had always faced life's challenges. As a single woman in her thirties, she had had plenty of proof to buoy her confidence. So when Catherine found out she was pregnant by a man she barely knew, there was no question about how she felt. "I was delighted and absolutely amazed," she says. "I was completely sure everything would work out. I wanted this, and because I wanted it, I would make it work."

Over the last few years Catherine's desire for a child had in fact been growing. Her work as a graphic designer was satisfying, and she shared an apartment with three other working adults in an area of Los Angeles known for its fine shops and restaurants and easy access to the beach. She had lots of friends, and life was "full and wonderful." But in her thirties, deeper dreams had been surfacing. As the years had passed without producing the "right" partner, Catherine had come to the point where she felt that "it wasn't necessary to have a permanent relationship in order to have a baby."

But there was something else Catherine had a passion for, something she was determined to do before settling down to parent: she wanted to live in Italy. "My grandparents came from there. I'd visited twice before and loved it. So my plan was to save up enough to go back and live for a year." With her job paying $35,000 a year, she was building a savings. The idea of having a child was on the back burner, along with dating. She'd be leaving the country soon and didn't want to set up any attachments.

Then Catherine went to a party one night. "I had a great time dancing with a couple of different guys. One of them came back to my house, and we talked until four in the morning. Then, *I do not know why,*" Catherine says, emphasizing each word, "I hadn't been in a relationship for four years, this was 1986 with AIDS and everything going on — but we ended up sleeping together. And in that one time I conceived a child.

"Here I thought I was working on getting to Italy, and it turned out I'd been saving up for a baby!" Catherine told her dancing partner what had happened and assured him that "I was totally fine with taking this on myself. I had intended to do so anyway at some point, and if this is what the universe had offered, then to me it was pure magic."

Catherine named her daughter Angelina, after a close Italian friend. Three months after the birth, she found a sitter to come to the house, and she returned to work. Life was vastly different now. Lunch hours were no longer spent reading over a cappuccino or chatting with a friend. "Most of my lunches were spent doing errands — buying diapers, food, all the things you need to keep a home and baby going. There wasn't time to do it after work. I had to get home so the sitter could leave.

"When you have a baby, after this great desire for a child, it's absolutely all-encompassing, and everything else becomes second to that. Everything." Not long after Angelina was born, Catherine realized she was going through a radical change. Out for a now-rare dinner with friends, she "could hear conversations at other tables — about what kind of restaurant it was, how the food was, what they liked about the place — and suddenly it all seemed so trivial. It wasn't a judgment about their values that I felt; it was more that it was amusing to me that I had been one of those people six months before. The fact that something could happen in a life to make you so different was amazing."

Soon even those occasional dinners with friends faded into the past. "I couldn't afford it any longer. A sitter could cost $20 for just a few hours. Add that to the cost of a meal and maybe transportation, I just couldn't do it." The financial realities of raising her daughter were not trivial. "Diapers alone cost at least $50 a month. My health insurance from work didn't cover the baby; I had to pay $90 for that. I was paying $600 for childcare, and that was more than my rent! Just to live in a relatively safe neighborhood with transportation nearby cost $550 a month for a room in a shared apartment."

Catherine got a raise at work. Still, rent and childcare entirely consumed one of her two monthly paychecks. "That's when I started living on my credit card. Every couple of weeks I wouldn't have enough money for Estrella's pay or for the insurance bill, and I'd have to take out a cash advance to cover them."

Catherine's lifestyle was far from extravagant. She lived without a car. Entertainment was something of the past. She continued to share a home with roommates. But there was no way around the basics of raising a child. Placing Angelina at age two in a daycare group didn't lower childcare costs. By the time Angelina was three, the picture was clear. Catherine had borrowed $3,000 a year on her credit card since her daughter's birth. Even with raises in her salary to $39,000 a year, she could no longer afford to live in L.A.

"I was determined to do whatever worked for Angelina and me, given the financial costs," says Catherine. She used her vacation time to investigate alternatives and ended up deciding to move to a smaller town hundreds of miles north. The standard of living was so much lower that childcare would cost half of what she had been paying, and it looked like a good place to raise a child. Although no full-time jobs in her field were available there, Catherine's company would provide her with some work and referrals. She was looking forward to working freelance for a while. Angelina's early years were slipping away, and Catherine hoped that having a more flexible schedule might allow them more time together.

Despite the promise of adventure in their move, the pain of leaving their large group of close and supportive friends was acute. These people were family. "Uncle Dylan," whom Catherine could call on to come over and help if Angelina was sick; "Uncle Joel," one of her housemates, who had spent nights on the sofa with Angelina when Catherine was sick herself and needed the refuge of her room alone. This longtime friend who Catherine felt was like a brother was dying of AIDS, and she wasn't sure when, or even if, they would see him again. But clearly there was only one thing to do. They said lingering good-byes and headed north.

Instability because of inadequate finances is common for single parents. Seeking affordable and safe housing may mean moving — sometimes many times. Seeking other or higher incomes may require new jobs or additional training. Suzanne, for example, reports that she moved fourteen times by the time Molly was four years old, trying to integrate work and affordable living. Noe took a six-month training course as a computer programmer to increase his earning power and then moved to the country to raise his three-year-old son in an environment more clement than the city. He worked part-time in a machine shop and part-time at a local state hospital.

We live where we must and piece together our incomes. "I never do less than three different jobs at once," says Julie, who, after her divorce, returned with her son to the midwestern city where she grew up in order to be near her parents and sisters. Julie works as a gardener, substitute teacher, editor, and office assistant. "I could get a regular job and make a lot more money, but then I'd be leaving Dana in before- and after-school care all the time. I just don't want that." Every choice in how we live and work revolves around that one central issue: how to afford raising our children and at the same time care for them in the best way we can.

When I first talked to Catherine, things were working out well in their new home. She loved the town; the daycare and schools were excellent. Full-time daycare cost only $300 a month at a center with the relatively rare option of flexible scheduling. They had their own apartment. Catherine had work, and Angelina was blossoming. Maybe they could begin to dream of Italy together. Catherine was still managing only the minimum monthly payments on her credit cards, and still borrowing to cover health insurance, now increased, without her coverage from work, to $200 a month for both of them. But she knew she'd make it. Whatever the challenge, "I just dig in and do what I'm going to do to make things okay."

The next time I spoke with Catherine was nearly two years after her move. After having talked to so many single parents who were struggling, I needed to hear some of that wholehearted confidence and indefatigable optimism. Instead, the story Catherine told was of a woman profoundly shaken. Continual financial stress, coupled with parenting alone, had worn her down.

"Last January and February were blackness," she related. "Suddenly it was like the lights went out. Financially, everything went down the drain. The impact of the recession hit us, and there was so little work one month that I earned only $300. I had to borrow on my credit card again just to get through. I don't know if I'll be able to make it financially, but I don't want to move again and leave everything this town offers Angelina."

It was not complaint I heard in Catherine's voice but incredulity. "When I've hit hard times like this before in my life," she explained, "there has always been a place in my mind where I could remember that things would change; *of course* they would get better. But I have come closer than ever to believing that it never will get better. Or if it does, by that time I will have run out of energy — or gone bonkers." Catherine almost laughed, but all mirth was quelled by what she had to say next: "What made me think I was a strong enough person to do this?"

Catherine's self-doubt, frighteningly uncharacteristic, hung in the silence. Then she went on. "Every single moment seems conquered by getting through, by survival. Every night seems difficult. I think to myself, 'I was never like this. I didn't let things get to me.' But they are getting to me. I lie there at night and I feel like my spirit is slowly leaking, leaking away. I wake up and wonder, 'How am I going to keep on doing this? What am I going to do? What is Angelina going to do?' I tell myself, 'I am responsible for this child, and this is my life. I made these choices, so just keep going.'"

By the following spring, a year later, Catherine's credit card payments were equal to her rent. She had canceled their health insurance, although she had gotten sick herself — "something they couldn't diagnose; I was extremely tired all the time." She was looking in national magazines for a job as a designer. "I decided I'd be willing to move in order to pay off my debts. But there just aren't any jobs I see that pay enough to keep me afloat in the area where they're located."

But something had to change. "I would never have believed it could get worse, and it did, because it began to affect me physically, and that really scared me." Catherine decided to sublet her apartment for the summer and go back to the East Coast to stay with her sister. She said she needed something she felt that only family could give her. She would take work along to do there and also would investigate some job possibilities in the area.

Catherine emphasized, however, that it wasn't the lack of money that was the worst part. "The real failure I felt was in the way I had started acting with Angelina." For Catherine, raising her daughter well was the most important thing in life. But the struggle for survival was swallowing up their moments. "I was short-tempered with her. I was rushing her around all the time to get the most number of hours of work in to earn as much money as I could. The kind of language coming out of my mouth was setting her up for something I didn't want her to learn. Things like 'Don't take so much time,' 'This is wasting time.' When I heard *her* start to say the same kind of things, like she was wasting time, it scared me. I thought, 'This is not what I want to teach her about how to live her life.' I felt I was failing as a mother."

This is one of the hardest aspects of the financial challenge — the impact it can have on our parenting. Raising children is not just about fulfilling our financial duty to them but about enjoying the extraordinary gift of their presence and encouraging a positive sense of life in them. But as Madeleine points out from her experience as a counselor, "When there is struggle for survival, that's when parenting gets difficult. When there's enormous fatigue on the part of the parent, that is the beginning of real chaos and pain and horror. This is when you're going to be screaming at your kid, hitting your child, doing all sorts of things you don't want to be doing. But you're at the end of your line."

◆ OVER THE EDGE

Single-parent families certainly are not alone with respect to economic challenges. Indeed, the biggest overall increase in poverty during the past decade has been among two-parent families.[1] But most recently, the fastest decline has been among female heads of household with children.[2] Nearly half of all families headed by single mothers are living in poverty.[3]

Although the lack of fathers in single-parent families has in the past been targeted as a cause of behavioral problems in children, some of the most recent research lays the blame on poverty. "Researchers found that problems previously thought to be caused by the absence of a father's emotional and psychological contribution to the family may in fact be related to the loss of his income,"[45] summarized a reporter. It is the pervasive financial stress at home that can lead to low grades in school, emotional trauma, and difficulties in social adjustment. This is not to say that fathers are dispensable but that a good paycheck isn't.

Nearly 87 percent of the parents raising children alone are women, but the "family wage" precedent, whereby men were enabled to earn more than women, remains entrenched. Women in the workplace have made some significant gains during the past decade; in general, however, they are still earning 30 to 50 percent less than men in equivalent jobs.[5] In 1991, the average income for single mothers heading households was about $20,000 for whites, $14,000 for blacks, and $15,000 for Hispanics. Single fathers heading households, on the other hand, earned an average of almost $32,000 a year for whites, $23,000 for blacks, and $23,500 for Hispanics.[6] That's average income — some earn more, many earn far less.

One of the consequences of this disparity is that following divorce, the standard of living for women goes down 73 percent while the standard of living for men goes up 42 percent.[7] Women who leave their careers in order to raise their children pay dearly. Sylvia Ann Hewlett estimates that a mother loses 18 percent of her earning power for each child she raises to school age. So a mother of two youngsters, suddenly on her own and faced with getting a job to support them, might well find herself returning to or entering the workplace with a 36 percent handicap in earning power.[8]

As studies on mothers without custody reveal, a primary reason mothers leave their children when they leave a marriage is economic. They simply can't afford to raise them.[9] Of course some single mothers earn more than some single fathers, but in general the difference between the financial struggles of men and women raising children alone is the difference between a challenge and a battle. For both, however, just the workday schedule itself can pose a threat to financial security.

Moshe is the full-time single father of a ten-year-old daughter and eight-year-old son. "I get up around five forty-five and leave home about seven-thirty. I have to drive thirty miles to my current job. I drop the children at the YMCA for childcare. They take them from there to school and pick them up again. I arrive back at six to get them and then go home to make dinner, which has to be very quick, because by eight-thirty or nine they have to be in bed or else I can't get them up in the morning. By Friday night I feel like I'm half dead. I don't think my life can go on this way for a long time. I am just exhausted."

It was because he was exhausted that Moshe lost his job with an architectural firm. "I am a good architect, but I was under so much stress taking care of the kids that my production went down. I told them I was a single parent and I needed some flexibility and understanding. But when they needed to lay somebody off, I was the first to go."

Moshe decided to turn his garage into an office. "I can do some small projects on the side there, and through an agency I found a part-time job which might become permanent." He also started marketing a communications device that gives him a percentage of sales. "Still, most months I can barely meet expenses," he says.

The YMCA gave him a 50 percent scholarship for before- and after-school care, so his monthly bill comes to $300 for the two children instead of $600. "But I owe them $3,000 because last year I couldn't pay when I lost that job and wasn't earning enough freelance." Health insurance is also an issue, as it is for Catherine. "I can't afford medical insurance, and with a temporary job I don't have it," Moshe says. "When one of the children got sick, we went to the county hospital. The bill was $300 and I just haven't been able to pay it. Hopefully, if we need to go there again for help, they will help us. It is a frightening situation. But I can't pay $300 a month for insurance. If my income were higher maybe I could afford it, but working forty hours a week already exhausts me."

Rent is another drain for Moshe. "I pay $785 a month for this house. It's small, the kids share one little room that I built lofts in to give them space for their desks and clothes. But we're near very good schools, and that's the point of living here. My landlord could charge me a thousand a month if he wanted market price for this place, but he's not greedy. So I'm very lucky. Still, a parent with two or three children has to spend $10,000 a year just on rent. That's not far from what mortgage payments would be. But I don't have the down payment. So I pay the rent, and basically the man who owns the house gets richer, and I stay the same.

"When all my income goes for rent and living from hand to mouth, I won't be able to help my children when they are ready for college," Moshe points out. Planning for the future is a common challenge for single parents. As another single father, Kevin, who raised two sons alone, aptly puts it, "There's an immediacy and a need factor that is so strong for most single parents that you don't do that kind of long-term planning. I didn't. It's very much a day-to-day problem for the longest period of time. You don't think long-term in the way two adults planning together might: 'Now, let's see, in five years, we'd like to buy this house . . . Remember, the kids have got to go to school . . .' Long-term plans just don't seem realistic."

It takes a certain minimum amount of money to cover the material needs of a child. Whether we have it or not, they need it. Whether we are living hand to mouth, like Moshe, with no nest egg for the future, or going into debt, like Catherine, the numbers have to add up. "I saw a program on television that talked about how much it costs to raise a kid to age eighteen," comments one single mother of two now-grown children. "I sat down with my calculator and figured out all the debts I've accumulated in the process. It turned out that the amount on television was right, and I had just borrowed whatever I was lacking. Now at the age of fifty with my kids gone and no husband, I have to look forward to working and paying back all that money. What a killer!"

The current estimate for the cost of raising a child born in 1991 to age eighteen is between $157,000 and $305,000.[10] That amount breaks down to between $730 and $1,400 a month for eighteen years for one child. That's the killer. And on average, the expenditures on a child in a single-parent family are estimated at 5 percent higher than for a child in a two-parent household, with higher costs for housing, transportation, and, for some ages, childcare.[11] No matter how hard we try, sometimes we just can't make it.

In general, single parents who *chose* to raise children alone were prepared, psychologically and financially, to do so. Those who may have assumed that they would have the financial help of the other parent often do not. Or they may find themselves in the kind of situation Claudia describes: "My ex-husband paid child support, but we split our debts in the divorce settlement, which was ridiculous, because I was earning less than one fifth of what he was making. But I had thought that money was not my issue, that all I had wanted was to get free of the marriage."

When money becomes a bargaining point, too many mothers and children lose out. An astoundingly small number of custodial mothers actually receive child-support payments. For those who do, the small amount of the average monthly payment is equally astounding.

◆ AND THEN THERE WAS ONE

"I think it's very hard for men to feel connected to children they don't see all the time," Madeleine acknowledges. "But it's also very hard for moms who are *so* connected to their children to understand why the fathers don't feel that. I can understand why psychologically it's hard for the absent fathers, but I approve of enormous amounts of child support whenever possible. For Leon, the father of my first son, it certainly is possible."

Madeleine, like Georgie, is one of the rare single mothers who receive anything near adequate child support. In the late 1980s, the *average* court-ordered support payment nationally for two children was about $200 a month — far less than the average cost of childcare alone in many areas.[12] That figure takes into account standard support payments that can start as low as $50 a month or less and averages them with the $1,000 a month on the high end that Madeleine would eventually receive. But Leon hadn't willingly offered that.

"After we separated, a friend asked me how much Leon was contributing to raising our child. I told him $400 a month. He was incredulous. 'That man makes a mint! He should be giving two or three times that,' he said." The cost of raising her son certainly required more, so Madeleine set out to get it.

First she appealed to Leon's ethics. "I wrote him a nine-page letter which I asked him to take to his church group and discuss with people he trusted and cared about. I knew that if he kept the issue under-cover and tried to make the decision himself without looking deeper, it would be too easy to put it aside."

Then Madeleine went to the district attorney's office to find out how support payments were assessed. Her monthly income, from work plus her inheritance, would be averaged with his to determine how much the absent father should pay. It turned out that although Leon had been known to tell associates that he earned $200,000 a year, he had claimed an income of only $45,000 to $60,000 when it came to the issue of child support. Faced with the prospect of a major monthly disbursement, a father might commonly ask his lawyer not only "How much do I have to pay?" but also "How do I bring that down?"

Court rulings often legitimate this attitude, with it being "very rare for any court to order more than 25% of a man's income in child support," as the social researcher Lenore Weitzman has discerned. "Men who earn $50,000 or more a year," she continues, "retain an average of 81% of their net income for themselves."[13] Despite attempts to increase collection, success rates in most states, as well as amounts assessed, remain too low to make a substantial difference for many.

"It's painful to see what women are going through to raise their children and to know what the fathers of those children are doing," Madeleine says, having worked many hours with single mothers in counseling. "It's criminal." Such men are mostly invisible — you can't identify a man who is not supporting dependent children — but they're all around us, depositing checks into their bank accounts, vacationing abroad, out with a date on Saturday night.

Bruce Low's decision to pay out 65 percent of his salary each month to support his young son was so noteworthy that his story was featured in *Mothering* magazine. The boy lives with his mother, Bruce's ex-wife. "I recognize that my influence on my son extends beyond my daily visits," he writes. "It reaches into what I do to support his entire environment. . . . I am trading my current comfort, as parents have throughout history, for his future." In this unique scenario, it is the noncustodial parent who worries about nickels and dimes.[14]

According to the sociologist Geoffrey Greif, "Women tend to have the same record of nonpayment for court-ordered support as do men. But often, due to the disparity in earning ability, they are asked to pay less."[15] Scott, who is raising his son, Braun, as his primary parent, relates, "For the first time in the history of our relationship, my ex-wife is earning more than I am, so this year is the first time she has given any money for Braun in the three years he has been with me. I asked for it. She had a little resistance, but once she saw the whole picture, she came to the same decision herself. She pays for half his school tuition — $210 a month." In fact, the contribution Braun's mother makes is higher than the average support payment in 1993 of $101 a month for the urban area of Minnesota in which they live.[16]

Eventually Leon did agree to pay $1,000 a month in child support, and Madeleine expects that amount to increase in the future. The more common response, however, is a complete abdication of financial responsibility. In 1992, only 58 percent of those eligible for child support even had court orders to collect it. Of those, only half were receiving full payment, a quarter were receiving partial payment, and the rest were receiving no payment at all.[17] Only about 25 percent of *all* single parents who could be receiving child support are getting anything at all from the other parent.

When "full" payment means as little as $50 a month, it is more the *idea* of support than its actuality that is being addressed. In Vera's case, the father of her child chose to work part-time and get an education in order to better his income. Vera had no such option. She worked for $7 an hour to make up everything that the $50 didn't cover, and paid $2 out of every hour of her wages for childcare.

Lorna, raising four children alone after her divorce, found that actually *receiving* the $415 a month her husband's lawyers had agreed to depended upon the quality of communication that month. If Lorna and her ex-husband had a disagreement about the children, he simply didn't send the money, keeping all of his $50,000-a-year salary for himself.

In many states, court-ordered support payments are based on the income of the noncustodial parent. In others, the amount is calculated according to the income of both parents. In neither case is the amount based on the costs the custodial parent incurs in raising a child. In Sweden, government policy ensures a minimum standard of living for single parents, making up the difference if support payments are inadequate.[18] In the United States, a single mother might work several jobs, fall into debt, or apply to receive the absolutely inadequate welfare grant that simultaneously prohibits her from increasing that amount without penalty. U.S. government policies have, in effect, ended up encouraging poverty as a standard of living. No matter what route a single parent may try, the children suffer, emotionally from the absence of a parent working long hours and financially from inadequate support. Currently 61.5 percent of all children of single parents now live in poverty.[19]

Nearly all other industrialized nations provide substantial support for parents and children; some provide special allowances for single parents. In Hungary, France, Germany, and Sweden, all families are supported by housing subsidies and allowances; meanwhile in the United States, rent can eat up between 30 and 85 percent of a paycheck — the poorer the family, the higher the proportion paid in rent. *Paid* leave after birth, often for periods of months rather than weeks, is the norm in most European countries and is available for fathers as well as mothers. Substantial allowances for childcare are provided and, of course, health-care coverage is universal, at least for children.[20] Although these social welfare nations are now struggling, in the emerging global economy, under the high costs of their substantial benefits, they have also avoided the enormous costs of extreme poverty and high crime rates in the United States.[21]

Such social welfare policies are not just a matter of heart. One third of the nation's households are doing the job of raising the future for all the others.[22] These children of today will fill the social security coffers of tomorrow by working when today's workers are too old to do so. It is also apparent that what we don't pay for at the beginning, we pay for in the end in terms of crime rates, quality of living, and human tragedy. The average cost of maintaining *one* prisoner for one year is $20,000.[23] In comparison, the average welfare grant, taking all states into account, for a single parent raising two children is $4,500 a year.[24] That means the sole permitted income for *three* people.

The cost of adequate and effective programs, however, would require substantial adjustments in government spending, and ingrained attitudes in our culture have been an impediment to such changes. "I've had people say to me, 'You chose to have those children, *you* deal with it,'" Madeleine reports. "There is no sense in our society of the incredible role that those of us who are raising children are playing."

While the stigma of bearing a child outside of marriage has diminished, the shame has been transferred to the economic hardship that pursues single parents. In a society in which money is the index of value, if I have none, I too am worthless. In our culture to be poor is shameful. These values have so pervaded our lives that even our sense of ourselves is determined by them. Struggling to support our children alone, floundering in an economic crisis of global proportions, we may still feel that our inability to make it is our own fault.

It's very hard to retain faith in our dreams and abilities when our options are limited by lack of money and our world is narrowed to survival. The wondrous possibilities of life as a family can get lost in columns of debits and credits. Generosity of spirit flees as we tighten. "I don't have enough money" translates into not enough time, not enough kindness, not enough love. "I've been realizing recently that I've been so frantic about making ends meet that I haven't played very much with Ivan," says Lisa, the single mother of a nine-year-old boy. "It's this feeling that you can't relax because all hell is going to break loose any minute. It seems that has become my excuse for not spending more quality time with my son. It's pretty amazing to realize that."

When our world is circumscribed by severe financial limits, how can we play with our children or be creative in our work? If our creative spirit is afflicted, it can become nearly impossible to imagine alternatives to the problems we confront. When our hopes and dreams grow dim, our trust in ourselves fades too.

◆ THE THREADS OF A DREAM

The California sun in December pours through the kitchen windows of Nicole's apartment. It sets aglow a painting on the wall next to the refrigerator — two bald and featureless androgynes held in a tender embrace. "I titled it 'Consoling,'" Nicole explains. "It came from a period in my life when I guess I needed that. I started it a year after my son was born."

On the wall opposite, light glances off a gold plaque engraved with Nicole's name. In finely etched letters beneath: CELEBRATING OUR PEOPLE. "That's the award I won in a video festival for the series of programs I did highlighting black people — talking about themselves, to each other."

Video production is Nicole's dream, the star that leads her on. "Eventually I want to do docudramas on African-American history. I want to show that we *were* there, we *are* here and have been all along," she says with a self-assurance that has been hard-won during the past nine years of raising a child alone.

Two months after Leroy's birth, Nicole returned to work with the company that had employed her for nearly a decade as an electronics technician. The renaissance she felt at her son's birth, a new determination to do great things with her life, smashed right up against "the same old environment. I was in a nontraditional role for women, so I was working with all men, and they didn't understand. They had even thought it was unfair that I could take medical leave because I was pregnant!" Laughing, Nicole adds, "All these men who were born from someone . . .

"I felt like I was always having to prove myself as a capable woman technician. They often doubted what I said, and every time I made a mistake, they'd be in my face. I was determined to get out of that, but here I was now with a baby. It wasn't like when I was nineteen and could just leave a job. So this time I thought, 'Look at this company and see where you want to be.'"

That's how Nicole got started in video production. "I thought, 'I can write. I can be a technical writer.'" When she checked out the communications department, she found a group of people who were doing trainings on communications equipment, using videos. "I went in talking about video like I knew what I was doing, and they hired me on."

Nicole's renaissance had begun. But ironically, the very thing that urged her on — caring for her son — would be the impediment that held her back. Leaving your baby for daycare is one thing; the prospect of leaving him for days on end is another — both emotionally and financially. "It turned out they eventually wanted me to travel in that job. But Leroy was still so little. They got to the point in my department where they said, 'We're not going to be able to keep you here because you have to travel.' I just couldn't. And that was it.

"That's when my road got real bumpy. I had worked with that company for so long. I grew up there, in fact. I didn't know anything else. So when I got laid off, my self-esteem really got knocked. For about a year, I just wasn't sure what I could do. I really didn't think I could do anything. I tried to get a job in video, but I kept bombing in my interviews." At the same time, Nicole's attempt to get back together with Leroy's father also failed. "It was a combination of things that knocked my confidence down.

"I was getting unemployment so I could pay a little rent, but I didn't have enough to keep a place of our own." Nicole stayed with a girlfriend for a while. "She really wanted to help, but you start crowding people's space and it doesn't work, especially when you've got a kid." So she rented a room in the house of an acquaintance. That soon turned into "sheer craziness." As a last attempt she moved in with a man she was doing some real estate work for. "He had said he would have a place for me to rent, but when that didn't come through, I just moved my stuff into his place. By that time we'd gotten involved, and I didn't have anywhere else to go. It was like, 'This is it, I don't care, I'm coming in.'"

Desperation. The arms of someone you don't even like can look pretty good when you don't have any money. As we all know, many marriages have been made and held together by desperation glue. "I was just there because I needed to be there, not because I wanted to be," Nicole admits. When the real estate business failed, so did that home. "All during that time I felt so bad for Leroy. I hugged him a lot and talked to him about what was going on. But it got to the point where he was saying, 'Mommy, where do we *live?* Where's our home?'"

Even the walls symbolizing home soon were no longer available. "We ended up sleeping in my car a few nights," Nicole says. "That year really zapped me. It gave me a whole different attitude about everything. For the first time I realized that anybody could be homeless. I ended up with a different kind of respect for people on the street."

Homelessness haunts single parents. We hear about it in the news. We see it in the streets. We hear about it from each other. Nicole wasn't the only talented, bright, caring single parent I talked with who had awakened to crumpled clothes, cramped muscles, and a disoriented child after a night parked on a strange but hopefully safe street. "I was poor," says Nicole, "but compared to some, I had a luxury. I had an automobile. And I could have gone home to my mom. But I really wanted to try to do it here because I felt this is where I can fulfill my dreams." The thread of that dream would eventually be Nicole's avenue out.

What are the options when we have no money? Catherine fell back on credit cards. Moshe got a scholarship for childcare and pieced together a living. Nicole had friends and a car. All of them were scraping bottom, dragging children behind. They, like many, will do anything to avoid what can look and feel like the ultimate failure — welfare.

◆ A MEASURE OF INTEGRITY

"You go in there with your head held high," Helen said to me. "You haven't done anything wrong." It was the same thing a friend had told her years before when, after leaving an affluent life as a married mother, she found herself needing to apply for medical assistance from the government.

You haven't done anything wrong. But you can feel like you have when you walk through the door of the welfare office professing poverty, publicly acknowledging need. The welfare system in general has done little to dispel that notion. Those who find themselves dependent on it must not only struggle to live on an income below the poverty threshold but also engage in a desperate battle to retain self-esteem.

I saw that battle in the faces of the mothers and fathers seated on rows of metal folding chairs under a low ceiling in a windowless room. They looked defeated. By the time I had waited three hours in this stark emptiness filled with restless children and beleaguered parents, I began to understand why. The worker who eventually looked over my application didn't once lift her eyes from the sheaf of papers. I was just one more in her endless caseload.

Did I need food stamps? she wanted to know. No. A monthly cash grant? No. Just medical assistance; I was in my third trimester of pregnancy, now alone and with no health insurance to cover the impending costs of childbirth. I asked, out of interest, how much the monthly allotment was through the program called Aid to Families with Dependent Children (AFDC). In our area, she told me, it came to $416 a month for one child, plus a little over a hundred dollars in food stamps. "How can anybody live on that?" I asked, incredulous. My rent alone, for a room in a shared house, cost nearly four hundred. "They do," she answered curtly, without looking up.

Today over 13.5 million Americans are receiving AFDC.[25] Currently one out of every five children spends some time on welfare before the age of eighteen.[26] While applicants come from a spectrum of socioeconomic groups, many would never have imagined themselves so needy. Those I talked with who had resorted to welfare were nurses, college graduates, artists, skilled workers — all taken by surprise, all ushered by some twist of fate into a club in which they would rather not be a member.

Some on welfare are ferociously determined to spend their children's early years with them, and they make this level of poverty a choice. Most, the majority, have no other option. Nearly half of all AFDC recipients are European Americans — white. (This group spends more time on welfare than any other.) An equal number are African-Americans. (This group has a higher proportion on welfare than any other.) The rest are Hispanic, Native American, Asian. Most are women. Half have never been married. The others are divorced, separated, abandoned, or widowed.[27]

No matter who they are or how they got there, this is not a popular citizen's group. In a survey that asked if the government was providing enough assistance to the poor in America, 65 percent responded that too little was being spent. When the same group was asked about government spending on welfare, only 22 percent said it was too little, and 44 percent were certain it was too much.[28] It is a hot and complex issue fraught with misunderstandings and misinformation. But categories and stereotypes fade when the focus is turned on individuals.

Meg, an old college friend of mine, worked at a day job while taking classes at night. But life always seemed to mean something more to her than the slow accumulation of credits that were supposed to promise a better job or a higher wage. Her home was always open to someone without one, someone needing to talk, someone with new ideas on how to change the world. She had a penchant for poets and

a passion for the downtrodden. In the late sixties, when baby boomers flooded the scene as social activists, Meg took up the banner,
collaborating with a church group to open a free clothing store in one
of the poorest areas of the city.

After graduation I went west. Meg moved east. I heard through
friends that she had married, settled down, and started a family. She
was happy, I heard — a dedicated mother. When I saw her next,
almost a decade later, she was living in a one-bedroom apartment
with her two kids, struggling to survive on a welfare check. Her
warmth hadn't diminished, but it was obvious that the breakup of
her marriage had been hard.

"I really did have a deep love for William. When I woke up in the
morning he always felt right. I missed that — a lot." She also struggled with guilt. "I was raised to think that marriage was a sacrament,
and you would go to hell if you broke your vows. There were no
divorces in my family. I hoped for a long time that he'd come back
and we'd all be together again."

Three years before, William had dropped Meg and the two children
off outside a government building on his way out of the country to
meet a lover. His move was not temporary, he said. With the freezing
air of winter as her only encouragement to go inside, Meg took the
hands of her five-year-old son and three-year-old daughter, pushed
open the glass door, and started down the dark corridor toward a
dubious refuge: the AFDC office.

"When I told the social worker that my husband had dropped us
outside and left, he said, 'How could you let him do that?' I just burst
into tears. I couldn't believe this was happening. He kept asking me
questions about what I had put on the forms and told me three times
that it was a crime to 'misrepresent my circumstances.' I didn't have
any intention to do that. I didn't know what the hell was going on.
I just knew I didn't have any other way to support my kids. By the
time I left, I felt like a dog."

The experience that welfare applicants have can vary greatly depending upon where they are and who they are. But those I spoke
with who had had positive experiences seemed to be the exceptions.
A nurse living in a small town who knew the workers at the welfare
office got the temporary boost she needed when her daughter was
born. Those who have been fortunate enough to enroll in training or
education programs have received the massive support of every avail-

able subsidy the system could provide. Many, however, report the experience as demeaning and demoralizing. "I wish I had never done it," says one single mother who applied for welfare so she could go back to school. "Emotionally, the price I paid for it so much outweighed what we got."

In Los Angeles, one mother tells me, she was checked at the door for weapons. On the other hand, in Seattle, another mother reports, the front desk passes out questionnaires asking, "How are we doing?" In Minneapolis a videotape on child development plays while clients wait in carpeted offices, and workers are kind. But no matter how hard individual communities and workers might try to humanize the process, the system itself remains confusing, humiliating, and punitive.

A morass of complex and rigid rules can prohibit parents and children who are destitute from receiving help. In one office, I watched a woman with long dark hair talking quietly with the receptionist behind the glass. This was in a rural area, the workers looked more relaxed than the urbanites, the building had windows. But the rules were the same. Gradually the client at the counter grew more agitated until she cried out in tears, "I have two sick babies at home! My check didn't arrive this month. I *can't* wait for two weeks for an appointment with a worker!" Stony-faced, the receptionist repeated the rules. She had seen desperation before.

In one midwestern family service office, the woman at the front desk was welcoming, the waiting room light and spacious. Tacked up near the door was a life-size photo in black and white of a mother and young child staring into space as they embraced. The caption read, "If being a single parent is tearing you both apart, let us help." A number was listed for a crisis nursery. But upstairs, where all the paperwork and interviews were done, there was the same regulated indifference. I stepped off the elevator into a pastel-pink hallway where a young girl with long red hair was sobbing. At her feet, a tiny baby was sleeping in a plastic carrier. Three other teenage girls holding babies surrounded her, listening, comforting. "They won't give me any help because I don't have a permanent address," she poured out, shaking. "But I don't have any place to live."

Other single mothers reported their tales of frustration to me. "My car was all I had left. Was I supposed to give that up too!?" asked Michelle. Because the two-year-old modest Japanese model she

owned was valued above the allowed limit, Michelle was ineligible
for assistance, even though her husband had transferred all other
property and assets into his own name before she knew what was
happening. "Was I supposed to sell that to buy a used car that might
not be safe for my daughter? And on top of that, risk the cost of
breakdowns and repair bills I couldn't pay?" Theresa refused to
reveal the identity of her children's father, which rendered her ineligible for AFDC. Afraid he would again turn his violence against her
and the children, she was trapped by the system's rules.

While states differ in the amounts they give in AFDC grants, virtually all are well below the poverty threshold. Texas, at the low end
of the scale, provides $476 a month, including food stamps, for a
family of three — a parent and two children. Before cuts to "balance
the state budget," California was at the high end, $850 a month for
a parent and two children. The national poverty threshold for a
family of three is computed at $940 a month.[29]

Yet any additional income a parent on welfare might earn or
receive reduces the monthly grant according to complex tables that
vary with different states. Gifts basically reduce a grant dollar for
dollar. Child-support payments can increase an AFDC grant by no
more than $50. Thus, a mother and child who receive $400 a month
through AFDC cannot through child-support payments raise their
total monthly income beyond $450, whether the child's father pays
$50 or $200. The state keeps the difference.[30] A welfare recipient
who works at a job can lose so much in benefits while simultaneously incurring expenses — such as childcare, transportation, suitable
clothing — that often working is not worth the effort. The Employment Policies Institute reports that "with every dollar earned by a
person on welfare, public benefits [to that person] drop even more
than a dollar."[31]

Even Robert Rector of the Heritage Foundation, a conservative
research group, calls this setup "the incentive system from hell."[32] As
nearly everyone involved in it recognizes, it's a system from hell,
period. Families with no other recourse are expected to live in absolute poverty, are discouraged from obtaining the means that could
reverse their condition, and are considered criminals if they "de-
fraud" the government by trying to make ends meet. Very few actually do manage to live on what the dole alone provides, and parents
secretly bringing in additional income, as they struggle to raise their
children, live in guilt and fear of discovery.

Alice lives on the fringes of an urban ghetto with her three children. "For three kids I get a little over $800 a month, including food stamps. If I were on just welfare, how would I survive? And if I was just working, I can't earn enough. Food easily costs $300 to $400 a month. Rent is the same. My daughter needs a bus pass to her high school. There's lunch money every day for her. They need clothes, and there are always things you have to buy for school. My son's fifth-grade class has a nature club that is going on an overnight, and they want $25. If he doesn't do it, he's left out of that learning. Maybe I could beg the school to pay it, but how do you feel about doing that all the time?

"I try to expose my kids to as much good stuff as I can. Out here in this area of the city, there are only a lot of people selling drugs. That's what's there when they go out. So I try to get them places — like to a show or even to the mall to munch on cookies. You have to do those things with kids. You can't keep them all locked up."

Alice refuses to let her circumstances limit her children's sense of themselves, but doing so requires a constant vigilance. Shy and soft-spoken, Alice grows animated as she says, "I will go out and fight for my kids," and she does. When a teacher kept failing her daughter in algebra, she spent hours at school getting her changed to a different class, where she now gets A's. Her three-year-old was enrolled in a daycare center that offered a government subsidy, but the financial advantage didn't outweigh the negative effect the place was having on her daughter. "I began to notice a change coming over her. She started with this mouth, cursing like all get-out. She was hitting other kids, and she'd cry and cry when I took her there. But when we'd go to church on Sundays, she'd go into the nursery and have such a good time that I had a hard time getting her to leave. I just had to take her out of that other place.

"I found a Christian preschool that I really liked. Now she's coloring and learning her numbers. She comes home: 'Mommy, I'll sing you my favorite song.' I have to pay $310 a month for that, almost twice the cost of the subsidized center. Some people say I'm crazy to pay that kind of money. That would be equivalent to rent. But, I'm sorry, I just have to."

In order to cover those extra costs, however, Alice is earning more than the amount she is allowed if she is to retain her welfare benefits, so she does not report the additional income. "I'd like to be financially stable on my own and not have to do this welfare and job thing, to always have somebody watching over your shoulder and to pretend I'm not working as much as I do. It's not trying to beat the system; it's trying to survive with my children. It's trying to *survive*."

The intensity in Alice's voice softens as she adds, "But I'm not a criminal. I don't want it to happen that I can't be around my kids. I read an article last week in the paper about how they are going to start prosecuting welfare mothers who work. I think, Oh God, I'm trying so hard to live. I'm not trying to do anything to outsmart these people."

Neither was Meg. "When the worker told me our benefits would be $423 a month for me and the kids plus $125 in food stamps, I could hardly breathe." Meg took the children home and began searching the want ads for a place she could afford to rent. Certainly they couldn't stay where they were. Now, kids in tow, she set out on her search. "When the landlords saw children, and then especially when they found out I was on welfare, it usually meant the place was no longer for rent. There's such a prejudice against welfare moms. The place also had to be set up so that I could sleep in the living room and the kids could share the bedroom. It had to be near a laundromat — no place with the rent I could afford would have washer and dryer facilities. We didn't have a car, so it had to be on a bus line. And I wanted at least a halfway safe neighborhood." Meg looked at nineteen places before she found one that worked — sort of. It wasn't until years later, when she entered a training program, that Meg would be told about subsidized housing.

Thus began the downward plunge. "I found it impossible to live on that amount of money. I was constantly borrowing and trying to pay it back. I finally wrote to William and begged him to send some money for the kids. He started sending between $150 and $200 every month. I knew if I reported it, they'd deduct it from my grant." Meg takes a deep breath. "But how can a person who was raised to have integrity continually lie each month without it deeply damaging her sense of self-esteem?" Meg had pinpointed one of the ways in which the system defeats even itself.

"I felt drained just by the amount of time it took to be poor," she continues. "In my mind I was continually trying to figure out what I could afford each month. I could lose control over a dime. I felt like everything in me shrunk. We'd go grocery shopping and I'd be telling the kids, 'No, you can't have animal cookies. We can't get those.'

'Who are they for, then?' my son asked me once. What was I supposed to tell him? 'You are poor and so you don't deserve treats'? What kind of message would that be?"

Getting to the counter to check out was another degradation. "I always wanted to crawl in a hole when I pulled out the food stamps to pay. I could hardly look at anyone around me for fear that they'd be thinking, 'I'm working to pay for her and her kids.' I'd have to keep telling myself, 'I *am* working. I *am* being productive. I'm raising good kids.'"

Meg's paranoia was not unfounded. The belief is common that those who work are being drained by taxes to support those who do not, notably welfare mothers. In actuality, during 1991, for instance, only 2.1 percent of all state source revenue went to AFDC, about $8 billion.[33] Of the total federal budget for that year, 0.9 percent went for AFDC: $12 billion. However, also in that same year, *$51* billion — 3.9 percent of the total federal budget — went toward the savings and loan bailout.[34] The sociologist Irwin Garfinkel of Columbia University points out that the *total* amount of money we've spent on welfare since 1930, when it was introduced, "doesn't come close to the money we've spent on the savings and loan scandal — not even close."[35]

Considering that kind of expenditure, and looking as well at, for instance, the considerable amount budgeted for national defense each year — anticipated to be $291 billion for 1993[36] — the average of $20 billion spent altogether each year by state and federal governments for AFDC[37] is minor. Yet the fear that "welfare leeches" are draining the country's coffers persists, and Meg's back crawled as she counted out those pieces of paper to buy food — minus animal cookies — to feed her family.

Meg *did* feel like a criminal. "I used to get so scared I'd get caught for not reporting the money from William. I'd see a police car and sometimes I'd actually think for a split second they were coming for me. I'd never committed fraud before! I'd report money I earned from babysitting or would get as a gift, I guess to make them think I was being honest. And I used to feel like throwing up every time I filled out those forms.

"One day my worker at the welfare office took me aside and said, 'Meg, the purpose is to get off welfare, but you'll never do that if you report extra income. The system doesn't work; it's crazy. Just don't

tell me when you earn a little money or someone gives you something.'

"I went home elated. I couldn't believe how relieved I felt. *I* was
okay; the system was screwy. I actually think that's when I first
starting moving up again."

After both of her children started grade school, Meg found a job
as a typist that paid $700 a month. She dutifully reported this major
shift in income on her monthly AFDC forms. By the time Meg had
worked for three months, the writing was on the wall. By working,
she could earn about $6,500 a year after taxes; on welfare she would
receive about $8,000 a year, plus medical assistance, and wouldn't
incur the additional expenses of after-school babysitting, commuting,
and clothes for work. "It was clear: I would actually lose income by
working!" She would lose more than that. "Can you imagine how it
felt to go to work every day and end up losing money? Who would
do that?"

While more than half of all AFDC recipients (55 percent) leave the
program within five years, the other half stay on, nearly a quarter of
them for ten years or more.[38] "No wonder," says Meg when I tell her
that. "I could have gotten off welfare much earlier if I had been
allowed to keep money I earned without penalties to my benefits.
That happened once when the Census Bureau needed people tempo-
rarily — AFDC had a special arrangement not to cut grants for those
who worked there, although they reduced our food stamps. I felt so
good going to work. I really liked the people and going in every day
to see them. They even helped me buy an old car. And my kids were
so proud of me having a job."

Meg eventually enrolled in a state-supported training program that
assisted welfare recipients in developing their own businesses. Run by
women who themselves were successful at business, the program
provided an extensive support system. Not only was Meg told about
subsidized housing and how to apply for it, she was allowed to rent
a computer through the program (owning one could have disqualified
her from receiving welfare), get training on how to use it, receive
loans to finance her business plan, and put the initial money she
earned through the business back into it without penalty.

Meg's plan was to open a store to recycle used toys. Parents could
leave toys on consignment and the store would receive a percentage
of sales. It was a business that had proven profitable in other cities.

She also planned to set up an area where people could sit and have tea while their kids played. An additional benefit of this endeavor would be that her own kids would have a place to come to after school.

The program also provided Meg free access to any legal aid she might need, and it supplied her with graphics assistance to develop her advertising and business cards. If she needed her kids taken care of at any point in the training schedule, that too was provided. But best of all, she was given encouragement and support to do her best. According to the philosophy of the program, it was as important to develop the business owner as it was to develop the business. This, Meg said, was the key.

"They had support group meetings where I got to meet other welfare women who also wanted to do something positive. And whenever I felt unsure about whether I could pull off my plans or not, I could call the woman who was my counselor there. She'd listen and always remind me to keep building my own self. 'Have you done your affirmations today?' she'd ask."

Finding a way out of poverty of spirit is essential to climbing out of the poverty of circumstance. It was this element as much as all the training and advantages that enabled Meg to begin moving off the treadmill and onto the walkway.

◆ IGNITING THE SPARK

Catherine's stay with her family proved to be something less than a refuge and renewal. Day after day she watched her sisters and their children go off to the beach while she worked on the design projects she had with her. Fortunately Angelina was willing to go with them. But in many ways the transition was hard for the five-year-old, so hard that Catherine felt she had to set aside her plans to interview with various publishing companies and visit old friends. She would not add to Angelina's trauma by traveling without her, and she wasn't willing to risk showing up for a visit or an interview with a distraught and frantic child. The most disheartening part of all was that Catherine had returned to her family desperately needing nurturing on every level and instead found herself entangled in old family disputes. "It turned out to be nothing like what I had hoped for in terms of emotional support," she says.

Then one day, a friend — a former college professor who had continued in her life as a mentor — called to see why Catherine had canceled the visit she had scheduled with him. "When he asked me what had happened, I couldn't hold back. I started crying and told him about the mess things had been." The professor started slowly to explain that he could afford to offer Catherine a major loan, interest-free, to pay off some of her credit card bills. "'I'd feel strange about that,' I told him. 'I would want to do something to make me feel like I'm paying my way.'

"He told me I might one day work out a logo for a small business he was starting, but it wasn't any kind of exchange he was looking for in order to make it worthwhile to him. And then he said — and this is the *biggest* gift he gave me — that of all the people he had ever met, I had the most integrity.

"That did it! Here was someone I greatly admired telling me he had faith in me. That I *was* strong. What no one in my family knew how to say to me, I got from somebody else: a clear expression of unqualified support. He had put me back in touch with something in myself I had forgotten, something I had almost given up on. 'Plop me down anywhere and I can make it work.' It was like I remembered who I was. He knew me, he knew he could trust in me. And that gave me the faith to trust in myself again.

"I got off the phone and it didn't even matter if the money never arrived. The money wasn't the issue. It was the fact that someone had offered something like that to me when I was so down. I had been looking at myself and judging myself in a negative manner. I had been doubting my own strength. I was engaged in a struggle with myself and my faith in my ability to cope, and I'd been losing.

"Some things are in your control and some things aren't," Catherine concludes. "But from that point on, something has happened. I have had steady work coming in. When interest rates went down, I transferred the remainder of my credit card loans to a lower rate, and that gave me a little more optimism too. But the first thing that set it all off was an act of grace, a gift of love and encouragement from another human being that opened the door again and gave me the push to open to the possibilities of life."

Our sense of ourselves has everything to do with how we approach the world. In lieu of such encouragement from others, it is the quality of our own thoughts and beliefs that can lift us up — or discourage us. As one single mother realized from her own experience, "You can be around the corner from exactly what you need, and you don't even see the corner to go around if you don't believe it could happen to you. You put up all sorts of blinders if you keep thinking, 'I'm not good enough for anything good to happen to me.'"

As single parents we may encounter many circumstances that chip away at our sense of worth and leave us low. We sometimes forget that we have any value at all. For Nicole, getting fired from her job was the beginning down. When she couldn't provide a home for her son, when she continued to fail at job interviews for video work, when her hopes of salvaging the relationship with Leroy's father were disappointed, she was left devastated. On top of that, Nicole knew that despite all of her training and experience as an electronic technician, she was at a disadvantage in seeking employment in an industry that was used to hiring white men.

"People act like opportunities are equal, especially in that corporate atmosphere. They believe that I have the same chance they do. But I'm black and I'm a woman. It's hard to get a job. Even when I have more experience than a man, they don't hire me."

Under this mountain of negations the spark was dim, and no one was rushing over to fan it into life. Near the end of that long year Nicole began doing some typing in a friend's office just to bring in some money, taking Leroy along with her. "At the same time I still had my love for video. I hadn't forgotten that. So I decided to do some volunteer work at a video production house. They didn't need to hire anyone, but I just had to do something I felt good about."

Not surprisingly, Nicole's confidence began to grow. "I was finally doing something I really liked to do. Not long after that I applied at another temporary agency, and within a week they sent me out on a job as a technician. They placed me with a good company, and I was earning a lot. I started feeling, 'I *can* do something.' Even though it wasn't a job in video, at least I knew I had enough skills that I could get a job making decent money. I knew I could trust myself and support my son. That's when I decided to go back to school and get my degree in electrical engineering in order to guarantee a way to finance my video work.

"I had seen that when I was trying to follow somebody else's lead — like my son's father or this guy with the real estate business that folded — it didn't work. When I follow me, I know I can count on it. My whole philosophy is to keep going, to keep pursuing that creative aspect. Even with working and taking care of Leroy, I squeeze in some video work so I have something to show regularly once a month, to keep my foot in what I love to do. Sometimes my classes may suffer a little in school because I choose to put that time into video, but that's what keeps my spirit up."

◆   WHERE YOUR TREASURE LIES

Perhaps Nicole could have kept her job in the video department of the electronics company had she been willing to leave her baby to travel out of town. Perhaps Moshe's production level would not have gone down if he weren't making good dinners every night for his children and spending weekends helping them build shelters for their baby chicks and guinea pigs.

As much as a roof over their heads and food in their mouths, our children need our presence, our comfort and nurturing. But the ax hangs over our heads on both ends of the tightrope. We have seen parents who lose their jobs, yet none of them would consider it better to "lose" their children. That their priorities are clear doesn't solve the problem, however. "I think it's a basic human right to be able to enjoy your children!" said one single mother. But the very fact that she had to declare it points to the struggle it can be to survive as well as enjoy them. Even when we're not struggling with the basics, trying to sustain a career and be available to our children pushes us up against the contrary values of the marketplace and forces us to define our own deepest values.

"It is definitely possible to do both successfully — work and raise a family as a single parent — although it is probably more difficult. You have to have very strong boundaries," says Ellen, who built a highly successful real estate company while raising her son and daughter alone after her marriage ended. "But it took many years before I learned to set those boundaries. I reached the point when I knew I had to tell clients who wanted me to come to see a house at seven at night, 'I already have an appointment from six to eight, but I can see you after that.' And that appointment every evening was at home having dinner with my children."

But it took an obvious message from one of her children to get Ellen to radically reassess her priorities. During his first year of college, Ellen's son became addicted to drugs and alcohol. "Devastating as it was to find out about my son's addiction, it was the beginning of a wonderful recovery for our entire family," says Ellen. "I had been working around the clock all those years, since they were six and eight years old, to provide a lot of money for material things. I was doing what I thought I had to as the breadwinner, based on my own upbringing. But what my children had needed was for me to be there for them physically and emotionally. In treatment I was able to see that my son's problem with alcohol and drugs was no more lethal than my major addiction to work. I began to see that both were a way to avoid the pain inside. The only difference between the two addictions was that mine got applauded by society."

In fact, when Ellen began to withdraw from her usual twelve- to fourteen-hour days in order to dedicate more time to her family, "no one seemed to understand the need, and some agents in my company began to feel I had lost focus and was no longer interested in the business. No one was saying 'Good job, Ellen. You're spending some time with your family.'"

Nobody pumps your hand for feeding your kids a good breakfast every morning, for teaching them values of cooperation and caring, or just being around when they're home. That behavior can, instead, be overtly discouraged, perhaps especially for men. Alan's friends insisted that men didn't raise kids. "And my father feels strongly that I have given up my life," says Alan. "He thinks that because of single fatherhood I have given up all opportunities to be a mensch, to do something great in the world."

Clearly, for Alan's father the Yiddish term refers to a man who attains wealth and status. In my own dictionary, however, the choices Alan made as a single father would make him the perfect example of a mensch. But it wasn't my world Alan was standing in when he made his choices.

Alan had been preparing from birth to assume a status and a salary that would prove his worth. As a successful Manhattan lawyer, he was on his way — until his marriage ended and he was left with his two girls, aged three and six.

"I know I could have gotten more help, I could have afforded it," says Alan. "And I did advertise for nannies. But I just couldn't seem to connect with the right person. Taking care of the girls began to cut more and more into my job. I wasn't willing to go out of town or to work nights. If I had to be in court all day and into the evening, I found it was so laborious planning out a patchwork of babysitters that it just wasn't worth it. Luckily I had some independent sources of income from a family business so that I could cut back on work. And I did."

What a triumph, to step outside the legal profession's tradition of long hours, its motto of "work first and family second," and choose a greater treasure! However, not only in the eyes of his friends and father but even at times to Alan himself, the price looked very high. "If I hadn't taken on the girls like this, I'd have had an illustrious career in public interest law. I might have been a world traveler. And — probably the hardest part — I might have attracted a woman as a new partner. When my relationships have failed, I find I can't help but indict myself, thinking if I had been these other things, maybe it would have worked out." What could be worth that price?

For Alan it was a simple and transforming discovery. "I really like children," he says. "I had never been around them at all until I was in my thirties. We had a big family when I was growing up, but I was one of the youngest, and all my years in college and law school, I had no interest in kids or contact with them at all. But by raising my girls alone, I probably know more than most fathers do about children. In Third World countries, people love children. You feel it right away. You never hear a child cry. People pick them up and care for them. They really like them, and I have evolved in that way myself. I spend time with my girls, I go on field trips with their school. I know how to relate to kids now. I wouldn't have had that if I hadn't made those choices."

As we cast our critical votes for what is of value in our lives, we face a challenge on two fronts — societal attitudes, and government and business policies that are only beginning to acknowledge the value of family, for both men and women. And we face our daily struggle with ourselves as we push our children out the door, tell them they are wasting time (which is money), put our best hours in at work and return, spent and exhausted, home to them. But as we acknowledge what is truly valuable to us and act accordingly, we will continue pushing the spiral of political and social change in the direction it is heading, toward supporting families and children.

"There are so many single parents today," Moshe points out, "that we could be a major political force to get what we need." He goes on to explain why he thinks single parents still have such a soft political voice. "First of all, single parents on the poor side tend to lack self-esteem, so they feel like they have less of a right to stand up and do something. And then most of us are working so hard to make our living, like me, that there is little time left to do other things, like make our needs clear. Other people in our society can't see what's going on in my life. They may think I'm just lazy or want a free ride."

But as we reach out, the story is revealed. A single mother raising her children in southern Minnesota graduates triumphantly from law school and takes her first steps toward her goal of making the changes in family law that will prevent others from going through what she had to. A welfare mother in Wisconsin starts a newspaper and support network to help others through the disheartening red tape of the system. A single mother working as a secretary starts a lobbying organization so that others won't go through the chaos she encountered when she lost subsidized childcare over legal technicalities. In California another single mother, one who resorted to welfare for a period of time after her divorce, wins a congressional seat in the state and begins her efforts at change. A welfare mother struggling against discrimination in finding housing receives a grant to start a nonprofit group to help single parents find rentals and roommates.

After her son's encounter with drugs, Ellen started an Awareness Hour on compulsive addictive behavior for parents and their teenagers. She also formed the first Codependency Anonymous twelve-step program in her city. "It's not enough just to achieve our own personal goals," says Ellen. "We must be willing to reach out and help other people by sharing our own experiences, our failures as well as our successes. We *can* make a difference in other people's lives."

◆ EYES ON THE PRIZE

It is in unlauded, inconspicuous daily acts that we make the difference in the lives of our children that only we as their parents can make. As single parents we may slow the advancement of our careers, we may struggle endlessly to make ends meet. Sometimes we may look like failures, or feel like failures. "True success comes from the inside out, not the outside in," Ellen says in her lectures to others who, like her, have discovered the wages of outward success. "Each of us was created as a unique, special, and precious human being, and as parents we owe it to our children to make certain they know and understand how precious they are. In our striving to succeed, it is very easy to become human doings. We are not what we do; we are not our professions. Money comes and goes, outward success comes and goes, but who we are as human beings — our honesty, courage, strength, faith and hope — is our legacy to our children."

We are not debtors, *we* are not welfare mothers, *we* are not the unemployed or the struggling. We are the vast human beings whom our children look to and adore. Our children depend on us, and we depend on so much more than money — friends and family who believe in us, the grace we cannot control but only receive, our own ability to endure and trust ourselves. That each of us is here alive at all is a miracle sustained by more than economic survival.

Our children may have little value in the world of human doings, but like nothing else they call us back to our human being. They call us back to the passion and the joy of life with no purpose. They call us back to the basic questions: What's it all about? What do we really need? Where's it all going so fast anyway? It can be hard to come skidding in from work to meet their halting little stories, to join the slower rhythms of the children who long for the presence of our being. But there they are — our treasure. There may be no VCRs and none of the latest anything, but to the degree that we have ensured our moments to enjoy each other, we have found our success.

One Sunday afternoon, I took Elias to an exhibit of Plains Indian art. He was especially intrigued by a collection of wooden batons, the tops carved with heads of horses. Reading the description, I explained to him that these were used in battle, not as weapons but to mark a warrior's promise to himself. In battle, the warrior chose his ground and, plunging the baton into the earth, vowed to fight to the death if necessary but not to move from the spot. "I like this," Elias said, pressing against the glass.

When we walked on, I reached for his hand, wanting to feel in that small warmth the remarkable reality of his presence in my life. Debts and bills and midnight fears seemed very far away. If anything has taught me to trust in life, it is living on the edge with a child. No, the battle to survive will not claim my spirit. It may take my hours, but it cannot steal our moments. This is where I plant my vow.

CHAPTER 8

◆

Working Around Our Children: Care and Childcare

Many things we need can wait, the child cannot. Now is the time his bones are being formed, his blood is being made, his mind is being developed. To him we cannot say tomorrow, his name is today.

— Gabriela Mistral

KIRSTIN FIRST CAME to the United States from Sweden as an exchange student at sixteen. She fell in love with the mountains and the vast, open West, and returned home only long enough to announce her permanent departure. In her new country she explored, earned a two-year degree in business administration, and settled in a resort town in the mountains. At twenty-five Kirstin found out she was pregnant.

"I had gone through a couple of years of romantic biological urges, and so I was quite happy to find out I would have a baby," she begins. "My boyfriend, Tom, and I had had a rocky relationship the whole miserable two years we were together. I suppose I could have expected it, but when I told him I was pregnant, he immediately said that he was not the father. Then after a few weeks he started saying the pregnancy was a good omen and it meant we should try to stay together. I saw it as a big *no*.

"Tom was an alcoholic. My father was an alcoholic, and I knew that I never wanted my child to grow up with what comes along with that. His inability to make up his mind about the baby was all part of it. So for me this was a test of whether I could stand up for my ideals or not. I was willing to do so at whatever cost. But I had no idea what that would be."

Tom turned uncertain again about whether he wanted to play any role at all in the baby's life, especially a financial one. With limited options for employment in a town with a seasonal economy, Kirstin took on a job cleaning houses for the winter; it paid well and she intended to save money. Knowing that she would have to work soon after the birth, she lined up a position as the receptionist at a local wildlife museum for the following summer. That would tide her over, she thought, until her winter job cleaning started again.

Kirstin sailed through her pregnancy, working and anticipating her baby's birth. Summer arrived, and with it tourists flooded the museum. At the end of June, in the height of the season, Alexander was born. What Kirstin would encounter in trying to care for him as a working single mother is something many of us who have been caught between our dreams and reality will recognize.

Unless we've been around babies a lot, it's hard to imagine how tiny and how helpless a newborn is. The task of caring for our infants is not only consuming, it can also be utterly compelling. Many working parents, married and single, who automatically assumed they would return to their jobs weeks after birth find themselves longing instead for months of time as they face the wrenching separation and the prospect of finding acceptable substitute care. For Kirstin, the impact of these emotional and practical considerations had to be dealt with during the first week of her son's life, before she returned to work.

"When you first have a baby you are so overwhelmed with all of it, with not sleeping at night, with the twenty-four-hour dependence. You live from day to day and you're glad you're still alive when you wake up!" As she talks about it now, five years later, Kirstin laughs, with perspective — and relief. "If I made it through the day, that was the best I could do. I cried almost every night. The whole thing was just so exhausting.

"And there was something else I hadn't really thought about. Even though I liked working and I intended to dedicate my life to meaningful work, I realized that I had an unconscious ideal: to me a mother was someone who stayed home with her child. Here I was now, with this baby and confronted with not being able to live up to my ideals. That was devastating. I could not be the kind of mother I thought a mother should be — number one, at home with the child. So I did the next best thing. I took him with me to work."

That was seven days after Alexander was born. "I was really allowed just a break for his birth, because it was the busiest time of the season, and this was a summer job. I had had a hard time of delivery, though, and I was pretty cut up, so I could hardly walk straight." That wasn't the hardest part, however.

"For almost the entire day, there would be anywhere from five to fifty people waiting to pay to get into the museum or wanting to know something. I was the only one at the front desk. My baby would be screaming because he was hungry. I wanted to breast-feed him — to me that was just another thing you did with a baby." But a steady stream of tourists left scarcely a moment for the kind of relaxed time nursing a newborn requires. Like many nursing babies, Alexander didn't want to take the bottles of formula his mother tried to offer instead. "My breasts would get so heavy and sore because my shift was eight hours long. Sometimes I'd be dripping milk out, and he'd be crying to eat, but I'd have to give my attention to the tourists instead. When the place would go quiet for a few minutes, I'd sneak him onto my breast, praying no one would come in. Then someone would walk through the door, and I'd have to tear him off. It was just awful."

The mother's body and the baby's hunger work in tandem. It's a perfect system, but the perfection is at odds with the way most of us earn our living. When we know what is best for the physical and emotional health of our children but our lives as working parents keep us from giving that to them, what do we do?

"I remember one time when there were about twenty people waiting at the counter, and I was holding the baby to keep him quiet, all of a sudden his diaper filled, and this warm, smelly ooze came leaking out through the blanket everywhere. I had to leave all those people standing there and run into the back office to change him. It was miserable. The whole thing was — packing my little baby in a carrying case every day and driving to work for that eight-hour shift. I had had an entirely romantic notion of what parenting would be like. When the cruel reality set in, it was devastating."

The rhythms of the eight-hour workday, the forty-hour workweek, have little to do with the rhythms of children of any age. Typically, the workplace is set up to accommodate the schedules of single men and women with no interfering commitments outside their jobs — not parents, and particularly not single parents.

Neither do government policies support parents. In early 1993, the long-awaited national Family and Medical Leave Bill was passed, ensuring (only for employees of companies with more than fifty workers) *twelve weeks of unpaid leave* for childbirth, adoption, and caring for a sick child. By that time, 53 percent of all mothers with children under one year of age were in the U.S. labor force.[1] While some companies provide extended, even paid, childbearing leave, that is still rare. We have babies and we return to work, many of us full-time. When we raise our children as single parents, we scarcely have other options. We may resign ourselves to "reality," yet the problem we face as individuals can't be separated from the social context in which we try to solve it. Our experience in the United States is vastly different from that of parents in nearly every other industrialized nation.

What would Kirstin's experience have been like had she given birth to a child on her own in Sweden? Exceptionally enlightened in its national policy toward families, Sweden is nonetheless just one of over one hundred nations that guarantee *paid* parental leave, in whole or in part, in many cases to fathers as well as mothers.[2] Of all major industrialized nations, the United States and South Africa are the only ones that do not provide such benefits.[3]

If Kirstin had been living in Sweden as a working mother, parental insurance would have enabled her to remain at home for twelve months while drawing approximately 90 percent of her salary.[4] She could also have opted for three additional months at a flat rate. Until her son's eighth birthday, she would retain the option to work for six hours a day.[5]

In Sweden, Kirstin would have also been provided with a special allowance for single parents and a guaranteed minimum income. In its efforts to "legitimize parenting," all Swedish families are provided with standard entitlements, among them housing subsidies, allowances for substitute childcare, income replacement for caring for a sick child, and universal child health care. "By these measures," writes the sociologist Ruth Sidel, ". . . the society is recognizing its responsibility to enable parents to care for their children without undue economic, professional, or emotional stress."[6]

This is an attitude that is written into national family policy throughout Europe. In Austria, four months of paid leave after birth at 100 percent of salary and another twenty-two months at a flat rate are guaranteed. In France, four months with 90 percent of earnings and up to two years of unpaid job-protected leave. Hungary, six months at 65–100 percent of earnings. Italy, five months at 80 percent of earnings. Finland, ten and a half months at 80 percent of earnings. Interestingly, our historical "mother country," Britain, "the country with the least-adequate overall child care provisions of any of the major European countries," provides six weeks of paid leave at 90 percent of earnings and twelve additional weeks at a flat rate.[7]

While the impact of moving toward global equity is forcing these countries to assess the feasibility of some of their overall welfare benefits, the principle behind them remains intact. "A deep-seated conviction still exists among many people that Europe has got some things right that the United States has wrong," writes Roger Cohen, reporting on the economic crisis in Europe. "The sentiment was summed up . . . by President François Mitterrand when he commented that the Los Angeles riots [in 1992] illustrated 'that the social needs of any country must not be neglected.'"[8]

That all children belong to a nation and are the responsibility of all its citizens seems to be an outrageous claim in our own country. We categorize children as private property, and thus view them as a choice and a luxury for which parents are individually responsible. Those of us with children are essentially on our own in caring for them, and we enter the workforce basically handicapped by their existence.

In the absence of guaranteed paid leave and with no other help available, Kirstin returned to work. Determined though she was to care for her son herself in his early months, she was unable to span the gap between her need to earn a living and the needs of her infant as a totally dependent human organism. His presence and his needs had no value in the workplace, and the arrangement was not working for anyone.

One afternoon near the close of the day, when nobody else was around, Kirstin's manager appeared and "very quietly, very subtly, very suddenly said that it wasn't working out for him. He was nice and kind, and I understood completely, but . . ." Kirstin packed her two-month-old infant back into his carrying seat one more time, gathered up his layette and the remnants of her bag lunch, and walked out into the glaring light of an August afternoon alone. She made her way through the carefree tourists, strapped her baby into the car seat, and squeezed the tears from her eyes so she could see to drive.

"I felt very lost. I was so scared. I had no money and none saved.

I had thought I would save during pregnancy but hadn't been able to. All these things you think you're going to do but don't . . . I had had some help from friends when Alexander was born, one hundred dollars here and fifty dollars there. His father was still confused about how he wanted to relate to him, so any money he gave was sporadic and very little.

"I figured I was just going to die. I simply didn't think I could live through that. I thought I'd never be able to sleep again, never be able to pay my bills. My winter job wasn't supposed to begin until much later. I didn't know how I could survive until then. And here was this tiny baby completely dependent on me.

"I was so exhausted when I got fired that I didn't have enough energy to even think of what I might do. I thought if things got any worse, despite the fact that I didn't like the welfare system and the reputation that came along with it — the stigma and what people thought of you — I would do that before I was going to bring my tiny infant to daycare every day for nine or ten hours a day. That was one thing I knew that I was not going to do. I refused, utterly and completely. I would rather live in total poverty than do that."

The dream of working while the baby kicks and coos on a blanket nearby is not uncommon, and not everyone who carries a baby along to a job encounters quite the same level of difficulty as did Kirstin. But the ingredients for success are highly specific.

By the time Mary returned to work as a receptionist, her daughter, Grace, was three months old. With welfare, a small savings, and help from friends, she had made it through those first months of getting to know her baby and helping her get established in a new world. A nurse by training, Mary knew the medical practitioners in the small coastal community she lived in well enough to find a job with two doctors who welcomed a baby in their office. "Grace was the third child to grow up in the patient waiting room," says Mary. "People would come to see the doctors and sit there holding Grace and talking with me about her, playing with her, tickling her. These are some of the same people I am caring for now in their homes while they are in advanced stages of frailty."

When Grace was about a year old, Mary took a job as a nurse for three long days a week, "in the office of the woman doctor who had delivered her. I found good childcare for her right across the street, right here in the middle of town. Even so, leaving her for that long a day was really hard. That first day I will never forget. But the doctor was so sympathetic and supportive that she let me go periodically throughout the day for fifteen minutes or so to nurse her, the whole time I was working there. This kind of closeness and connection is an advantage of living in a small community. I would say that that one fact — living in a small, close community — has just about made all the difference in the world to me. I have always known who Grace was with and that I did not have to worry at all about her well-being."

For Kirstin, the circumstances that made this dream possible for Mary were not available. Throughout Alexander's early years Kirstin would continue to search not only for ways to have more time with him herself but also for quality substitute care. What she encountered would be a story in many ways tragically typical of raising a child as a working parent in the United States today, where, as the editor of a major professional journal puts it, "Child care . . . is a national scandal."[9]

In most cultures, the role of "motherhood" has not meant that the mother is the *only* one to care for a child. The mother is not even the only one who nurses a baby in most tribal societies. When the entire social context supports parents, they are freed to engage in their other tasks. Our working at a job is not in itself harmful for our children and can be beneficial, providing models of involvement and capacity. However, trading the emotional well-being of our children for financial security and job commitment is simply not a viable option, either for us as individuals or for our nation.

As single parents, most of us *must* work,[10] and many of us also *want* to. The difficulty we face is in finding the right combination of circumstances to make it possible to work without sacrificing our children. And that depends not only on our own choices but on those of the society in which we live and the places where we work.

As it is now, when we set out to work, we are usually faced with a long and disheartening search to find acceptable and affordable childcare, especially for very young children. Once we have found it, there is no guarantee that it will last. We may be lucky enough to find a caregiver who provides our children as much — perhaps even more, in some ways — than we might. But it is luck, not adequate resources, we rely upon. All working parents face the childcare challenge, but for single parents the problems are amplified because we face them on one salary and one person's limited time.

◆ BUY ME LOVE

We have taken the need of children to be nurtured and tended twenty-four hours a day and coined a word that fits into the current economic thrust — "childcare." Yet there is a dilemma built into the system. Childcare is marketed as a commodity, like gas for the car, which enables me to get to work. But it's not. Childcare is a major issue of hearts and souls. I'm not looking to park my child so I can work in peace; I'm looking to buy him love.

Absolutely nothing has been harder in raising my child alone than finding good childcare so I can work. In fact, research indicates that "the overwhelming factor in determining whether working mothers are happy is day care."[11] I would with certainty amend that statement to read "good, reliable, loving, nurturing daycare." All of us carry our children to work, whether we do so in a baby seat like Kirstin or in our hearts. Knowing that my son is well cared for and loved has made the entire difference in how and sometimes even *if* I have worked.

I unabashedly want those who care for my child to love him — that is, to genuinely extend themselves for his spiritual, emotional, intellectual, and physical development. This is what is required of all participants in this enterprise of caring for our children — for parents, caregivers, and society. Yet I feel slightly uneasy saying that, knowing that many might feel I am asking too much. I feel as if I need to justify my ferocious commitment to raising my son well, as if that impulse so many of us feel is not to be commended but rather considered neurotic. But there is a tremendous voice lifting for the children, and the single parents I spoke with, those who were committed to raising their children well, are part of this voice. And the choices we struggle to make in how we care for them as we work are the substance of that sound.

"I was crazed on the subject of choosing Sierra's nursery school," begins Cheryl, whose daughter is now five. "Ever since she was a baby, she had been in a small play group with a wonderful sitter who took care of the children alternately in each of our homes." That also meant that one or two days a week Sierra could be in the familiarity of her own home, where Cheryl's office was as well. "She knew I was nearby, and that means a lot. When she turned four, however, it was time for something else, and the other children in the group were enrolling in preschool. I was faced with trying to find a place I felt good about and that would be good for her. You better believe I tried hard!"

As a single parent, I know without question that the people who care for my child while I work are the most important adults in my life. I feel completely vulnerable to them, dependent on their whims and choices in order to sustain my livelihood. I count on them to hold up the other end of the blanket as the other, most consistent, nurturing day-to-day presence in my child's life. They hold his well-being — and therefore my own — in their hands. The few times I have left Elias without being sure that he would indeed be cared for well, I have felt torn apart. As Cheryl puts it, "I think the quality of childcare means a lot more for single parents because that is 'the other' for our children." To find that other is not easy.

When it came time to choose that preschool for her daughter, Cheryl made a long and thorough search. She still recounts the story with some agitation — and a degree of embarrassment, perhaps, that a woman who teaches leadership skills and problem solving in the country's major corporations should be thrown into a quandary by the choice of childcare for her daughter.

First Cheryl checked out the possibilities, asking friends, looking through the local parenting paper, calling for information. "I pared the choices down to six places that sounded good and were close enough to be practical. Then I took Sierra with me to visit all six. With my work schedule we could really only fit in about one a week, so this process took a long time. When Sierra's father came to the United States to visit her, he went back to each of them again with me. He was willing to do that because I was going crazy trying to decide."

Cheryl returned two or three times to several of the schools she was most interested in. "When I went back for my third visit to one of the places I was considering, I felt a little embarrassed to be there again. When I laughed and sort of apologized to one of the teachers at being so careful, he said, 'Oh no, this is great. Virtually no other parents have come and hung out like you have to see what the school is really like. They just find a good and convenient childcare and put their kid in it.'" Cheryl's point was proven. The other parents, virtually all couples, didn't lack concern for their children; but they probably considered themselves less dependent on childcare to provide the "other" in their children's lives.

As single parents, we may feel that it is not just important but *critical* that caregivers and teachers, from infancy through high school, be supportive and understanding for both us and our children. These may be the primary adults our children can count on when we are not available, and they have a major influence on their development. And for us these others who share the minutiae of daily care for our children are also the ones who tell us stories about their antics, who listen to our stories and concerns about them, and who celebrate with us their accomplishments. If we are fortunate enough to find them, they are the ones who love our children with us.

◆ STARTING AT THE VERY BEGINNING

Children need care, guidance, and love. Although individual children differ in their requirements — and many influences form the character of a human being — too much information is available about the importance of the early years for any of us to ignore. The findings of some of the research in this area can place us, as working single parents, in painful binds. It touches on passions, fears, longings, and guilt. To say anything that counters the movement toward increased childcare for infants and toddlers sounds regressive. I certainly do not advocate a wholesale return of women to the home and a central identity as "only mothers." But I think it is essential that we acknowledge the weight of our responsibility to ensure the kind of care our children receive.

I hold my breath as I read the research. With every line of evidence, I look at Elias and wonder: Has he gotten what he needed? But it is better to know what is needed and try to approximate it than not to know at all. One of the most authoritative — and most passionately contested — researchers, Jay Belsky of Pennsylvania State University, holds that "children who experienced twenty or more hours per week of nonparental care in their first year of life of the kind routinely available in the United States . . . are at elevated risk of developing insecure attachments to their mothers and of being more disobedient toward adults and aggressive toward peers as three-to-eight-year-olds."[12]

"Insecure attachment," researchers say, results in inability to trust and empathize, to form enduring intimate relationships as adults. Frightening. Then what do we do? Some, like Kirstin and others we will meet in this chapter, arranged in some way to work with or near their children. Some, like Meg in the last chapter, remained on welfare while their children were young not only because it was difficult to get off it but also because they wanted to be present for their children. "It was the best gift I knew how to give them," says Meg, "and I almost died trying!"

Noe became sole parent for his son when Oliver was two and a half. Feeling he needed to get training in order to earn enough money to raise a child well, Noe enrolled in a course for computer programmers. "That was the most difficult time of our lives. I almost wish now that I had just collected AFDC and stayed home with him instead of leaving him in childcare from seven in the morning till four, five, six in the afternoon. I think young children really need that direct contact and thoughtful, sensitive, caring connection with one consistent person. And I think it's the best if it's their own parent, but at least the same person.

"I know, though, that I would have had a conflict of feelings about not working," adds Noe. "I would have felt like I wasn't being a productive member of society. Our whole training, especially for males, is that way." The attitude doesn't apply only to males, as any woman who has "just raised kids" would attest. The work ethic is so honored in our culture that welfare policy in some states proclaims, in effect, that it is more important for parents to be down at the fast-food restaurant turning burgers than home with their children. New state programs to limit AFDC grants to two years seem to give precedence to saving money for the state rather than seeking to ensure the welfare of children. Media stories praise single parents who work at three jobs to support their families as paradigms of industriousness with the implication that anyone else virtuous enough could do the same. But where are the children? Who is taking care of them, and how?

I am certainly not condemning those who take on that enormous burden. They have no other option for survival in our society — except welfare, and that is hardly an option at all. But to make our children priority is to struggle against the philosophical underpinnings of our culture.

Whether we want to or not, we get jobs and find childcare. Certainly substitute care is not in itself harmful. The essential point to note in the research lies in Belsky's phrase "nonparental care . . . *of*

the kind routinely available in the United States." The evidence thus
far points with surety toward the fact that *quality* of care is the
primary factor in whether a childcare arrangement is harmful or
beneficial.[13] The question is, what is considered "quality"? Summa-
rizing the most recent evidence from a large body of research, Martha
Zaslow of the National Research Council draws some very specific
conclusions. The elements in childcare that are essential to the well-
being of a child include a "warm and caring environment," which
means small group size, trained workers, and well-organized physical
space, "a relatively higher proportion of time spent by children in
interactions with care givers rather than in solitary play or play with
peers . . . and more interactions with care givers that involve sharing
of information."[14] These are the circumstances that result in the
positive development of children.

Another specialist, Alice Honig of the Syracuse Children's Center, the oldest federally funded infant/toddler childcare center in the
United States, says: "The primary ingredient to help young children
flourish consists of loving, responsive caregivers, generously committing energy, body-loving, and tuned-in attentiveness to their child's
well-being. And every ingredient counts!"[15]

That is what I call a definition of love, and it is love at any age
level that cultivates the full flowering of our children into healthy
adults. Anything less than this may be harmful to some degree,
from hampering potential through cultivating pathology. As Dorothy
Conniff, the director of Community Services in Madison, Wisconsin, writes: "When children under 3 are put into impoverished or
chaotic environments with inexperienced, discouraged staff who ex-
pend most of their energy just trying to maintain order, the children
suffer. . . . We have no idea how destructive a situation we have
created. It is a social experiment on a grand scale with virtually no
controls."[16]

Some research even points to the fact that academic progress,
school skills, and behavior problems may all be affected by quality
of early care. "Children who had engaged in more positive interactions with day care adults at [age 4] were rated at age 8 as more
socially competent, accepted by peers, and empathic."[17] Isn't that part
of what we want for our children?

Yet the number of daycare arrangements available with such standards are woefully small in relation to the need. In 1990 almost 29.5

million children thirteen and under had working mothers."[18] A national survey reported that in the same year about *five million* spaces were available in licensed childcare facilities, and three million more in nonlicensed.[19] Of course our own approved caregivers — relatives, sitters, family daycare — may not be licensed but may qualify as loving. As most of us have discovered, however, quality caregivers in any arrangement are not easy to find.

Nor are they easy to keep once we find them. Constancy is one of the primary ingredients in quality care. Indeed, in the morass of conflicting research results, the importance of continuity of care, particularly during the first eighteen months, is widely accepted.[20] Yet a survey conducted by *Working Mother* magazine found that among 1,733 readers, "Ninety-seven percent of the respondents say they had to change their caregiver at least once within the past year; 48 percent had to change their arrangements two or more times."[21] Does that sound familiar?

◆ THE COST OF LOVE

Ben was lucky. While he reports that the hardest part of raising his three children was "juggling the daycare situations and trying to figure out the logistics of getting them there in time to get to work," he managed to find a childcare arrangement that lasted — for six years! "When my older daughter, Ruby, was almost three, I stumbled onto a really good daycare center. My younger daughter also went there, and when they went on to grade school, they were able to go to the same place for before- and after-school care.

"I still had to drop them off at somebody else's house at five every morning because the center didn't open until six-thirty, but it was a set routine. That was the benefit. And for them the place was wonderful. It gave them a social life, provided swimming lessons, lots of field trips. It was a relief after struggling through all the other alternatives I'd tried, like live-in sitters who were unreliable."

The constancy of care was a benefit to both Ben and his children. But Ben, a skilled carpenter, had a couple of other major advantages as well. "I was lucky enough to have a lot of latitude in my job. If I had to, I could just quit, which I did regularly, and most of the time I could get the job back. There was a period when all three of my kids came down with chicken pox, one after the other. We spent five solid weeks with chicken pox. I just said to my boss, 'I have to quit. My kids are sick. And I'd like to have the job back later.'"

Besides that, Ben was lucky enough to be able to afford the quality care he found. "Not that I was making great money, but I did have a trade. I didn't realize how lucky I had been until several years ago. When my kids got older, I started making more money, so I could hire someone to move in to help drive them around. We lived in the country by that time, so getting to school and activities meant a lot of driving for three kids. I put an ad in the paper saying I was looking for a single mom or a college student as a live-in. I would pay all their room and board plus a few dollars a month, and all I basically needed was transportation to and from school for my kids. I wasn't looking for anybody to babysit at night or bathe them or anything.

"I had over a *hundred* phone calls from single moms who were totally distressed with the life they were stuck in, because they couldn't afford daycare. It was so expensive they couldn't afford to go to work. It actually paid more to be on welfare! It was a real eye opener. Made me feel lucky I am a man as a single parent. Most women with families alone don't have the means to support them as well as I did, let alone the flexibility in their jobs."

Even *married* professional women with young children can find that when they return to work, "their earnings are barely enough to pay for child care, taxes and the other expenses of working."[22] For me, childcare, even when it was not full-time, was the single highest cost item in my budget. Unless we can find a trusted relative willing to care for our children for free or for minimal monetary compensation, we face major costs when we try to arrange the care we want. Once again, government policy not only doesn't help, it can actually discourage us from doing what we need to do. "Nannygate" made that clear.

When Catherine, whom we met in the last chapter, returned to her job after Angelina's birth, she was convinced that hiring a babysitter to come into her home to take care of her infant daughter would be best. She had read the recommendations of child-development specialists and was reluctant to do anything else. And she knew what she required in a caregiver. "I was looking for not just someone who would babysit but a certain kind of person. I saw a sign a woman had posted in the church where I went for my mothers' group. It was a miracle that she turned out to be that kind of person."

Estrella was from Central America. She was warm and experienced in caring for children. She had been a teacher in her own country and was a sophisticated woman in her late thirties. "And coming from a child-oriented culture, she loved children," Catherine says. "She loved playing as much as Angelina did. It was the greatest thing to see them together. If I hadn't found someone like her, I would have found a way to work at home or something. Taking Angelina out to daycare at her age was just not a choice. I didn't want to risk all the sickness, for one thing. And I just knew this kind of one-to-one care in the home was best."

The only problem with Estrella was that she bore the gruesome-sounding label "illegal alien." Hiring illegal immigrants to care for children was such a common practice, however, that Catherine says she just didn't think about it. "Frankly, the first question I asked someone who applied to take care of my child was not whether they had a green card but whether they loved children or not."

According to the rules, however, Catherine was now an outlaw. What would have happened were she to have complied with the law? The first consequence would have been losing her wonderful caregiver. "When Estrella's American friends who were helping her suggested she might want to go to the government for asylum, she was very hesitant. She was afraid they would send her back to a situation that was untenable." Were Estrella to have applied for a green card, she would have gotten in line behind more than eighty thousand others waiting to receive permission to work legally. Since 1991, only ten thousand "unskilled" immigrants a year have been allowed green cards.[23] By the time Estrella would be able to work legally, Angelina would be in grade school.

If Catherine had complied with the law, she would have entered that intricate web of conflicting requirements that came to light during the Zoe Baird nomination for attorney general in early 1993. It would also mean filing five to eight complex federal forms each year and perhaps state forms as well. It would mean paying taxes for Social Security and Medicare and withholding unemployment and workmen's compensation and income tax. This would mean even lower wages for Estrella and higher costs for Catherine — both of which were impossible for either of them. "I paid her $3.50 an hour. I knew she was living with friends and wasn't relying on this income to pay her rent and food. I don't think I could have in conscience hired someone for that if they were just living on my wages." Even at that rate, Catherine was paying $600 a month in childcare expenses — more than her rent.

Wages for sitters who come into the home are generally at the top of the scale. Those who work legally, paying taxes on their wages, ask for $7 to $12 an hour plus paid vacations, which is the least they deserve for the vital job they are performing. But who can afford it? Often the only alternative is to find someone willing to work for minimum wage, or less — usually someone who wants to receive his or her pay "under the table."

What else might Catherine have done? Care for infants at centers can easily cost $600 a month and is in the greatest shortage. Were she lucky enough to find a place she liked and could afford, she would be extremely lucky if they had an opening and if it were en route to her job besides. I can imagine Catherine waiting for a bus before dawn in the driving rain of winter, laden with infant, diaper bag, umbrella, and purse. Too many do it. And if Angelina were sick, it would automatically mean lost time at work, since centers or homes with other children usually can't take sick babies, who will contaminate the others. According to Ruth Matson, who started the first daycare center for sick children in the United States, children under three are sick an average of twenty times a year. She adds, "The head of a national chain of childcare centers told me that on any given day, ten percent of their total population is out sick."[24] That's a lot of missed work for parents.

So Catherine continued to break the law and to pay for her wonderful, illegal, at-home childcare. "This law is making lawbreakers out of hundreds of thousands of people who are otherwise law-abiding citizens. They're desperate," says Sam Bernsen, a lawyer who formerly worked with the Immigration and Naturalization Service. A spokesman for the IRS estimates that "75 percent of the two million households that employ domestic workers [including child caregivers] fail to pay the required taxes."[25]

When Angelina turned two, Catherine did take her down the block to a family daycare that accepted toddlers, and she returned once again to the right side of the law. Care at that age tends to be somewhat easier to find, especially if the child is out of diapers — a requirement of many centers. However, this next step brings up another set of challenges, as Kirstin would find.

◆ ROUND AND ROUND AND ROUND WE GO

During those terrifying weeks following the termination of her job, Kirstin put on weight and slept little. "I looked horrible. One day on the street I met up with the man who managed the houses I would be cleaning that winter. The next day I got a phone call from him. Our boss had come to town and had asked him how I was doing with the baby." The manager had told him what was obvious — Kirstin was having a hard time. "The next thing I knew, my boss gave me a check for $2,500, just like that. It wasn't an advance on pay, it was a gift. He is actually a very kind man. He put me on salary immediately and made sure they found enough work to keep me going until the heavy winter months arrived. It was bare kindness. It was really a miracle."

The miracle enabled Kirstin to care for her child herself while she was working until he was seventeen months old. With Alexander strapped in a frontpack or a backpack, Kirstin made beds, decorated Christmas trees, stocked cupboards, swept out garages. In those early months, the only time she needed to hire care for him was on weekends or holidays when her boss was in town and Kirstin had to serve at parties he was hosting. Then she left Alexander with an older couple. They seemed rather like grandparents. A welcome surrogate family for her son, she thought.

By the time Alexander was eighteen months old, it was clear that the time of sitting in a backpack had come to an end, as had playing alone while his mother worked. The time had arrived for someone else to care for him. First Kirstin decided to hire someone to come in and babysit at her home, thinking that would give her son the advantage of a familiar setting. But she found that the only people she could afford to hire were those who wanted to work short-term. "Actually the only reason the two women I first found were looking for jobs in childcare is because they were pregnant and they felt they were limited in the kind of work they could get. The moment they weren't pregnant anymore or were too pregnant, they were gone." And so was the bond her son was developing with them.

Even in a small town, Kirstin had to pay $3.00 an hour for someone to come to her home. At over $100 a week, it was a substantial addition to her budget. "This wasn't really working. First of all, I couldn't afford that amount. And then I didn't want to deal with the constant changing of people. It took so long to find them, and I had this stream of strangers coming into my house."

Looking at it from the perspective of the caregiver, it is no wonder there is such turnover. The job is isolating. The pay — while high for the parent — is miserable at less than minimum wage, with little opportunity for advancement and no benefits. Most sitters are on their way to something else.

"I felt if we're already going to have this kind of life," Kirstin goes on, "with so much stress built in, I at least wanted some continuity for both my son and myself. So I decided to put him in a daycare center. I thought if I could find the right one, maybe we'd be straight on with it until he was six and so we'd be settled." That's what we look for in raising our children — to settle in. But it's often just not in the cards. The only consistent caregivers Alexander had were that old couple on occasion.

"The first daycare center I took Alexander to didn't work at all for him," Kirstin relates. "The employees changed so often there too. And I think the institutional atmosphere just didn't give him what he needed." Kirstin was back to square one. Perhaps Alexander was especially sensitive, but his protests were an honest and understandable response to his experience.

The rate of turnover is indeed very high in the average daycare center — 41 percent of the workers come and go during the course of a year.[26] The way many centers are structured can be exceptionally demanding for both child and worker. In trying to shed light on the problem, Dorothy Conniff calculated what actual care would consist of in a typical infant center. For a caregiver responsible for four babies (a low ratio — in many states, the number allowed is six or even more), it would require seven hours and twenty minutes of the day just to dispense with the basic physical care of feeding, changing, cleaning up, and handwashing for hygiene. On top of that, the worker is supposed to be talking to the babies and playing with them.[27] At eighteen months, Alexander might require less attention to his physical needs, but keeping up with a toddler's emotional needs and activity level is a time-consuming task.

Yet despite the tremendous demands of the job and despite the fact that we as parents consider caring for our children one of the most important jobs in the world, there is little prestige connected with caring for children in any setting. In fact, *The Dictionary of Occupa-*

tional Titles ranks the job of childcare at the same skill level as parking lot attendant![28] Standard pay rates for a full-time job are in the lowest tenth of all wage earners, often with no benefits or health insurance.[29] According to Child Care Action Campaign, if childcare workers received salaries comparable to those of others with similar training and responsibilities, annual fees per child at an average center would increase from $4,070 to $8,425.[30]

"I looked around at a number of other places after that one, and eventually I found Patricia, who took care of children in her own home," Kirstin goes on. "She was a wonderful person. However, she didn't take children under two, and Alexander was just barely two by that time. And he was not potty-trained, which led to some conflict with her as well. But she gave in and took him, I guess because I really wanted her to. I liked her a lot personally.

"But for some of the same reasons as at the daycare center, Alexander just did not cope there either. There were twenty-two kids with just Patricia and her husband taking care of them. He cried and whined all day. I would pick him up at night and he would be completely frazzled from crying.

"I was hysterical at work myself sometimes, not knowing what to do about him at Patricia's house. I felt terrible leaving him there. I'd be crying at work, saying 'I can't cope, I can't do this anymore, I can't do anything.' My manager got angry and told me to stop bringing my problems to work with me. I got very angry about that, but I thought, yeah, he is really right. I do. But that is because I don't have any place else to bring them. Where the heck am I going to bring my problems? I don't have any family here, where I could say, 'Mom, please could you take care of him for a while?'"

It used to be that grandparents and other relatives cared for the children of working parents. Now, however, only about 16–20 percent of all working parents rely on relatives.[31] As in Kirstin's case, many grandparents do not live nearby. And these days many of them feel entitled to their own lives and don't want to get tied down with taking care of another family. Working parents who do have willing, able, and gracious care available from relatives are fortunate, and in the minority.

Patricia, the caregiver, eventually said she didn't want to deal with Alexander's crying anymore. Kirstin was back to the hunt, her difficulties multiplied by the fact that she now had a little boy who "was shy, wouldn't talk to anybody, wanted to be held all the time, and wanted his blanket constantly." The childcare round was taking its toll. "I looked for something small. I put him in a home daycare with five children for the rest of the summer. Then in the fall I took some time out from working to be with him, and he started getting better. I put an ad in the paper for a 'caring person,' knowing he needed more of that individual attention, and a woman from Eastern Europe visiting her daughter responded. She was available for only two days a week and for only four months, but she was willing to work for $3.00 an hour, and I could tell she was great. She was a puppeteer, and was experienced, and she just sort of took over. She is the one responsible for getting him out of that sorrowful state he had been in for a whole year. He turned into a laughing, funny, outgoing little kid. I hadn't even known that was in him. He was growing so beautifully those months with her."

Our children give us undeniable clues as to what works for them. But their feedback can demand a lot from us. When Shay, a nurse, got a new job, she found a childcare center nearby and transferred her three-year-old daughter to it. She thought it would be convenient and give them both more time together mornings and evenings. But it wasn't right for Jenny. "She really rebelled. She didn't want to go. She begged me to send her to another school instead. I thought, 'A kid can't be any clearer than this.' So I got off work early on several different days and popped in at unexpected times to see what was going on. That was when I saw how rigid the place was. They did everything in twenty-minute segments.

"I also asked Jenny what she didn't like about it. She said they didn't let the kids talk when they were going in and out of the classroom. I thought maybe if we switched teachers it would work. I asked if they could switch her to another room. The response was, 'Why don't we get a social worker to talk to you about this.' And then they said the classic line that lets you know you never want your child in that center. They told me they had 168 kids and I had one, implying that they knew more about mine because they knew so many! I moved her from that place. The big thing you learn through all this is to trust yourself, and to listen really carefully to your child.

"I did find a wonderful school that Jenny really liked after that," Shay continues, "and then after about a year, I was recruited by the best hospital in the city, and they had an excellent daycare center right on the grounds. They had a nursery school and kindergarten with eleven kids, two full-time teachers, and an aide. It was fantastic. She was there for two years. I could pick her up from there some afternoons and take her to work with me. She'd sit on the floor in the middle of the treatment room where the patients were waiting for chemotherapy, and she'd draw pictures for all of them. They loved it. She had a very clear concept of what I do as a nurse, and she was so proud. When I'd come to get her for those afternoons, she would put her thumbs in her coat and say to the kids in her class, 'My mom's here, and she's a nurse.' It was like, 'Eat your heart out, guys — she's *my* mom.'"

Good daycare can provide a lot of advantages. For our children, it can mean stability amid changes, learning social skills, having opportunities we can't give them ourselves, providing different role models. For us it can mean a great deal as well. Claudia, the creator and administrator of a daycare center expressly designed to serve Minnesota state employees, points out, "A good center can provide a single parent contact with people who can understand what you're going through if you've suddenly been thrown into being a working parent, people who can give you clues on development phases in your child when you're feeling worried or guilty, people who can point you to resources like support groups. When I first got divorced, I know it helped just knowing someone who could recognize the grieving process you go through. And if you don't have men in your kids' lives, it can be great to find a center with male caregivers. I have often felt in this kind of work almost like extended family to single parents."

Maybe that's what Shay and Jenny had finally found. "The people at that place are the most marvelous people in the world," says Shay. She and Jenny were lucky. But it can be very hard sometimes to understand what our children might be trying to tell us if they do not seem happy in daycare. Leaving a child crying in the arms of someone else is one of the hardest challenges we encounter as working parents. Why is my child crying? Is she really okay here? Is it a phase, or is it a message? Am I too attached, or is something wrong? This difficulty in being able to interpret our children's feelings is why placing them in the hands of someone else, especially when they are very young, can be so hard to do. As Kirstin would later find, it can also be very hard to listen to and respond to our own feelings.

◆ THE BEAT GOES ON

The challenge doesn't end, of course, once our children are in school. Then we are faced with before- and after-school care. It is estimated that 3.5 million children between the ages of six and thirteen are "latchkey kids," returning home to an empty house after school, to wait alone until their parents are back from work. This figure might in fact be much higher. According to the National Research Council, the number of children alone caring for themselves and sometimes younger siblings could be as high as 15 million. Less than 38 percent of all children have a parent who stays at home.[32] Well over half of all working women have children under eighteen; 53 percent have preschoolers.[33] Many working parents, single and partnered, find leaving their children alone for periods unavoidable. The Search Institute reports that approximately 60–70 percent of single-parent children in grades six through twelve were spending two or more hours a day at home alone. (For perspective, up to 56 percent of children in two-parent families also did.[34])

"I came home from school every night to an empty house and a refrigerator," says Terra, now nineteen, who was raised from the time she was three in a single-parent household. Her mother, Marian, blinks back tears as she says, "It's something I suppose I repress more than anything about what the realities of single parenting were."

Marian's job as a secretary allowed virtually no flexibility in her schedule, so arranging care for Terra after school and during vacations was a major endeavor. "At first, when she started grade school, I had a teenage girl come in at three and stay until I got home. When she got a little older, she began going to the house of a neighbor after school. Milly had five kids and was always there, so it was a family structure rather than an institution, which Terra would have balked at. The summers were the worst to cover, especially when I got a better job and had to work extra hours.

"By the time she was ten, Terra resisted any kind of 'babysitter,' anytime, and it just wasn't a battle I could fight. So she started coming home after school alone. She said that's what she wanted to do." Near tears, Marian adds, "But it was like a knife going in to hear her make that comment. She was so alone."

The research on latchkey children reveals various effects of being home alone, but probably few parents and few children would consider it ideal. While we place a great deal of importance on adult presence and guidance for preschool children, older children, including teenagers, also need that. Being home alone and the excessive television watching that often accompanies it, are two of the behaviors that place children at risk, according to the Search Institute's study on youth.[35]

As Stephanie Coontz points out, however, much of the effect depends upon the individual child and the circumstances. The media widely reported the results of a study that found that regardless of sex, race, or socioeconomic status, eighth-grade students who took care of themselves for eleven or more hours a week were twice as likely to smoke marijuana or drink alcohol as those who were actively cared for by adults.[36] To complete the picture, Coontz reveals that more than three quarters of that group had, in fact, never tried either. While some studies indicate higher stress levels in latchkey children, others report a greater sense of responsibility.[37] There are so many variables to take into account that all we can do is assess our own circumstances and do what we can in a less-than-ideal situation.

While Helen was at work, her teenage daughter began entertaining her boyfriend at home. "No matter what I said or did, it kept happening," says Helen. "I could see that she was lonely and wanted company, but I was exasperated. One day, I hit on it. Knowing how much she liked animals, I said, 'Pamela, how would you like a dog?!' Well, that dog cost me a fortune in veterinarian expenses, he was impossible to housebreak, and I found him to be a very annoying animal. But it was exactly what Pamela needed. She loved the dog, and sure enough, she lost interest in the boy."

The obstacles we encounter as single working parents may seem insurmountable. Sometimes, like Helen, we can come up with a creative solution. But without a doubt this is a crisis — one we cannot solve alone, for we are tied into a system that delimits our choices. For those of us, the majority, whose lives are sustained by "nine to five," the only way we may be able to change the way we care for our children is with the cooperation of the businesses and corporations we work for.

"I used to laugh when I read those books that would talk about whether you should go back to work or not after your baby's birth," comments Diana, a commercial litigation lawyer who was working with a large law firm when she got pregnant. "I'd think, 'What about me? I have no choice, because I am my own support. What do *I* do about nursing? What do *I* do about caring for my baby?' I was desperate to figure out something."

Desperate. The term is striking. In one of the wealthiest nations in the world, we live in such a way that *we are desperate to care for our children.* Do we point to government, business, culture, values, or the human condition to blame or petition? All are part of the web in which we rest, yet only with tremendous individual effort do we find solutions that work. Diana's desperation was her motivating force, and it got her what she wanted.

◆ MIXING BABIES AND BUSINESS

Two very different avenues have led Diana and Conita to this downtown office on the thirty-first floor of a high-rise. But both are single mothers, and both have found that the existence of one little room where their children are welcomed has made a tremendous difference in their experience as working single mothers.

Conita, the mother of two school-aged children and the comptroller at this company, meets me at the pink marble reception desk. The sound of our footsteps is absorbed by plush gray carpet as I follow her down a hallway lined with doors. She stops to open one of them, and the gray expanse explodes into primary colors. On the walls of this office room hang posters of Thomas the Tank Engine and illustrated nursery rhymes. The fact that they are mounted two inches above the baseboard might seem odd were it not for the fact that many of the things in this room are less than waist high — a playpen, a baby walker, a shelf stuffed with picture books, and assorted things to push and pull in bright colors.

The only "desk" is in the corner, covered with a pad and blanket and cluttered with a stack of diapers and an assortment of baby toys. Above it are drawings by children, several of them signed NICKY. "That's my seven-year-old," Conita explains. "Both she and my twelve-year-old son come in during school vacations and breaks." Beyond the table, a sheet of glass opens onto a breathtaking scene. We are floating above the tops of most buildings. Cars and buses look like toys below. This is a nursery room with a view.

I notice I'm towering above two of the occupants myself as I look around to respond to a friendly little "Hi!" Someone introduces me to the small person with blond curly hair so confidently serving as the welcoming committee. "Sophia has been here since she was a baby, and she is the second child in her family to come to work with her mother." The program started with Sophia's older brother when he was a nursing baby, five years ago.

"How old are you, Sophia?" I ask. "One!" she answers proudly, and her mother, who has stopped by, explains that she is not quite two. In a walker a few feet away, a small baby with pitch black hair and almond eyes reaches her arms up to her own mother, Diana. "This is Leslie," Diana tells me as she picks up her baby. "She's seven months old." Hannah, the young woman who cares for the children, gives Diana an update on Leslie's morning.

We finish the tour with a look at the adjacent kitchen. A highchair is stationed next to a table where chairs for big people surround a tiny suspended seat. This is the on-site, full-time childcare that the employer and employees of this firm have fought for and enjoyed during the past five years. "This is what corporate America *should* look like," says Conita. We all nod in agreement.

With Leslie in her mother's arms, we start walking back to Conita's office to talk. "You see how outgoing Sophia is," Conita comments. "I think her verbal abilities and her confidence come from all the loving interaction she has with adults here. And when my kids come in, they play with the babies too. A lot of the kids of the parents here drop by and visit whenever they can."

"It's not unusual here to see a child," Diana adds. "In other offices, you'd probably think that someone was sick or the babysitter had died if a kid were there. But here it's an entirely different frame of reference."

We pass another employee in the hall. "Hi, baby!" she says with a smile to Leslie as she heads on by. The attitudes I see of the employees here clearly seem to support a claim made by the head of the company, the man who first encouraged his employees to return to work with nursing babies. Writing about the success of the program, he reported that "morale in the office seems higher than before the nursery project began — a few of the employees even use break time to hold or play with the babies." Another critical success, he reports, is that "there has been no drop in productivity."

"People love it," Diana comments. "*I* love it. Leslie is so loved here and so cherished, and she knows it. She has so much affection from everyone. The people here are like Leslie's family." For Diana this is of more than casual importance. Even though she hadn't expected it to be that way, she has been basically on her own since she gave birth.

"Leslie's father very much wanted to have a baby with me, but he has trouble with the 'C' word and the 'M' word," says Diana. "Commitment and Marriage. When I told him I was pregnant, he broke out in huge red hives all over his body and disappeared for three days! He has remained in our lives to some degree, but if I'm really honest with myself, I know I'm doing this on my own without him. I have some girlfriends whom I see now and then, and some mothers in support groups, which I think are very valuable. But my own family hasn't been any help at all, really."

Diana has a brother not far away, but her mother and other relatives live in Hawaii. The geographical distance is not all that separates them, however. "I would say that it's a strong stigma that is still in the Asian community about what family is supposed to be," Diana explains. She was born in Hawaii of Chinese ancestry, and the old ways hold fast. "I'm not married, so I have done something 'bad.' They like Leslie — she's a very sweet baby, so there's no way you can't like her — but it's hard for them to accept this. She's outside their experience. It's just not how it's done."

So this place where Diana works has become the family who greets and cuddles and daily shares her baby. She wouldn't have to be a single parent to appreciate that, but it adds a special blessing to her experience as one.

"Before I got pregnant, I had noticed that there were babies around this office building," says Diana, launching into the explanation of how, as an employee of a different company on another floor of the building, she comes to be sitting here in this office. "I'd see them on the elevator, and I kept wondering why. I finally waylaid the mommies with their babies and asked, 'Is there a daycare center here?' They sort of abruptly answered, 'No, there isn't. No.'" Conita joins Diana in laughter. "They seemed to be trying to hide something. It's like they were all saying, 'Babies? What babies?'

"I finally got to know the mothers over time and met the babysitter and took a tour of the nursery here. I thought, This is so wonderful. I also found out why they were so evasive." The head of the company had been greatly pleased at the success of their on-site daycare, and he offered to give lectures to other companies on the model. When word reached the guardians of the city and county codes, an inspector arrived to tell the company that paying a hired babysitter constituted establishing a daycare center in the building, which meant they had to comply with legal codes. The center had to be on the first floor, have running water in the room, have special insurance, and on and on.

Threatened with the demise of their treasure, the forty-five employees of the company — who were mostly women — rallied, each signing up to take care of the babies an hour a week, thus eliminating the contract for pay that was at the base of the problem. The boss was glad to subsidize the program in this way. "But that plan lasted about a week," Conita explains. "It failed miserably. It was just too much for the babies to have that much change in their care. The moms weren't getting any work done. But no one was willing to give up. So we made sure we addressed all safety requirements, and then we were . . . well . . . *creative* in solving the issue of paying for childcare." However, it is due to this creativity that the company must remain anonymous — a statement in itself.

When Diana found herself pregnant and faced with the imminence of the childcare issue, she remembered the creative solution upstairs. Diana approached her law firm — most of whom were men — to propose a similar setup. Three of her colleagues were having babies within a month of each other — two lawyers and a paralegal — and the timing seemed perfect. "The firm's response was, 'No way. We're not having babies here. What if the clients hear them crying?' The truth is, clients don't come in very often at all," Diana comments. "It really was a standard prejudice on their part — that babies and business don't mix."

Diana proceeded to contact the owners of the office building and proposed a regulated daycare center on the first floor. "After several weeks of consideration and lots of questions, they declined, saying there were too many problems with insurance. There is always something. It takes a really strong person to say, 'I'm not going to let the hurdles bother me.' I guess that's what the owner of the business that has the nursery here felt.

"His support was essential, but in my case, really it was the women here pushing for another woman that finally made it work. They had been following what was going on with me as I was trying to figure out how I would take care of my baby when she was born. And they never let up. They said, 'If we can't do it this way, we'll do it this other way. And then if that doesn't work, we'll do something else.' And we worked it out so that I could bring Leslie up here. Even my own law firm came around eventually, letting me move my desk up here to work while remaining with them.

"I returned to full-time work when Leslie was just shy of three months. At first I nursed her every two hours. Now it's every three or four. You'll see me sitting in there at my desk working on things while she's nursing. I can actually dictate at the same time!"

The babysitter comes in to take Leslie, who seems a little tired of sitting in one place for so long. She goes away happily in Hannah's arms. Not long after, the two of them appear at the window that separates the office we are in from the next. Leslie is fast asleep. "I knew she just needed to be rocked a bit," Diana, the proud mama, comments. Diana knows how lucky she is. She nurses her baby, sees her sleep, sees her happy, sees her part of a loving "family."

Conita gets up to answer the phone. When she returns, she explains that it was her kids. "Soccer practice is canceled because it's raining, so we had to figure out when I can pick them up now." Her children were already three and eight years old and enrolled in other primary care by the time she came to this company. But even when they were babies Conita had been lucky. She was still married at that time, and her mother-in-law, who was from Nicaragua, took care of the children when Conita went to work. "It was simply a part of the culture. So my son got all that holding and warmth from his grandmother.

"When my daughter was born, Grandma took her too. I actually asked the CPA firm I worked for by that time if I could bring her in for a while, but they were very offended by the proposal. I was even hassled for pumping my milk to throw away just for my own comfort. It was horrendous. The man who heads this company where I work now was one of my clients at that time, and when he and his wife came up with this idea about letting mothers with babies return to work, I thought, 'See, you *can* mix babies and business.' I applied here eventually because that meant a lot to me."

Even though her children are in grade school, the company's attitude makes a big difference to Conita. "In the former company, if my kids were sick, I was in such a bind because I couldn't use my own sick days to cover. The time wasn't prescheduled, so they knew it wasn't vacation. It's really a problem in a lot of places. The wife of one of my co-workers here lost her job because of what her company called 'an unscheduled absence' when their child had an ear infection.

Here we never have those dilemmas. If Nicky is sick, it's a sick day for me, and I'm home with her."

This solidarity with the family helps to solve another critical challenge of parenting — vacations and school breaks for grade-school children. "During Christmas vacation, both my kids come in on the days I work. There's a room here with a TV in it, and there are the babies to play with. My twelve-year-old, Danny, comes in on days when there are teacher conferences at school. He especially likes it during breaks because sometimes there are a lot of kids here. They hang out in the kitchen or the nursery.

"Nicky, who is in second grade, comes in about once a month. Sometimes she says she has 'mommyitis' and just wants to be near me. I feel like I work so much that it's a good chance to give her a little more time. I set her up with coloring and things to do. And she goes into the nursery and goes out for walks and to the park with Hannah and the babies. Once they all went to a nearby museum together. I love having her here like that.

"Actually, I feel I've been pretty fortunate all along, because at least I had their grandmother to care for them when my kids were preverbal. If your baby is crying when you put them in someone else's care, you don't know how much of it is just the change, or how much of it is that they are being hurt in some way. And sometimes the hurt is not even abuse but simple neglect.

"But here, we all *see* Hannah, the babysitter. We see how much she holds the kids and interacts with them. The moms can pop in at any time to see their children. They're almost in a fishbowl. That makes a big difference in how you feel when you're working. I think the worst part about childcare when they are little is not knowing what is going on with them."

For Kirstin, that would be the very worst part.

◆ REWRITING THE BOTTOM LINE

"It was Christmas and Alexander was three and a half," Kirstin explains. "As I had to do every year, I worked on Christmas Day for my boss and his guests, leaving my son with Grandpa and Grandma, as he called the old couple. Since I was gone during the day, I would always try to make the nights extra-special for him. So that evening we snuggled up together to read some stories, and I asked him, 'How did your day go, honey?'"

Alexander's answer hit her "like a giant lightning flash through my entire body," Kirstin puts it, to describe how she felt when her son revealed the story of sexual molestation he had undergone at the hands of Grandpa. "I believed him instantly. I knew my son, and he did not even know terms and concepts like the horrifying things he was telling me."

The possibility of abuse, physical and sexual, is something that those of us who leave our children with others have to consider. Despite Marian's very careful search for a good preschool for Terra, she later found out that spanking was the method used to maintain the lovely order and attention apparent in the children there. In one daycare center in Minnesota, surveillance cameras and microphones are being installed to assure parents about what goes on there and assuage the caregivers' concerns about being unfairly accused.[38] The extent of the fear and these extreme measures to alleviate it seem equally frightening.

More horrifying is the invasion of our children's innocence. Although evidence shows that sexual abuse is primarily perpetrated by someone close to the child, that very fact can also give us pause in relation to caregivers. As single parents, we may feel that our children are particularly vulnerable. We may have to scramble more often to find substitute care or accept a situation that is less than ideal. Although it can be hard for children in any family to reveal to their parents that they are being abused, one teenager reported that he hadn't told his single mother that he had been molested as a child "because she already had so much to deal with." And also, because we are extremely dependent upon childcare in order to sustain our livelihoods, we may be more likely to deceive ourselves.

"I was instantly mortified when Alexander told me this," Kirstin continues. "I remembered two or three times when I had dropped him off there and felt a great uneasiness. I had even wondered, 'Is something going on here?' Something felt not right. But I would leave him and drive away and make myself forget about it. I remember that thought of molesting would swish through my mind, and I would just quickly go on to forget it. I had to get to work." Listening to ourselves, trusting our gut feelings, is vital. But we can get so locked into the need to earn a living, to the commitment we have to our jobs, that we may hush the voices that warn us.

The next day, when Kirstin reported the story to the authorities, the hell only deepened, ending in a futile attempt to make the couple acknowledge what had happened. She went from full-fledged depression to rage. "I think trying to confront this alone as a single parent makes it twenty times harder," says Kirstin. "I felt so alone." She saw a counselor a few times but couldn't afford to continue. Within a few months Kirstin found a support group. By that time the lid had already been lifted on her own molestation as a child, and the healing of her son would become her own healing as well. "The damage with sexual abuse comes with having to keep a secret. The good thing is that Alexander is not having to do that. We talk about it very openly. Because of that, he will never be as damaged as I was."

Kirstin made it through this tremendous upheaval, but it left her work life in shambles. She limped through the remainder of the season at the cleaning job and then left it for good. "I had to do something different. I was sitting on the couch one night and this idea came to me of starting a business of my own — to give me more flexibility and to have Alexander with me sometimes as well. A lot of people who come here in the summer to climb or in the winter to ski bring their kids and want to have a break. Why not provide it? And I could hire others to do it as well.

"I have had great ideas before that I haven't followed through on. But something drove me invisibly to do this, like a force within me. I thought, 'This is my way to make it work.'"

Kirstin did start the business, and in time it did take off. But she has had to take on several other jobs as well to make ends meet. She cleans occasionally and works part-time in a variety shop. When Alexander started kindergarten, she was hired to do the after-school program. She has even begun making dried flower arrangements to sell at a Christmas bazaar. "It's something I can do at home. It's not what I want to do with my life, but it keeps that creative spark alive.

"The whole cause of this huge shift is that Alexander comes first, before my job and before my career. I *want* to drop him off every day at kindergarten. I *want* to pick him up every day. That's the kind of freedom I want, and if it takes three jobs, juggling around, driving me nutty, then I'll do that. Because when it comes right down to it, what's number one here? For now, my child is still more important to me than my job. That's the bottom line."

If we are to raise our children in a way we feel good about as we work to support them, their care has to be our bottom line. Increasingly, businesses are finding that this value also makes economic sense.

"Our boss brings clients in here and he says, 'Here is the nursery, and here are the babies,' and he is very, very proud," Conita reports. "But when he gives talks on this to businesses, he emphasizes what to him as a businessman is most important — the bottom line. You've got these trained employees, you've invested a lot of time in them, and it's downright stupid not to facilitate their return as quickly as possible."

As the boss tallies the specifics: "It would cost $10–15,000 each to replace these employees. We are giving up about $6,000 a year in rental space to save $45,000 in retraining costs." But this man joins Kirstin on *her* bottom line when he adds, "But there's a much more valuable gain I have made as an employer. These people can't be price-tagged. They are typical of the people in our office that I like to work with and who make our day one of association rather than toil. It's as if a piece of home has been taken to the office." A grandfather five times over, he says that stopping by the windows of the nursery gives him a chance to "look in at a bit of tomorrow."

As more men who cherish their grandchildren make choices in support of their employees, as more women who understand the needs of parents and children move into positions of power in business, as more men care for their children and understand what it means to be a working parent, the face of corporate America will change and more nurseries with a view will fill those windows of the high-rises, humanizing the downtowns of our cities. Slowly it's beginning.

"I ran out to get a bagel for lunch one day," Diana relates. "The man at the counter was irritable, demanding in a surly voice which spread I wanted. When I opened my coat to get at my billfold, out popped a little face and two brown eyes. 'Oh! A baby!' the guy said. 'Hi there!' It was a total change in him. Suddenly he was saying nicely, 'What was that spread again?' and 'See you next time.' Children make us remember what we're doing," says Diana. "They make us remember what it's all about." Diana eventually resigned from her law firm and became lawyer-in-residence for the company with the nursery, "realizing just how important that was to me." She got good child-care. The business got a good lawyer.

For the last seven years, Milton Moskowitz and Carol Townsend have compiled for *Working Mother* magazine a list of the best companies for employed mothers. The first list, in 1986, contained thirty companies. By 1992 the list topped off at one hundred, and literally thousands of firms applied for the 1993 selection. Companies are rated in four areas: level of pay, opportunities to advance, childcare, and family-friendly benefits. The authors write: "Flexible work options — which allow parents to make time for school plays and doctors' visits — continue to multiply, as companies recognize how alternative work schedules can attract and retain skilled people. Working at home, job sharing and compressed workweeks are all on the upswing." Over half the companies profiled in 1992 and 1993 have on-site and near-site childcare centers; the others offer various forms of childcare support, including subsidies, before- and after-school programs, and training daycare providers. It's a small drop, but the bucket is bound to fill. Moskowitz encourages employees to speak up and to organize to get what they want. Changes will happen through the dedication of the parents — single and married — who strive to keep this dream building.[39]

"But you do have to take chances," says Kirstin. "I used to feel that with a child you had to be even more cautious and make sure you had stability. And it's true, taking chances with a child is much more complex than taking chances without one. But now I'm feeling more like I really have to do what's needed and to trust. Because when you're a single parent, flexibility in your job is one of the key things."

In the last part of this chapter, we will look at some of the ways other single parents I spoke with managed to combine work and caring for their children in ways they felt good about.

◆ MOTHERS OF INVENTION

"I didn't want to go out and work and leave my baby for somebody else to raise," says Jacki. She did what many single parents I spoke with found worked for them, throughout the years their children were growing: she worked around her child. "I knew if I went to work in a regular job, it would have meant not being with Piper practically all day long. I started the business so I could work at home and be with her and wouldn't have to put her in daycare." That business — Jacki's Magic Lotion — sustained them for eighteen years. "I'm moving on from that now that Piper has just moved out, but it did what I wanted. It supported us and raised her. We didn't get rich, but we made enough to get by." It was enough to enable

Jacki to take care of her long-awaited daughter in the way she felt best.

Jacki's marriage of nine years had produced no children, even though she and her husband had longed for one. But in one of those "miraculous conceptions," she got pregnant almost immediately after her divorce by someone she scarcely knew. A tubal pregnancy ended in loss not only of the baby but apparently of Jacki's ability to get pregnant at all. "The doctors told me there was no way I could have another pregnancy. I had other reproductive problems, and this had finished it off. I was grief-stricken because I was thirty years old and wanted a child, even if I didn't have a husband. I got really depressed."

Jacki left her home in northern California and headed for Berkeley. While working in a bookstore on Telegraph Avenue, she met an intriguing man, and they started seeing each other. "I explained to him that I couldn't get pregnant, what the doctors had done and said, and that there was no need for birth control." Duty done, Jacki broke down and told him how much she had longed to have a baby. "I'll do some magic on you to get you pregnant," was the man's response. "And he did!" says Jacki, still amazed.

A few weeks later, unaware that her longing had been fulfilled, Jacki left the city and moved into a small cabin on some land near friends. It was the early 1970s and "it was the dream at that time, to go back to the land." Soon after, she found out that she was indeed pregnant. Knowing that her magician had no intention of acting as a father, and not even knowing any longer where he was for sure, Jacki set up a home and prepared to parent alone and figure out how to support herself.

For years Jacki had enjoyed making body lotions for her friends, so she decided she would start manufacturing them out of her house. The months of pregnancy flew by, however, and Piper was almost four months old by the time Jacki was ready to begin the business. "I packed her up and took her down to San Francisco to hunt for plastic bottles. I was so ignorant of the business world that I didn't even know I could get a phone directory, look under 'Plastics,' and have them send me samples. I got a bag of bottles in the city, went home, and filled them with what I had mixed up. It was a very basic process.

"I got a friend to draw me a label, and I copied them and glued them on." Then, with Piper in arms, Jacki peddled her lotion to small stores near her home and in San Francisco. "People actually bought it! Eventually a distributor saw it, and the business grew."

Working around a baby wasn't easy, however. "It drove me absolutely nuts a lot of the time," says Jacki, laughing. "Especially doing the paperwork. I'd be trying to figure out something I didn't know how to do in the first place — like tax forms — and Piper would be wanting to eat, wanting me to play, pulling papers off the desk, knocking things over. I'd have a wonderful typewritten letter and she'd knock baby food all over it.

"I had friends who either traded babysitting or took her on a regular basis as well. That was really helpful. But it wasn't until she was four that I felt like she was finally independent enough for me to feel like I wasn't on call every minute anyway. Looking back, though, I am very glad I did it that way. I felt like I was a good mother and gave her what she needed. And we have a really good relationship. Piper turns out to be quite a capable person. She saw me being disciplined in working, and she is that way. She has been working the last two years, first as a dishwasher and then she worked her way up to being head cook in a very good restaurant. And now she's going to college. I'm proud of her. She's strong, intelligent, trustworthy, very creative. I think I did a good job, and I'm sure I couldn't have done it if I'd gone to work eight hours a day."

Angie's first major step, after her excruciating decision to leave her marriage, was to define the best way to proceed. "I sat down and thought, 'Here I am, with a year-and-a-half-old baby. What are my priorities?' I was fortunate to have a little money, so I didn't need to work immediately. Although earlier a career had been of interest to me — I had planned to take a doctorate in chemistry — by this time it clearly wasn't. Parenting was. I wanted to structure whatever I was going to do around my daughter."

Until China was four, Angie worked as a midwife, which gave her flexible time. China often went to births with her, and housemates and friends with children filled in if necessary. Living with others helped financially, but by the time China was four Angie needed to find a livelihood that would pay more. "I decided on teaching because it meant that my time was basically similar to the kind of holiday time she would have at school. So I went back and got my teaching degree.

"I intentionally chose to teach in an alternative school that was very community-oriented. The staff was part of a support group for each other, and there was a tremendous amount of support for each of the kids. That gave us an additional extended family. China was in my class her whole time through school, until she was fourteen."

While career wasn't of utmost importance for Angie, for Cheryl, the leadership trainer who so carefully chose her daughter's preschool, career was one of the main purposes of her life. In order to cover the unpredictable demands of writing and conducting trainings, Cheryl found another single mother with a daughter to rent the downstairs unit in her house. In exchange for getting a rent reduction, the woman occasionally picked up Sierra at school and took care of her when Cheryl had evening work or an engagement out of town. The arrangement had an additional advantage: the daughter was Sierra's age, and the two girls became like sisters during the course of the time they all lived together.

The combination of accessible help from others and flexible hours at work seems to be optimum. Bryce, a single father, arranged something similar. When he divorced and took on responsibility for his four children, the youngest was seven and the oldest was sixteen. Like Cheryl, he had a downstairs apartment in his house which he rented to a single mother whose schedule allowed her to be home by the time his children returned from school, so at least someone was on the premises.

Realizing he needed to earn more than his job as the director of an alcoholism council could pay, Bryce went into real estate, a career path a number of single parents I spoke with entered for the flexibility it allows. Bryce was able to set up a home office in addition to his office at the company, although eventually he found that "when the kids were home, I had to be somewhere else if I was going to work, because they'd want my attention."

Having that work flexibility allowed Bryce to do the kind of parenting he wanted to do. "I'm a serious parent," he says. "I spend a lot of time with my kids. They know I'm here a lot. Kids make the equivalency between attention and love, and I make sure they all get plenty of both. And that's for me too — I mean, I like them! We hug each other a lot, and we talk a lot."

Part of that talk goes on at meals. Dinner is harder to coordinate with so many different schedules for sports practice and other activities, but Bryce makes a point of always fixing breakfast. "I want to have that initial contact with them every day. It's just about the only time the whole family is together in one place. It means I have to get up an hour earlier, and I spend probably two hours every morning just at that, but it's worth it. We all used to sit down to breakfast together. But now that we have kids going to school at different times every day, first one comes in, then two more, like that. At least I get to see all of them. And I'm either standing there cooking or sitting down at the table with them. But we talk every morning. I think that has paid big dividends in terms of family closeness and keeping things together."

Bryce has also had success with summers. "They were a hard time to handle. But my kids were all school-age by the time I was the parent, so I didn't need to get full-time childcare, even that first summer when David was eight. The woman downstairs was around later in the day, and she could be some support for him. The older kids were there, of course. And all of our neighbors knew I was a single parent. I established pretty close ties with them, and that helped a lot. But I got through the days in a very accountable way. I'd always come home for lunch, every day. That worked really well, because the kids would usually do a lot of lazying around the house in the mornings, and I'd be there just about the time they were ready to go out somewhere. So they could tell me where they were going.

"I also never discouraged them from calling me at work. I felt like I had to maintain that communication and contact, so that we were tied. If they wanted to go someplace, they had to call and get permission.

"The thing that used to drive me bananas, though," Bryce says, smiling, "was when one would call and say, 'He hit me' or 'She's got my beachball.' I'd try to offer some kind of solution over the phone or tell them that if they couldn't handle it we'd deal with it at lunch. That was also an advantage of being able to get home. And because I basically make my own time, I could also just pass through at odd times. So we made it through summers pretty well like that."

Bryce echoes the refrain of the others in talking about the success of his choices. "I just made the decision a long time ago that one of my prime purposes in life was to raise these kids, and I'm going to do whatever it takes. It's more a matter of commitment than of 'how to' — you kind of make it up as you go along, no matter what comes up. I'm committed to my kids taking a lot of my time until they are twenty or so. I have to cut a lot of other stuff out of my life. But I just love 'em."

Raising children requires sacrifice, especially when we do it alone. Like Bryce, we all have to "cut a lot of other stuff" out of our lives. In a system where money means time, that also means that when we cut time out of livelihood and put it into our children, we have less money. As Billy, the carpenter and sculptor we met in an earlier chapter, puts it: "I could go the route of going to work real early and having Aaron in childcare and somebody taking him to school. Then in the afternoon somebody else could take care of him so I could work real late. But it's not worth it to me to spend that time away from him. The whole country is geared toward getting more. I'm not real big on changing other people, but I've got to act the way I believe, and I think unless we start wanting less, it's downhill with the planet. Aaron and I have our needs taken care of, maybe not all of our wants, but we're together a lot more, and that's real important."

"Quality of life," writes Joseph Chilton Pearce, "depends little upon standard of living." While of course galling poverty can truncate the ability to love, Pearce reports that when researchers tested the intellectual capacity of children from countries with a very basic standard of living and compared them with the performance of privileged children from the United States, the former outperformed the latter. It is not material advantage but rather the quality of life — which Pearce says means love and caring — that develops all innate capacities.[40]

Caring for our children confronts us with some basic choices and questions about quality of life. What *is* important for us and for them? How do we care for them? What do we really want for their future? We are engaged in a way of life that has essentially no precedent. Perhaps the most wholesome way that we can build a positive future is to base it on a standard that characterized those societies that endured for centuries, even millennia — the well-being of children.

As single parents we have an advantage. Because we have no illusion that anyone else might be picking up the pieces, we are obliged to be committed fully. Yet we cannot do this alone. Caring for our children is a social issue. Caring for them well while we work can be solved only with the cooperation of government and business. It can be solved only with the involvement of friends, family, neighbors, social action groups.

Certainly we need more and better childcare arrangements. A few major companies and numerous small ones across the nation are discovering the value of on-site and assisted childcare and are themselves granting the paid leave not ensured by government policy. Yet because these benefits must be offered with the best interests of the *business* in mind, the best interests of the children are not necessarily ensured.

However, the basic answers to the questions about childcare do not lie in creating more childcare centers or centers for sick children, or in lengthening the school day in order to sustain the efficiency of the workplace. Those solutions often only more effectively separate parents from children. As individuals, we may be able to make certain choices that work for our families. But ultimately, perhaps the only real answer lies in changes as radical as restructuring the workplace and the workday, guaranteeing flexibility in jobs, shortening work hours for parents, ensuring more generous parental-leave policies, and joining with other industrialized nations to adopt, in addition to tax breaks, other supports for families. To effect such changes requires a transformation in a habit of our culture to act as if we are each an isolated individual, leading a life separate and distinct from all that surrounds us. We are, in fact, intricately connected to one another, and the choices we make as individuals ripple out to affect the direction of our world. Children do belong to everyone, and how we care for them will affect the future of us all. To begin to think in this way requires a monumental cultural shift, but this may actually be the only truly realistic solution.

The "quality-time" argument that supposes we can squeeze our parenting into a couple of hours each night and on the weekend, along with everything else we need to do, is simply another way of quantifying our lives, and it doesn't work. *Presence* is quality time. And presence requires quantity of time. If I were in an adult relationship with someone who proposed limiting our direct interactions to, at most, eleven minutes on weekdays and thirty minutes on weekends, the standard for working parents and their children, I might begin to question whether I was valuable in their eyes or not.

Granted, not all parents are cut out to spend time with children, and good substitute care is their best choice. But if we were to ask our children what they would like, how many of us might hear, as we often do anyway, "I want to be with you"? They like being around us.

Sacrifice for our children doesn't require our entire lifetime. Now that China has moved into her own life, Angie has resigned from her teaching job and is training for a job that will support her priorities next in line — travel and study in India. Jacki, in her third year of international studies, is leaving her lotion business behind her as she prepares for a year-abroad program in South America. Billy is sculpting late into the evening while his son sleeps, and he knows that one day this will be his primary work.

Kirstin is determined, once Alexander is in grade school, to find work that is more meaningful and personally fulfilling than the patchwork that has enabled her to get her son through his early years. As she puts it, "The future will have to include fulfillment for both my son and me and not just be geared to the needs of one. If I deny myself that, in the long run he would be unhappy too."

When we make our children our priority, not only are we doing the only thing that makes the whole thing work, we are also, by virtue of the amount of time we spend with them, developing close companionships. In the next chapter we will look at what it means in our lives as parents when our children become our friends.

CHAPTER 9

◆

When Our Children Are Our Friends:
Love and Limits

Oh, Mama, how can you really say yes,
if you can't say no?
— Eric, four years old

Let your yes be yes and your no be no.
— James 5:12

WHEN I WAS A CHILD my big sister had a bracelet with a golden heart on it that spun on a tiny axis. I was six years younger and everything she owned held important secrets. On either side of the heart were embossed letters, hieroglyphs that made no sense on their own. But when you set the heart spinning with a flick of your finger, a message would magically appear: I LUV U. She'd hold it in front of my eyes and spin out the silent words I fervently hoped she meant. When she was out of sight, I'd quietly remove it from her jewelry box, examining each side of the heart, then set it spinning to watch as the flip sides joined to broadcast their ephemeral message: I LUV U, I LUV U, I LUV U. Not only the mechanics but the message itself mystified me, and I am as intrigued now by what it means as I was then. But now it is my own heart striving to bring flip sides together to convey one message as I am learning what it means to love a child as a single parent.

Raising Elias alone, particularly during the times when we have lived without housemates, I find myself in an intensely close relationship with him. Our love for each other is undistracted and undiluted by the presence of another parent for him or a partner for me. Daily activities I would share with a partner or that Elias might with another parent, he and I do together instead. *We* are the primary relationship in each other's lives.

Elias is the one I spend my evenings with after work. He is the one I please with a delicious dish, and the one I talk with over meals. He is the one I cuddle with to watch movies or to read books together. He is the one who helps me buy groceries, the one I go swimming or bicycling with on Sundays. He is the one I sing with in the car and dance with at home. He is the one I make plans with and around. He is the one I wake to greet at the start of each day and the one who gets my last kisses at night. We have "lovers' spats" and then later we whisper sweet nothings to each other. "I love you more than all our friends and the universe put together," he says in my ear. "And you are the most important person in the world to me," I return. "You're a lovesend to me, Mama," he chirrups, smiling up at me. "And I'm a lovesend to you," he adds, completing the circle. I have known no love like this before, so unquestioned, so encompassing.

And then come those moments when I am compelled by virtue of parenthood to turn and tell him no, to restrict his choices, to go against his will, to draw lines he cannot cross, to don a face and posture that doesn't look like love to him and scarcely feels like it to me. "How do you feel when I tell you to go play because I must work right now?" I ask him. "I feel like you hate me," he says with trembling chin. When I'm holding fast to a "no" for some reason apparent to me, and he, angry but with no one else to turn to for comfort, falls into my arms crying, I experience a painful dissonance of heart. Unless the issue is clearly one of safety, I invariably doubt and question my stance. Am I doing the right thing? Is there a different way? It can be a lonely precipice we stand on.

All parents struggle with these issues of loving and limiting, but within our single-parent family, there is no automatic hierarchy of two adults defining the power structure, there is no one to advise me as to whether I am being too strict or too lenient, there is no alternate support for either of us. Although I am free of conflict with another parent, the conflict takes place within myself.

I never realized until having a child how much of love has to do with limits. I set limits on him for his sake, I set limits on him for my sake, and I set limits on myself for his sake. There are limits which allow us to separate and limits which permit us to be close. My love for my child is an intricate balance of embracing and delimiting. And I struggle with trying to get the overall message to read I LUV U.

Many single parents I spoke with also acknowledged having an especially close relationship with their children. The "boys' clubhouse," as Billy calls his home, is clearly a scene of love and warmth. "Aaron and I take care of each other a lot, and it's really fulfilling. I haven't even missed relationships with women. Psychologically and spiritually, it has been so healing and nurturing to relate to Aaron, and it has been that way right from the moment he was born."

"I'm just in love with her," says Dawn, a young mother of an eight-month-old baby. "I can't even say how much." Married mothers and fathers fall deeply in love with their children as well, but eventually they must turn their love back toward their mates and reestablish that central bond. If they don't, the marriage fails. However, with no other pull on our heartstrings, single parents can flow right into that pure and sweet intimacy we experience with our children.

Uncomplicated by the intricacies and intrigues of sex and romance, our bond with them can allow a genuine love to blossom in our grown-up hearts. Gwen's entire adulthood had been on the fast track. Romantic involvements had never been deep enough to cut through the drive that allowed her to gain success in politics by her mid-twenties. But giving birth to her son as a single parent changed that. "He is already teaching me about intimacy," she explains. "The first time I told him I loved him, it was such a foreign sound coming from my mouth.

"That was a pretty telling moment — sad, sort of," Gwen says quietly, "that I'm not someone who says that much in my life. It just touched me very deeply that it was genuine. And I didn't have to be questioning, as I have so often with lovers, whether or not this was someone I really loved."

Gwen cried when she spoke of love for her child, as did so many other single parents I talked with. Perhaps we cry because love is the standard by which we measure ourselves, the height to which we aspire. "I don't think I really understood love before being a parent," says Madeleine. "I know I didn't. I thought I loved . . ." She pauses, glances away to reflect for a moment, perhaps running through her scrapbook of memories. "And I did love. There's no question about that," she says, tears rising in her eyes. "But when you get to be a parent and you have to take care of somebody, you get to see that love is action, love is doing for somebody else. It's attending to, taking care of, cleaning up after. It's teaching, nourishing, hugging, laughing, crying, being present with and listening, listening, silence and listening to find out what and who somebody else is and what's important to them, what's hurting them, what's pleasing them, what interests them." And all of this attentive presence is not to a mate but to Madeleine's two little boys.

"The relationship between a single parent and a child is something special that you can't really have with anyone else," comments Jacki, who raised her daughter alone from the beginning. Now a young adult, Piper has just made her first move away, to a small city three hours from the home she and her mother shared.

On the wall above the couch where Jacki and I sit is Piper's graduation photograph, crackling black eyes and dark flowing waves scarcely harnessed by the frame. Jacki, quiet and self-contained in contrast, smiles up at the image. "She really has that Latin spark. Her father was half Gypsy and half Indian from South America." When she turns back, I notice for a moment in her own deep blue eyes a kind of wistful joy.

"Piper is just a very special person," Jacki continues. "All these years I knew I'd really have to take care of myself when she left, because I am very attached to her. I've not had any other connection with anybody else like the one I've had with her. Not my husband, not my parents, not my boyfriends. I mean on an everyday level, she has been the main emotional contact in my life."

Piper has not been her *only* emotional contact. Jacki has always had many good and close friends, including boyfriends all during Piper's growing years. Piper herself is an outgoing teenager; she was elected homecoming queen the year after they moved to this town for high school. Energetic and ambitious, she also held a steady job during her last two years of school. But despite their obviously healthy independence, this mother and daughter also had that "something special that you can't really have with anyone else."

Perhaps because Jacki lived alone with an only child, their bond was particularly close. But parents with more than one child have also reported growing closer to their children after divorce. After Nora and her husband separated, she developed real friendships with her children, especially with her three teenagers. "Some of it is due to a kind of emotional honesty that spilled over from the divorce. Some of it is that in the marriage the whole house revolved around what worked for Greg rather than what worked for the rest of us. Now we have open conversations about what's going on with them, about what's happening when I'm not feeling good, and they come to me more easily when they're not feeling so great themselves. It's not that I wasn't close to them before, but now there is definitely a different relationship."

Children of single parents have told me that their parent is like a best friend to them. They direct their unconditional and boundless love toward that sole constant recipient. "If my dad was around, I probably would feel about the same for both of my parents," says eleven-year-old Paloma. She and her fifteen-year-old sister live with their mother, Drusilla. "But since he's not here," she continues, turning toward her mother with a smile and unabashed fondness in her voice, "I kind of picked out Drusilla."

"My mother is a girlfriend, a sister, a person I can count on," says Monique. Her parents divorced when she was nine, and now, at twenty-five, Monique feels close to both of them, but especially to her mother, who was her primary parent. "I've seen her at her absolute worst, and at the same time we are very affectionate. I have some other good relationships — with my fiancé and with a couple of close girlfriends — but the one with my mother is the richest relationship I have. I know her so completely, because she has been so open with me. I think that the best thing a parent can do, even if they screw up everywhere else, is to let a child in on who they are completely. That is what has made me healthy and excited and secure about life."

The structure of our families has a profound effect on our relationships with our children. In the single-parent family, the delightful companionship that can develop between us and our children is one of the benefits of parenting alone. However, the fact that our love is not automatically circumscribed, as it can be by the structure of the two-parent family, compels us to carefully establish boundaries and limitations.

◆ HOW CLOSE IS TOO CLOSE?

As a psychologist and a pioneer among women who have chosen to raise a child alone, Cynthia has paid close attention to the unique relationship she shares with her daughter, Kyra, now nine. At this point, Cynthia notes, she doesn't miss having a partner for herself, nor does she have a particular desire to find one. Kyra is her companion. "We take the most exquisitely fun vacations together," says Cynthia. "Of course they're geared to her age level, but we have the most wonderful times."

One vacation Cynthia remembers, which they took when Kyra was four, was spent living with a Mexican family. It revealed to Cynthia a major contrast between the way she and Kyra relate and the way in which the parents and children in that family related. "One of the things that was so telling for me as a single parent was watching the parents in the Mexican family function as a unit. The children were distinctly of another level — not 'lesser than' but 'other than.' The parents were a tight team, and the siblings hung together and did their own thing. I became really aware of the fact that when you are not partnered, there is a way in which your children psychologically move up into the level of partnering. Kyra and I *are* like a wonderful couple in some ways. You can't fully prevent that, and in some ways it's very positive. But you can prevent some of it, and you have to."

When two adults are partners in a family, they form a strong primary bond that automatically changes the dynamic between parent and child. This is one of the reasons why dating, discipline, and issues of dependence can be so harrowing for single parents. Without that automatic hierarchy, we and our children enter into a dynamic that implies equality.

Sheila raised her first daughter, Hilary, alone while finishing graduate school. Now remarried and a tenured professor, she and her husband are bringing up the child they had together. "One of the major differences I see in childrearing now as opposed to when I was a single parent is that to my younger daughter, Thea, I am clearly Mom, and Mom and Dad take care of Thea. My older daughter really grew up feeling responsible for me. Hilary and I always said we were growing up together." Not only may children with one parent feel more responsible, they also become entitled to more responsibility.

"Now that Greg is gone, I think I also give the children much more say in all of the decisions," says Nora, "from what we should get at the store, to what we will eat, to who's coming for dinner and which of their friends is staying over. Before, I probably didn't do that. There is a way that we run the house now in which the older children are more equal participants. It's their house as much as mine now."

Nora's children are no longer living in their *parents' house,* they are creating a home together. It's a difference that shifts roles and assumptions.

"There is so much going on between the parents in two-parent families, with and about their children, that doesn't exist when there's only one parent," observes Alan, who is raising his two daughters alone. "If something is on the floor in our house, either I have to pick it up or they do. I don't have a spouse to fight with about who is supposed to do it. The kids can't appeal to one parent or the other to do it. It's either them or me. They see their impact directly on me, and they see that everything can't get left to me. If I say, 'Set the table,' and they say, 'No, we're watching TV,' I tell them, *'I'm* not, I'm making dinner, so you set the table.' They can see the whole picture and how they are part of it. There is no model for selfishness."

Recognizing their own importance in creating the family develops a sense of belonging in children and an awareness of their own effect on others. This can be very empowering for them. The psychologist Janet Surrey emphasizes that "knowing how to perceive, respond and relate to the needs and feelings of the other person" is an important part of self-development.[1] In a society where individuality is so highly valued and altruism and cooperation are too often considered out of place, the special closeness we share in our families can be an opportunity for our children to develop a strong knowledge of mutual caring.

On the other hand, this closeness and implied equality can lead to feelings of too much responsibility — emotional and practical — and to enmeshment and misunderstandings. There is great danger for a child in having to feel like "the man of the house" or "the little wife." Cynthia notes, "That psychic partnering is something we have to be constantly aware of as single parents, because it doesn't necessarily give all positive messages for a child. It can not only mislead them about their degree of importance in relation to other people — as parents we are more adoring than they would expect to find in most other relationships — but it can also give them more responsibility than they should be having for our emotions and psyches.

"I feel the need to be continuously repeating to Kyra that she is not responsible for me, but I don't really know if I am getting through. I notice, for instance, that sometimes if I am feeling sad, she tries to fix me in some way. I say to her, 'I can understand your wanting me not to be sad because you love me, but you don't have to fix me. It's really okay for me to be sad. And you don't have to be responsible for how my life is going. You can care about it, but you don't have to fix it.' I try to draw those distinctions between caring for me and *carrying* me. I don't really know how to do that, but that's the best shot I've come up with so far."

It's a subtle distinction, as tricky to define as it is to comprehend. Even if we tell our children that they are not responsible for us, they can still see that they have an impact on our lives. The important point that Cynthia is trying to convey to her daughter is that Kyra has a *choice* in the matter. Kyra's feelings of concern don't mean she must either fix her mother or face failure, but when no other adult is around to deflect the emotional intensity or give support, it is easy for a child to feel compelled to take on the task.

Laurinda's thirty-year-old son, Eric, looks back now at his childhood and remembers "the role I took on from an extremely young age of being a partial parental figure in reverse. I remember it making me feel important and giving me a sense of having a place. It might even have made me feel a little more secure to have such a role. But it also meant I felt responsible for my mother's well-being, and because of her chronic depression, I got into a habit of feeling like a failure because I couldn't make her feel better."

Our children can end up "carrying" us, often without our being aware of it. Especially following a divorce or separation, they see and feel us struggling alone and they want to do something to help. When Elias and I moved out of the home we had shared with several housemates — a difficult change, but not as wrenching as the breakup of a marriage would be — he made playdough figures to keep me company while he was in school. The positive part is that, wanting to feel free to play with others but fearing I might be lonely, he hit upon a plan and executed it. The negative potential lay in the fact that I had no idea that he was worried about me in this way.

Sharon made a surprising discovery when her six-year-old son, Jed, couldn't make up his mind whether to spend Christmas with his father or stay with his mother for his entire vacation. "I kept being supportive, telling him that whatever he decided would be fine with me," explains Sharon. She had thought Jed was simply unable to decide which he wanted to do. A week before Christmas the real source of Jed's dilemma came out. "It turned out he was afraid that

I would be all alone on Christmas and he didn't want me to be sad. So even though he really wanted to go, he wasn't going to in order to take care of me." Once Sharon assured him that she had several great places to spend Christmas, Jed was happily off to see his father. "But I hadn't even known that was what was behind his indecision," says Sharon. At his age, Jed himself may not have fully understood his feelings.

Rick's three teenage children have no trouble pinpointing their feelings, and — to Rick's credit — they also have no trouble letting him know what those feelings are. "We have a real open communication," says Rick, who has been raising his children alone for the past fifteen years. The early days when he returned home from work to bathe and diaper and cuddle have given way to evenings of conversation over dinner. "We talk about everything," Rick goes on. "Sex, relationships, money." He admits that "the kids accuse me sometimes of talking too much about those kinds of things. But I get worried about money, worried about bills, and I talk about that to them. Because I don't have a wife, I kind of use them as sounding boards more often than I should. It's not like I'm really talking to them about it, more *at* them, because there's nobody else to talk to about those kinds of things. But they tell me flat out they get tired of it."

Children can be wonderfully honest in their own defense if, like Rick, we allow them to be. But this is one of the places where setting conscious limits on ourselves may be imperative. When we're overwhelmed with trying to make ends meet, it can be nearly impossible not to talk about it. Our children, however, may feel very vulnerable, aware of their contribution to the burden but with no ability to help solve the problem.

This quandary can be especially overwhelming for our children when our unhealed emotions become a sustained weight on their shoulders. As a teenager, Kelly was filled with a rage she continually directed against Meg, her single mom. When Meg went to a counselor for some advice, he recommended that she try reflective listening with Kelly. He demonstrated the process of mirroring back to the speaker what has been said to clarify needs and avoid an instantly defensive reaction.

The next time she and Kelly had a run-in, Meg began with "I think I haven't been listening to you very well . . . ." Aiming for the heart,

Kelly thrust back, "It's too late now! You were so depressed so much. You never got it that Dad left you."

In the face of the awful truth, all communications skills deserted Meg. She sobs again now, recalling the memory of that moment. "I felt awful," she says. "I knew that Kelly's point was that she had had to take care of me. She had said that before." Maybe what Kelly was also saying now, as a teenager beginning to define her separateness, was that Meg could have, indeed should have, defined her own separateness as well. Meg managed to regain what the counselor had suggested. "I said to her, 'I understand what you are saying, and yes, I was depressed a lot. And yes, you did have to take care of me at times.'

"This is something that happens with single parents," Meg comments, "because your closest tie is with your kids. Your husband or some other close family member or friend isn't there to take care of you by acknowledging your pain, giving you strokes and love. The kids see you unhappy, and they are young and wonderful and they want to help, so they figure out how to do that. But when they get older, they are so angry about it, because it's not their role. *You* are supposed to take care of *them*."

Our children are bound to witness our emotional ups and downs. To a certain degree it is healthy for them to see the full range of human feelings in adults. Even healthier is for them to observe how emotional states change like the weather, and how we can successfully move through them, either with our own tools or by reaching out for appropriate help from others. In lieu of that, however, they do take on the burden. When we are so quick to say "You *make me* so mad" or "You *make me* so happy," how would they not conclude that they too *make us* sad, depressed, poor, or lonely? Without adequate boundaries, and without our taking adequate responsibility for our own states of mind, our lives become enmeshed with theirs in a way that blurs where we stop and they begin.

Lydia was only twenty years old when she gave birth to her daughter, Sabrina. "I looked young and acted young, and so we had a lot in common as she was growing up. But there is a real danger that a symbiosis can develop between a single parent and a child in that situation that is not totally healthy. You have what amounts to buddies." Buddies who encourage and support each other in their lives are no problem; what Lydia feared was the entangled constancy that can develop in which well-being depends upon the presence and emotional state of the other. Looking back, she feels that it was her own "healthy amount of selfishness that made me want to seek male companionship, hang out with my own friends, and have my own life. It kept me from totally falling into making my daughter my main friend."

Lydia works as an administrator at a small private school. "I do see single mothers there who are too close. There is a dependency that develops where the mother has lost herself and she is living through the child. There was one parent, who I think represents the extreme. She had recently separated from an alcoholic partner, and she was so anxious about her child, whose development had been arrested academically because of emotional tension. Sometimes that mother couldn't even separate herself from her child in her talk. She would refer to 'we' when she meant 'I.'

"This is not a phenomenon limited to single parents," Lydia adds. "But if someone's emotional life is hindered in some way, it is very easy to latch on to the child, this creature who needs you so much, who gives you a purpose in life. For that little person to grow up and individuate and separate is such a threat to the well-being of the parent that it is very difficult for the child to become healthy."

Clarifying and sustaining these boundaries, these limits of our own individual lives and those of our children, is such a subtle task that it can catch us unawares. Often we are not sure what has happened until the patterns that were formed in early childhood explode in our children's teenage years. Marian's job had required leaving Terra five days a week, usually from 7:30 in the morning until 6:00 at night. For a few years she added some evenings away on to that while she finished her college degree. With so much time apart, Marian spent as much time with Terra as possible on weekends. How could she leave her yet again to go out on a date or be with friends? So they were tight weekend buddies.

Marian is amazed now to look back and see that for a number of years she virtually never dated, and even when she had the opportunity to spend time with adults, she took her daughter along or refused the invitation. When an aunt invited her one Saturday night to a special dinner, adults only, Marian brought Terra. The other relatives there were couples, all with children, none of whom were at the dinner party. She notes now that "those couples may also have spent long hours working and away from their children but would think nothing of getting a sitter and going out on Saturday night."

A number of single parents told me they simply didn't go anywhere that they couldn't take their young children. For some, that was how they preferred it. For others, prohibitive childcare costs meant that taking children along was the only way they could go anywhere at all. The critical point is not how and when we do things with our children but whether it is clear to both us and them that each of us can also have our own friends. Acknowledging that preference and need, however, can feel like rejection all around.

For Marian, spending as much time as she could with Terra had meant doing a lot of children's activities. "If we went to a movie, of course it would be a kids' movie. And we did other things centered around what she would enjoy. That was fine with me. It's part of the fun of having a child." Marian was also used to being with Terra's friends, driving them places, having them at the house, taking them on outings. In her own mind, Marian was almost "one of the gang." But for Terra, by the time she had reached thirteen, what her mother's role should be wasn't so clear anymore.

"Terra asked if I would like to go to an amusement park an hour or so out of town," Marian remembers. Marian would drive, of course, and they would pick up some other friends of Terra's who wanted to go. "Well, I don't like carnival rides myself, but I thought this would be so much fun for her that I was willing to do it. Why not? We'd done things like this before. I liked her friends, and I looked forward to an enjoyable day.

"We piled into the car and laughed and talked together all the way. I knew all these girls. The difference this time was that two boys from their class were also along. We got to the gate and bought our outrageously priced entry tickets and bounded through the gates together. Just after we got in, Terra turned to me with raised eyebrows and said quite emphatically, 'Catch you later.'" Ten years afterward, Marian still chokes on the words. "It was devastating. I had known I wouldn't be going on rides, but somehow I had thought I would be included. I spent the day wandering around alone, waiting for them, every once in a while catching sight of Terra and a delighted gang of kids leaping past, having the greatest time."

As an individuating teenager, Terra very clearly defined her limits and preferences. But Marian, as a loving and devoted parent with some measure of guilt, had a harder time establishing hers. This would become even more apparent in an episode that happened shortly after the amusement park debacle.

Marian met a man at church who asked her for a date, a rare outing that she was greatly looking forward to. Terra returned from a babysitting job next door in time to see them off. Instead, however, when she walked through the door, she took one look at the date and — it had nothing to do with what she saw — fell flat on the floor, throwing her arms around Marian's feet, wailing, "Please don't leave me! You can't leave me here alone." The date mistook the signal as the protests of a child suffering from extreme abandonment. The evening ended early with no follow-up phone calls. Marian gave up dating once again. "Enmeshed," she says now, looking back on it all. "That's what I call enmeshed."

◆ I SAID NO, OKAY?

When the limits of our individual lives as single parents and children are not clear, we can end up controlling each other, overstepping our bounds, and coming up against some stinging realities. To set limits in any context can signal separations between us and our children that are painful for everyone involved. The closer we are, the harder it tends to be to define separation. This is perhaps one of the reasons why taking on our role as the authority can be difficult for both us and our children, especially in the area of discipline.

"You can't be a dad and be a good friend at the same time, it seems," says Rick. "How can you be a power structure when you're being a friend? I'm kind of juggling one against the other all the time, especially as they get older. I feel like I lose my authority by becoming too friendly. I'm still trying all the time to balance that. I probably let it go too far, then I react and knock it back. It's that old seesaw — I wait till it gets out of control, then I react."

We probably never attain a balance between authority and friendship with our children, and the dynamics change continually as they mature. Cath, the single mother of twelve-year-old Danielle, relates, "There was a long period of time when we were so close I wouldn't have even imagined disagreements between us. When I had to limit anything for her, I hated it. It felt awful. I still have a very difficult time prohibiting or outright denying her what she wants. For example, she called up today and said, 'Mom, can I have a hamster?' I said, 'No, I don't want an animal around right now.' Well, she went ahead and brought one home anyway, and now she wants us to talk about it.

"So much of our relationship has been based on mutual exploration, discussion, and understanding, not on setting rigid limits, that it just seems impossible to start doing that now. I think Danielle might even like me to set rules sometimes — she pointed out to me once that I overcompensate by not standing up for myself. But I think to just lay down the law would be like asking her, 'Will you accept this as a rule now because it might make your life easier?' Even though it actually might, I don't see that she's going to do that."

The psychologist David Elkind, in his book *The Hurried Child,* points out that "authority often exists as an 'echelon' structure that has a natural hierarchy or chain of command." He explains that in a two-parent family, the parents can support each other in their authority; and most decisions are ultimately made by them, even when children participate in the process. In the single-parent family, with no backup for the parent, the *children* become the only ones to support parental authority. As Cath makes clear, when we are used to relating to our children as friends and engaging them in decisions, we are then left with placing them in the almost untenable position of granting us *permission* to take authority: "No, you cannot have a hamster, okay?" "In effect," Elkind writes, "this means that contracts are rewritten so that children are full partners."[2]

At least, that's what it can feel like to them, and the difficulty sets in because in reality they are not. "Yesterday Lana cut her afternoon classes at school," says Hallie. "When she finally admitted it, I told her, 'Listen, I want you to know that it's your job to go to school. I'm your parent, and based on my age and experiences, I'm the person who has to guide and direct you. We're just not equals here. I may not be right all the time, I'm going to make mistakes, but I have your well-being at heart.'

"She said to me, 'No. We are the same here.' Well, sure, we hang out together, people sometimes mistake us for sisters, I'm this kind of zany person. So she ends up thinking like that.

"I told her, 'No, I'm the mother, and you're the daughter. You can talk to me about these things, you can go ahead and get a tutor or counseling or whatever you need, but you can't make decisions that go against you.'

"That's the hardest part for me," says Hallie. "I just want her to be good and skate through, but it's not happening like that. She wants to live on the edge, she wants excitement. So I'm constantly trying to set boundaries and limits, reward her for positive stuff, and tell her what the consequences will be — because I know. I've been there."

When we talk as friends and have fun together as buddies, confusion sets in when as parents we are responsible for teaching and guiding. We may include our children in the process, but whether subtly or overtly, we are directing their course. Assuming that authority makes us different, separates us. Our very young children don't like it any better than older ones, but we have more control over the consequences of their actions. If we must, we can put them in time-out or remove them bodily from the scene of temptation. But as they get older, more independent, and can challenge our authority more effectively, what do we do?

◆ THE FINAL PUSH

It was young Diego who was the first thought in Julian's mind when he woke and his last thought before he slept. At night they lay side by side in their tiny new home. When Julian taught his classes at the university, six-year-old Diego went with him. When Julian decided to leave his profession as an architect to become a therapist, eight-year-old Diego sat in on training sessions. "This kid has had so many hours of observation in therapy that if he ever decides to be a therapist himself he is going to be extraordinary!" Julian jokes. They shared the cultural delights of Buenos Aires, taking in concerts and films together. Julian cooked Diego's favorite dishes and hovered over him happily as his son wolfed them down. When Diego was fourteen, the two moved to Texas, where Julian took a teaching position; living in a new country together only deepened their bond. "There was such a tremendous togetherness between us," Julian comments. Diego, now twenty-five, concurs. "My father was everything to me. He was God."

"I would say to him explicitly, 'Besides being your father, I am your friend,'" says Julian. "I wanted him to feel he could talk to me about things. I considered him my equal, in the sense that as human beings we both had rights. For instance, in the house, he had as many rights as I did. It was *our* house. By telling him that we were equal in our

rights, I wanted to convey to him, 'You are as important as I am.'"
But what Julian said and what Diego heard turned out to be somewhat different, and that difference would prove formidable.

Considering himself a progressive parent, Julian leaned toward the
negotiating end of the spectrum in discipline. He laughs now as he
remembers a favorite story. "Once when Diego was little — maybe
six — he and I were at the university on the way to the class I was
teaching. We were walking through the open courtyard of a building
under renovation. I ran into a friend and we starting talking. The next
thing I know, I hear Diego's voice — far, far away, somewhere. 'Papa-
a-a! Papa-a-a!'" Julian replicates the rising and falling cadence.

"I look up, and there is Diego, leaning down from this scaffold,
twenty to thirty feet above me, and all around on the floor is broken
glass. Oh, my heart!" Julian catches his chest. "I run over and begin
talking up to him, the way I was then, explaining everything. 'Diego,'
I am saying gently, 'now I want you to understand that it's not a good
thing for you to do that.' Diego calls down, 'Do you want me never
to do it again?' I begin to answer, 'Well, I just want you to see how
dangerous . . .' when Diego interrupts me with the no-bull tone of a
six-year-old. 'Do you want me to come down right now and never
do this again? Just say it!'"

Julian smiles and pauses for a moment, his eyes cast down, remembering perhaps that cheeky child who was the light of his life. Then
he meets my eyes with a direct gaze and tells me intently that it's
important for me to give Elias clear directives. Julian goes on, "In
general, though, there seemed to be very little reason for restrictions
or establishing consequences or any of that when Diego was little.
You know, I think at that time I was the only single father in the
whole country of Argentina! People actually used to say that I would
screw my kid up by raising him by myself. I think Diego must have
made a silent pact with me to be this great kid in order to justify my
single parenting.

"So maybe it was moving to a new country that did it," Julian
muses. Not long after their move to the States, Julian fell in love with
a woman, and she and her young daughter moved in with them. "It's
true that my father had always pretty much let me do what I wanted,
but this woman wasn't like that," says Diego. "We were living in the
same house, so she had to lay down some rules. I was a child, and it
was unavoidable. But I was so used to having my way."

Around the same time, Diego began discovering that his peers in the local high school didn't think or act at all like his father. "They didn't want to *talk about* things. What my father had taught me wasn't the *real* world." In many ways the "real world" seemed distant from his father's strong ideals. Julian's tendency to minimize material aspirations began to make the wealthier lifestyle Diego's mother was offering him back in Argentina increasingly attractive. For a teenager in the throes of an identity crisis, the contradictions spelled chaos. Even when Julian's woman friend moved out again, things didn't return to normal between father and son.

"*El infierno puro* — the pure hell of single parenting," says Julian, smiling and rolling his eyes. "Here we had been like friends, such close companions, and everything was changing so drastically.

"One day when Diego was a teenager and we were into some kind of argument, I started scolding him, which had become typical for me." Julian's ideals were eroding under the pressure of raising an adolescent. "When talking didn't work, sometimes scolding did. There I was, shaking my finger at him, doing my routine, almost as if I'm talking to a little boy. All of a sudden I notice that I'm not doing this to *this* size," Julian says, laying his hand on an invisible head that is waist-high, "which I don't like doing anyway. But here I am going 'La, la, la, yammer, yammer . . .' when I realize that I'm doing this to somebody bigger than me. I'm doing it to someone who suddenly, it feels like, is towering above me." Julian bursts into a laughter that brings tears to his eyes. "I immediately changed to my negotiating mode. I tell you, I got scared! The two of us have laughed about that since together."

These shifts as an adolescent grows can feel as sudden, dramatic, and confusing for the parent as they do for the child. "I was in the kitchen preparing dinner one night, and Diego came in and started arguing about wanting this or that. He wanted blue jeans, he wanted money to go out. I didn't have it. I was very much into this thing that clothes were just to cover the body and I wasn't going to support expensive designer blue jeans. But no matter what we were fighting over, it would always escalate and escalate. At one point during that argument, I looked down at myself. I had grabbed the knife that I was cutting vegetables with, and I was holding it like a dagger." Julian makes a white-knuckled fist, the knife almost materializing with the intensity of the memory. "Here I was, someone who had worked very hard at evolving nonviolence in myself, and that was how I was feeling.

"What Diego has done for me, especially during that time, is he has humbled me. I saw things about myself that I didn't know about. I'm a humanist. I believe in the efficacy of nonviolence and communication, confrontation without insulting or hitting. But during that time . . . I would wonder sometimes, 'Who *am* I? This is my *son*. We were friends, and now this.'"

All we want to do is love our children, and then this — this heavy mantle of having to guide, limit, direct. These passionate confrontations during adolescence occur in most families of any structure. But for Julian and Diego no one else was around — no one else to check their feelings out with, no one else to get guidance, relief, or support from, no one else to diffuse the intensity. And the depth of the friendship they had shared only made it harder.

"There were times when things were very difficult between us, and I would just say to him, 'God, Diego, I wish I was your pal and not your father.' As a pal, I could just go along with him. Why not cut classes? Why not get stoned? I wouldn't have to put up that figure of authority. 'But this is the way it is for me,' I'd tell him. 'I'm your father in this relationship.'" But that wasn't the way Diego had heard it before, and he wasn't willing to accept the hierarchy Julian was now struggling to clarify.

"It went on and on, getting worse," Julian continues. "We were standing in the living room having one of these escalating things one evening. The TV was on, but we weren't even hearing it. There we were face to face, screaming at each other, fists clenched. All of a sudden, in just one instant, we both heard some news being broadcast. *Marvin Gaye . . . killed by his father, a minister.* We were electrified. Like this could be us. And it could have been. It could have. We both got that. They were no different from us. We just became mute in the realization, and we stopped. We dropped it.

"When you get that close, all these things come out. It was a frightening time. I remember the scariest part. I remember one day getting to a point of feeling so extremely vulnerable and not knowing what was going to happen between us. That day I found myself feeling no love for Diego at all, feeling like I really could say, 'I don't care, I don't give a . . .' I think that's the scariest thing I have ever felt. It wasn't like being angry with him. It was *not caring*."

"Ambivalence and conflict are woven into the fabric of family life," writes Arlene Skolnick in *Embattled Paradise,* her book on the American family. "They arise from the intimacy and commitment that provide its distinct benefits."[3] Perhaps the greater the intimacy, the more the potential for conflict, especially between an individuating teenager and a parent. And for the parent, not caring feels like the ultimate sin. Perhaps it is the ultimate defense against the pain of inevitable separation.

"Diego had stopped going to school, and I had tried everything in my power as a nonviolent person," continues Julian. The rules of friendship no longer applied, and in the distance that now grew between father and son, Julian resorted to absolute authority. He tried grounding and curfews, which, unheeded, warranted last-ditch punishments, like locking Diego out of the house and forcing him to sleep in the garage. He tried consequences, taking away as many "privileges" as he could, save withholding food and water. He threatened to call the police when he found Diego smoking marijuana in the house again, after having been warned. But nothing worked. "I felt stripped," Julian says, "as if nearly everything had been taken from me. Finally I had no options left except the car his mother had bought him. So I said, 'If you don't go to school, you can't drive the car.'

"'It's not your car!' Diego said. 'You didn't give it to me.'

"'Yeah, but you live here,' I told him. 'This is *my* house, these are my rules.' It had gone from 'our house' to 'my house,'" Julian acknowledges. And Diego hated that. Julian was stripping Diego of the privileges of equality as Diego was stripping him of authority.

Julian continues the story in a soft and strained voice. "He didn't go to school again the next day. When I confronted him, he got very nasty, very provoking. He said something ugly to me." The reins let loose and Julian flew against Diego, pushing him to the wall. "He looked at me, he smiled and said, 'Got ya. You have nothing else to take away from me, and now you've become violent.'" Four days later Diego left.

What had happened to that friendship between father and son? Does such closeness compel such distance? Is it simply part of the trauma that goes along with the teen years? Could Julian have done anything different? Patterns begin early. Maybe it was something that started with Diego calling down from that scaffolding. I searched for clues in the stories of other single parents, trying to fill in this intricate picture of loving and setting limits.

◆ SWITCHING HORSES MIDSTREAM

"I think it's even more important for single parents than it is in a two-parent family to have it established that the parent is the boss, not the child," says Cheryl. "With two parents, you can trade off — one can alternately be the good guy and the other the boss. I have seen that work a few times when Sierra and her father and I have been together for a few days. Even though all children push to be in charge, it's incredibly confusing for them if they are. Worse than that, it's intolerable for the single parent, who already is stretched with limited time, money, and resources. But I've had to learn that the hard way."

Cheryl approached relating to her daughter with the same high ideals that she had brought to her search for the right nursery school. "I always felt it was important to give her choices, to acknowledge that she was getting to be a big girl and had some control over her life," Cheryl explains. "You know, I was being a modern parent, always explaining, always trying to be fair, to understand her point of view. I erred on the side of giving every possible choice. And I guess I did overdo it." Cheryl laughs. "I'll never forget one time we were in line at the ice cream store. I had bent down next to her and was reading off all twenty-one flavors to her so she could make her choice. The man in line behind me said, 'I can't *believe* this.'

"It's hard, I guess, to maintain perspective with our kids. With babies there's no choice. That makes it easier. You give them all the love, you give them everything. They have a need and you respond to it. But as they get older, it's easy to keep on giving and giving. I think between the ages of one and two the shift happens from all needs to increasing wants, but I didn't do too much about it until between three and four. I had a lag period, and that made it hard. I could still see so clearly what she needed in every way, and I wanted to give it to her, especially my love and attention." With no one else around, like the man in the ice cream store, to provide some perspective, "all of a sudden you end up with a real unhappy kid, and you're miserable yourself."

Cheryl, herself a teacher of cooperative leadership, started going to parenting seminars looking for some pointers. But the most effective parenting lessons came from an unexpected source. "This past summer Sierra and I went to the mountains for a few months together. I took along a young woman as a nanny, and she had a completely different style from mine. She had grown up on a horse ranch and was well versed in training horses, and she treated Sierra sort of the same way! She barked orders almost like a drill sergeant, and Sierra would respond."

Cheryl recognized that it wasn't the nanny's authoritarian measures themselves that Sierra was responding to. Rather, it was the nanny's clear inner conviction. "The point is to be clear in your own mind what you want. It doesn't mean I always get it, but I have really raised the odds by being totally clear. I knew I had to do this. Earning a living, taking care of a house, taking care of a kid, I was going crazy with trying to placate or deal with endless demands."

Effective discipline depends a great deal on inner conviction. Another single mother, Lynette, discovered that too. "It was hard for me to make the rules and then do the endless repetition it took to enforce them," she says. "I just hated to see Lisa cry. Sometimes I'd just feel wiped out by the effort and start wondering whether it really was that important that she not throw toys or play with my things." In an attempt to choose her battles, Lynette finally resorted to writing down in her journal the rules which she felt were important. "*I* was the one who needed to know what the rules were," she says.

"I'd read them to Lisa in the morning and in the evening — no throwing things, no hitting, holding hands when crossing the street . . . But interestingly enough, once I had written them down, some of them I never needed to say again. It became clear to me that she could tell when I really meant what I said."

Children read us loud and clear, and they feel every wobble and nuance we feel as we attempt to carve out a comfortable and manageable level of authority. Their ability to play the edge may seem controlling, but it's by pushing our buttons that they discern the limits of their own power. "Having a set of rules to remind me of what my own limits are keeps me from losing it and getting angry because I hadn't set my own boundaries," observes Lynette. "Then I don't have to go through feeling so bad like I do when I lose it. I also give her choices in the process — like 'You can sit here on this chair or you can go up to your room.' But the main point is that I have to be fully ready to accept the rule myself in order to be effective at discipline."

"But to break the bad behavior patterns," Cheryl continued, "required a period of hard separations and crying. I hated to go through that. There were times when Sierra would go screaming to her room when I knew she desperately wanted to hug me. She'd be really disconsolate. But now she can have a time-out and know it's not the end of the world. And I can also start using some of the other cooperative methods, which I prefer, as well. I can acknowledge her feelings so she knows she's heard, and then there can be some decent negotiation.

"I've learned that in my relationship with Sierra I need both ways of relating. In the leadership trainings I talk about them, in fact, as the 'command-control model' versus the 'cooperative model.' There has been a lot of the top-down, ordering-around model in all relationships in our society, and the cooperative system is now growing in demand. But you need both. There are times in every situation when you have to say, 'Do what I say.' I found that if I was always being the cooperative friend with Sierra and then suddenly tried command control, it didn't go over very well. I've had to change my preferred style somewhat. And it's been very successful. It's now clear to her that no amount of crying or whining or bad behavior is going to get her what she wants. What a relief!" says Cheryl. "We're both much happier."

♦   GETTING IT TOGETHER

After that ultimate confrontation Diego returned to Buenos Aires to live near his mother. Over a year passed before he would even speak to his father again. It took another couple of years before a death in the family got them across a table from each other. And another four years lapsed before they spent any extended time together again. Diego's wound was still gaping, and he wasn't going to let his father miss that fact. Then, finally, when Diego was twenty-four he paid an extended visit to Julian. During the six weeks they lived under the same roof together again, they laughed, cried, and fought their way into a new world.

I first spoke with Diego shortly after he had arrived for the visit, and he still seemed to wear the face and shoulders of a teenager. As he recalled the years of growing up with his father, what struck me was how often he spoke of feeling betrayed.

"Many times my father said to me, 'I'm your friend as well as your father.' His preaching was 'I respect whatever you do, you are your own person.' But then I saw that that was not true, and it became a lie to me. Things in the household went as *he* said. Things in my life went as *he* said. He was controlling the household completely, and he wanted to control me."

It wasn't that Julian hadn't been sincere, but there did seem to be a confusion about friendship and authority between them. And a teenager who had "pretty much had his own way all along" wasn't suddenly going to submit to parental authority, particularly when he was used to assuming equality.

"Maybe having some conflict is inevitable," comments Diego, "because there does have to come this separation. You have to have it to establish yourself as an individual. But with me it came so hard because his preaching was 'I respect what you do, you are your own person,' and then I saw that that was not true.

"God knows what my kids will be doing when they're in high school," says Diego, smiling. "There are no rules for parenthood, so I don't know. But in my own experience, once a kid is fifteen or sixteen they are just not under your control anymore. You may expect them to go to school and not smoke pot in your house, but you can't expect them not to smoke if they choose to outside the house. Control doesn't work.

"I'll tell you what would have been helpful for me. Engaging my participation in solving the problems would have helped. Acknowledging the problems would have helped, and warning me that there will be some drastic measures if certain things happen again — but doing this very clearly before everything blows up in your face. Saying, 'These are the rules of the house' — not 'my house' but '*the* house' — and 'if you don't respect them, you can leave.'"

The external "authority" that both parent and child must bow to is valuable in diffusing power struggles. It is easier to break a stalemate when a *timer* goes off after five minutes to signal the end of time-out, or when a *signed agreement* specifies behavior, or when, as Diego points out, the *house* has rules.

"But for me," Diego points out again, "it got to that crisis point mainly because he told me *he* was not making the rules in the house, that we were *both* making them. But that was a lie."

There are layers of complexity in every story. Julian actually remembers trying out everything Diego now suggests. The betrayal that

Diego genuinely felt was not devised but rather arose from the errors and misunderstandings so woven into any parent's attempts to love. The significant point here is Diego's suggestion that absolute limits might have been easier to deal with than a misleading idea of equality. Parent and child "do not make a fifty-fifty relationship," Diego says now. While discovering the world together is one of our shared joys, learning from each other in this area of communication and discipline is one of the hardest parts of being in a family.

"You really can't count on any particular method to guarantee results," Julian comments. "You have this monumental task, and you're the only one to do it, so of course you give it everything. And of course you and your children get very, very close. These kids are our lives. That closeness is part of what causes the intensity of the conflict. But is the answer that we shouldn't get close to our children? Of course not. And of course they feel betrayal. When they're little, they think we can turn day into night! And then we're the only one to blame when we can't.

"The way I see it is that Diego needed to push that hard at the end precisely because we were so close. It was like a birth. You can study Lamaze breathing techniques or any other methods in preparation for labor, but when it comes down to it, birth is usually extremely hard."

During those six trying and sometimes explosive weeks together, Diego and Julian hammered out their new relationship. Every day brought a new confrontation, some days a new resolution. Gradually the pouting teenager in Diego's face disappeared. "We said good-bye at the airport," Julian relates, "and I watched him walk to his plane. It had been a boy who came, and it was a man who left."

Diego is now, of course, no longer under his father's control, so the rules of equality are more realistic. Yet so too are the differences more easily accepted. "I love Diego as a person and as a friend," Julian affirms. "It is very important that we develop that friendship. But I will be his *father* always. By that I mean, if I see him doing something to himself I consider harmful, I am going to tell him. I am going to be there with unconditional love and truth he can count on." Maybe in this formulation true friendship and good parenting meet.

In this area of discipline, as in other areas of family life, we as single parents are forced beyond the traditional modes. Our circumstances compel us to discover methods of discipline that encompass the equality implied by our family structure and the authority required of our parenthood. Research shows that single-parent families often allow early autonomy for adolescents and utilize a permissive mode of discipline. As we know, both of these can result from lack of time, energy, and resources as well as from a different dynamic between parent and child. Some of these circumstances we can do little about; others we can work to change.

The fact that permissive parenting is associated with poor school performance in children of any family structure offers a direction to pursue. Interestingly, the mode of discipline used in families of children *most* likely to do well in school sounds much like Diego's proposal. Defined as *authoritative,* as distinct from authoritarian, this style emphasizes setting clear standards for our children, expecting mature behavior, firmly enforcing rules with established consequences, encouraging independence and individuality, openly communicating with our children in ways that encourage discussion and negotiation, and recognizing and respecting the rights of both parents and children.[4]

Individuation isn't something that happens only at adolescence. It starts at the moment of birth. And learning how to lovingly express limits is something we learn anew each step of the way. Madeleine, whose two sons are now school-aged, wisely observes, "I find there's a great taboo on not knowing how to discipline your children. You're not supposed to not know how. You're somehow supposed to produce, without a great deal of work, children who behave according to the custom of the area you're living in, with impeccable table manners and no desire to beat up on other kids. I think the biggest thing that helped me is to realize that I don't know everything. It's the safest premise as a parent." It's a process of discovery, one in which, as single parents, we have a good opportunity to engage our children.

When Sheila was raising her first daughter alone, there were times, she recalls, "when I would look at Hilary and say, 'I've never been a parent before. I don't know what to do. You are throwing a temper tantrum, you want to do this, I want to do that. I don't know what the heck to do. Maybe you can tell me!'

"Sometimes Hilary would go away and get it together herself. Or she would come and say, 'Okay, Mom, let's see. Can we figure this out like this, this, and this?' Then I could say, 'Okay that's a good idea, let's do that.' What it developed in her was a sense that if she knew she wanted something, she had to figure out a way to get it. She had to come up with some ideas that worked for both of us."

That defines the ideal — something that works for both of us. Do we all have to go through the radical separation that Julian and Diego went through? Will we all inevitably find ourselves abandoned abruptly by our teenagers at the gates of the amusement park? One single mother who survived the teen years with three daughters testifies, "Nobody warned me how difficult it was going to be. With the second two it wasn't as much of a shock, but I don't think it matters what you do. It's a hard time. It's so hard on them, and so hard on the parent." Still, is there a way we can learn to define our limits and pass through that birth into a new relationship without limiting our love?

◆ LIMITLESS LOVE, LOVING LIMITS

Right from the beginning, Angie and her daughter, China, were very close. Angie taught in the same alternative school China attended. "In fact, China was in my class her entire grade-school segment, so our lives were intermeshed. We were together all day. We even ate lunch together. Until she was fourteen, China watched me play with other kids during the day, and I played with her. For a lot of kids, starting at five, their lives go in quite a different direction from their parents. When she and I came home, it was from the same environment."

Whatever methods of discipline she might use, Angie wanted to ensure that they took the unique needs and qualities of her daughter and their friendship into account. "What I wanted for China was for her to be an empowered person. To me that meant allowing her to make a lot of decisions early on in life, even little decisions that normally parents take away from their kids. Generally, for my discipline style, the line was safety, physical or emotional. If her decisions ran counter to my own ego, that's when I would pull back and let her do something that might seem unusual but not dangerous. I was very clear in myself about the qualities I wanted to nurture in her — that she would become really independent, that her creativity would have a free range of expression, and that she would know that she was really loved in whatever she did."

Respecting China's choices extended into many areas of their life together. "She had a lot of say about which house we bought when she was twelve, for instance. A lot of decisions we made were fairly equal. But along with that freedom came the responsibility of maintaining the setting." All along, greater responsibility for China accompanied greater freedom of choice.

Whether they were sharing a home with housemates, as they often did, or living together as just two, they held weekly family meetings. "We would spend a lot of time at a meeting acknowledging each other for the things we appreciated. And we would also talk about chores, what needed to be done and who would do them. Starting at ten, China was responsible for cooking one meal a week, and that increased over time. Whenever it looked like she was able to take over a part of her life that had been one of my chores, we made the transition. So by eleven she was doing all of her own laundry. Maybe it was because it was an expectation from such an early age, but it was explicit that chores went along with greater say in how things went in our home.

"With China helping to get things done, it also meant I had more time to spend with her. So that was a good motivation for her. However, she certainly didn't willingly and automatically do every chore she had. We tried different methods to help with that. For a period of time we had a job chart up on the refrigerator, but she hated that. She felt as if everyone who came in the house knew how she was doing. So we stopped it."

China even contributed solutions to the clashes that inevitably arose between them. "I always tried to make sure that the consequences of her behavior were 'natural consequences,'" says Angie. "And we argued a lot about what they might be. It was really important that we had the space in our relationship to have discussions like that."

One of the classics — getting out the door on time in the morning — became a major issue. "Tomorrow I'm going to leave at eight o'clock regardless of who's in the car," Angie finally told her daughter. China protested that the consequence — having to take the bus — wouldn't work because she wasn't old enough at ten to do that. "Okay," Angie said to China, "can we arrange that you go to the neighbor's? Or what are the solutions you can find if I can't? I still need to leave on time, and it's still stressful for you." China did, in the end, decide to learn how to take the bus.

"But the main point of all this," says Angie, "is that through discussing a problem, we could hear why it was a problem for us. Instead of getting madder and madder, she would hear why it mattered so much to me to get to school on time, rather than thinking that I was just unreasonable or authoritarian. I can't emphasize talking enough."

Talking, discussing, arguing, deciding — Angie says unequivocally that "the key to the success of our relationship was that we both had the habit of dialoguing." When the hard times came along in China's adolescence, that would be one of the major factors that would carry them through.

"Starting around fourteen, China really pushed me away to create her own space," Angie goes on. "I responded with deep hurt more than anything. I'd walk through the door and she'd say, 'Oh, God. You. Home again?' It was really hard because we had been so close. But a few things brought us through that very hard time. Just hanging in there, of course, as well as my own practice of meditation and inner work every day that helped me disentangle and let my own anger and resistance go. But two other elements were indispensable: community and, of course, communication. Underlying that hard time we were still talking all the time."

It wasn't a skill that just came naturally to Angie; she worked at it. "First of all, the school I taught in emphasized interpersonal communication skills. The kids and teachers spent a lot of time practicing, making sure they knew how to ask questions, how to state what their feelings were, how to claim ownership for their own feelings.

"I also took a lot of different courses, like Parent Effectiveness Training. I had to learn all those basic formal skills. One of the most critical ones was owning my own feelings and making 'I' statements. I learned how to make clear what my feelings were and say them without blaming China. The other part, which was probably the hardest for me, was learning to listen without presenting my viewpoint. It didn't always mean saying yes to what China was saying, but it meant receiving it with an open heart and in an undefended way, and also allowing her to have her different viewpoint.

"I had a fairly authoritarian upbringing myself and I knew I didn't want to repeat that with China, but I had to really work at developing a different way. In parenting we're undertaking one of the biggest jobs we do without much explicit training. Communication skills are parenting skills and probably the most important ones we can have."

So it turned out that even in the midst of some of the most painful times, parent and child continued to communicate. "One time when China was seventeen, she had been out until five in the morning," Angie relates. "In high school she had had curfew hours, but now she had graduated and was moving into another phase of growing up. When I asked her where she had been, she was infuriated. She thought that at her age it was an invasion of her privacy. By that afternoon she had packed and left. However, she came back every day to feed her horse and to let me know that she was okay. She wouldn't tell me where she was, because she wanted to drive home her point, but she also made sure I wasn't in agony.

"After about a week of this, I said one afternoon when she was back that I really needed to talk about this. We spent about four or five hours going through how she felt and why it was so hard for me to let go of my concerns out of fear for her safety. We ended up coming to a new agreement. I had to look at the fact that part of letting go as a parent is that I wouldn't always know where she is. I had wondered for a long time at what age you let go of that, and I finally had to say we'd come to that age.

"That sense of what is empowering to them shifts as a child grows up. As a parent you have to keep shifting with it. It's never stagnant. Being her only parent, I found it especially hard because I felt so totally responsible. I'm a fairly in-charge and controlling person, and ultimately I had to look at parenting as letting go of being in charge."

The second major element in their lives that padded the impact of that furious adolescent struggle to separate was community. "Living with someone else was critical to the success of our relationship throughout childhood and particularly through the teenage years," says Angie. When China was twelve, some good friends, a married couple, moved in with them. "I know that because we weren't living in isolation, we didn't become convoluted. We had some way of maintaining perspective. I had somebody to talk to; China had somebody to talk to. It kept things in balance.

"We were also fortunate that our friends were people with wisdom, so they did not take sides. When China and I were sorting out something, we might independently talk to either one of our house-mates, and they would never say, 'I think you're right and she's wrong.' There were certainly times when China would say, 'You adults all think the same way,' or she would feel that. Or one of our housemates might echo something I had said. But there was always the sense that in the midst of working out what we had to between us, there were supportive people there for both of us.

"Sometimes one of them would say to me, 'It sounds very difficult right now. Why don't you just go sit and meditate for a while.' Or they'd ask me, 'Do you remember a time like that before when it all seemed so hopeless?' And it would take me out of the tunnel vision of that particular incident. I'd remember, 'Oh yeah, this will change. I can probably count on that.' If we had been on our own, it would have been easy to magnify a lot of situations which were diffused by the presence of other people. Often just having the chance to say to the others what was happening could diffuse a conflict."

Research indicates that "additional adults in single parent households do indeed reduce adolescent deviance."[5] As we saw with Angie and China, having housemates gave both of them support and also provided perspective during conflict. It offered China adults other than her mother as role models, and it gave her the opportunity to observe successful adult interactions, in daily life and during house meetings.

Using authoritative discipline, learning good communication skills, and involving other caring adults in our daily lives are all ways to support loving interactions between us and our children. The common message these elements convey to our children is that they are worth adult time and attention. As Rick puts it, "Attention is love, and you can't give them enough of it. It's the one thing I could afford to give my kids."

This is also why our being nearby, even without interacting, is so important. In his list of what he considered helpful for teenagers, Diego included "having somebody at home." He goes on to explain his reason: "When you're a teenager, you're really still a child, trying so hard to be an adult." But with the pressures many of us have in our daily lives, offering our presence can be hard to do.

Madeleine found that she just had to set aside a specific time to be available for her boys. She unplugs her phone every evening from 6:00 to 9:00. "I also don't have dinner parties unless everybody coming over wants to focus on the boys. Children need so much attention at that time. Not just my kids but all kids."

Madeleine refers to that bedtime period as "the cosmic hour." She reads to her boys, rubs their backs, tells them stories about what happened in her day or when she was a child herself. "It doesn't matter what I say especially; it's the sound of my voice talking about something important to me in a very soft, easy, truthful, kind, and generous way that's very comforting to them.

"I also think that it is really important for them to be able to communicate their love and care for me. This is the time when that can most easily come out. I think a lot of the reason for distress at bedtime in children is that there is nobody around to listen to these extraordinary, deep thoughts they have, deep concerns about each other and the universe and about love in general."

Children are extraordinarily deep. I still recall my feelings as a child, contemplating the magic words on that golden heart spinning in the air. It's love that is the heart of the matter, and what an extraordinary balancing act it takes to convey that.

◆ THE CONDITIONS OF UNCONDITIONAL LOVE

This unmitigated love affair we have with our children insinuates itself into our lives so deeply and naturally that sometimes we cannot even see how encompassing it is, how close we are, how close it allows us to be — and how different that might be from other families around us. So many single parents "confessed," fearful of misunderstandings prevalent in our culture, that they shared their beds with their children, for instance. While all children seem to love climbing in with their parents, most partnered parents in our culture sooner or later make very clear to their offspring just to whom that bed belongs. Many single parents, on the other hand, say, "It seems so strange to have each of us sleep alone. Sharing a bed is a way to give my child the presence I can't otherwise. Why not cuddle?" Depending of course on the ages and sexes of our children, it can be hard to come up with reasons why not. And so the closeness of the day spills over into the night.

In the current climate of our culture, which is so conscious of sexual abuse and its damage, red lights can flare when we speak of intimacy and love in connection with our children. Establishing absolute sexual boundaries is one of the ways in which we must circumscribe our relationships with them. Still, we *are* physically intimate with our children. Colleen, who is a pediatrician raising her son, Simon, as a single parent, draws a careful distinction between sexu-

ality and sensuality. "Our relationships with our children are very
sensual," she says. "The delight we both experience in touch is an
essential part of their development. Massaging the soft, tender bodies
of our babies tells them we love them. Simon is eight years old and
still loves back rubs. It calms him and gives him a healthy contact
between us that is nonverbal and reassuring. And I still love to touch
his warm little back and hold him close."

Starting with birth, our children are intimately connected to our
bodies as women, especially if we nurse. In our puritanical culture,
the fact that some nursing mothers experience orgasm when they
begin nursing their babies is a secret sparsely revealed. For a married
mother this might be confusing, but her sexual impulses are clearly
defined by having a mate. For a single mother, alone with her baby
night after night, this can lead to a terrifying fear of being deviant.

One single mother, Sophie, confides that she also "had several
dreams when Trevor was younger of us making love. I had one of
him at about two years old in which I actually climaxed. I felt really
guilty about even having such a dream. I finally mentioned it to
several people, who all admitted that they too had had erotic dreams
with their male children. I think it must be very natural."

These fears can be particularly prominent for parents raising opposite-sex children. But we are sexual beings, as are our children,
increasingly so as they mature. What happens when we alone are
available to provide guidelines for appropriate behavior, or information and support through critical phases of puberty? "Go ask your
mother" or "Go talk to your father" is often not an option for us.
While some single parents feel at ease in talking about sexual issues
with their children, others, like Alan, already feeling uncomfortable
in "a world of women raising children," found his first daughter's
menarche in some ways perhaps more trying than she did.

"I was and still am shy and uptight about discussing sexual matters
with my daughters. I used to worry when they were little, 'How am
I going to handle puberty?' And actually — despite excellent education programs at her school — the actual moment when she began
menstruation was quite traumatic and upsetting to her. She was too
embarrassed to tell me what was going on, but I was able to surmise.
I thought, 'Oh why can't she have her mother here to help with this?'
Here was a classic mother-and-daughter moment and all I could do
was kind of wring my hands. I didn't want it to be a traumatic event,
but I didn't know what to tell her. Somehow we passed through that,

and now she's more comfortable with it. She'll tell me, 'I'm having my period and that's why I'm not feeling well' or something like that."

It is in the everyday moments of our home life that we find ourselves in situations that can seem magnified by the absence of a partner. Colleen describes one night when she and her son, then five years old, were sitting on the couch together, watching a television program. Simon began to masturbate, something relatively new for him to do intentionally. He turned to Colleen and said, "Mom, give me your hand. I want you to feel this. Touch me." Colleen froze.

"I know it's common practice to sexually stimulate babies in some cultures to comfort them, but it hadn't been part of my culture!" Colleen says. "And it wasn't about to be." Colleen explained to Simon that it was all right for him to touch himself but not appropriate for her to do so, and that it is better to do that kind of thing in his nice cozy private bedroom. "I didn't want to convey that there was anything wrong while at the same time I needed to make it clear that this was not something like me giving him a back rub."

Similarly, Sophie describes a Saturday afternoon when Trevor was seven. "Trevor called me over when I walked through the room where he was watching a movie. 'Mom, how come every time that girl walks across the screen, my penis wiggles?'" Sophie was not going to say, "Call your grandfather to talk about it." "'Um,' I started, trying to think fast. At that age, Trevor didn't know yet about sexual intricacies. I had to give him an answer appropriate to what he knew. So I said, 'She's a beautiful woman, and that's a natural response in a man. When a boy gets to be a man, when he sees a woman he's attracted to, it makes the penis feel alive.' He said, 'Oh, how interesting,' and that was that."

Sophie feels that it is important to convey to her son that he can freely speak to her about sexuality — that it is not off-limits between them. "I have not always waited until he asks about some things," she explains. "They already learn so much more about it at school than we're aware of. And sometimes it is hilariously, but potentially dangerously, off base."

As our children blossom into sexuality, becoming more private about their bodies, establishing physical boundaries, not wanting to be kissed or cuddled, we face a loss of one of the sweetest parts of our relationship. But our greatest love at this point is to honor the limits. "Sometimes I wish I still had a little boy who I could just cuddle," Jane Anne admits now that Jonah is seventeen and soon off to college. "I wish I could come home and just crawl into bed with him sometimes. I can understand the urge parents have to keep their children bound to them."

Lex has shared parenting of his daughter, Shana, for the thirteen years since his divorce. Watching her flower into a teenager, he went through an awkward period of time as he began to shift his behavior toward her. The little girl who used to cuddle on his lap and run naked from the shower to her room was undergoing vast physical and emotional changes which both of them had to keep up with. "I'm still her main squeeze," Lex says, "but I find that I don't kiss her on the neck anymore like I used to when she was younger, and in lots of other little ways we're a bit more distant." To make sure Shana didn't feel less loved by him in the face of these limits, Lex had to look for new, more appropriate ways of expressing his love for her.

Our children themselves will usually clue us into their emerging needs. "When he was about seven, Jed started closing the door of his room when he dressed, and I started closing mine," explains Sharon. "It just naturally developed."

Limits on our sensual intimacy are a part of letting go as our children move on into their lives. Many single parents with grown children report that even though the emotional intimacy and affection they had shared earlier went for a bumpy ride during the teen years, eventually they met anew to share affection as adults.

In a letter to her mother during the first year after China left home, she wrote: "I really am lucky. I am realizing there are very few people I can talk to about meaningful, important things. I'm so glad you are one of them. You are a teacher, a mother, and a best friend, all in one. I think it's a reflection of how well and differently you raised me from how you were raised in that as soon as you became independent and left home, you formulated a whole new code of values and life's purpose from that which you'd been raised with, where now that I'm starting to become independent, I'm realizing the truth of the ones I was raised with."

Our children may indeed be the "greatest love affair" of our lives, as Germaine Greer suggests.[6] Our love for them may be the closest we ever experience. Yet, with all of this passion and intensity, that love is circumscribed in so many ways. And in the end, all the love we give them is only to let them go.

CHAPTER 10

◆

Dilemmas of the Heart: Dating and Seeking a Partner

I wouldn't be attracted to someone who didn't adore my child.

— Julie

IT'S SUNDAY AFTERNOON AND Elias has fallen asleep next to me, his face nuzzled into my neck, his small hand resting on my heart. Lying together like this, so close, I catch the fragrance of his warm breath — peanut butter and jelly — and for a moment I feel wistful at this fleeting scent of childhood. As we lie there, our breathing falls into rhythm. This may be as close to the ease of love as two people can get. Complete, fulfilling. But this is not the love that has been sung and celebrated through time. There is another kind of love my heart can remember, similar in essence to what I feel for my child but so different in expression.

Long before I gave birth to Elias, I used to think that a child would be secondary for me to a partnership, the fruit of our love. I assumed that the love my partner and I would share for the child would increase our love for each other. But in my mind, the partner and I would be the "we," and the child would extend from us and be held by us. As a *single* parent, I and my child are the "we." He is my primary relationship. It's not that I am a single person who happens to be a parent; I am a parent who is single. That's the order it goes in. And just as every aspect of my life as a parent is lived in reference to my child, any new love who may enter my life during Elias's growing years will also have to be in reference to him. That changes everything.

"Mama, what does 'single parent' mean?" Elias asked from the back seat of the car one day as we were doing errands. Ever since he was about a year old and I started working on this book, he had heard the term in interviews and conversations. He was nearly four now and it had never occurred to me that the meaning wasn't obvious to him. In fact, he had informed me not long before — one evening when he wouldn't come to dinner because he was "working," pounding away on a toy keyboard — that he was himself writing a book on single parents. I figured he had a lot to say about the parenting part. And I had just assumed that the single part was clear to him from our friendships in various families, some with one parent, some with two.

But he was asking, so I answered, trying to keep the definition simple. "It means a mother or a father raising children on their own."

"No," he said, "that's not what I mean. What does *single* mean?"

"Oh. Single. Uh . . ." I began, tripping over the functional reality of who I had become as a parent and the memory of myself as a woman who once had, and perhaps one day again would, love someone in that intimate, vulnerable, frightening, and fulfilling way we call *relationship*. "Uh . . ." Elias was still waiting. Keep it simple, I told myself. "Well, most people . . . no, *many* people like to have another person in their life they spend time with. Someone who is very special to them. That's their partner. So if someone has a partner, they're not single."

There was a long silence in back. Then, hitting little high notes of delight, Elias said happily, "That's like you and me. *We're* partners!"

Another little fissure opened along that crack in my heart that seems to come with loving a child. "Oh, sweetie . . . We *are* partners in a way. We're buddies, and we are very special to each other. But big people like to have other big people for partners. Like Laurinda and Ted, they're partners," I offered, naming two of our housemates. "And sometimes two women are partners and sometimes two men —"

Elias interrupted, "But you don't have a partner then."

"No, I don't," I answered, wondering for a moment if I should feel lacking in something. "I'm a *single* parent."

The term has a double meaning. It means we're raising children on our own, without the day-to-day presence of another parent. But it also means, as Elias pushed me to define, that we are raising our children as single people, as opposed to married or partnered. In some ways our children do become our partners, the main emotional contact in our lives. Relating to them can be not only consuming but also very fulfilling. As Billy says, "Aaron takes care of a lot of my need for relationship and affection. So I don't feel a need to go out and date or find someone. I have enough going on here after work with Aaron, and with my music and my carving. For the first time in my life, I'm feeling fulfilled and not expecting a relationship with a woman to fulfill me. It might be nice if I met somebody, but I'm not into going out and looking for a stranger to be my friend."

As human beings we need connection. We need to belong to something or someone. We need to love. While there is a strong compulsion for that connection to be with an adult intimate partner, many single parents would agree with Billy that the bond with their children can be deeply fulfilling. In many ways it satisfies our criteria for true love. We trust each other, we adore each other, our relationship is long-term and committed. Even when they leave, we know the love will not end. Now that I have Elias, it's a love I know I missed all my life.

Yet sometimes we can get to missing that other kind of love. And when we set out to look for it, the unique reality of our situation strikes us immediately.

"I don't even know how to describe myself to women I meet," says Denny, the part-time father of two boys. "I usually say, 'I'm single — with children.'" We are single but not unattached, and that fact has a profound effect on whether we date, whom we date, when and how we date, and what it means to enter an intimate, loving, and sexual partnership again. To an undeniable degree, we are already "spoken for," committed, even partnered; we no longer are single-hearted.

"Single parents deserve to have a romantic life," Tracey declares, "and their children need to see them having loving relationships. I've seen far too many children get enmeshed with their parents, and the child becomes the be-all and end-all for the parent. I don't think that's healthy for anyone. But it's tricky to have relationships. As I have found out, you have to be extremely careful. When I broke up with a man my sons had gotten really attached to, my kids were the ones who suffered the most. I can't just willy-nilly jump into something with someone anymore like I did before I had children. Now it isn't just my own heart I'm playing with. It's also the hearts of my children."

Some single parents, like Tracey, find it important to date and have partners. Some, like Billy, aren't looking for now — which doesn't mean Billy is emotionally enmeshed with his son. It means that he has found freedom from feeling compelled to have a relationship with a woman to fulfill his need for connection. Not dating can also be a healthy choice for both parent and child.

Sophie deliberately chose not to look for a partner until Trevor was five years old. "For one thing, I didn't want to do a rebound. I knew that any relationship I would get into right away would bring up all my anger with my ex, and I didn't want to work through all my stuff about relationship when I had a child in his formative years. They sense too much. But it was not a supreme sacrifice just for the sake of the child. It was also for me. It was a good opportunity to be on my own and at the same time give him as much as I could. I dated once in a while, but it wasn't a major part of my life during those early years."

Some, like Nora, leaving a defeating marriage, found that dating a kind man who really saw and appreciated who she was gave her a sense of herself that she needed in order to make the transition into her new life. But Nora wasn't looking for a new partner, nor did her children need a father. They still had theirs, even though he lived elsewhere.

On the other hand, some, like Vera, are desperate for both after years of parenting alone. "When people would ask, 'How do you do it all?' I used to say, 'You do what you have to do,'" Vera relates. "But about six months ago, all of this façade crashed. It just came down to the fact that I want to be married. I'm tired of this. I want a long-term relationship. If it doesn't work out with the man I'm seeing right now, I'll move on. I just want it with someone. What I'm saying is, this is hard. I need help. My sons need a father. And I want them to see a relationship that works."

Some want a daddy or a mommy to complete their families. Some want an intimate partner for themselves but "don't want anyone around telling me how to raise my kids." Some find both parent and partner. No matter what their wishes or circumstances, those in this chapter have been caught in dilemmas of the heart as they are pulled between their love for their children and their desire to love another adult as a partner.

♦ SINGLE AND PARENT

One of the most basic considerations is, of course, how do we find someone when so much of our time is dedicated to our children? "The one biggest problem I had as a single parent," says Kevin, "is not only what woman would want to take on all this havoc, but how could I possibly meet her? I couldn't go out looking. I couldn't go out to bars, even though I had never done that anyway. I had kids to raise. It was not accidental that I chose to get a house by the beach. On Saturdays I sat on the porch and played my guitar while everyone strolled by. In fact, a woman I eventually married did walk right past the door. That's just how it happened, because," Kevin says, measuring out an inch of air with his fingers, "my world, between work and home with my boys, was only about this big."

How to meet the "right" person isn't just a challenge for single parents, as the personals columns in every newspaper attest. But single parents come as a package, and that can make it doubly difficult. "The way I look at it," says Sophie, "is that anyone I date is dating two people. Some people say, 'The kids will get used to them,' but I will not make Trevor second in importance to anyone. That's too insecure for a child who has nowhere else to go. But that sure makes it harder to find someone. It's a bit much to ask most people to do." Yet that's what many of us are asking.

"Having children certainly does compound the difficulty of finding a new partner," says Jennifer, the single mother of nine-year-old Matthew. "I was in one relationship that looked good, but he said that, frankly, it scared him that I had Matthew. Well, it scares *me* that I have Matthew, the complete responsibility for another life. So I certainly understand someone else being reticent to take on a person with a kid, when they're perfectly able to date someone without one."

Among the Pygmies of Africa, children are so highly valued that a woman who is pregnant, by anyone, is considered a double prize in marriage because she comes with a treasure. In our own current culture, a child might more readily be regarded as a burden or a bother. For this reason, some single parents try to narrow the field down to people obviously interested in children — those who already have them. Support groups made available through community services, singles groups sponsored by churches, and organizations such as the nationwide Parents Without Partners provide opportunities to socialize for those who understand what it means to raise children.

Carmela, a freelance writer and the mother of a five-year-old, was already so involved in activities — community projects, her daughter's school, a small business organization — that she wasn't inclined to join another group. She found a different route instead. "I took out a lifetime membership in a dating service," she says. The high-tech system she enrolled in not only catalogs members but makes a videotape of them for interested participants to view. Her tape, of course, included her daughter, Alicia. Carmela was especially taken with the video of a man who "in the course of his four minutes changed costumes four times," she recalls. "His three daughters were all in there, laughing throughout. The tape was so funny, I really cracked up." Carmela ended up closing her file in the dating service when she got engaged to the star of that show.

Single parents meet potential partners in the same ways that everyone else does — both intentionally and randomly, through ads in the personals or through friends, through organizations and in the workplace — but always aware that their children too are involved. Whether it's through miracle, calculation, or creative enterprise that we meet people, who we are as single parents is likely not to be who we were before we had them and began to raise them on our own. We have changed, and that changes the game.

From the outset, there are the basic, practical ways in which our lives are so different from those of single people. When Elias was fifteen months old, a friend thought it was about time for me to get out a little and look for that man we were all sure was waiting for a ready-made family. She arranged an afternoon date with someone who sounded on the phone as balanced, mature, and kind as she had described. But the difficulty I had in even finding the time to fit that conversation in should have been a clue. I still didn't comprehend how vastly different dating as a single parent could be from dating as a single person.

When you're single, you simply get ready and go. Your biggest problems are what you look like and what you might talk about, both of which are somewhat in your control. This time it was between loads of laundry, diaper changes, and feeding lunch to a toddler that I tried to curl my hair, get dressed in clean clothes and keep them that way, and stay relaxed. In the end I wasn't able to find a sitter and couldn't really afford one anyway, so I took Elias along. We ended up having a pleasant afternoon with a very sweet man, but I breathed a sigh of relief when it was just me and Elias again, riding the ferryboat back across the bay at dusk. Parenting was more than enough for now, and I just didn't have the energy for any of the emotional drama that seemed to be a part of romance. After that day, dating faded into the background. My life had become Elias.

Sometimes it's just easier that way. One mother who gives lectures on single parenting at the high school in her town reports that when the kids there ask her what dating is like, she has just bluntly told them, "It's a joke. You come home from work, you're supposed to clean up your house, dress up yourself, get your child ready for bed, pick up the babysitter, and then be energetic enough to have some man walk into the house and be ready to be entertaining and fun. Who in the world even wants to do it?"

This is one of the dilemmas of dating for the single parent. Even if we fantasize about finding a partner who might lighten our load, that load is so consuming we don't have time to look. "You get overwhelmed with so many things to do raising kids alone," says Alice. "Being on call, being a taxi driver for them . . . It makes sense that you don't want to go out and try to meet people. Somebody comes along and says, 'Hi, who are you?' and you're supposed to say, 'Oh, I'm this mass of problems . . .'? What are you going to do, make up a big lie?"

Even when we do meet someone who understands what our lives are about, we often don't have enough to give them. "A lot of my relationships have fallen through," says Jeff, who is raising three boys alone, "because the people I dated needed a lot more attention day after day than I could give them, everyday stuff I just didn't feel I could do. I think single parents have no idea how much of their energy is already tied up. So it's real easy to get overextended if you try to add on dating. Some people sacrifice their kids' needs for a period of time, trying to get a relationship together, but I've never been able to do that."

Playing the double role of a single parent easily fills twenty-four hours already. Even more significant, it can change us subtly and profoundly. As Sophie says, learning how to fill all roles as a single parent made her feel as if she had become more masculine. She describes the effect that had on dating. "The more functional and masculine I got as a single mother, the fewer dates I had. In one of my classes there was a guy I thought was a good potential for dating. We were friendly. Then one day suddenly he turned up engaged to someone and with the wedding date all set. I said to him, 'You didn't even give me a chance!' He was really surprised. 'I didn't know you wanted to date somebody,' he said. 'Why would you need a man in your life? You seem to be so . . . self-sufficient.'

"I hit the ceiling. 'Do men date only needy women, then?' I asked. I was angry. 'If I'm "self-sufficient," it's because I'm not willing to become a martyred female who is not functioning until I get my other half. I have learned to be whole!'" Sophie laughs now to recall her reaction, but she still holds to the truth she put forth in her defense.

Even if we are no longer waiting for completion in our "other half," however, we might still dream of someone to carry part of the load and take on the roles with our children that we can't. But until they appear we are *it*, and no matter how desperately we may long for a partner or pray for rescue, putting off addressing our needs and concerns doesn't work. So we are forced to get beyond what Billy calls "the myth of need." Yet that poses another dilemma for single parents if they want an intimate relationship.

"The better you get as a single parent, the less desirable you become as a partner," says Priscilla, who is raising two sons on her own. "I mean, I find it difficult to be both autonomous and efficient in the way that's required to parent and also feminine in the way we're accustomed to in partnering. You just don't have time to do much acting when you're a single parent.

"On top of it, you set up a system that works for your daily life, and you become accustomed to it. You might like a man to come into that system, but you don't really need them. But if they feel like they're just extra or in the way, they can feel threatened as the dickens." The same is true, of course, when a single father introduces a woman into a tight family system.

The most basic dilemma of all for the single parent is, as Tracey puts it, that "it's not only our hearts but the hearts of our children" that are involved. We are single *and* we are parents, and in many ways those two states are at odds. For most of us, the only resolution may lie in finding someone interested in us and also in our children. But, as Jane Anne points out, "we are so passionately attached to our children that it's hard for someone else to match that. I don't even think the man I'm dating right now is nice enough to my *dog,* let alone my son, because he doesn't lavish attention on them like I do. Besides, he wants a relationship with *me.*"

"But if somebody dates a single parent and doesn't understand that the child or children are number one, they are doomed." Lydia, who raised her daughter alone, makes no apologies for her feelings. "There is no need to excuse that feeling, no need to explain it away. It's simply the truth. When push comes to shove and you have to make a choice or a decision, you will make that child number one. You have to. It comes with being a parent."

These deep bonds with our children absolutely change who we are and what we seek in a partner. "Before I had Piper I was into whoever was exciting or good-looking and good in bed and fun to be with," Jacki reflects. "Of course, after her I had to have a man into children, someone who wanted to do things you do with kids as well as with me. It's hard to find someone who wants to come into a family. To take on another person's kids is just not easy. You've got to be a really special person."

The job description is formidable. We want someone for the "single" part of us — a companion, a friend, an intimate, a lover, maybe even a soulmate. That's hard enough to find. On top of it, we want someone for the "parent" part of us, someone who will selflessly love and share our children. It's a tall order. If we can't find both, what do we do?

♦ PARENT OR PARTNER?

"Get married as quickly as you can find a woman to move in," Alan's friends and family told him when his wife left him with their two girls, aged three and six. They even resorted to legal history, hoping to influence Alan, a lawyer, on his own terms. The reason the law gave children to women in court so often, his friends insisted, was that it was "meant to be" that way. "Men don't raise kids," they said.

Over time Alan's own views on that began to change as he spent time with his girls. Yet he continued to feel he owed them a mother. "If I couldn't keep their own mother on the scene, then I felt they deserved a female presence they could relate to, someone who could snuggle up with them and give them the kind of closeness that I had such a hard time doing. I have always had a hope that I would find someone. I think they did want a stepmother. I think they still do, even though they're now adolescents."

For some, the idea of *sharing* parenting almost seems to be encoded, deep down at that cellular level where the egg and sperm meet to begin a new human life. At least on the practical level, it's obvious that raising children requires the participation of more than one adult. Even cultures that did not recognize biological fatherhood developed other forms of caring units in which men and women were bound in committed relationship to children. Our own culture, despite the divorce rate, holds to the nuclear family as its ideal.

Rick, who began raising his three teenagers alone fifteen years ago, knows that "what I have given my kids is better than what they might get in a bad but intact family. But at the same time, you know that the other way is the right way, it's the natural way, it's the way it's supposed to be. I sometimes feel a little guilty or a little lost for it not having been like that."

Gabriele, who is raising her son, Christian, on her own, feels certain that "single parenting is not the real thing. Everything operates on balance. The seasons, man and woman. A single-parent unit is not a balance to me. My ideal is a man and a woman and a child. Deep inside, I believe that God intended it that way. You can strive and strive, and you might get close to it, but I don't think it will ever get as close as the real thing. Something is always missing, for me and for my child. Something to make this complete."

Gayle stands in the park on a Sunday afternoon, watching her two healthy boys playing ball on the green. As a doctor, she doesn't struggle with the financial traumas that many face. Still, when I ask how she is doing as a single parent, she takes her eyes off her boys and, turning to me, says, "I call it the unnatural act."

Unnatural act. Not the way it's supposed to be. Not the real thing. These are strong terms, absolute and nonprovisional. Our own convictions about how children should be raised can sit in judgment upon us. The overwhelming tasks of our daily lives can feel like testimony to the lack of balance. Our hearts too may cry out that something is missing. "The only part of single parenting that I could absolutely not tolerate again is the pain of not sharing Trevor with anyone else," Sophie says. "Whenever he succeeded in something, whenever he was in his fullness, whenever he had words of wisdom — it was like Christmas morning with nobody else around to watch you unwrap the present."

Sophie doesn't fight back the tears when she talks about this one. "I had more nights sitting at his bedside, looking at this angel, this growing and wondrous human being emerging, and realizing that I am the only one in the world who knows the secret of this person. That loneliness was the greatest pain. Not being able to hold somebody's hand and say, 'Isn't he wonderful?' or 'Aren't we doing a good job?' I could call up someone on the phone and say, 'Guess what he did today?' They might say, 'Oh, how nice.' But it doesn't make them lose a night's sleep out of ecstasy because he pooped on the toilet or said his first word. It did to me because I was so excited. Not having anybody else to share that with was a loneliness I had never experienced before. Never."

All the solutions to whatever we lament or lack can in our fantasies get gathered into that one basket of the perfect partner for us and the ideal parent for our children. Perhaps the fact that Alan is raising daughters made him feel especially compelled to find for them the presence of a woman. Certainly Billy in his "boys' clubhouse" felt he was nurturing enough to give a son what he needed. Studies show that fathers raising daughters alone do tend to remain more aloof, emotionally and physically. Taboos hang heavy over a father snuggling up with a growing daughter. But whatever sex our children are, we may still feel this deep pull to find them a mommy or a daddy — especially when they ask us.

Elias hadn't talked for a long time about wanting a daddy. When we were living in our big shared household, our men housemates seemed to satisfy his need for male presence, and his godfather Sypko lived close by. But one day when we were living far away from those men who had so welcomed him, he took me by surprise. We needed publicity photos, and the photographer who came to take them turned out to be a warm and humorous man. Elias took to him completely. They played and sang through the session. As the photographer was leaving, Elias asked me to bend down because he had a secret. He whispered in my ear, "Maybe *he* could be my father."

I was so taken aback by this sudden revelation that I drew back and looked at him a long moment, my heart aching at his sweet innocence. His eyes were aglow, his whole little body alive with hope and pride in his great idea. "That's such a sweet thought," I said, trying at least to acknowledge his resourcefulness and his tender feelings. But not wanting to mislead him or embarrass any of us, I suggested, "Let's talk about this later, okay?" And I clumsily added, seeing that he was still on the verge of popping the question, "This isn't exactly the way it happens."

I did have a talk with him later that night, a delicate attempt to support him while trying to convey something about human relationships. I explained that someone who would be his daddy would most likely live with us and that they would have to be someone I also felt very close to. That person, in fact, would probably have to be my partner. But it's as hard to describe this complex role to a four-year-old as it is to find someone to fill it.

"I have found it very difficult to find someone who wants to walk into an existing family," Alan says. "Someone who doesn't have children already often doesn't want to marry someone who does, because either they don't want children or they want to have them with someone who is going to begin a family with them. I've had three or four relationships during the last eight years, but none has led to marriage.

"We were all really happy with the last woman I was seeing — Rebecca. She even moved in here for a while. The girls really had expectations, so they were deeply disappointed when it didn't work out for her and she left. For me it was probably the most grave blow of all the women I've dated, because I had high hopes too. It knocked me back for a long time. When that kind of thing happens, you can't help but indict yourself. That was when I began to think about all the things I wished I could have been, thinking if I had been them, then the relationship would have worked out. I thought because I'm in this predicament with kids alone, none of us gets what we want.

"I do feel like I have deprived them of a mother by not remarrying and bringing a new woman into their life. To have children and then to say — even though by actions that are essentially out of my control — 'You won't get a mother or a mother's love' . . . that's what I did to them. I think that has been the hardest part of all of being a single parent — feeling that by not being able to bring them a stepmother, I deprived them."

The hard part wasn't actually that Alan couldn't find a willing woman. In the end it was that he had to admit that his desire to give them a mother simply couldn't force his heart. "There actually have been a few women who would have been stepmothers to them," Alan explains. "But one night I found myself telling a friend, 'I just can't do it. I know it would be great for the kids. I know the food would be a lot better around here, the house would look better, but I just can't do it. I can give the kids everything, but I can't give them that last thing — which is my own freedom to choose who I can love and live with as a partner.'"

Alan pauses to introduce his two daughters, who have just arrived home from school. They smile graciously and talk for a few minutes before heading off to their rooms. Not having a stepmother certainly hasn't impeded their development into self-possessed young women. When they leave, Alan responds to my unexpressed thought. "I think it's a miracle that they can grow up without a female presence and feel pretty good about themselves as young women. It's wonderful. It goes to show what can happen almost automatically, because I certainly didn't do anything in that direction."

Alan stops for a moment to make sure the girls are out of hearing range, then returns to complete his earlier thoughts. "I know in the previous generation someone would write to the old country and ask to have a wife sent over. A farmer on the frontier would order a wife and mother through a catalog, and everyone would take what they got." But no matter how deeply Alan wanted that "female presence" for his daughters, those methods didn't fit the life of a lawyer in Manhattan at the end of the twentieth century. Yet it's hard for Alan to accept that reality without regret. "You could say that if it's appropriate for a man to raise daughters, then what I've done is okay. But if it's not, I might have made a mistake. I might have been guilty of selfishness there."

As useless as regret is, it does arise in the package of human emotions. Jacki faced the same crossroads as Alan, and like him, in the end, she made the choice for herself rather than for her daughter. Now she sometimes wonders. "There was one guy who really was like a daddy to her. He'd take her places, he'd spend time with her if she didn't feel well, he was willing to give up his time, or even time with me, to do something with her. She liked him a lot, and he also had a kid her age she could play with. If I had married him — and I could have — we would have had a totally different life. I tell myself that I wouldn't have been who I am now, and she wouldn't be who she is. Yet at times I regret that I didn't keep that relationship, because he was a wonderful daddy. None of the others have really been daddy material."

It's hard to find daddy material or mommy material, and some single parents definitely don't want that. "David *has* a mother," says Ed, who is raising his thirteen-year-old son. "He visits her weekends and vacations. But I'd like to find a woman *I* could have a relationship with. Still, she'd have to be someone who can relate well to David. In my life, he's still number one."

◆ A TUG OF HEARTS

Romantic love as we know it is built on the assumption that lovers are "it" for each other, primary in importance in each other's hearts and lives. What happens when we already have a number one, our children, and yet we long for love and companionship with a peer?

"For me the hardest thing about being a single parent was trying to have a relationship with a person of the opposite sex," says Jacki. "That was much harder than doing all the grocery shopping, fixing the car, staying up with Piper at night when she was sick, being there when she was hurt, even harder than getting through her early teenage years. All of that is hard, but it's possible. But having a romantic and intimate relationship with someone . . .

"In the beginning, when Piper was just born, I must admit I assumed that I would get another husband who would be her father. I had always had a husband or a boyfriend, and I just figured that the next one who came along would take the role of playing a daddy to this child, and he would love me and love her. It took me a couple of years to realize that that was probably not going to happen."

What did happen instead is the deep relationship Jacki developed with her daughter. "When you're the single parent, you put this real special energy into your kid. Because I was single with Piper, we did a whole lot together. We were very involved on an everyday level — the cuddles and hugs and discussions and giggles and just sitting and watching TV together. I did those things with *her.* So when I would date, there was always this kind of pull between the man and the kid."

Jacki was the rope in a tug-of-war between hearts. "Very seldom did Piper not like a man I dated. But even with that, there was always jealousy. Even with my last boyfriend when Piper was seventeen, although she would never admit it, in subtle ways she was interfering. When he was around, she'd want my attention more or do irritating little things.

"But when she was young, it was outrageous. Whenever a man I'd be dating would be around, she'd crawl into my lap, pull on me, get upset about some little thing, hurt her finger — just tacky little things to get my attention. Whatever was my button at the moment — and I had different ones over the years — she would push it.

"I would find myself placating her so that she wouldn't come between me and my date. Nighttime, for instance, was always an issue if there was a man visiting me who was waiting for her to go to bed so I could spend time with him. I always read her stories before she fell asleep. If someone was waiting in the living room, she'd invariably want more stories. If I said no, she would cry and scream her head off, knowing I didn't want her to cry in front of the guy. It would be noisy and he'd be disturbed. So I'd give her more stories.

"If there had been no guy there, I would have said, 'No more,' and she might have whimpered for a minute or two and that would have been it. If it had been her real dad in the next room, it would have been okay with me for her to be acting like that. But when you're trying to have a romance with someone and your kid is screaming down the hall, it just doesn't work."

And chances are the person waiting in the living room doesn't understand why the kid doesn't just behave — particularly if he hasn't had children of his own. Alan reports the same problem.

"My kids would go out of their way to assert their territory, even when they really liked someone, like Rebecca. If she and I were talking, invariably they'd need help with their homework, or they couldn't find such and such. Rebecca was someone who really didn't like having her attention broken up like that, so I think that was particularly effective in discouraging her.

"But I felt torn. I could see that part of it was a con, an attempt to be divisive, and part of it was they really did need someone. Rebecca, who was a school counselor but didn't have any children of her own, didn't seem to realize what kids are really like. She'd say to me, 'Children need to know that after nine o'clock you're not available.' I told her that frankly I had never heard of anyone who actually has a kid assert with confidence a statement like that. But she thought I was a patsy and let them walk all over me."

Alan really loved his girls, and he loved Rebecca as well. The difference was that he was responsible for his children and their lives in a way that he wasn't for Rebecca. Was he supposed to refuse to help them with their homework so that he could give his time to Rebecca? But was he supposed to give up his desire and opportunity to build a relationship with her because of his children? Which of them was he supposed to listen to?

One single mother, Ann, who raised her three girls alone after her husband's death, laughed as she recalled an event that symbolized the dilemma. "The first man I had started dating was over for dinner, and two of my girls were there. We were all sitting at the table, and I remember my head going like I was watching a ping-pong game. The man would say something that demanded my attention. Sharon would immediately say something entirely different. She was nine years old, my youngest, and she felt most afraid that I might get involved with someone."

If that unknown person at dinner were to become part of the family, what would that mean for Sharon? For one thing, she'd be gaining a housemate she might not have chosen herself. For another, as Ann related, "Sharon told me eventually that she was afraid that if I got married again, she'd have another parent who might be stricter than I was." Just by virtue of his being another adult, the man's presence would indeed tend to establish a hierarchy of power. As we saw in the last chapter, in single-parent households there is a tendency toward implied equality rather than firm hierarchy between parents and children. Sharon and her sisters knew they could negotiate with their mother on most things. If she had a backup, would her policies get stricter?

That was only one of their worries. The ping-pong strategy might work at the dinner table, but can success in holding on to the parent's love be assured? When we bring home a potential partner, our children can react with the kind of desperate jealousy, fury, and fear of abandonment that we might feel were an intimate to do the same to us. Jealousy is a dark flower of fear — fear of being left out, fear of being expunged in the eyes of those who matter most. We may say, "They want attention." But attention is the tip of the iceberg; they're fighting for their lives.

Even a child in a two-parent family will vie with one parent for attention from the other. Often children interrupt their parents' private time, feeling left out of that adult echelon. But actually the intimacy and closeness of their parents is reassuring, a glue that holds the family together. As David Elkind points out, "In the two-parent family, the loyalty of parents is taken for granted because the adults are the biological parents and this imposes a sort of automatic loyalty. The affection of one parent for the other is not seen as a threat to loyalty, since both parents are biologically bound to the children."[1] But introduce into a single-parent family a man or woman who has little relationship to the children, and loss looms in their fears.

Not only might children be struggling with the fear of losing the only remaining parent they have at home, they often struggle long and hard with the loss of their two parents as a unit. They may dream, long after any real possibility exists, of their getting back together again. Sheila was surprised to discover that even after she had been remarried for three years and her twelve-year-old daughter had a wonderful stepfather, Hilary continued to harbor fantasies of her own two parents reconciling. "I was so amazed because Hilary had been two years old when my first husband and I separated, and she adores Jack, her stepfather."

The revelation presented itself one day when Sheila and Hilary were visiting the city where they used to live. "Hilary's father and I had spent a lot of time together with her that day. The next morning when Hilary woke up, she said, 'Mom, I just can't imagine you and my dad being together.'" It was then she confessed to Sheila that "all these years I have hoped that you guys would get back together, and I fantasized what it would be like. But it's just really clear to me that you and Jack belong together. I can see how you and my dad wouldn't live well together at all."

Even when our children tell us that they want us to have a relationship, the actuality can be more than they are prepared for. When Evita, Ruth's adopted daughter first arrived from Central America, she wanted her new mother to get married "in the worst way," Ruth reports. Evita was a lively and romantic four-year-old, and the idea of a lovely wedding filled her mind. "She picked out a friend of mine and figured out where we would go on our honeymoon and all the details of the wedding." At the time, Ruth had just ended a long-term relationship, and marriage was far from her mind.

Later, however, when Evita was eight, Ruth did begin dating. "Evita went berserk," Ruth remembers. Despite her skills as a social worker, Ruth says, "I was so shocked that I really handled it poorly. I just didn't know what to do. Evita was brutal and horrible. This guy kept trying to make friends with her and she would say all these horrible things to him. She was really scared that she would lose me to him. It brought up everything about loss for her.

"But I know it wasn't just Evita," Ruth emphasizes. "My friends who are single parents with children of the same age all said it has been brutal when they connected with someone. Every day Evita would sit there and say to me, 'How could you do this to me? I thought you loved me. We were so good, just us together, and now what are you doing with this other person?'"

Betrayal. Bringing someone else into our lives can make our children feel cast aside. Why do we need anyone but them? Even our casual friendships can feel to them like a threat to their place in our lives. I was lamenting to someone one day about how much I missed having time with friends. Overhearing me, Elias drew himself up very tall and pronounced, "Well, *I'm* your friend!" If I needed others, then did that mean he wasn't enough?

Actually, it did. He wasn't. We may love our children more than we ever love anyone else, but just as they need peers, so do we. But stepping out to build a separate, personal, private, intimate life with someone else can even feel to *us* a little like we are betraying them.

Nothing Ruth could say or do seemed to cut through her daughter's fears, but a counselor she found for Evita had some skillful methods that helped. "They talked about different kinds of love and they did things like drawing hearts in different colors for each kind," Ruth explains. "Those sessions seemed to help Evita feel much less threatened by my being close to someone else. My relationship with that man did end, but it really made me think, 'How am I going to pull this off?' Evita even told me later that she would prefer if I would wait until she moved out of the house before I got involved with anybody! I said to her, 'No, Evita, I can't do that. That's a long time.'"

It takes a lot of reassuring to let our children know that they will not lose our love. During fifteen years of raising his three children alone, Rick kept his single social life completely separate from his family. "For years and years, I just didn't have the time or the interest in a serious, long-term relationship," Rick says. He just wanted to date now and then. "My kids knew I was going out, but that was never considered a threat because the people were never part of our family life.

"But recently, in the last year, I've gotten involved with someone for the first time. I have brought her home and introduced her to them. I tell them it's not with any guarantees about the future, but just that I've reached a time when I need and want someone in my life." Rick's daughter is just going off to college and his two younger children are both in their teens. But the fears still arise.

In what is probably an understatement, Rick describes the response his family has made to this change. "It has been a bit of a struggle and has brought up a lot of questions for everybody — questions of authority and possessiveness, territorial things. It has caused us all to face a lot of situations that maybe we put off through the years."

Open communication has been a hallmark of Rick's parenting style, so his children "have an awful lot of say about what goes on in my relationship, which is unusual for a lot of families. For the most part it's pretty good," Rick says, "but sometimes it feels a little awkward, and I wish it were a generation back, like my parents, where kids just weren't involved in that kind of stuff. So we talk a lot about it. Over time it's gotten better, and they feel less scared. But it just takes an awful lot of talking. Time and lots of talk. The biggest fear is that somebody is taking me away from them. I tell them it's not a problem, that nobody could take me away, that there's plenty to go around."

Plenty of *one* to go around. But the practical and emotional logistics can make that distribution hard, sometimes impossible, to pull off. Even a broken heart can have its advantages compared with the shredded mass the pull between our children and a potential partner can make of our hearts.

"You just have to choose which is most important," Jacki concludes. "And I definitely chose Piper. I wasn't willing to stop the way I felt about her. Men are temporary, kids aren't." The bond we have with our children can scarcely be broken. We share a past and a future. We know that they will be in our lives, no matter what happens. Even if we suffer an emotional break with them for a period of time, we remain their parent. We will always be their parent, they will always be our children, in a line of connection that is the life of humanity itself.

With a lover we share a different kind of intimacy, in some ways much closer than with our children. We are vulnerable and meet naked in body, soul, heart. We are not the caretaker; responsibility is a choice rather than a given. Yet one of the mysteries of this love is that no matter how profound it is, in a moment it can break. "I don't care if you're married for a long time or whatever, that relationship can end," Jacki says. "But the child is always there. Even when they grow up, you continue the relationship. A man can be replaced, but a child can't."

The fact that relationships do come and go brings up questions about *how* we date when we have children. Do we bring our dates home or not? If so, when? What about sex? What do we do if a relationship ends? In these issues, as in all others, the welfare of our children has to guide our choices.

Our children's well-being, however, depends greatly on ours. Dating and seeking a partner may be invigorating for us in ways that are good for them. It may also release them from feeling that they are the only one to care for us or that they have to be our partner. As Laurinda's grown son, Eric, recalls, "The absence of a permanent male figure was hard," but the several long-term relationships his mother had "got me in touch with some wonderful and different men who I could get to know deeply. It gave me some very good role models."

For some single parents who find a partner, the love does multiply and become all-embracing. Ryan, who has been raising his daughter as a co-parent since she was an infant, reports that she "flowed right into my relationships with women and really got along with them. She fell in love with each one, and seemed fine when each was over. She just seemed to take it all in stride. And now she is great friends with the woman I am married to, and she has chosen to live here with us most of the time. We have a lot of love and affection in our house." That's the ideal, and it is a blessing to find it. Unfortunately, what seems to be more common is his daughter's negative experience with her mother's remarriage — another reason why she chooses to live with her father.

Each child's responses to a parent dating will be unique. But there are guidelines that some single parents have found helpful in caring for those small hearts.

◆ WHO KNOWS WHERE OR WHEN

"I never went out with men who thought my having a child was an issue, and I never went out on a date before eight o'clock," says Shay, who raised her daughter alone for four and a half years before remarrying. "That meant that I really wasn't taking any time away from Jenny." Shay's daughter met only a few of the men her mother dated, and only after Shay knew them pretty well. This protected Jenny from developing attachments and expectations and then being disappointed.

"I think another part of why it worked so well may be that I never felt guilty about wanting a partner for myself, just as I never felt guilty about going to work to earn a living. I think kids can pick up on that guilt and uncertainty in a second, and if they think they can keep you home with them, they'll try."

A number of single parents found that keeping their dating lives separate from their family lives worked best for everyone. This approach, however, has its drawbacks. Past experience has led another single mother, Jennifer, to her adamant stance "to keep any boyfriend away from Matthew until I am sure this is someone I want to have stick around. But that means it will be extremely expensive to date. Where I live it can cost at least twenty-five dollars to pay a sitter for an evening. If you want to see someone a couple of times a week, babysitting can end up costing a couple hundred a month."

This policy also brings up another of the dilemmas of dating for the single parent. We don't want to develop a serious relationship with anyone who couldn't have a good relationship with our children, yet to find out how they might get along means risking hopes, fears, and attachments by introducing them. "Trevor has met a number of the men I have dated," says Sophie, "because I don't want to date people who don't seem to have a positive connection with him. There's no reason even bothering with it for me. I can tell a lot about a man from how he relates to my child and how Trevor feels about him."

A number of single parents reported how accurate their children were in sizing up the potential of those they dated. They want to protect us and make sure we have the best. "With some men Trevor has actually moved closer to me and wouldn't even leave the room. With one man he stood right in the middle, between us, while we were talking. But with a man he liked, he was quite different. When we went to a restaurant together, he ran to a chair on the opposite side of the table. The man asked him, 'Wouldn't you like to sit in the middle or next to your mother?' Trevor said, 'Nope,' and quite happily sat across from us to make sure this man and I were together. I think it's his way of saying it would make him feel good if his mom were being loved and cared for by somebody he trusts."

No matter when we choose to introduce a date to our children, sooner or later, it is up to us to hold their hearts carefully. When Rick finally did bring his woman-friend home to meet his family, he was careful not to build an illusion for his children, careful to let them know there are no guarantees. Tracey, whose sons felt so disappointed when her relationship ended, looks back now and realizes that the "shock had been so extreme for them because I had told them that I was madly in love and that this was 'the one.' If I had been more tempered in my approach, I don't think the end would have been as big a shock."

If a relationship ends, the loss can be hard on everyone involved. "The breakups weren't easy for my daughter because she did bond with a few of the men I was seeing. And she was important to them, too," says Lydia. "But thank goodness I'd chosen such nice guys to go out with! Two of them actually remained very much in touch with her, sending her cards, talking to her on the phone now and then, sending money for her birthday, that kind of thing."

This kind of continuing care on the part of someone we have dated is a real treasure, because our children can easily end up thinking that they caused the relationship to end. "Psychologically, they can't help but feel that they did something that drove that person away," comments Alan. "For sure, part of a kid would wish that the person would just go and leave their parent alone. And they certainly can be bratty, even if they like the person. But then if they feel they have accomplished what part of them wanted, they feel very guilty."

When Rebecca decided that Alan and his family were not what she was looking for, she wrote a letter to the girls and asked Alan to read it to them. It assured them that she loved them and said, as Alan paraphrases it, "Just because I'm not there doesn't mean that it's your fault." "She did everything a psychologist would say was important," says Alan. "But when I read it to the girls, they didn't seem to really care. Kids have a great way of tuning things out that they don't want to hear about. I know they were disappointed, and they didn't really want to talk about it."

This double pain is one of the unavoidable risks of seeking a partner. Most of our children will one day themselves look for a partner. One of the best gifts we can give them is to model our ability to respond to loss and disappointment by honoring our feelings and then with resilience moving on into life with an open heart again. If we can convey by our example that the value of our lives is not determined by whether we are in a relationship or not, that being a full and loving human being doesn't depend on having a "lover," and that the value and quality of a relationship is not necessarily judged by its longevity, we are offering them a gift they can carry into their own lives.

♦ WHAT ABOUT SEX?

If sex becomes a part of our romantic involvements, we face another set of critical logistics. The increase in sexually transmitted diseases has almost relegated "casual sex" to the archives. Still, "single parent" is not synonymous with "celibate" — although considering the difficulties in finding partners encountered by both single mothers and fathers, it can sometimes seem like it!

Single mothers report an additional challenge. While they may want to have a sexual relationship with a potential partner, a number of those I spoke with felt profoundly disturbed by the assumption some hold that single women with children are easily available for sex. Not only did women relate stories of the heavy "come-on" from men once their circumstances were revealed, but one woman, Joan, raising a daughter alone, relates how the woman next door to her who was divorcing her husband arranged for him to take Joan to a movie. She accepted, thinking that for both of them this was just a chance to get out. "When we got home and he wanted to come in, I realized that my neighbor had thought she could pawn her husband off on me, as if I were an easy mark."

Sexual standards and mores are very personal, but all the single fathers and mothers I spoke with felt that this area had to be handled very carefully in relation to their children, and that being embarrassed or deceptive about sex only encouraged their children to be the same. While some of our concerns about the impact of our sexual involvements can be eliminated if we restrict such intimacy to times when our children are not around, for many single parents the only available leisure time is at home after the children are sleeping.

Everyone I spoke with was concerned about being discreet, but sometimes we are taken by surprise. "You guys are bare naked!" two-year-old Holly announced to her mother and her boyfriend when she walked into the bedroom one morning and found them just getting up to dress. Gretchen answered with aplomb, "'Yes, we are!'

I wanted to be just straightforward, because I don't want to convey to her that bodies are bad, or that expressing affection between adults is something to hide — but I don't mean we'd ever make love in front of her. If I was having a different boyfriend over every week, I do think it would be a problem for her to find us naked, but Mark and I have been together a long time."

If Mark had been a stranger to Holly, the situation might have been very confusing for her. Kirstin describes an altogether different scenario that happened when Alexander was two years old. "One night a man I had been seeing casually was visiting and we decided he would spend the night. I hadn't done this ever since my son was born. The next morning Alexander came into my room very early. He was shocked to find a man there, and I felt really uneasy.

"For weeks after, he did not stop talking about Rob sleeping in my bed. Even months later, when Rob, who had become just a friend, stopped by to visit, Alexander asked if he was going to spend the night. I felt so uncomfortable about it all that I asked Alexander if he had liked Rob staying over. He answered something like, 'No, it was not good.' That was hard for me to swallow, because I think sexuality is a beautiful way of sharing when you are with the right person. I have tried since to convey that to him, but he may have picked up as well that I didn't feel that special way about Rob."

What Kirstin didn't know at that time, however, was that her son might already have been experiencing sexual abuse at "Grandpa's" house. It might well have been that which caused his very negative reaction. In any case, Kirstin took Alexander's feelings seriously but she also considered her own. "What Alexander said made me have to think about what I wanted to do in terms of sexuality. Ever since he was born I have felt that I wanted to wait for the right person, but it's pretty hard because you have your human needs too. It felt really good to sleep with Rob, and I really enjoyed the intimacy because it had been so long."

If anything in a relationship can make our children feel isolated from us, it's the privacy of sexuality. Our bedrooms and our beds are such a focal point of intimacy that, with our very young children especially, we can expect to face some painful situations. Alexander may have come into his mother's room earlier than usual that Sunday, but it was his habit anyway to crawl in every morning — as many children do with their parents. But when the bed is Mommy's alone or Daddy's alone and someone else is there, the child can feel suddenly very left out.

If Mommy's or Daddy's bed is also the child's bed, the issue is intensified. Some version of "the family bed" is not uncommon for very young children in single-parent families, or even for older children of the same sex. Those who share report distinct practical and emotional benefits. Children, of course, tend to be in favor of this arrangement. But in addition to fearing the misunderstanding of others, single parents who share their beds with children often worry about how they will get the children out if they want to have a relationship. Indeed, one mother reports that her six-year-old daughter, who had her own bed but customarily slept with her mother anyway, shouted at the man who entered their life, "You've moved right in on top of my place!"

The purpose here is not to assess the pros and cons of sharing our beds but to relate something of the realities we face when the two meanings of "sleeping together" collide. Some who might want to share a bed with their children choose not to in hopes of a future intimate relationship. Some who do share their bed find it a struggle to reclaim it whether they want to have a relationship or not. Some who share report that the issue resolved itself with probably less of an overall struggle than the total hours that might have been spent trying to keep the children in their own beds night after night. In any case, all the pulls single parents can feel between their children and an intimate relationship can meet symbolically in the bedroom.

For Piper as a child the fact that she had to sleep in her own bed instead of with her mother when a man slept over seemed to be an issue no more fraught with competition and concern than any other about dating. Jacki attributes that to the fact that "it was never something we couldn't talk about if she did feel threatened or uncomfortable. We have always talked openly about everything to do with sex. She has asked me questions about all of it, and she talks about her own sexuality in a way that I wouldn't ever have talked to my own mother. She has a very healthy attitude."

Certainly Jacki's own sensitivity to her daughter's needs contributed to that healthy attitude. When Piper moved beyond childhood and into her teen years, Jacki's pattern of sleeping with her boyfriend at the house changed. "I haven't slept with anybody here for four years, from the time when Piper was about thirteen to the time she was seventeen," Jacki explains. "Because she was entering her own sexuality, I think it would have in fact bothered her to be in the house and have me here sleeping with a man. I think it would have been very embarrassing for her at her age to hear us making love, and very intrusive for her to come into the bathroom in the morning and have a man be there."

Puberty and the teen years are such a vulnerable time in so many ways for our children that our sexuality, when we are single, can bring up a confusing intensity of feelings in them. For children of divorce, someone new in bed constitutes a graphic displacement of their other parent as well. Jonah's parents separated when he was fifteen. Not long after, when his father began living with the woman he was seeing, Jonah cried to his mother, Jane Anne, "How can he do that? Doesn't he care about *us?*" A year later, when Jane Anne began having an intimate relationship with a man, she describes how "Jonah went through a long period of time when I couldn't even touch him. He wouldn't come into my bedroom at all. I think he was just terrified. We must be such a threat to them at that age if we are ourselves being sexual."

Sexuality is a powerful and mysterious force. When it is exploding in the hormones of a teenager, trying to control and clarify its boundaries can indeed be confusing and even frightening. Jane Anne reports that when Jonah fell in love with his first girlfriend the following year, he grew more at ease with his mother again. "He'd even come in and sit on my bed at night again to talk. It was a total change." The boundaries had been secured.

What effect does our children's burgeoning sexuality have on *us* as single parents? For instance, what is it like for us to have teenage children dating, particularly if we are not? We might feel as abandoned and left out by their intimacy as they can by ours. Marian's response reveals a spectrum of feelings. She herself had forgone dating most of the years she was raising her daughter. So when she related that Terra had become sexually active at the age of sixteen, I asked her whether she felt uncomfortable about it, perhaps even resentful. "Actually, I felt quite relieved!" Marian told me. "I had been afraid that because I had been largely celibate during her growing-up years that she would have a skewed perception of sexuality and intimate relationships. So when it became apparent to me that she was sexually active, I was glad to see that her nature hadn't been somehow repressed by my choices.

"Another thing I felt good about was that all of her choices in boys seemed healthy. They were nice, they were her own age. Their relationships felt young and innocent and exploratory rather than exploitative. The whole tone of how they related was very fresh and sweet.

"The difficult part for me was that our bedrooms were too close for comfort," Marian added. Both bedrooms were upstairs, side by side, in the two-story house Marian rented. Not wanting to bar Terra from having boyfriends in the house at all, and recognizing the probable futility of the attempt anyway, Marian asked her only not to have anyone stay overnight. "Even though she didn't like that, no one ever did. They'd be discreet and quiet when they were together, but you don't really want to be in a bedroom next to someone, especially your daughter, when they're making love. You do need privacy. And I also didn't want to come down in the morning and encounter her boyfriend in the kitchen. I told her, 'Your private life is your own, but we live together in this house.' I would have extended the same consideration to her."

For Laurinda, having a son had its own considerations, both when she was dating and when she wasn't. "When Eric was twelve, in puberty, he would get really jealous of my friend, the man who was living with us. One night this man and I were downstairs together and Eric called me to come upstairs. He wanted me to stay and talk with him for a while, but there was a kind of sweetness with a sexual overtone in the way he was behaving toward me, kind of needy and seductive. I really understood that it was jealousy he was feeling, and because a man had my attention, he was trying to get it back in this way. I did stay there talking with him for quite a while, because I could see that he truly needed some attention from me, he needed to know that he was special."

Eric at thirty, remembering those days, acknowledges having had a "multitude of feelings about my mother having a relationship with a man. Sure, sometimes there was resentment and anger at somebody taking away some of the attention I could be getting. But at times I actually didn't feel threatened by it at all because I knew those relationships weren't going to encroach on me. The pattern had shown me that they'd end! And it would not have been healthy for her *not* to have had those relationships. Besides, I liked having the father figures. But maybe something in me liked having them not be continuous, too."

A few years later, when Laurinda was no longer in a steady relationship, the issue was different. "When Eric first had sex with a woman, I think he told me within a day or two of it happening. When I told my therapist about it, he strongly advised me not to talk with Eric further about that part of his life. He felt that not only is this such a sensitive transition for a young man, but that being a single mother with no steady man in my own life, it was best to keep the whole issue as separate as possible. He felt that Eric was already so attached to me that this distancing would enable him to continue with the healthy separating his emerging sexuality was a part of."

Like Marian, Laurinda reports that she felt relieved when her teenager started being sexual — "partly because it felt important that he make that step into his manhood, but also because I could see that he *could* let go of me. Actually, the hard part of his being sexually active is something I realized only years later," says Laurinda. "It was that he had become the model of the kind of man I was looking for in a relationship. I don't mean age-wise or oedipally or any of that. It was just that he was actually much more mature in so many ways than many of the men I could find to date!"

As our children in their teens become increasingly aware of peer pressure and seek to conform to the values their friends hold, our own sexual choices may make them uncomfortable. It can be hard to have a single parent who is sexual, and even harder if the parent is gay. Now that her older daughter is seven, Jane can speak easily to her about her own preference "to have a woman as my best friend," and she can even convey to her the fact that "some people just don't understand that, so we don't need to talk with them about it. That's what I tell her, and she's fine with it. We talk about racism because she's biracial, so she already has a grasp on prejudice.

"But I expect there to be issues related to lesbianism when she's a teenager," Jane acknowledges. "The woman I was in a relationship with when I adopted Jordan had teenage daughters, so I already went through the experience of them adjusting to their mother having chosen to be a lesbian. Even though they had been brought up with a very liberal value system, it still touched their lives.

"I remember something that came up for the fifteen-year-old daughter. She thought the paintings I had in the house of female nudes were lesbian art because she had never been exposed to nudity in art before. She felt like it was an advertisement on the wall that she lived with lesbians, and she was worried about what her friends would think when they came over. The children ended up having a selection of friends who knew we were lesbians and felt fine about it, but they also had other friends they just didn't want to have to get into it with. Their mother and I respected their need for privacy, so we were discreet about our relationship, and the kids were free to introduce me as their aunt if they wanted to. I think I'll give my daughters the same option, to tell their friends or not, because I don't think they should have to deal with all the repercussions if they don't want to. Of course, I'll also want them to have a certain level of respect for my privacy as well and not have them advertise it to everybody either."

"I don't think I will tell Abe at all about my sexual choices," says Nancy, a lesbian adoptive mother of a two-year-old boy. "Society is so shortsighted and so one-dimensional that it may be devastating for him. And though we have a deep bond, I want to protect him from the cruel part of people's personality by keeping that part of myself unknown to him."

Jasmine, on the other hand, feels that being open with one's children gives them the strength to stand up to prejudice. For her, telling her daughter that she was gay meant coming out of the closet altogether, because she felt it was confusing to ask Mindy to hide the fact as if it were shameful. The whole experience has brought Jasmine and Mindy closer.

As single parents, we walk a precarious path in the area of sexuality. Our sexual choices do have an impact on our children, whether it is our choice of partners or our choice to be sexually active at all. We want our children to develop healthy attitudes toward sex while at the same time understanding boundaries. Some single parents who want to have an active sex life legitimately fear that their teenage children will take a cue from them and feel that they too are entitled to have sex with their dates. Tracey points out, "I feel like it's fine to make it clear to my kids that sex is for adults, that it's something they will have plenty of time to enjoy later as a natural privilege and choice of adulthood, like having a career or driving or traveling alone — things that require responsibility and maturity and the capacity to understand and take on consequences."

Whether we choose to forgo sexuality while raising our children or to be sexually active, either choice is healthy as long as it is made with the well-being of our children in mind. "I don't think it's fair for a person not to be able to be fulfilled sexually if they want to, just because they are a single parent," says Lydia. "Looking back, though, I do think I'd do it differently myself, considering what it must have been like for my daughter sometimes. But I'm talking from forty-two now, not twenty-eight, when the hormones were still raging around inside." Lydia is also talking about being that age in an era before AIDS and other considerations began to make us very cautious and more likely to look for commitment before getting involved sexually.

Yet commitment itself remains an issue. "The chances of finding someone to take on a parent and child seem pretty slim," says Lydia. "So that means you're with an uncommitted partner if you're with anybody at all." We are bound to have some starts and stops in our dating record as single parents, and how we answer for ourselves the questions about the beginnings, the depth of intimacy, and the endings will qualify the impact on our children of "new love" in our lives.

◆ THIS FOOLISH DREAM

Undeniably, those entering a single-parent family are in some ways outsiders — outsiders striving to make friends with the "brutal" Evitas, outsiders waiting in the living room as Jacki reads another story to her insistent daughter, outsiders who also claim a piece of our heart. Does the outsider ever get in? What happens when a single parent does find a partner? The majority of divorced parents do remarry, men at a higher rate than women. A quarter of all children today will live with a stepparent by the time they are sixteen.[2] But stepparenting and blending families bring their own considerable challenges.

"By the time I met Nick I had given up looking," Sheila begins. Her daughter, Hilary, was nine years old by that time, and they had been basically on their own together for seven years. Most of those years had been spent living in a big house in Seattle with two housemates while Sheila went to graduate school. Sheila and Hilary were best friends with another mother and daughter just two doors away, and Hilary's father continued to see her every week. Their lives were full and connected to a world of supportive friends.

"Still, I went through a period of being traumatized and unhappy because I desperately wanted a mate," Sheila continues. "My natural tendency is to be partnered. I didn't necessarily want a husband, but I wanted that intimate connection with someone. I actually went a little crazy trying to figure out what was wrong with me, and where did I fit, and was I supposed to be single the rest of my life, and what would that mean? I would obsess on those questions, and for a while I was so emotional about it all that it made it very hard to be present for Hilary. I had to keep pulling myself back to be there for her.

"I finally came to the point where I decided I would have lovers now and then and seek out close connections with many people. That's what was important — there were a lot of different parts of me, and I really liked having friends, both men and women, whom I could connect to in different ways. I was trying to let go of attachment to a particular formula. I had had the formula in my happy little marriage, but I hadn't been happy."

So Sheila stopped looking. She cultivated her friendships, and "Hilary became my pal and my partner. I took her everyplace with me. We went to bookstores and movies together. Looking back, she has a very positive, romantic image of our years together. It was such a bonding time."

When Hilary was nine, Sheila's own father remarried. Sheila and her daughter traveled to the Midwest for the ceremony. "Jack was the son of my dad's best man. There were no sparks, but something deep clicked between us." A number of the single parents I spoke with reported the same experience of being attracted to a different kind of person now that they have children — someone with whom there are perhaps no sparks but something deep. Maybe one of the gifts of raising children is to bring us to a deeper understanding of love and release us from the flash and drama of more superficial romance.

"He lived halfway across the country, so we wrote letters to each other for a year. Something about that letter-writing made me trust him. And he was so willing to take Hilary on. That is rare. Other men I had met thought it was sweet and romantic to have a mother/daughter team, but they didn't really want daddy responsibilities. I knew, though, that such men did exist, because my own stepfather had been such a wonderful dad."

During the same year that Sheila and Jack were growing closer by mail, a colleague of Sheila's at the college started courting her — and

Hilary. In Sheila's heart, Jack was the one. But the other man was present in Hilary's life, and what was best for her? When her colleague proposed, Sheila went to her daughter, uncertain what to do. "'This is going to sound really weird,' I told her, 'but I am feeling confused.' And I told her what was happening. I made it real clear to her that I wasn't going to marry anyone she didn't approve of. She said, 'Oh, Mom, I'd much rather have Jack as my stepfather.' She hardly knew him, although we had talked about him a lot, and I'd read parts of his letters to her. I said to her, 'You are part of this decision, Hilary, and it is really important to me that you are willing to make it work. Because if you're not, you're my number-one priority.'"

Just as it is important for someone dating a single parent to respect the depth of the bond between parent and child, it is vital to keep that bond in view if a marriage or committed relationship is to work. Marriage is not an automatic solution to the pulls we feel between our children and someone who has come into our lives as a partner and mate, although one single father, Bryce, had hoped it could be.

When Bryce and his wife divorced after twenty-one years of marriage, he took on responsibility for raising their four children himself. "Actually I was very pleased when she wanted to leave the kids with me, because I really like kids," Bryce says. "She does too, but she doesn't do as well on the day-to-day stuff. Even though she doesn't see them a lot now, I've never encouraged them to reject her, and we're still good friends. In fact, I think that is one of the most successful things we've ever done together — we never made the kids choose between us. They never had to give up one of their parents."

About a year after Bryce became a single father, he began to date a woman he met at church. They were both Mormons, and family was important to them. As they got to know each other, some issues about priorities and what "family" meant for each of them came up, but both seemed to feel that commitment would help solve the problems. About a year after they met, Bryce and Linda married; two and a half years later, they divorced.

Linda's two children were in their late teens and no longer around home much, so, as Bryce says, "integrating our kids with each other was not the problem. We did have differences about how mine ought to be raised. But the real problem was that I had this romantic notion that we were going to put this together and be a tight little family again. My former wife and I and the kids had always been a tight family, and I thought we could be the same."

For Linda and Bryce, however, trying to create a new family only seemed to intensify the tug of hearts that had occurred while dating. "I tried to make sure Linda knew that she was important in my life, but she's very perceptive. She could see how important my kids are to me, and it put me in a bad bind," Bryce says. "Out of her feeling a little insecure, Linda would set up situations where I'd have to choose between her and the kids. Maybe I'd be doing something with one of them, and she would say, 'Let's go out and get a salad for dinner.' I wasn't going to drop the kid and run out the door with Linda. And it happened the other way around too. I'd be trying to have some quiet time with her and the kids kept coming in, one after the other, until the whole evening was taken up by kids coming in. They probably wanted me to choose too."

But the choice was already made. "Linda wanted my bond to her to be stronger than it was to the kids," Bryce says. "And even though I thought it should be true too, it still just wasn't the case. I had bonds that went back fifteen or twenty years with the kids, and with her for about a year. And definitely those older bonds were stronger. The kids are my flesh and blood, and by golly, that was more important to me deep down inside."

Bryce's bright, shining, confident kids are the flowers of his dedication. But does the cost have to be the sacrifice of that other chamber of his heart? And is the parent the only one compelled to stretch the heart's capacity? Everyone in a newly forming family may know what they want to get, yet find themselves faced instead with what they must give.

"Both Jack and Hilary wanted all my attention," says Sheila, continuing her story. "Now they have a very nice relationship, but it took a long time. Jack was strongly aware of the fact that Hilary and I were the primary dyad in our family. He told me later that he didn't fully understand my connection with Hilary until our own child, Thea, was born, five years after we got married.

"So at first the three of us had what I would call in my communications courses a 'toxic triad.' I had a connection to both of them; they were the weak link. It started to change when I got a job teaching at night, which forced Jack to be the primary caretaker. Now they're great together. He taught her all about baseball and they talk the sports page together. They still go on an annual ski trip. But it took that kind of time.

"In many ways I found parenting in a marriage much more challenging than it had been doing it on my own. In my courses we talk about the fact that a dyad is a much stronger system than a triad. When it had been just Hilary and me, the rules were clear. We negotiated them, and they were set; but we made them together. If we decided we wanted to do something together, we did it. If we wanted to do something separately, that was okay. There was just a lot more control over how the communication between us went. When there are two parents, like Jack and I with our own daughter now, there always has to be discussion.

"Also, when I was parenting alone and would come home from work, it was just Hilary and me. She and I could spend our time with each other or by ourselves together. When you come home and there are three people, it increases the amount of interactions you feel responsible for. There is just something easier about the energy of two. It's much easier to set a mood and a field to work within. It takes a lot more work for three to dance together."

Strengthening that third connection, so one's partner and one's child can begin to dance, requires, as one single mother put it, "a lot of communication and a conscious process of turning over some of the responsibilities. A person coming into your life really has to carve their own niche." And we have to be willing to let go and allow some of that. It is an intricate dance.

The man Shay finally married started it off on the right foot. He brought two rings to the wedding — one for Shay, a sapphire amid diamonds, and a tiny sapphire for her daughter, Jenny. "In the ceremony, he gave her a ring as his daughter. Here's a man who never thought he would marry anybody with children, but he's a natural."

Even when we do find a partner, that bond with our children remains, deep and unique. "Hilary is engaged now, at twenty, to a very sweet man," says Sheila. "She called the other day from the East Coast, where she's in school — we have these huge phone bills because she just likes to chat, and we're still such pals. She was thinking about her wedding and wondering who should give her away. She said, 'It would hurt Jack's feelings if my dad did, and I could never do that, because Jack has been much more of a father than my father. But I don't want to hurt my dad's feelings either.' I said, 'Well, have them both.' She wasn't sure by the time we hung up.

"Then she called back a few days later and said, 'Mom, when Frank asked me who he should ask if he could marry me, I said you. Then I realized that *you* are also the one who ought to give me away. You are the one who ought to walk down the aisle with me — because you have always been there.' My very traditional daughter is breaking the formula." Sheila smiles. "It was so sweet. Those are the kind of statements we make to each other that indicate we still are a strong primary dyad."

Even in the best of all new worlds, like the one Sheila and Jack seem to have, the bond with the child is still perhaps primary. From the steps of his beach house, Kevin serenaded a new partner into his life and into the lives of his two boys. But it was the man who married, not the father. "I saw that the ultimate responsibility for the children remains with the one who brings them into the marriage," he says. "It's far different from that of a two-parent system. So even though I found a mate, I was still a single father, and I have been one ever since." The guidelines for forming a successful partnership when we have children are highly specific, and it requires a conscious effort to learn them.

Bryce and Linda remained friends after their divorce. "We always liked each other. It was just that all that other crap had come up." How that "crap" could so thoroughly interfere with their love for each other was a mystery they didn't want to leave unsolved, so they decided to take a stepparenting class together. "The thing I found out in taking the class," Bryce reports, "is that of course the tight little unit won't happen again. You're not a nuclear family. You might be able to do better if you start with kids at age three, but not with teenagers. It's like I'd been chasing a foolish dream the whole time. It was a sad thing to me to realize that, because I had really enjoyed being a good close family in my first marriage, and I really wanted it again. I finally came to the conclusion that my kids are getting grown and it isn't going to happen. Linda and I had learned all this stuff the hard way instead of having those realistic expectations at the outset.

"Taking that course let us know that these problems we were having that seemed so hard for us to solve and resolve are the same thing that everybody has. We had just thought that *we* were doing it wrong, and that we were defective. But we came to see that we actually were operating off different expectations. Hers were more in the nature of just how devoted to her I could be and still raise a family. And mine were just how tight we could get this family together, and how devoted she could become to my kids. But she couldn't — they weren't her kids, and I hadn't looked at it that way."

Within a year of taking the class, Bryce and Linda married again, ready to try a second time. "We can probably be plenty tight as a family anyway," Bryce comments, "but I had just had this picture in my mind of how it was supposed to be." Bryce had to give up that dream for one that would work.

Perhaps our pursuit of love is always a foolish dream insofar as we hope to harvest the beauty of love without the pain of its human expression. But the pain in love serves to break us open, to move us beyond our limits and into something greater than ourselves, greater than our categories and conceptions.

"I love being partnered with Jack," says Sheila, "but I know that he's not everything in the whole wide world. Having been a single parent, I got a sense of myself that I never would have otherwise, I'm sure. I got a sense of autonomy and strength and identification of who I am that I would never have gotten by continuing to be partnered. I got a sense of community and how you can create family with people you trust and who love your child. I don't fear now if circumstances would bring me back to parenting alone.

"But I do really value parenting with Jack. The physical part is lots easier — if Thea gets sick I can ask Jack what his day is like and we can decide who can stay home when. I remember when Thea was almost three years old and how much it meant to her running back and forth between Jack and me. I remember thinking, 'Hilary was this age when this got taken away from her.' But I also miss the special closeness Hilary and I had together. It's sort of the yin and the yang of parenting. I love both ways.

"Really, what it comes down to is, how do we create that sense of family? It doesn't require any one formula. There are lots of ways to get that feeling."

Whether it is through Bryce's acceptance of his "plenty tight family anyway," or through Sheila's family of friends when Hilary was a child, or through Jacki's ultimate decision to choose her daughter because "a man can be replaced but a kid can't," as single parents we are redefining our conceptions of family, of relationships, indeed of what is most important in life.

"We tend to focus on the singleness of our lives as the cause of our problems," comments Priscilla. "We think, 'Well, maybe if I just have a relationship, these things will change.' It's not that. No matter who we are — rich, poor, blind, single, or married — we're all having to face the same basic issue. I think it comes down to trying to figure out what life is supposed to be about."

If it's about love, which is essentially what all those love songs of the ages proclaim, then these changes that are happening in our families and in our relationships may be some new avenues for its entry. Our concepts about marriage and partnership are changing radically. When partnership simply can't mean two half people completing each other's lives — because as single parents we can't wait for our other half in order to raise our families, because as single parents we already have a completion of love through our children — then even the formula for what a relationship is or can be for us changes. "The way I see it," muses Billy, "is if you don't have a need to be in a relationship and you have other deep satisfactions, like Aaron is for me, and my music and carving, then if a relationship does come along that's right, you're a much better person to get into it because you are already a whole person."

Now at the other end of the parenting journey, having seen her daughter off on the first great venture of her life, Jacki admits that "it's no longer a priority to find a man. I would still very much like to have a man in my life who was a really sweet guy and a good companion, even someone I could spend my life with, but it doesn't seem to be all that important. I actually have a better time hanging out with my women friends — and it's a lot easier! Even though I would like to, it's not like I've got to meet a guy or I'll go nuts, or that I won't ever be a whole person without one."

For some single parents, the childrearing years do pass without the partner so many once felt they couldn't get along without. What once seemed so essential becomes "an illusion," as Marina, a mother raising her son alone, calls it. "The hardest part of becoming a single parent was realizing that my conviction that I had to have a partner in order to be happy was a fallacy. I thought I needed a man around to make me complete. Now, raising my son, I get a different sense of myself and realize that no one can make me complete from the outside."

Our children teach us a great deal about how to love and relate. If, like Sophie, we can take the time when we are focusing on them as a time to heal our wounds, we may be able to invite a partner into a functioning family unit as a welcome expansion of our love rather than as a hoped-for solution to our problems. We can use the pressure of providing our children with stability as an incentive to look carefully before we leap and to deal with our own self-destructive patterns before we choose a mirror of our deficiencies in a partner.

If we don't find a partner while our children are growing up, the "school" of raising them may well prepare us for one later. Laurinda feels not only that she learned how to love through her son, but also that raising a son helped to heal her wounds about men and enabled her to see a man as a person rather than as a threat. Now thirty-one years after first becoming a single parent by divorce, she is partnered with a man with whom she does have the first true love of her life — after her son.

Friends sometimes ask me if I miss having a *relationship*, pronounced in that way that carries the momentum of romantic history. "I do have a relationship," I sometimes answer — one of the deepest and most intense of my life, one in which I am learning more about love than ever before. If I do someday enter an intimate partnership with another adult, it will not be for the perfect romance but rather, as Elias has shown me, as a further opening into love with all its pain and glory.

CHAPTER 11

———— ◆ ————

There Is Always an Other:
Talking To and About the Other Parent

A child can live through anything, so long as he or she is told the truth and is allowed to share with loved ones the natural feelings people have when they are suffering.

— Eda LeShan

KNIGHTS AND DRAGONS had become Elias's latest passion. His quest to sort out "good" and "bad" was playing itself out through stories of noble adventurers saving innocents from the fiery scourge, and he was bent on becoming the hero. So when he saw "real armor," molded from gray plastic, at the toy store, he was certain he needed it. I hesitated. Fighting had not been an earnest part of his play before, and I wasn't sure how much I wanted to encourage it. In the end I relented, and we carried it home.

More than delighted, Elias began the transformation immediately, wielding the sword as if he had been born to it. I pulled a string through the belt slits on the gold plastic scabbard and tied it to his waist. Slipping his arms through the straps of the breastplate, I turned him around, kneeling to secure it in back. Meanwhile, he investigated the helmet. With one size to fit all interested heads, this one was large enough for him to pull the visor down as a chin strap while it still covered his mouth and nose. Disguise complete, he turned to meet me, armored in plastic from navel to crown — all but the eyes.

I saw them alone for the first time, isolated from the soft features and fine, blond hair that had defined his face from baby into boy. All at once I was hovering between a surge of love for my little knight and a sudden impulse to flee. There, framed in armor, were the eyes of the father he had never seen. Inside me, those eyes had frozen into the cold stare of adversity. Now there before me, they were melting my moment of confusion as they lifted into a smile.

There is always an Other. Whether they are part of our daily lives or not, they are present in our children. The Other may be our children's other biological parent or our adopted children's birth parents. The Other may be someone we once loved or someone we have never seen. Whether he or she is actively involved in the lives of our children or not, the Other is present in the nucleus of each cell of their bodies, present in the depths of their psyches. For our children, the Other is not *other* but part of them. And in whatever way and to whatever degree we can, we must honor their right to that part of themselves. For us that may well mean learning how to relate to and about that Other in a way that supports our children as they carve out their relationship with their other parent, whether that relationship is solely within our children's minds and imaginations or whether it also involves interaction between child and parent.

Their journey may begin with questions: Why don't I have a daddy? Why don't you and Mama live together? Who is my other parent? They seek out their origin story as intently as a scientist delving into the secrets of the universe. How we answer them depends a great deal on how we hold our own story of the Other in our hearts and minds — whether we see the Other as ally or adversary, as one who helped us to fulfill a dream or a traitor who destroyed one. What we tell them can contribute to a story that heals the division or conflict they may feel, that addresses a void or soothes a rejection — or that perpetuates the search and the pain.

Those who consciously chose from the outset to be single parents will inevitably have questions to answer. But their answers can focus on their own longing and love for their children rather than on conflict or loss surrounding the other parent. Those who intentionally conceived or adopted may choose to help their children search for biological parents. These children may have to come to terms with a void in their lives, but they are not caught in the trauma of divorce or separation, pulled between two parents or repeatedly rejected. For parents who chose, the questions were perhaps anticipated and prepared for long before they arose.

"I felt it was very important to be as truthful as possible right from the beginning so that I wouldn't end up in the position of losing my daughter Willow's trust by later getting caught in a lie or having to redo the story," explains Ruby, a woman who conceived her daughter by donor insemination. "So many people knew our story, and I didn't want another child to suddenly drop a bombshell on her one day."

When Willow was about three years old, she watched one of the family's roosters jumping on a chicken and started asking why. "I seized the moment!" says Ruby. "I told her that men have seeds and that I had to go to a special place to get some so that I could start growing her. The details have gotten more filled in as she gets older." As far as Ruby can tell, Willow has been comfortable with the explanation. Now that she's eleven, other questions come up. "I wish I could meet my real father," Willow said one day. "I'm sometimes curious too," Ruby told her, "although it's not possible to find out." They talked a little more, "she wondering what he looked like, me wondering what his career was. We keep the story open and alive."

For Ruth, who adopted her daughter from Central America, there was no story to keep open and alive. Little, except for war and poverty, had been told to her about four-year-old Evita's past. Evita herself had to tell Ruth. "She wouldn't talk much about her parents and family, but one night when she was about eight, her best friend was over. We had built a fire, and Evita ended up telling us her story. She just started pacing up and down in front of the fire, talking. It wasn't with a lot of feeling, just 'This is what happened. My mama said, "You need to go away." And she combed my hair and cut it before I left, and she cried and cried. And then they came in this van and a soldier I knew took me away to a house where kids who have no mommies and daddies live. They said, "You're going to America."'"

"It was amazing," Ruth says softly. "Her little friend and I just sat there. I used to say to her, 'We'll go back someday to visit,' and she would say, '*No, esta cerrado,*' it is closed, meaning that part of her life has ended for her."

For others too, those who have come to single parenting through pain, loss, or conflict, keeping the story of the Other open and alive can be a challenge. The stories of parents who conceived their children together can end in devastating pain. How ironic that the passion that once drew two people together can with equal intensity blow them apart. For many, the other partner looms large as a source of pain, fear, perhaps continuing and unresolved conflict. Mention of the Other may catch in our throats or rise with a surge of anger. Some of us have to chop through a dense thicket to remember the love that called our children to life.

Among the single parents I spoke with, the story of the Other was one often told in anger or tears. One mother painted a terrifying picture of fleeing through city streets, infant in arms, pursued by the baby's father. One father remembered with pain his little boys waiting for Mama to come back from the store where she said she was going when she left. Another mother reported having made a dedicated effort to keep her child in touch with his other parent, "because I felt it was important for him to know his father," and then opening her door one day to discover she was being sued for full custody.

Less dramatic but no less grim are the stories of those who struggle to survive financially alone or those who with inadequate answers face the searching eyes of their children. An astounding percentage of noncustodial parents take little or no emotional or financial responsibility for their children. On the other hand, some, paying the state-ordered minimum in child support, feel entitled to interfere at every juncture with their children's upbringing. Those who try to co-parent may find the unresolved problems of their dissolved marriage heightened.

While children may be spared, by divorce or separation, the damaging effects of conflict between their parents, their inner healing must still take place. Our role in that is essential. There are no easy ways to resolve this issue of the Other, because unlike some other challenges we face as single parents, this one may have no apparent solutions to make it right for everyone involved.

Some do manage to work it out, as we will see in this chapter. But the issues are complex and require delicate and dedicated work. "I have this saying that you never know someone until you say good-bye to them," Sheila comments. "I've seen people who seem very loving and caring suddenly rip their kid apart emotionally to get back at an estranged spouse. My ex-husband and I had to fight that impulse. There is such a pull in romantic relationships to be so angry about the ending and to blame each other that you get into hateful and mean-spirited kinds of behaviors. But we both loved Hilary, and we understood that we had to come out of this as friends with each other for her sake. We held that strongly as our goal, but it was hard. We created a saying for all three of us: 'The family is in the heart, not the home.' We weren't going to badmouth each other, and we were going to talk about childrearing practices together. When Hilary's father comes and visits her now, he and I do stay up all night and talk. But I could never live with him."

Even though these two parents worked to resolve their conflict, their three-year-old daughter still felt pulled apart by the separation. "Hilary went through a period of kicking and screaming, with both of us. She'd scream, 'I hate you, I hate you!' At me. At him. We would just hold her and let her cry. I'd say, 'I know it feels really bad. We feel bad too, but we can't do this together.'" Even at that, it took Hilary until she was a teenager to finally accept her parents' divorce.

But when conflict remains unresolved, within ourselves or between us and the Other, it can settle deep into our children. They struggle, often in silence, to reconcile the two, for unless they can claim the Other, either actually or figuratively, a part of them is missing.

◆ A P A R T O F B O T H

"They told me they were unhappy together, and that they fought." Twelve-year-old Danielle sits poised on the couch, speaking with the clarity and sophistication one might expect from the child of two creative and successful professionals. "They told me stories about each other. She told me that my dad was not kind to women, and he told me that my mom only married for money. I felt like I was part of both, but instead of being part of two good things, I was part of two bad things. So I always felt I must be something bad, because that's what my parents were."

The depth of children is scarcely determined by their age, although we may sometimes be misled by their elfin voices or limited vocabularies to assume that their feelings or psyches are only half formed. Our children, no matter what their age, ponder vast issues. And at a time when they are still trying to establish simple categories of good and bad, they are faced with having to comprehend subtle shades of gray.

Danielle was three and a half when her parents separated. As an infant she had been left primarily in her mother's hands by a father who had been very unsure about having a baby in an unstable marriage. However, by the time Danielle reached eighteen months, his walking, talking living doll had become irresistible to him. "They bonded just like this," Cath says, crossing two fingers. "By the time she was three, she was so close to him. It was very hard for me because there was no way for her to see that in some ways he was quite dangerous."

Cath herself had come to see that, but by the time she realized that she had to leave, half of Danielle "belonged" to Daddy. "I think it would have been better for her to be with just me from the time she was quite small," Cath says. "But neither of them would have permitted it, even though over the years it was clear that it made her practically crazy to be with him for any extended period of time. I saw it, I suffered it, I wanted total custody of her. But I felt there would be no way to control it legally, considering who he was, his status and his public character. Besides, he would have just come by brute force and taken her, and she would have gone with him. It was impossible to control. So I resigned myself to playing the role of mediator and of being there for her no matter what happened . . . and hoping eventually that she would see it and choose to live with me full-time."

Battling to define herself, suspended above an abyss, Danielle tried to force the plunge. "I tried committing suicide twice," she says candidly. "It had to do with my family. I felt my parents were not the way *I* wanted to be." Did she have a right even to live if she was indeed "part of two bad things"? But perhaps that was why she felt compelled to defend her father and seek his redeeming qualities as well.

"Whatever is supposed to be good about me is supposed to be from my mom," she says. "Nothing is ever given to my dad as praise. Even though a lot of him has been very destructive, he has given me a whole lot — my spiritual self, my ability to compensate, to give a lot to people. And even though he might be a jerk, everybody has feelings. I think if people don't care for someone, they should still love them, because the person can't help how they are."

Danielle's compassion could lift her beyond the absolute categories of good and bad that were pulling her apart. For our children, this issue of who or what is good or bad is a critical part of their attempt to define the world — and themselves. "Does a bad person know that they're bad?" Elias asked me once. The answer opens out into a world of questions. Are people bad or are actions bad? If someone hurts me, are they bad? If my mother or my father hurts me, are they bad? And if they are, am I? Children pulled apart by unhealthy conflict between their parents in any family structure are engaged in an internal battle which to them is as serious as life and death. And they are compelled to find a way either to escape or to formulate some image that makes them feel put together again.

"I make up families, and that's what keeps me alive," Danielle tells me. She has filled dozens of spiral-bound notebooks with penciled stories illustrated with images cut from magazines — stories of families where children and parents live together with no conflict, stories of what she dreams her own family might be when she grows up. There are also pages of her poetry. Opening one notebook, Danielle reads a poem which defines the split she has been trying to mend:

> I am a bait
> Between two hungry eagles
> That claim I am their supper.
> Who is right?
> Who knows?
> Their reasons are equal
> But judgments and intentions vary.
> I hope that I am the right bird's supper.

"She wrote that when she was ten," her mother offers in a small voice. "Isn't that just chilling? And it's really . . ." — Cath lets out a pained sigh — ". . . accurate, accurate. I have been at such a loss about how to handle this split Danielle feels in herself because her father and I are so distant and so different. I feel like this desire to have the mother and the father and the baby all together is almost something inherent, something very deep. Sometimes I'd find her awake at night when she was young, carrying on conversations with the invisible figures of Jesus, Mary, and Joseph, who, she said, were sitting at the foot of her bed. I feel like this Holy Family model is a kind of archetype, a deep symbol in the psyche — and I don't know if archetypes can change. Children know they come from a man and a woman. They want to put that together, but I don't know what can be done.

"And even though I have been so aware of the lack she has suffered, and I have so much wanted to address it, have wanted even to be both things to her, I am astonished that I have not been able to do that. I wanted her to be happy without that. And yet she has obviously experienced tremendous fragmentation. When she was very little, it focused on a deep necessity she felt for all three of us to be together. Once around the time when her dad and I first separated, she was riding behind me on a bike and she said, 'Oh, I love my mom so much. I can press a button on her back and she turns into my dad.' In her eyes, the three of us always had to be a unit, no matter how separate we were. That pull of trying to get the two parents back together again has got to be a way of trying to reunite a fragmented sense of self."

A fragmented sense of self. Is this, then, what we are dealing with when our children ask those questions: Can he come back? Why isn't she here? Elias at three wanted to know who made his daddy go away. "Did *you* make him go away?" he asked me. Then, cautiously, his deeper, more critical concern: "Did *I* make him go away?" Who is good and who is bad here? To answer their questions truthfully and appropriately can challenge us to our bones.

"It just broke my heart each time Trevor would ask me the question 'Why don't I have a father who loves me?' How do you answer that?" Sophie asks. She is remembering back to the days when Trevor was five or six. "Each time he asked, I had to take a deep breath and say, 'God help me with this one.'

"A few years later, when a girlfriend of mine got pregnant, she asked if she could stay with us and have her baby. She was someone Trevor liked a lot. I told him she was coming over and had a baby in her tummy and that we were going to help her have the baby. His first question was, 'Where's the father?' I told him that the father was not coming. 'Why?' he asked me. 'He has decided not to be a father,' I said, as evenly as I could. Trevor just slumped. 'Mom,' he said, 'I don't understand how a man can do this. This is his *baby*.' What he's saying is, 'How could *my* father do this?'"

Trevor was not facing the kind of expressed conflict between separated parents that Danielle was, but he struggled as well with issues of love and conflict. And seeing his father only once a year, Trevor was struggling with a void. As Sophie puts it, "These concerns and questions are Trevor's attempts to develop his own story. Even though I would like him to be able to do that with as little pain in it as possible, he will have pain. That will be part of the chiseling tools of his life. But how do I answer him? He is going to be a man someday, and he is asking, 'How can a man do that?' He's also asking, 'How does a man *not* do that? What would it mean to be a father?'

"I can't say to him, 'Your father knows what he's doing, and when you grow up you too will leave your son.' I can't say, 'Your father is an awful man and you have a right to feel betrayed.' I do say, 'I'm sure all those men hurt because they don't know how to show love.' I do say, 'I don't really understand either, Trevor.' Then I go on to tell him, 'Someday you are going to be a man. Someday it's likely that you will have a child of your own. You do not have to be the way you see these men being, because you have an opportunity to construct for yourself the kind of father you feel a child needs.'

"He knows what that is. He knows what he needs, he knows what he has a longing for." The steps Trevor would take to define that for himself would challenge Sophie to understand and support him in a way she hadn't anticipated, as we shall see later in this chapter.

What do we do as parents to help our children feel "put together"? How does *our* relationship with the other parent affect our children? How do we assist them in resolving the conflict or confusion they may feel? The answers are as unique and varied as our circumstances. But the inescapable challenge we all share is facing the reality of the Other and acting with full integrity for the sake of our children.

We cannot save them from the pain of their own life stories, but we can make choices we hope will enable them to move forward with a sense of their own strength and integrity intact. We may choose to minimize a draining conflict with the other parent by negotiating rules of conduct. We may make choices about how we talk about the Other to our children. We may decide to minimize and even prevent contact when necessary. We choose how we will stand by and support our children as they seek their own healing.

In all instances, we also have to resolve some of our own inner conflicts. In the end, perhaps it is the compassion or forgiveness we hold for the other parent, whether he or she is in our lives or not, that is most healing to our children.

◆ BREAKING THE ICE

"Shannon basically thinks of her childhood as positive, and I look back on that mothering time as a good experience." As Margaret talks softly about her years of raising her daughter alone, I sense a deep and private world behind her gentle warmth. The story she tells reveals that for her and Shannon the Other had been ushered away into that inner world long ago and had remained there, hidden and inaccessible. "Even though things fell into place in many areas of our lives, I see now that there was an enormous iceberg of energy, in me and also between us, that Shannon and I simply did not acknowledge — and that had to do with who her father was."

It wasn't that Margaret hid a uniquely shameful secret about Shannon's father. Like others, his crime was that he turned away from a woman he knew little about and a daughter he met once when she was three weeks old. It was the late sixties, and being a single mother was becoming acceptable, maybe even desirable, at least in Margaret's circle of hip and creative friends. Besides, Margaret "had a distinct feeling that we weren't really meant to stay together, even though I thought he was a good person. By the time I found out I had gotten pregnant, he had stopped calling. I don't know if it was pride or what, but combined with my not being that interested in him, I just went ahead and went through the whole pregnancy myself.

"After my daughter was born, I decided it wasn't really fair not to tell him, so I called him. He came over and met her and was happy to see her. But in the meantime he had married a woman with three kids, and they were pregnant with their own child. He didn't call again after he left, and I thought that if he didn't feel like building that connection, I didn't really feel like pursuing him to do that."

But there is another significant part to the story. "My parents had wanted me to give the baby up for adoption," Margaret explains. "They were not at all supportive of my parenting alone. Actually my father was irate, and he repeatedly threatened to kill whoever it was that had gotten me pregnant. I knew he wouldn't actually do that, but I felt very afraid. I didn't want anyone in my family to find out who he was."

It wouldn't be until years later that Margaret would recognize how her father's threats had sealed her choice to keep Shannon's father out of the picture. But at the point when she moved back to her parents' house with a month-old baby, it was clearly best to keep quiet. Soon enough, the memory of Shannon's father was buried.

"It wasn't that I was deliberately trying to hide from Shannon that she had a father," says Margaret. "But the hidden part turned out to be that she didn't get any sense *at all* of who he was. And I think it had a tremendous effect on her. I could see a tendency in her to push other things away as well. If she didn't want to discuss something, it absolutely didn't exist." It was a response that gave Margaret pause. Although our influence accounts for only part of who and what our children are, the choices we make when they are young certainly do bend the branch. Now, twenty-five years later, Margaret says that a pattern of denial took root in her child of "immaculate conception."

One thing Shannon couldn't deny, however, was her mother's dedication and love. The child thrived, strong and confident, surrounded by a loving community of friends. Margaret recalls neighbor children running in and out of their big old house, a Great Dane and a German shepherd patrolling the yard, and a little girl happy with her life. "Whenever children would ask Shannon about her dad, she always replied simply that she didn't have one. I'd hear her tell them, 'My mom conceived me by herself.'" Those few times when Shannon asked her mother where her father was, Margaret simply told her that she didn't know — which was the truth.

Shannon grew up, moved out, and, a year after starting college, met a man and married. Perhaps it was when they began to consider having a child themselves that the reality of Shannon's own void became apparent. Conception was not immaculate; it was real and human and intimately bound up with a father. Somewhere she did have one. Where? At twenty-two Shannon came to her mother to say she really wanted to meet him.

"After all those years, I found I had a lot of emotion attached to the issue," Margaret recalls. "I felt afraid, really afraid. If I found him, I wondered how he would receive my daughter after all that time. I assumed he still had a family of his own. How would they react? And what about all the expectations and feelings Shannon had built up? I wanted to protect her. But I wasn't even sure why I was so scared." Perhaps Margaret could still hear the voice of her own father, twenty-two years before, threatening havoc. Perhaps she feared admitting into her own life again — even if just through her daughter — someone who had had such a profound impact on it. Even after years of separation, we may still find our hearts leap at the sight of the Other, or our jaws set hard as if to ward off an assault.

No matter what lay behind Margaret's fears, however, she had to do something. Her daughter had asked. "I was the one who had the pieces that would allow Shannon to go ahead and meet her dad and see who he was." Time passed, however, and Margaret kept *thinking* about trying to find him. "It was so hard for me to do. Eventually I had to admit that I just wasn't doing it, and that I needed some help." Margaret asked a friend, who agreed to do what was needed. "I told him what the man's work had been, where he had lived, and anything I could remember. I had no idea where he might be."

After some weeks, Margaret's "detective" found a phone number for someone of that name and description living in a neighboring state. He called and asked whether the man remembered Margaret and coming to meet the baby daughter. "That child is now a young woman and would like to meet you," Margaret's friend told him. The man on the other end of the line listened to the stranger with this momentous message, took down his name, said, "You must have the wrong person," and hung up.

"I'm sure it must have been such a shock to him," Margaret acknowledges. "But then he called my friend back and apologized and said that yes, he would like to meet her. He and his family were actually scheduled for a vacation near here the very next week, and he would get in touch with her himself."

There are so many children today who have no contact with their other parent, especially with the father, that this search for the Other is becoming a primary mythos of our time. Two, so intimately linked, perhaps even resembling each other, find themselves face to face as total strangers. For Shannon, the man who stood up and walked toward her across a restaurant was almost a complete mystery until that moment.

"Shannon went alone to meet the man and his family. That's what she wanted to do, and that was fine with me," Margaret relates. "They all were, at least that first time, very welcoming." The ice had been broken, and something frozen had been released in the young woman.

And so too in her mother. "When I was finally willing and able to talk about her father with Shannon openly, I was amazed at the release I felt. There's so much tied up in us when we're not honest about things or able to feel that we can be honest. We deprive ourselves and our families. I think that whatever is hidden or unknown in families affects everyone.

"The important thing for both of us that came out of her meeting him was seeing that when something so enormous as the identity of a child's other parent is hidden, it distorts the child's life. And it also distorts the parent's life to hide something like that. One of the gifts to Shannon of my finally going through that difficult process of enabling her to go ahead and meet her dad is allowing her to look at a lot of things she hadn't looked at before."

In the years since that time, Margaret has found herself working in her healing practice with people who have been adopted or have not known one of their parents. "I started to notice some patterns I found interesting. Often these clients reported that they would grow very close to people and then push them away — until they made contact in some way with that absent parent. I have come to conclude that everyone who has an absent parent should at least be able to see a photograph of them, even if they don't have a relationship with that parent. This at least gives them some way to connect with and answer where they came from on that level."

Shannon had her answer. Even though the relationship with her father didn't become all she might have wished for, at least she could sink her teeth into her own destiny and grapple with it, and in Margaret's mind, she and the shadowy Other could proceed on into their separate lives, disentangled now that they had met in their grown daughter. "Even though I hadn't been interested in the man myself, it was important for my daughter to have some sense of him. More important than I had thought," says Margaret.

She is quiet for a moment, pacing some avenue in that inner vastness. "Maybe I might have kept that relationship more open," she offers, musing aloud. "He closed it down, but I maybe could have sent him photos or asked for one or something. Maybe I could have done more of that on behalf of my daughter." Margaret hesitates again. "Actually, though, I don't think I *could* have done it differently, since at that time I was so afraid that someone would get hurt."

Taking a deep breath, Margaret offers now with no hesitation, "The one thing that I do feel I would do differently is to address that issue of her father with her more directly. What I am saying is that it's important to be as honest with our children as possible, and to find help in looking at the issues if necessary."

◆ KICKING AND SCREAMING

When Carmela found that she and her partner of several years were pregnant, there was no question in *her* mind about whether to keep him in their lives, but there were a lot of questions in the mind of her partner. Determined that her daughter would know her daddy, Carmela waged a campaign to adjust her outer world as intense as Margaret's had been to adjust her inner world. Jarrett wouldn't budge. By the time Carmela was seven months pregnant, he had basically disappeared from her life. "But I had this whole thing in my mind that my kid needs a father, that he was making a really big mistake, and that it was my job to correct it," says Carmela.

Meanwhile, she attended birth classes with a girlfriend and tried to heal her wounds. "I felt desperate most of the time — emotionally up and down," says Carmela. "But I was bound and determined I was going to keep my life together," and she worked right up until the day she went into labor.

With her first contractions, determination kicked in. Carmela hadn't talked to Jarrett for weeks, but she picked up the phone and called his office to tell him she was in labor. His response hadn't changed: "I don't want anything to do with it." Undaunted, she carried on, shopping to stock the house with groceries, buying cheeses and champagnes for the celebration she planned with her friends and family. "I was having a great time walking around town announcing, 'I'm in labor!' The pains were serious but nothing treacherous.

"At one point I went over to Jarrett's office. He had a line of clients, and I waited there with my huge belly until everybody cleared out. He turned to me and said, 'What are you doing here?'

"I said, 'I'm in labor. You have to know this. I am in labor *right now.* I'm going to the hospital sometime in the next few hours, and I want you there. I think it's really important.' His response was the same: 'Nope, just leave. Go have your baby. Leave me alone.'"

As she put away the groceries back home, labor intensified. "I called him every hour. 'Now I'm down to four minutes. It's getting really close. Time is running out. You really have to do this.'

"'No.'"

Carmela tried persuasion. "'It's a once-in-a-lifetime opportunity. Your kid's being born.'" She tried reason. "'The likelihood of your getting into another relationship and having a child are somewhat slim with your personality the way it is.'"

No again and again. "Each time he'd say no I'd get off the phone and cry and cry. My girlfriends were with me, all saying, 'The bastard! Why do you keep calling him?'

"Sure, I was angry with him and I was bitter about his behavior, but I never hated him. I always loved him. Part of it was the love drama. You know how love is. I was attached to him, and I had his baby. Part of it was that my kid needs a father. Yes, we can have our kids by ourselves and be single parents, but I just think it's vital that children have their connection to both their biological parents. And I was determined to do my damnedest to make sure that could happen.

"In my last call from home, I said, 'I'm down to three-minute contractions. I'll be at Memorial Hospital.' His answer was no, and he was very firm about it." Carmela gave up on Jarrett's being there and went into full-fledged labor — hours and hours of it. "The staff kept saying C-section, but my doctor was great. He was very aware of my psychological strengths and needs. He kept saying, 'Let's wait a little bit.'"

Then literally in the eleventh hour Jarrett appeared. "It was around eleven-thirty at night, and I felt tired and weak, sort of resigned. I didn't have any drugs but I got real passive, which is not my style. All of a sudden Jarrett was there. I thought, 'My God, he is so brave,' because everybody in the room hated his guts. I was astounded that he had come.

"At that point my labor got really bad and I passed out. When they revived me with sugar-water and oxygen, everyone was getting robed up for the delivery room. I heard someone saying, 'Aren't you going in?' and Jarrett's voice answered, 'No, I'm not going to be there.'" That familiar no.

Carmela's friends went into action. "'Damn it, you've come this far. Go all the way!'" They forced him into getting scrubbed and robed and into the delivery room. "My girlfriends were at my feet, and Jarrett was at my head. He was the sweetheart he can be. He can be such a wonderful, nurturing man. And he was all there for me, totally there, in every way he could be.

"The baby was blue when she came out. They rubbed her down and stimulated her, then handed her to him. Jarrett said, 'No, no, no.' Someone answered, 'Take your baby. It's your daughter.'

"After I had nursed her, he went with her for all the procedures while they stitched me up. The nurse came in and said, 'Boy, I've never seen a prouder father in my life down there in that nursery.' Jarrett stayed with the baby and me for the next twenty-four hours. He changed her first diaper, took care of her in every possible way.

And then he disappeared again. Poof! Gone. But I had done it. I had wanted him to feel that bonding, which he did, for her and for him. Then I think all his old stuff just flooded him again.

"My next goal was to get him in her life," Carmela continues. In an operation that resembled extracting wisdom teeth, Carmela sought Jarrett's further involvement in their daughter's life, pressing him to appear for birthdays and holidays, taking photographs on each occasion. She sent photos to Jarrett and to his parents, and saved some. "When Alicia is twenty years old and looks at her family album, I want her to see her dad present throughout her entire life, with no gaps," Carmela declares. Eventually she pressed for child-support payments, which Jarrett finally agreed to. She answered her daughter's questions as best she could — "Your daddy does love you. See, he gives you this money every month." But personal appearances were rare.

"During that first year he'd stop by for a little time, then freak out and go away. He couldn't stand it because the baby cried a lot." Crying babies are notorious for driving parents up the wall, but Jarrett's discomfort had perhaps an extra ingredient. "Even to this day," explains Carmela, "he feels bad. He came the other day with an article that says women under stress have babies that cry a lot. So at that time he was putting two and two together. This kid was just freaking out all the time.

"I was totally exhausted myself. I shut down my business because I realized I was in no shape to deal with that. I had some money in a savings account and I wanted to stay home and try to recover from the emotional trauma of the past months." Carmela continued to see her counselor and, except for the baby, "forgot for a while that the outside world ever existed."

When Alicia was three and a half, Carmela called and invited Jarrett to spend Christmas with them. "We ended up talking for a couple of hours on the phone. If Alicia sees Daddy once, she'll want more. How often could he see her? We discussed the emotional risks this would bring up for her. Jarrett made it clear that I would have to be present if he was going to spend any time with Alicia. He was afraid of what would happen if she had a tantrum or freaked out and cried. We covered a lot of bases."

At the end of the conversation, Jarrett started to wobble again. "You've got to understand I might back out at the last minute. I might chicken out," he told her.

"Okay, I got it," Carmela told him. "I won't say anything to Alicia."

She just waited. "Alicia and I celebrated Christmas Eve together and went to bed." No daddy appeared that night. The next morning when the doorbell rang, despite the nature of the day, no one was expecting the person they found on the doorstep. Santa Claus stood there with hat and beard and literally a bag full of presents. He had "tons of presents. He had an entire year's worth of presents for Alicia. And he had the presents he had bought for her for Christmas the year before but had chickened out sending to her. Alicia was dancing around shouting 'Daddy, Daddy Daddy!!!' It was all very emotional for me. So much must have gone on in his mind and heart without us even knowing it."

Jarrett continued to see his daughter occasionally, but only if Carmela was present. It wouldn't be until Alicia was five years old that Jarrett would spend time with her alone. During the course of those years, the child's two parents struggled to figure out what would work best for their daughter. "To me the fact that we didn't trust each other had to be dealt with," emphasizes Carmela. "You don't just pretend that the problems don't exist and then try to relate with the other for the sake of the kid." But eventually both had to recognize that "every time we tried to communicate about our conflicts, we would get uptight and our goal of having two parents for Alicia would get knocked aside. So we decided to put all that on a back shelf and simply practice being in the presence of each other in harmony. In essence we were creating a new habit."

Over time these two parents have managed to minimize their conflict. Jarrett still hasn't become the devoted father Carmela would wish for her daughter, but Alicia knows who he is and she is forging her own relationship with him. For some single parents, however, no amount of communication or negotiation with the Other can lead to harmony, and for the sake of our children we choose a different way.

♦ CHOOSING WHAT WE MUST

"There are some absolute basic musts in co-parenting, and one of them is that you don't talk against the other parent to the child," Tracey declares. "And you don't involve the child in issues over their heads, issues that simply do not concern them." Tracey's cherished dream of harmonious co-parenting after divorce had fallen on the rocks. "I had held on to that ideal of how we were going to do it, the way I thought it was supposed to be. I just hadn't wanted Dillon to go through that sudden separation of parents that I did as a child. I never saw my parents together again until right before my father died, and I was twenty-eight by that time. It's a great shock for a child to have such a total split."

For a few years, even after Reid had remarried and Tracey had gotten involved in a new relationship, they managed to sustain a friendship, celebrating Christmas and Dillon's birthdays together, meeting to make co-parenting decisions, staying in touch for Dillon's sake. It was not a seamless fabric, but Tracey was determined to do whatever it would take to make her ideal work. When Reid began to increase the time Dillon stayed with him, Tracey complied, even though their divorce agreement had specified that she would be the primary parent during the early years and even though Dillon begged to stay "home" a few more days before going to "Roseanne's house," as he called the home of his father and stepmother.

The summer of his eighth year, Dillon started returning upset from his week-long stays at his father's house. Tracey couldn't get from him what was happening. Was it hard for him to come back? Did he want to stay at Roseanne's longer? Did he want to stay home longer? The boy was silent, sullen. When our children participate in worlds that are off-limits to us, we may find ourselves foundering in a sea of guesswork when something seems amiss.

Indeed, the transition from one house to the other is difficult, as a child snips the web of connection — to one set of values and rhythms, one set of bedroom furnishings, perhaps one set of clothing or pets or foods — and begins rebuilding another. Often they need hours alone to complete the transition. But Dillon was withdrawing for days, and Tracey was worried. Reid wasn't helpful on the phone or particularly friendly.

Then one day when Dillon returned from his father's house, he blurted out, crying in frustration and fury, "Roseanne says you are a liar!" As he filled in the details, Tracey got the picture, and it was not a surprising one. "I knew through friends that Reid had been talking against me, even to them. And now I could see that Roseanne had gotten downloaded with all of his unresolved stuff about me as well, and it had been spilling over onto Dillon. That was immature and inappropriate for her to do, but at the same time I could understand what had happened. I had once been in her position myself, as the emotional basket for all of Reid's stuff about his first wife.

"I had been telling myself all along, 'Turn the other cheek, it will pass, he'll grow up and get it clear.' What I hadn't been doing was admitting my own anger about what Reid was saying. I had told him it was off-limits to talk to my boyfriend about me the last time he did, but because I had wanted to keep up this whole thing of the extended family with him, I had been compromising in a lot of ways. But now this was ripping Dillon apart, and I wasn't going to sit by and watch it happen.

"I wrote a long, very straightforward letter, basically saying let's call a spade a spade, confronting what was going on. I asked Reid to sign an agreement not to make derogatory remarks to Dillon or in front of him about me, my friends, my work, my relationships, my lifestyle, and not to involve Dillon in disagreements between us. And I agreed to make the same commitment to him in return.

"I had to be willing to say, 'This is not working for me.' I had to be willing to call things as they are. This is part of my becoming healthy and really breaking the co-dependency patterns that I've had with Reid all along. But what I also had to be willing to let go of was my desire to have this harmonious, open, extended family type of relationship. I had a lot of myself locked up in that.

"After sending that letter, I felt great, I felt liberated. I felt like after four years we finally were divorced. All of this had been really hard on Dillon, but it ended up being good for both of us. I saw how much I have compromised to try to create this relationship with his father in the way I thought it was supposed to be, meanwhile denying my own anger and also denying what I was seeing going on with Dillon.

"In the past I had not supported Dillon when he'd say, 'I want to stay with you longer, Mom.' I've said, 'Now you've got to go be with your dad. This is your agreement. Your dad wants this.' And so on. I've done it in the name of co-parenting. I felt I couldn't say to Dillon, 'Okay, take a couple more days here, and we'll talk to your dad.'

"I have begun to realize that I have to look at this whole co-parenting endeavor more from the child's point of view than from the parental-need point of view. This ideal that the parents want, of fifty-fifty time between them, makes our children into ping-pong balls. They're always a visitor, going back and forth. Reid's need to have Dillon fifty percent of the time at this point is not necessarily Dillon's need. His need is to be with his dad and to see him, but not for the length of time his dad wants him for.

"I understand the concept of trying to get co-parenting to work, but I think in practice the child needs to feel that there is a primary home and primary caretaker, especially when they're young. I'm not saying that should be the mom. I am saying that the child should be listened to. Of course, it's very difficult because they also need to get into a routine or rhythm that you stick to as well. But I think sticking too tightly to Reid's needs had sacrificed Dillon's needs."

With her second son, who has a different father, Tracey realized early on that there were deep problems between herself and her son's father that could not be resolved. "But this time I knew I was not going to carry on with the relationship just for the sake of supposedly giving the child two parents, either living together or sharing parenting. I was much more willing to face up sooner to that mistake and say no.

"And actually I have had a far easier time parenting Corrin because our lives aren't so focused on conflict with the other parent. It's hard to say of course which way is best for the child. How do we ever know? I can speak pro and con for both ways. But to be caught in the middle of two parents in conflict is very destructive. I know, from my own childhood."

Taking such clear and resolute action can sometimes be the best choice for our children. For Billy that meant finally deciding that Aaron wasn't going to live with his mother again. Maybe Aaron's plummeting grades were his own cry for help; changing schools four times during the year he lived with his mother undoubtedly contributed to his difficulties. Once again with no warning she had arrived to drop the boy at his father's house, saying, "I'm going. I can't do this anymore." Billy finally stood behind what he felt — he was going to raise Aaron himself.

Carmela pursued her baby's father long after most women would have quit. Margaret hid the father away inside her, and then stood against her fears to face her denial. Tracey firmly said no, so that she could say yes to the best interest of her sons. Billy took charge when he no longer felt his wife could handle parenting. These are awesome choices we make, for they profoundly affect the lives of our children, and we can only trust that we are making the best, perhaps only, choice for their sake. We will never know what it would have been like had we taken a different course or had the Other made different choices. *This* is the life we have. Sooner or later, our children will let us know what they need, as did Sophie's son, Trevor, when at age seven he presented his mother with his unexpected request.

◆ STAND BY ME

"Douglas was coming through town and was on his way to pay Trevor his annual visit," Sophie begins. Before she continues, she explains, "We had stopped calling Douglas 'father' or 'daddy' by that time. Since Trevor was so deeply exploring what father really meant for him, he felt good with that. And it worked for me because I feel as if the title 'father' is sacred, and I hoped to reserve the specialness of that role. And 'daddy' felt like an active role rather than a title. So we just called him Douglas."

The afternoon Douglas was due to arrive, Sophie reminded Trevor in passing. "To my surprise, his response was, 'Don't let him in. I don't want to see him.' I was taken aback a bit. He hadn't said anything about feeling this way before."

Even though it had seemed hard on Trevor to see Douglas for those brief visits, Sophie had made it a point not to interfere, based on her experience that when she had tried to discourage the contact, both father and son blamed her for getting in the way. Still, Trevor would be disturbed for weeks after seeing Douglas. A couple of years before, he had spent a week traveling with his father, and had returned refusing to wear seat belts because his dad had said that seat belts were for wimps. Trevor also reported watching murder mysteries on television late at night, and he "even began talking about being afraid that Douglas would hit him," says Sophie. A counselor advised her to monitor the relationship but to recognize that it was *theirs*. "He also told me it was better for Trevor to have some sense of his father and be able to draw his own conclusions than to have no contact at all and end up with some idealized image. I knew Trevor would forever blame me if he thought I had kept him away from his father." Besides, Douglas assumed that he could see Trevor when he wanted to.

"This was going to be just a short visit," Sophie continues, "so when Trevor said he didn't want to see Douglas, my first thought was that we would talk it through and then everything would just go on. I figured that he was probably in that age when he was afraid of hurting my feelings, maybe thinking that seeing Douglas was disloyal, or maybe that he felt shy or a little afraid. I decided to set up a play session with his miniature cars and things so we could talk without him feeling cornered for answers. I lit some candles and we got really quiet and focused on moving these little cars around. It was about four in the afternoon, and I said, 'Hmmmm, I guess this is about the time Douglas would be getting off the plane, according to what he said.'

"'Um-hmm,' said Trevor. Play, play, play.

"'What if there was a knock at the door right now and Douglas was here?' I asked him. 'What do you think would happen?'

"Still playing, he said, 'Oh, he would come in and he'd smile and laugh. And he'd have tears in his eyes. And he would pick me up and swing me around and tell me how much he loves me and how I'm the most important person in the whole world to him. And then he would have all these presents for me. And he would tell me how much I'm just like him.'"

Sophie stops her story for a moment. "All of this is quite likely," she comments. "Trevor was recounting it all from the visit the previous year." She picks up the thread again.

"'Then what?' I asked him. Play, play, play.

"'Well, then he'd put me down, and then he'd say that he has an important meeting he'd have to get to soon.'

"'So what would Trevor do?' I asked after a few more minutes of pushing little cars around.

"'Well,' he said, 'I think I would have to take the presents and throw them all away, and then I would have to turn to him and I would have to say to him, 'Don't come back. I don't want you any longer as a father, because this is not what I want a father to be.'

"Those were his exact words," emphasizes Sophie, making sure I could comprehend not only what her seven-year-old son was facing but also what *she* was. Douglas was not what Sophie wanted a father to be either, but she couldn't keep Trevor from him. Should she now keep him from Trevor?

"'What do you mean?' I asked him.

"'He doesn't love me, Mom.'

"'Well, I'm sure your father loves you in the way he knows how,' I said, still assuming we were just working through his feelings.

"'Mom,' Trevor said, and he stopped a moment, staring down at the car in his hand. 'Mom, if a man loves a boy, he wants to stay and read him a story. He wants to miss his meeting and spend the evening with him. He wants to drive him to school sometimes. He wants to live nearby him. He wants to see his bedroom. He doesn't love me. When he tells me those things, it hurts me. And I don't want him to do that anymore.'

"Then he dropped his car, and tears welled up and he said, 'Mom, please don't make me do this. Don't let him in.'

"'Maybe it's important for Douglas to hear this from you, Trevor,' I tried.

"'No. His feelings will be very hurt, because he won't understand what I mean. And I don't want to have to hurt him. Don't make me do it.'"

And what about Douglas? Even though his behavior as a father was outrageous in Sophie's estimation, he was Trevor's father and should have some right to see him. Should she let Douglas in and force Trevor to visit with him? Should she, in effect, teach Trevor to hide his feelings? Sophie could see that there was nothing to be gained by complaining to her son about his father's behavior, and she wasn't about to defend it. She was also well aware from the past that having it out with Douglas about the nature of his involvement in Trevor's life would do no good at all.

"All I could do was say, 'All right, Trevor.' He was saying he was too young to have to do this, and he was right. I would have to do it, if I wanted to feel good about myself.

"'I will not let him in the door,' I said. 'I will stand by your side. But I do think Douglas needs to hear this. Will you give me permission to meet him someplace else and tell him what you said?'"

Trevor agreed to that, and when Douglas called, Sophie made the arrangement. "I went into Trevor's room and said, 'I'm going to have coffee with Douglas now,' and told him the neighbor down the hall knew I'd be gone for about an hour in case he needed anything. He looked up and said, 'Okay, Mom, good luck.' I noticed that he didn't stumble or question or seem frightened. It was just 'Good luck.'" For three years beyond that day, Trevor would refuse to see Douglas. He would himself know when he was ready again.

With Sophie's support, Trevor had written a major turning point into his story. "What he did was decide what a father could be, and acknowledge that it was not what his own father was," Sophie says.

"Through that he has come to a healthy conception of fatherhood —
so he can be a father someday himself.

"I think Trevor doesn't feel betrayed by Douglas personally because
he doesn't really know him. We never lived with him, so Trevor didn't
have to go through that kind of major rejection a child can feel when
someone they're attached to leaves. So he doesn't miss *that* man. He
misses that sense of one man loving him the way his mother does.
But he has a strong sense of himself and a secure foundation to work
through that void.

"But I never say to him, 'It's not important that you don't have a
father, at least you have a mother who loves you,'" Sophie adds. "I
say, 'It's sad that you don't have a father here, but what's important
is that you do have a parent. Everybody needs one person who really
loves them and listens to them — and you also are loved by many
other people. And there are people out there who are going to love
you who you don't even know yet.' In other words, I try to direct
him toward not focusing on what he doesn't have but on what reality
he might discover."

Douglas met with Sophie, then went on to his important meeting, this
time without seeing his son. Billy's ex-wife agreed that he would be
the better parent and sees her son occasionally. In many of the stories
of the single parents I spoke with, the Other seems to disappear into
the wings. What has happened to these other parents? Either they too
have suffered some degree of pain at the loss of their children — even
if it was by their own choice — or, more tragic, they had already been
lost to themselves long before. But in order for the children not to
pass on this legacy of loss, they will have to acknowledge its magni-
tude and mourn it.

"I think Trevor has a lot of grief about it all," Sophie says. "That's
one of the things that can make me cry. It's one of those areas where
I can love him, tell him he's okay, but I can't heal him. I can support
his choices, but the healing is something he will have to do himself.
Basically, it's men's work, and he'll have to do it with other men."

When Eric, at thirty, and his mother, Laurinda, sat side by side
relating their story, they both recalled their happiness those years ago
when they were reunited after Eric's two years of living with his
father. For Laurinda that moment was pure joy. But for Eric there
was something else as well. "When I think of my mom and me

jumping up and down outside my dad's house that day I left, I also think of him inside and what he must have been feeling. Here my mom and I were happy, and his new wife was satisfied with what had happened. He was the one left out in the cold. That makes me quite sad. I relate to the wounded feeling as a man. As I get older I get much more in touch with how painful and difficult that time must have been for him." Indeed, Eric's father would later tell him that it had been the most painful decision of his life.

Although we might want to dismiss the Other from our lives once the romance is over or the marriage ended, for our children it's a different matter. They may claim immaculate conception, like Shannon, or they may choose to stop seeing the Other for a while, like Trevor. But within them the Other lives as part of their story, and many will not rest until they can meet the eyes that gave them their own.

♦   STRAIGHT TALK

For Danielle, the struggle would be to reconcile her love for her father with her increasing recognition that his abusive behavior was not something she wanted to be around. In order to separate from him, however, she had to claim his goodness for herself. After all, unless she could prove he was good, how could she know that *she* was?

This left Cath in a dilemma, particularly when Danielle returned from her father's house confused and reeling from his criticisms. There was no way for Cath to explain to her sobbing child that what her father was saying had nothing to do with her and her abilities but rather with himself. Any negative comment about him sounded to Danielle like an attack and sent her into battle in his defense. Cath could only try to counterbalance the debilitating effects. "I really tried to reflect her back to herself in positive ways," Cath relates. "But her self-esteem still suffered. In the face of an extremely critical other parent, I felt like I couldn't get through to her with a positive sense of her life."

For Cath, seeing what was happening to her daughter yet being unable to acknowledge it directly placed her in a difficult bind. Uncapping her tremendous frustration, she blurts out, "I tried, tried, tried not talking about him for so long, and I tried to acknowledge the good things about him. But from time to time I would have to explain some of his behavior to Danielle when she found it confusing or hurtful. During these past four years especially, it was clear how confused and upset she was when she came back from his house. The suicidal times also have been when she was with him or when she returned after an extended visit. But I really tried not to say very much about what I thought about him or what happened that precipitated our getting separated. I didn't want to make her carry it."

It would seem less than human for Cath not to feel enraged when Danielle, sobbing, would relay the image of her father on a sudden rampage, smashing her favorite toys against the house and verbally stripping her of her right to existence. What could hold back the raw honesty of Cath's feelings at those times, what could keep the truth from crashing through the gates of principle — "Say only nice things about the other" — to win the moment?

As these human passions rise up from the depths, they get compounded with all the untended hurts and residual anger of our lifetimes. Suddenly the Other is the "cause" not only of the suffering of our children but also of every challenge we face in raising them alone. "If it weren't for your father . . ." "It's your mother's fault things are like this . . ."

All of Alan's training to become a successful lawyer, all of his practice in composure and detachment in the courtroom, couldn't cut through the rage pouring out of an open wound when his wife left him with their two girls. Now he wonders whether that unleashing may have left his daughters with some scars.

"Probably the most psychologically tender stuff is what happens right away when children are young, but I was at my worst then," says Alan. His girls were three and six when his wife left with another man. The anger erupting with his sense of betrayal settled over Alan's actions like thick volcanic ash. "I had not met the man who would become her new husband, and I didn't want to. I didn't even want to catch sight of my wife. I would let the girls out at a prearranged spot when they were going to visit their mother, and drive off before I had to look at her. When I'd pick them up, if they would so much as say, 'Jim took us to the park today,' I would stop them. I didn't want to hear about it."

When Brigitte announced that she would be moving to another state, leaving the girls entirely in Alan's hands, he remembers, "I felt like I was going out of my mind with the sudden developments. I felt like she was the cause of this tremendous confusion I was going through in trying to take care of kids and a house and work all at the same time. I guess everyone in that kind of situation is over-wrought. You hear all the time about slamming doors and court orders and a lot of aggression. Brigitte and I never were violent, but certainly the girls picked up from me disapproval and tension. Even though I knew it was my duty as an adult not to act out in front of my kids, I know I gave them a negative feeling. I undoubtedly said harsh things to them about her."

This is one of the areas where compassion for ourselves is crucial. No matter how much we know about the "right" way to talk about the Other, we sometimes slip and are humbled once again. We may need to allow ourselves to express our anger in a way that leads to personal healing. Denying the pain doesn't serve anybody in the end, but neither does bleeding all over our children.

In general, the rule is a good one: say nice things about the other parent; don't let your own conflicts interfere with your children's relationship with their other parent. If both parents are basically balanced, this standard advice is valuable. It saves the children pain, and as Alan and many others have found, time heals wounds. It is hard to erase or build over a legacy of aspersions — and confusing for our children — if and when we do reestablish connection with the Other.

But how to talk about an Other who is indeed hurtful or dangerous can place us in an ethical bind. Isn't it essential to validate the experiences of our children and try to help them protect themselves? Yet how do we acknowledge negative behavior on the part of the other parent in a way that doesn't make the child feel emotionally and psychologically torn and "part of something bad"? Not talking about these things can be a dangerous denial, yet doing so requires a delicate advocacy. And when the "talk nice" rule becomes a deception purportedly for the sake of our child, we can run into a massive tangle of concerns. In fact, a one-dimensional presentation of the other parent can create even more confusion for the child.

For years Helen made a point of promoting her ex-husband's virtues to their daughter. "I harbored a lot of resentment for him," Helen admits, "but I was very careful so that Pamela could develop her own relationship to him, free of my stuff." Certainly there were times when Pamela might return from a weekend at her father's house with hurt feelings over his criticisms or emotional distance, but Helen stuck to that guideline.

When Pamela was twelve years old, the confusion became clear. One day, after yet another discussion with her mother about why her parents were not together, Pamela shouted at her, "If he was so good, then why did you divorce him!" Now, years later, Helen reflects on what her daughter must have felt. "Her father had told her the divorce was my idea, so Pamela assumed that I had done this capricious thing that had ripped her life apart. Who knows what kind of fears haunted her. Maybe she thought if I could do that to him, I might do that to her too. Whatever it was, she carried a tremendous resentment, and not until she was twenty-one and we talked more openly about all of it did she really understand."

Only after Angie's ex-husband had called and threatened to kidnap China did Angie sit down and reveal to her eight-year-old some of the facts about her father and how their relationship had ended. For the child's safety, Angie's lawyer had advised her to do so. "To my surprise, what happened is that China started opening up to talk about some of her own hurt, the fact that her father hadn't written her more often and was in touch so seldom. We just really hadn't talked about these things at all before. I saw that my attempts to not prejudice her about him, to say good things, had meant — unknown to me — that I had blocked off a whole avenue of communication between us of her hurt about it. I feel that telling her those things made honest something between us that had not been quite honest before. But I'm also glad I hadn't told her negative stories about him when she was very little. By the time she was eight and this happened, I think she was old enough to deal with it all in a different way than if it had been part of her younger experience."

Angie's story points out the importance of taking into account the age of our children as we talk to them about the other parent. We need to be sensitive both to what they want and what they are ready for. But ultimately, the truth, as pure as we can make it, will be the only reality we have a right to give them. As the psychologist Leah LeGoy points out, "The truth allows them to move forward in their lives," not held back by a vacuum or by the dark threads of family history.

"Every time I'd say to Melissa, 'Your dad loves you,' I'd cringe inside," admits Michelle, who had struggled since her daughter was nearly two to explain why her daddy was suddenly not there. Now that Melissa is five years old, Michelle wonders how to talk to her about his alcoholism. "Sometimes I'd say, 'Your daddy has a sickness, and so he left you because he loves you and didn't want to hurt you.' But she knows what love is. Love is when somebody is there for you over and over and over again. Love is when someone nurtures you, like when you have to water a plant or it dies. Melissa knows that. So when I'd try to tell her in that way, she knew it was a lie, and I knew she knew it. It created conflict in her for me to say that, because then she was left with trying to figure out, 'How did he love me and leave me?'

"The truth is that he doesn't love her. I don't completely know where I stand on this issue of what to tell her, but it tends to make sense to tell her the truth. He's not capable of love. He doesn't love himself, and you cannot love other people if you hate yourself like that."

Being honest with our children about their other parent is not a simple endeavor. Talking in terms that are too complex or that convey a burden too great to bear can be overwhelming for them. Children feel a loyalty to both parents and may be convinced that unless they reveal anything negative they have been told by the other parent, they are hiding something or taking sides. Or, as in Danielle's case, negative remarks can make them feel "bad," or make them feel they have to defend the other parent. For Cath, honesty would be possible only when Danielle herself was ready.

◆ WITH BOTH AS PART

By the time Danielle started seventh grade, she was living primarily at her mother's house. Her visits to her father's house had grown less frequent over the past year, and only when her stepbrothers were there did she not take along a friend. This was the change Cath had been waiting for, and she looked forward to a less traumatic year than the previous four had been.

Then Danielle came home from school one day with what looked like a flu, but it didn't go away. After weeks in bed and multiple visits to doctors, she withdrew from classes. When severe headaches developed, along with exhaustion and depression, Cath took her to specialists for CAT scans and to check for encephalitis. "I was terrified,"

Cath relates, "because we didn't know what was going on. They couldn't detect anything." With Danielle scarcely able to sit up for more than two hours a day, Cath sustained a rigorous schedule of going into her office for a few hours at a time, then rushing home to tend to her daughter. If it weren't for a young single mother and her baby who were living with them at the time, Cath admits, "I wouldn't have been able to work at all. I was just stretched beyond capacity."

Weeks went by, and Danielle began spending her limited time awake working in her notebooks, on her "stories." But now there was a difference: the families were not always happy; sometimes they had problems — and resolutions. One story even featured a single-parent family. During this time Danielle's father split up with his new wife and began calling his daughter every day, asking her to come live with him. Danielle refused. "As she began to understand how debilitating it had been for her to be around her father, she began to talk more about it with me," Cath remembers. "She decided on her own that she would see him only if he came to town, only on her own turf." Establishing boundaries was one of the major steps Danielle was taking to resolve the conflict she felt about her father.

In the end, the healing of Danielle's illness would also see the resolution of the turmoil she had undergone for years. Seeking a cure for her headaches, "I took Danielle to a husband and wife who were both osteopaths and worked together as a team doing cranial sacral work," Cath explains. "It was an absolute miracle. The first time we went, they were both bending over Danielle, working on her head. Suddenly there was a moment when I swear I was seeing Mary and Joseph hovering over the child. When Danielle got up, she said, 'I have never felt so good in my life.'" Cath laughs now, recalling the immense relief she felt.

Cath is certain that, besides the physical healing this couple accomplished during the year of weekly treatments Danielle received, they also provided her daughter with the image of a man and a woman functioning together in a harmonious way, and that this model mended something very deep in Danielle's psyche. Perhaps that child, talking to the Holy Family at the foot of her bed, had finally heard them answer, had finally felt them enfold her in their embrace.

Reflecting on Danielle's experience, Cath points out that "it's important not to make the mistake of mixing up that inner process with an outer structure. Those images, like the Holy Family, are archetypes that are a part of the *inner* life. The 'mother' and 'father' are symbols of different aspects of ourselves that join to bear the fruit of a child. In symbolic terms, that fruit is any creative act.

"Of course it can be helpful for our children to have some external models of how opposites can work together effectively — and I think that's why that couple meant so much to Danielle. Yet to say that the only way they can develop their wholeness or heal their fragmented self is by having parents who are married would be an error."

As Danielle's depression and headaches began to lift, she made other decisions that would anchor her healing. At thirteen she became very involved in the Catholic church, the religion her father had grown up in. "I think it was an attempt to reconcile him in a huge way," says Cath. "She knew he would approve, and so would his parents." But there was much more going on for Danielle than a wish for parental approval. Joseph Chilton Pearce, author of *The Magical Child*, points out that around this age, children develop a sense of their vast potential and a tremendous longing to unfold what he calls their spiritual capacity. If that step is not taken, the impulse can backfire into cynicism and deep disappointment. Danielle herself holds that when her spirit began to turn, her health came back. She had found a way to take that profound step in her development and simultaneously redeem her father within her by laying claim to something deeply connected to him.

Now, with both her inner and her outer relationship to her father clearer, Danielle no longer needed to temper the truth. "Finally in the past couple of years we have been able to talk about her father's childhood and how things must have gone terribly wrong," Cath relates. "We talk about how his life as a child was really devoid of the comfort and love everybody is looking for, and how that meant he got really smart but not emotionally nurtured or nurturing."

The last time I spoke with Cath, Danielle was fifteen and had been enrolled for two years in a school she loved. "It is so thrilling to see what has happened to her," Cath said, almost laughing with delight as she talked. "She is so healthy. She used to miss so much school, and now she is hardly ever sick. She went through that great crisis and came out changed. She does see her father now, but she has herself carefully defined the limits. She knows what works for her. And I think she has a whole different perspective on him."

Sometimes only a motivation as deep as the love we feel for our children could get us to face our anger and resentment and move beyond them to frame the life of a hurtful other parent in the compassionate way that Cath did. For Billy, perhaps all those late nights spent facing the serpent-headed Medusa emerging from that gnarled wood led him to a resolution. "When Aaron asks me why his mom is so weird," says Billy, "I explain to him how she grew up and how I grew up and why we're so different. I tell him that everybody has reasons for being the way they are, and just because that's the way she might be doesn't mean all women are like that; and that this is the way I am, but it doesn't mean that all guys are like this. I tell him that it takes all kinds. He still has a lot of love for his mom, which I don't try to diminish at all. And she has a lot of love for him. I tell him that anything he notices between me and her is only between us, and that how they relate to each other has nothing to do with how she and I might."

If the grief and sorrow our children encounter as their stories unfold can develop in them the heart of compassion, they enter their lives with a victory already in hand. The same is true for us. "I look at Jed sometimes and I realize that his dad was once a little boy just like him," says Sharon. "I can see it in so many ways. Some of those beautiful qualities I love in my son, I once saw in his dad — that's why I married him. But that man was so distorted and crippled by his upbringing that he just couldn't develop those qualities himself. So even though now I can't relate to his father at all, I see that in this boy I have a chance to nurture and bring to flower the person his dad could have been."

Along with these choices we make about the lives of our children comes the responsibility to care for their feelings and help them understand in a way that opens their hearts, not closes them. Tracey has given careful thought to how she will tell Corrin about his father and why he is not part of his life. "I am hoping that I will be able to present Corrin's personal myth to him in such a way that he will feel very special about how he came into being — not that he lacked anything but that this is part of his uniqueness. My thought is that I would tell him about how I dreamed, the summer he was conceived, that I saw a child running toward me who felt like a great presence of love. And then I will emphasize in terms of my relationship with his father how much love he and I shared that summer. It was glorious, and I think I will actually say to Corrin that he is a love child, created through this extraordinary experience with his father. I neither want to harm the image of his father for him nor do I want to idealize it. I want to make him as real a person as possible for

Corrin, with his shortcomings and his good sides. I want to weave a personal myth for my son that gives him a very strong and positive sense of who he is.

"So many mothers who have a child on their own feel apologetic," Tracey continues. "One woman I know felt so bad when her child asked where his daddy was that she felt she had to say, 'I love you but he doesn't love you enough to come around.' The way I see it is that women who go ahead and have children on their own need to impress upon them how much they were wanted and how much it means to have the children in their lives. It takes so much intention and courage to say, 'I really want a child and in spite of the fact that I don't have a relationship that supports it, I will go ahead.' They need to let the child know that that's just how important they are, and then do what they can to give them a good and balanced sense of their other parent."

◆ BEYOND BETRAYAL

"It took me almost two years," says Alan, "before I was able to say to my daughters, 'Well, she's your mother,' and put in a good word as well as a bad one. Then finally I got to the point where it was almost entirely good things. At this point, as they get older, I try to tell them all the good things about her. And the bad things, I tell them that's just the way she is. Sure, she is irresponsible and scatterbrained, but the good thing is that she is so creative and such a loving person. I finally got to the point of view even that it wasn't a failure or malevolence on her part that she left but that there was a real difference between us. She wants A, B, C, and D, and I want other things.

"Psychologists tell me that deep inside, the girls might be filled with anger because they were abandoned, but if it's there, it's beneath anything I can reach. At least they know their mother is a good person, and we keep her presence alive here. We'll say, 'I wonder what Brigitte is doing right now?' and we might laugh fondly and say, 'She's probably stuck in the mud somewhere or has lost her keys.' They understand now that she isn't here because she really needed to live somewhere else. And as they get older, I'm almost shocked at how easy it is to talk with them about it. I find myself speaking as I would to another adult."

These parents are not denying what the other parent has done; they are not justifying hurtful or irresponsible behavior. Forgetting is not a part of forgiving. Just as history unremembered is bound to repeat itself, so inappropriate, harmful, or cruel action is not to be dismissed or swept under the rug of the unconscious mind only to be repeated again, in ourselves or our children. An attitude of "no blame" doesn't mean no responsibility. That we are all making the only and best choices we can doesn't mean that we don't try to make those choices with care and awareness. Neither does no blame mean no action. If it's important to us, for instance, we should indeed pursue a deadbeat parent for financial contributions, or strongly encourage the other parent to participate in our children's lives, or prohibit bad conduct. But effective action needn't be powered by unresolved anger.

The anger and hurt we feel that is triggered by the actions of the Other may wake us up to ways we have allowed ourselves to be mistreated and force us to work on healing those wounds; it can remind us to teach our children not to abuse others; it can compel us to reach out to help others who are also suffering. However, until we can act rather than react, we are still trapped, entangled with the Other, keeping the pain alive that continues to place our lives in the Other's hands.

Releasing herself from that trap was, as one single mother puts it, "empowering." For the past fifteen years Mudita has successfully shared parenting of their daughter with her ex-husband. But only a dramatic shift in her perceptions made this possible. "I just had to stop having Wes and what he did be the reference point for my life. If I wanted to feel happy, I couldn't wait for him to do something or to be the solution. It was *my* anger and *my* hurt and *my* sadness that I was stuck with, and eventually I wanted to move on from that. And just from a pragmatic view, it didn't work to keep blaming him for how I was feeling. The animosity was self-poisoning."

Yet despite her desire and willingness to forgive, the process took time. We cannot force forgiveness or compassion. "At the time we broke up, I would have been happy to have never seen Wes again. I would have just moved on," Mudita admits, "if we had not had Rose." That fact pushed Mudita to do what she now describes as "one of my life's biggest challenges."

That struggle to genuinely forgive eventually led Mudita to understand that "no one thing, no one incident, no one person makes us into who we are or is responsible for how we feel. There are such a great number of variables in our lives that we can't point a finger at any one of them and say, 'That's what is to blame for how my life is and how I am feeling.'"

That understanding freed Mudita to make clear choices for the good of her daughter, but she couldn't have developed their model co-parenting arrangement through her own efforts. Wes too had to be willing. "You just have to stretch beyond your sense of 'I am right' and be able to forgive — over and over," says Wes. On virtually every count of what can make shared parenting work after separation, Wes and Mudita score. Shared philosophies in childrearing, shared financial responsibility, clear agreements, supportive new partners, friends in common, trust and goodwill — it's a tall order, and perhaps nothing less can work.

"When I think about what some people have, I feel so lucky in my situation," Rose says, acknowledging the success of her parents' efforts. "Even though sometimes it's kind of weird — I mean, it's not a normal situation, and I have to explain to my friends that my parents are divorced — it feels comfortable and natural to have what we have." At sixteen, Rose, like many teenagers, wants to fit in and be "normal." But unlike many, Rose has an intact family. This doesn't mean that her parents live together. It means they are raising their daughter in a way that clearly has helped to integrate, not pull apart, this child whom they both love. "I think it's great," says Rose, smiling, "because I think by working together to raise me, they refound why they were ever together in the first place — because they were friends, and of course to have me!"

The fact that there *is* an Other forces us to face them, either in person or within ourselves, for the sake of our children. We can't control that Other. Perhaps we can't even really understand them. And compassion certainly doesn't mean self-righteously pitying them or condoning harmful actions. Maybe in the end it means simply letting them go, acknowledging that life brought two individuals together who in a magical moment created a child and then moved on again into separate lives. The welfare of the child rests appropriately with both, but if the other parent doesn't take it on, spending time blaming them doesn't make us more effective as parents. Perhaps the most profound level of forgiveness is recognizing that whatever has happened between ourselves and that Other is simply part of *our* own life story — a story that has left us with the gift of our children.

◆

CHAPTER 12

No One Can Be a Single Parent:
Extending the Family

Let us put our heads together and see what life we will make for our children.

— Lakota Chief Sitting Bull

OUR BACK DOOR OPENED onto the kitchen, and like most families we preferred it to the more formal front entry. At times, nonstop as a cuckoo clock at noon, it delivered and released us. Laurinda would just be returning from an early morning walk, carryout cappuccino in hand. "Hey, Button-Nose, I brought something for you!" she'd greet Elias, slipping a croissant from a white paper bag. Max on his way out to yoga class would gently tease a grumpy toddler awake. "Good morning, Marmaloris," he'd call softly with his favorite nonsense word. "Don't smile now . . ." A little face peeking in at the window would signal that Morgan had arrived, lifted by his mother for his usual greeting; he and Elias would run off to play until the babysitter appeared. "Uncle" Wes would return from delivering his early-bird newscast, and young Rose would be off to school. For the first three and half years, that door opened into a world Elias came to know as "family" — eight unrelated adults, one teenager, and him, in a grand old three-story house on a corner.

A few faces changed as housemates moved on and were replaced, but the sense of family remained. In my memory the images of that time weave a tight web of support. Max pacing the floor with a feverish baby while I lie in bed, myself flushed with flu. Laurinda soothing and supporting me as I struggle to set firm limits with Elias.

Sandia and Jasmine under the dining room table giggling at Elias's antics. Ted reading him *Winnie-the-Pooh*, in a house they made of cushions from the couch. Rose juggling fruit in the kitchen. Will working past midnight with Sandia and Mike to make a papier-mâché tunnel for a train from Santa. Oscar strapping Elias into the stroller and bumping out the door while I fulfill my monthly duty as cook for one of the two house dinners we scheduled weekly.

Because we shared a home with friends during the first years of Elias's life, many of the challenges I faced as a single parent were tempered. I had contact with other adults, he had the presence of good men, I was relieved from the burden of daily cooking by sharing preparation with others. Elias's world was friendly and alive and much bigger than me and whatever my state of mind happened to be. Because we lived with others, I wasn't alone to hear his first word or to see him try his first steps. I wasn't even the one to get him to sleep through the night.

Like any family, this one had its own challenges. There was always someone else to consider. But that is the point that remains with Elias still, two years after we have left — there was always someone else, and to him that means family.

From the moment I found myself on my own and soon to be a mother, my definition of family began to shift. The *single* part of single parenting that had so ominously threatened isolation and loneliness turned out to be anything but that. In fact, my life and Elias's have been far more filled with the support and love of others than it might have been if we were part of a supposedly self-sufficient nuclear family. A broken dream of "family" in reality has become a family broken open to the love and participation of many.

Indeed, the idea of family is being redefined in the thoughts and experiences of our entire society. Today only 11 percent of American families are made up of two parents functioning in the breadwinner/homemaker model.[1] While the proportion of adults choosing to live alone tripled over the past three decades,[2] there is a simultaneous move to shared housing, motivated by both economic need and desire for community.[3] What we have come to call the "traditional" family is in actuality far from traditional. Throughout human history, the nuclear family has been actively infused with relatives, friends, and a variety of "kin," as well as sustained by neighbors, extended family, village, and tribe.

In many cultures, families with open borders still prevail. A friend who lived in the Middle East with her husband's family talks about missing the typical household she lived in of twenty related adults who all participated in caring for the children. Another friend, who lives in Ecuador as an anthropologist, is, by invitation, *co-madre* — co-mother — to several Quechua children. In that culture, every child has a number of genuinely involved co-parents who are considered blood family *hasta la tumba,* until death. Lillian Rubin writes, "Most anthropologists today argue that kinship is as much an *idea* — a system of belief — as it is a biological fact."[4] That our own ideas about family are changing is apparent in the results of a national poll conducted in 1989 in which nearly three quarters of the participants chose to define family not in terms of blood ties but as "a group of people who love and care for each other."[5]

As single parents, we cannot be and do all things for our children. Even two-parent families are stretched on the rack of this expectation. But raising children alone, single parents live with little illusion about the possibility. Thus we have the challenge and the opportunity to reach beyond the borders of biology to weave for our children a web of support made up of many others who want to encourage their development into healthy and wholesome human beings.

As single-parent families, freed from the patterns and expectations that might be automatic in a two-parent family, we have the potential to stretch in many directions. Over the past nine years, since Alan and his wife Brigitte divorced, they have reestablished communication and developed an increasingly interactive relationship. "Now it has come to the extreme point," Alan says, "where she can stay here in the house, along with her new husband and their two young children, when she is visiting our daughters." To Alan this is still rather extraordinary. As he speaks of it, he shakes his head in amazement at this situation he could never have imagined happening when he first divorced.

"My friends and relatives, disapproving, say, 'Isn't it very New Age to have your ex-wife and husband staying in your house?' My answer is, 'Where would they stay? They don't have money for lodgings, and if they stayed with Brigitte's friends, they wouldn't have a comfortable place to just hang out with the girls." What Alan's associates aren't aware of is that this kind of "extended family" is happening with increasing frequency, and that those who can reach beyond the barriers of convention are contributing to a model of family that is helping children of divorce and separation feel put together.

"It's funny, but I also feel really affectionate to Brigitte's two little kids," Alan continues. "At first I had thought I just can't get involved, but with each passing year I feel more and more like their uncle or grandfather.

"And something else I find amusing is that I have extended this bizarre openness to my ex-wife's family to also include her relatives! When her mother or father want to see the children, they come here and stay. I don't even have a direct obligation to have my ex-mother-in-law in my life, and here I've got her in my house, and I'm taking care of her and listening to her complain about everything. I get up in the morning and there is Yvette, blustering away in the kitchen, cleaning up. But she deserves to see her grandchildren.

"One summer I took the girls to France to leave them with their relatives there for a visit. All of us met in Paris — Brigitte, her husband and their two children, me and the girls. I remember saying to them, 'This is as crazy a situation as I could imagine.' Here were all these different kids together. There just was no model I had for it. Maybe in retrospect people will say that in the 1980s and '90s this kind of family evolved, but when you're living through it, you feel like a complete jackass," Alan confesses. "I can laugh about it now, but then sometimes I'd say to myself, 'What am I doing? Why am I spending my vacation in France with ex-relatives I don't even like? Why am I taking this extra trouble?' But it's definitely worth it. I can see that it has enriched our lives for me and my daughters to have all these connections."

Family ties don't break when hearts do, and as hearts mend, this "bizarre openness" can indeed enrich our lives, assuring us that we belong to a world much larger than the tiny unit confined to a single household. Family *is* being redefined in the 1980s and '90s, but actually it is simply returning to forms that have defined human civilization since its beginnings. Stephanie Coontz unequivocally states, "There has never been a natural family economy in which families have been able to take care of all of their needs — taken care of elders and fully provided for children. Families have always needed help from outside the family unit."[6]

The "economics" of the family does not revolve only around material needs. Equally important are emotional and spiritual needs, to love and be loved, to know and be known, to count on others to carry our needs as their own and to be counted upon in the same way. These qualities, which have been assigned to families of biology or marriage, are increasingly being extended to others as well.

Diana finds family for her daughter through the on-site childcare at work, and it is a friend rather than a relative she names as legal guardian in case of her death. Angie and China share a house with friends and find community through the school where the mother teaches and the daughter is a student. Shay finds male role models for Jenny by joining a social organization for single parents in her city. Sophie finds the models Trevor needs through the boys' choir at her church. Catherine leaves her family of friends in Los Angeles but finds a neighborhood of families in the small town she moves to, with "kids running in and out of each other's houses and sharing bathtubs after dinner." Through babysitting co-ops and support groups, we find family. "Aunts" and "uncles" and godparents fill roles as close and committed, or even more so, than blood relatives. As Nicole puts it, "I think everybody you know becomes extended family when you have a kid. You depend on all of them to teach your child certain things."

"Being a single parent really taught me that I need more than one person in my life," says Shay. "I saw clearly that when your foundation is built on only one person, it's just not real. They could die. They could do anything. So could you. You need a lot of friends." When Shay remarried after four years of raising Jenny alone, one of the things she liked most about her new husband was that "he has so many people in his life besides me — deep, significant friends who would drop everything and come and be there for him if he needed it. That's what I found too as a single parent — but I really had to work to build that."

It doesn't just happen. Establishing those connections with others takes time, and the results aren't guaranteed. "All of these community things that make it work better take a lot of time to arrange," Cheryl admits. "And then there's the cost of including other people in your lives, because you inherit their problems and crises along with them. That's the paradox. But ultimately I think you have to be willing to make that time and take that risk. We need other people."

Of course having others in our lives brings challenges. Every family structure and arrangement has its advantages and drawbacks. While living with others who loved and appreciated both of us certainly afforded Elias and me a bit of heaven, it didn't come without its little hells as well. The attempt to blend a multitude of needs, varying schedules, and differing standards of house maintenance into a working unit can be overwhelming. But without the entrenched and often largely unconscious patterns typical in blood families, such shared households have a good opportunity to develop communications skills and methods of conflict resolution. In that household, Elias saw grownups argue and disagree, but he also observed conflicts being resolved and people listening to and learning from one another. Equally important, he learned, as Cheryl puts it, that we need other people.

When Ruth proclaimed, "Single parenting really works!" she wasn't talking about parenting alone — far from it. "By the time I adopted Evita, I was pretty settled into a home I had actually bought with kids in mind. The house has three floors. Evita and I live on the first. Upstairs was a friend and her two children. They were older than Evita, but my friend was like another parent for her. I'm not very good myself when people get sick, for instance, but this woman is great, so Evita could go upstairs and get taken care of by her in that way.

"On the top floor was a woman from Mexico with two little girls Evita's age. She could go up there and speak Spanish with them. The doors were almost always open in the house. We'd trade sleepovers for the girls when one of us was working or going out, and they could come home from school and do homework together. Different people have lived up there at different times during the last eight years, but always people who either have children or are interested in children. It just didn't work if they weren't. So here in my house there has been this entire community."

Ruth, a social worker and college professor, not only had a small tribal unit at hand, she also had "a lot of other people who were close to us and supportive. My parents were terrific, I have a cousin who lives nearby, as well as my brother and his wife. And I have several other friends who've been around us a lot. A couple of them are bilingual in Spanish and English. I knew quite a bit of Spanish, but sometimes it just wasn't enough to do what was needed. When Evita first came from Central America, she'd go through times of getting hysterical. She'd scream, 'I want my 'nother mother, I want my mom!' She wouldn't let anybody near her. *'No me toca!'* she'd scream. 'Don't touch me.' I would cry and she would cry. My friend Marisa would get on the phone with her, and she'd talk to her in Spanish and tell her stories, in a way I couldn't do with my own level of Spanish, until Evita would fall asleep with the phone in her hand. Years later I heard Evita telling a friend, 'Can you imagine — when I came here no one understood me except Marisa. She was the only one I could talk to.'"

Ruth's wisdom was that she recognized she could not be all things for her daughter, that she was in fact a better parent by extending her immediate, day-to-day family to include others — both adults and children — and to reach beyond to include many more. Extended family can make the difference between a life that has room in it for finding the joy in raising children and one that is often little more than a daily grind. Whether we live under a shared roof or not, whether we are friends or relatives, in extending our families we can find the abundant nurturing our children need as well as the essential support and companionship we do.

◆   THICKER THAN WATER

"Without family I don't know what we would have done," Rachel says of the eleven years she has been raising her daughter as a single parent. "It's not that it always has to be relatives, but you need a certain amount of support. And especially for me, in the position I was in . . ."

Being nineteen years old, unmarried, pregnant, and "not a real marketable commodity," as Rachel puts it, was a terrifying position to be in. It wasn't one she had ever imagined for herself. "I didn't have a very clear direction in life, but I certainly was not 'the girl who turns out to be an unwed mother,'" Rachel says. "That was not part of my concept of myself." As a freshman in college, Rachel at least had a wide open field of possibilities ahead of her — until she found out she was pregnant.

"I used to lie on the floor and pray that it wasn't really true," she says. "I didn't tell anybody that I was pregnant until I was six months along. No one. I knew I was either pregnant or quite ill. I finally went to a doctor to have a test. I didn't understand that a pregnancy test shows negative after a certain amount of time. So when the doctor told me it was negative, I said, 'There's no way.' At that point, I didn't show at all yet. He examined me and said, 'Oh, my, you're very pregnant.' When I put my jeans on after that examination, I couldn't

zip them up! It was like the baby was saying, 'Well, here I am!'"
Rachel smiles, remembering. "The body has tremendous control."

By that time the father of her child — Rachel's first sexual relationship — had disappeared. "He had told me that he was not fertile. When I look back now, I know it was foolish, but I didn't use birth control. I thought that I loved him and trusted him. I wouldn't lie to him about something, so why would he lie to me, is how I thought.

"I told my friends and my sisters and my brother, who are all older than me, before I could tell my parents. To me that was the scariest thing. I made my sister Marian come along when I told my mom, I was so scared." Marian, whom we met earlier, had already broken with family tradition, having left her marriage several years before and returned home to live for a year with her three-year-old daughter. Rachel continues, "I told my mom first because I didn't know how my dad would react, and I felt I was at the end of my stress limit already and couldn't handle a negative reaction. It turned out that they were both very, very kind about it and very supportive."

They invited Rachel to live with them. Marian went with her sister to birthing classes and stayed by her side through labor and delivery of a tiny red-haired girl. "It was so nice to have my older sister there as my birth partner. Otherwise it would have been like being thrown to the wolves," Rachel comments. Thus the nest that had appeared to be emptying resounded again with the midnight cries of a newborn. Rachel and her daughter, Mahala, were home.

"I can see how for centuries and centuries, and in a lot of cultures still, people do live with their parents when they have children," Rachel comments. "We get along quite well, and since my father died when Mahala was two, it has been a very mutually beneficial living arrangement. I pay the utilities and half the groceries, and my mom owns the house.

"She really has taught me a lot of things as well. Of course we do fight with one another occasionally and we have our griping sessions — we wouldn't have a relationship if there wasn't a little friction — but I really enjoy her company. She's a very intelligent and lively person. I just can't really see what life I'm possibly missing in my mix of things — except for sex, which doesn't seem to be an issue for me right now anyway."

The success of this type of extended family depends upon a special blend of characters, circumstances, and, perhaps most important, values. Living with our own parents can be an even greater challenge than raising our children alone. For some of us, however, it might be the only refuge, at least for a period of time. The option of going "back home" seems to be our ultimate psychological safety net.

Whether we live with them or not, grandparents and relatives can take on a new value when we have children, especially when we are raising them alone. "When I left home as a kid, I was into drugs and rock-and-roll," Billy admits. "For a long time I didn't communicate much with my family at all. But now that I'm raising Aaron, I see myself telling him the same things my mom told me, I use the same clichés, and I begin to see more and more how well she raised us, even though I didn't realize it at the time. So when I talk to my mom now, there's a real untold bond. I feel like I'm one of her favorite sons, because she knows that I'm doing this, and she knows that I know that she did this alone too, raising us after my dad left. We talk to each other real lovingly now."

When her husband's death left Maxine and her two daughters on their own, she moved back to the United States from Britain to live near her own mother. "For me Grandma is the one other person who is truly interested in my kids," she says. "She goes out of her way to take them into her life. She even changed the date of her college reunion to take care of them one weekend when it turned out that I had a teachers' conference scheduled that I couldn't miss."

On a practical level, our own parents might be the only ones in the world we feel we can really count on to help out, from occasional babysitting to full-time childcare, from making loans and gifts to opening their homes and larders when we're down and out. It is not uncommon for grandparents, in cultures around the world, to raise their grandchildren. In the United States over three million children are currently living with their grandparents, 28 percent of them with neither of their own parents present.[7] Our parents, if they are retired and able, may also be the only people we know who have any time available to help us in a consistent way.

"One of the reasons I moved to the town where my boys grew up was because my parents were there," says Kevin. "They lived just a few blocks away, and they were probably the best support group I had in raising my boys. But I never really wanted to need them unless it was absolutely necessary. They made it very clear that I was the one in charge of the kids, that they were my responsibility. Yes, they would babysit, but I was not going to be able to drop them off in the morning and pick them up at night. So even though they needed to put that limit on it for their own sake, it was still somewhere for us all to go on Wednesday nights to have tacos. And they really loved the kids. That in itself helped. They got extra love there."

Grandparents can sometimes provide emotional and spiritual sustenance that our children might not find in any other way. This is what primarily lay behind Sophie's decision to settle, while Trevor was young, in the small town where her parents and other relatives lived. "Although I think you can have an extended family of committed friends, I think a sense of legacy is important too," Sophie says. "And forming those deep bonds with relatives takes away from the parent being the main bond."

The benefit that blood family uniquely offers is connection with that odd assortment of people we might not have chosen as friends. As Sophie points out, that can have real value for our children. "There are things happening in my family that aren't all so great," Sophie says, "but I use that. I can say to Trevor, 'This is an example of what happens when you use drugs. This is what happens when you don't wait for the right mate. And we love them anyway.'

"Part of the reason for staying in that town was also to keep Trevor around his great-aunt Harriet. She had never had children, and she was crippled. My mom and grandmother cared for her, and Trevor and I took care of her on weekends. She loved Trevor and was convinced she had been kept alive to meet him. I think what is important in that bond between a child and an older person is that the child is not going to them to get taken to the circus or something, because they can't do that. Harriet could give him nothing but love. And he could hardly wait to get over there to see her. He would massage her foot where the toes were amputated. He would help give her the insulin shot. He would help transfer her to the potty and pat her on the bottom the way I would. He just loved her. She was teaching him compassion.

"When Trevor was four, he chose a ring for his great-aunt's birthday, against my mother's wishes. 'Get her something big so she can see it!' she said. But he was adamant. He chose an opal with gold around it. He was sitting on top of Harriet on her hospital bed when she opened it. He put the ring on her finger and said, 'Now, Aunt Harriet, when you can't see me, you can just feel your finger and know I'm there.' That's what she gave to him."

Another thing relatives can give to our children is an active connection to their heritage. When I spoke with Vayla, who was raising her two daughters, eleven and eight, she was torn by indecision — should she accept her parents' invitation and move back to the Southwest to regroup, or should she remain in the West Coast city that had become her home? With her parents' help she could go back to school and save money and, equally valuable, put her daughters in close touch with their heritage. "My mother is Pueblo Indian, and we have lots of relatives back there. My grandfather, before he died, was chief of the reservation. When we're home, we go out there for First Harvest Dance, for All Saints' Day, and whenever there are dances or celebrations. My own father is part black and part Indian. The girls' father is a mixture of English and Irish. And I want my kids to know all three of their cultures."

Perhaps more than anything else, having children can bring us closer to our relatives, for our children "belong" to them too. While Nicole includes many in what she calls extended family for her and her son, Leroy, she considers herself "lucky that my brother moved out here too. Extended family can be people who aren't related, but it means so much more when you have your relatives who are part of that." For Nicole and her brother, who lives close by, extended family has meant being able to count on each other to care for their children. "My brother has four kids, and we trade off a lot. They are like siblings to my son. In fact, they all lived here for months at one point. The relationship they all developed in that tight situation was really valuable.

"We've always had a tight sense of family, but with kids it's even more. I have learned that in African culture, there are no nieces or nephews; rather, your siblings' kids are your own sons and daughters. I told my brother that. Now he even says to me about his kids, 'Remember, they're your children too.' I do take it on like that, I accept that responsibility to nurture them, and he does with Leroy. I can call on my brother for anything. Not only that, I can say to him, 'Be a father for my son.' I can't do that with anybody else."

Until her daughter, Mia, was three years old, Tammy and her sister, also a single mother, shared a home. "We did a kind of extended, alternative family together. She was on AFDC and she watched Mia as well as her own child while I went to school and worked. She was a terrific mom." When Tammy moved to do graduate work in social policy, her life raising Mia underwent a major shift. "I found out how difficult single parenting is when I moved, because I don't have any family here. Friends are a different kind of support system. Single friends have their own lives. Families tend to stay home at night and just enjoy their own families. Back home it was nothing to drop Mia off at Grandma's or leave her with my sister. I could do things on the spur of the moment. Here, absolutely not."

There is a kind of entitlement we may not feel with anyone other than relatives. But for some, that entitlement comes at a price. Our parents tend to assume the right to advise us, assess our parenting style, or sit in judgment on our choices much more freely than friends do. When Maggie adopted an eight-year-old girl who had been removed from her family because of abuse, the only people who didn't support her decision were her own parents. "They were frightened at this whole idea. 'Who are her people?' they wanted to know. Tessa was going to carry their name, and that disturbed them. So there was no support from them at all."

Another single mother, Marge, on the other hand, was offered lots of support by her parents — but she found it too conditional to accept. "Whatever they offered always came with some hidden agenda. Nothing was free. It had always been like that. So even though they were on the other side of the country I wouldn't accept any help from them."

Marge's parents wanted not only to help but to do the parenting as well. When we haven't been passed off safely into the hands of a mate, our parents can feel that they have both a duty and a right to fill in. "There was a point when they even talked about trying to take Taylor from me and have her stay with them because I was living on my own," Marge says. "I was raised with a lot more material privilege than my daughter has had, and they thought that she should have been too. They figured that if I wasn't going to avail her of this privilege, they would just have her live with them.

"At one point I even tried to get myself disowned from them and to cut all the legal entanglements that bind me to my siblings. Even though it has been a struggle financially without their help, I know I can take care of myself and my daughter, and for me, nothing replaces that."

The ties with our families of origin are so deep that we use terms like "disowned" to define separation, acknowledging that a sense of ownership is indeed a part of this bond. This is the family we "belong to," whether we want to or not. So indelible do we consider these bonds that only death can truly end the connection and responsibility.

Our blood families are the roots of our physical existence, where we have come from. But the self we once were can be very different from the self we strive to become. Even short visits "home," intended to cement relationships between our parents and our children, can nearly strain them to the breaking point. Laughing in acknowledgment, one single mother, Sharon, explains why she lives in her hometown again. "It was easier to move the two thousand miles back here with Jed to live in the same city and be near my parents than it was to visit them once a year and have to stay in their home for two weeks!"

Rachel's older sister Marian describes the year she spent at her parents' home as a "mixed blessing. In some ways it was really very good because there was economic and emotional support," she says. "If I wanted to read a book or take a bath, I could do that. They would play with Terra, and I was not alone. It wasn't just the parenting support, it was the human support — friendship and family." But there was a trade-off. Marian had returned with her three-year-old daughter to a family still raising children. Rachel was in high school, and another sister living at home was in college. Their mother and father were still very much in their own parental roles.

"The hard part was merging back into the household where I was also a child," Marian remembers. "I had become a different person living with my husband, and I had left behind some of the familial patterns of behavior. I stepped back into a household that was still operating basically in the same way. The tone was that you didn't say anything negative, you didn't say, 'Something is wrong here' or 'I'm angry.' Always, on the surface, everything was fine, whether it was or not. And that was hard.

"When the tensions would build and something would be wrong, if I would say, 'What's happening? It seems like you're angry,' everyone would say, 'No, nothing's wrong.' I felt like I was going crazy. I remember telling a woman at work how I was feeling. She said, 'You're not going crazy. You left your own home and are living in your parents' home with a different dynamic, and it's pushing buttons because you were raised this way.'"

When we go home, no matter how deep-seated is our new identity as adults and as parents, we are still the children of our own parents, and on some level we do become children again ourselves. In addition to that, we are introducing our own children into a context that may still be very much the same as when we left. In light of those circumstances, our refuge can turn out to be a minefield.

During the many years since I had left my parents' house, I had come to know myself as a person with a certain set of values which were sustained and supported by the friends I chose and the people I lived with. In some ways the values were similar to those of my parents; in other ways they seemed to be a world apart. And although I could talk with my mother like a friend over the phone, living with my parents again was to me "the solution to be avoided at all cost" — until the cost became too high. It became eminently clear that the intense effort still needed to finish this book would require long hours of help with Elias that I could ask for and afford only from my mother. I returned with him to my parents' house to live.

Immediately I seemed to be overtaken by my worst self. All the communications skills and rules of social restraint I had learned as an adult were swallowed up by the unmitigated emotions of a child — me. I was seventeen years old again, fourteen years, five, two. I was faced now with all the unfinished business of my childhood, not only through raising my own son but also through reliving some of the same dynamics I grew up with. Every cell in my body felt engulfed by family patterns. I seemed to get hooked into them despite myself. The person I had become didn't fit, she stuck out. My child-self, although recognizable, felt long outworn, her reactions uncomfortable, downright despicable. I simply couldn't manage to draw up the loving and mature responses I had worked for years to develop. I could remember precisely the dilemmas of my childhood yet I felt helpless to change any of them. And it was terrifying to see Elias begin to replicate some of the same patterns.

I found myself suspended between being an adult and being a child, and when the two clashed, I was wrenched into overwhelming rage. Simple questions from my mother — "Do you have enough gas in your car?" "Shouldn't Elias have a sweater on?" — sent me into a fury. For months it felt as if my mother and I lived in different worlds that could never meet. Despite the inevitable conflict, however, despite the fact that I resented having to feel so dependent, I also had to admit a deep sense of relaxation that I had not felt since Elias was born. I knew that no matter what happened, we would have a place to live and he would be taken care of. I knew that when I had to work late nights, weekends, anytime, someone else was there.

Perhaps when parents and their grown children live together it is in arriving at agreement on some basic values — namely, the value of children — that is the key to success. "I like a real neat house. I thrive on that," Lorraine admits when she talks about what it has been like living with her daughter Rachel and her granddaughter. "I'd think to myself, 'Here I worked all these years to get things the way I want them, and now I've got these two going through here.' But I had to see that this is not going to work if I'm going to be thinking all the time, 'Why doesn't she pick this up?' and 'Why doesn't she keep this clean?' I've had to tell myself, 'You're going to drive yourself crazy if you dwell on this. You might just as well say I prefer to enjoy them being here, and what's the difference if the house isn't absolutely perfect and if Mahala is breaking something or what have you. That's a small thing in comparison to having her around.' It's still one of the things that comes to mind more than anything else, though, so when I get discouraged sometimes, I think to myself, 'Well, what do you want? A sterile home or do you want their companionship?'"

As Rachel points out, "For women of the Housewife Era, like my mother, the state of the house was a real reflection of who they were." For us of the Working Single Mother Era, it's quite different. It may be very difficult for someone who didn't work while raising small children to understand how low down on the list of priorities tidy and uncluttered quarters can fall.

Like any relationship, the one between Lorraine, Rachel, and Mahala took time to work out. When I asked Rachel how she had to change in order to make the relationship work so well, she laughed and said, "I had to learn how to be more patient than I tend by nature to be in terms of making small talk!" I laughed with her, understanding from my own experience how annoying it can be to hear about how shoddily a neighbor's lawn was cut by a hired gardener or which distant relative is now in the hospital.

But for Rachel, other changes were much more profound. "Being her youngest child, I found it difficult for a long time to accept what my mother said as anything other than a directive. It had been a habit in our relationship that she would tell me what to do. So even though a lot of her advice about how to raise a child was really wonderful, it was hard not to take it sometimes as judging me as being incompetent."

Some of it was habit, and Lorraine learned to remind herself that "Rachel is raising her daughter the way she thinks best. It's another generation. There are many times of course when I would think I would do something differently, but I bite my tongue rather than say, 'You're not right.' I don't think I have the right to do that. That little girl belongs to her."

Much of what lay behind their successful adjustment to living together was Rachel's coming to terms with her own role as a child and as an adult. "Frankly," she says, "I needed to grow up, I needed to get beyond viewing her as 'mother.' When I felt so dependent on her, I resented that. Now that I'm at the point where I can regard myself as a capable individual, we are able to be more like peers than mom and kid. I take what she says as advice, not orders; I take it as her imparting information and not so much as instruction.

"Another thing that made a difference, especially after my dad died, is that our roles have changed," Rachel continues. "My mother relies on me for certain things now, just as I rely on her. This also allows me to be an adult. She turns to me for advice and emotional support in a way she wouldn't expect if she viewed me as a child."

Both agree that if Rachel's father were still alive, she would probably not have stayed as long. But in his absence Rachel's presence became prized companionship for Lorraine. "I was able to live with someone I have known all her life," Lorraine says. And Rachel had vital companionship as well. "I think it's very hard to live alone with a child without having input from other adults," comments Rachel. "Children are wonderful, and Mahala is like my primary partner right now. I enjoy her; she's insightful, intelligent, fun. But you just relate to adults differently, and I need that."

For everyone involved, this extended family is a success. "As far as I'm concerned," says Lorraine, "the advantages have been far greater than anything you could consider a disadvantage. I get to have this child around without having to take care of the disciplining aspects. I get to have companionship. I think I have the better bargain!"

Mahala, at eleven, perhaps feels she has the best bargain of all. "It's nice to have someone home. I like to come home after school because my grandma is here. If I get sick at school, I'm not scared because I know that she'd be here. And because she lived before, she has a different point of view, and that's interesting." Plus she knows that Lorraine is an advocate for her. "My mother is very much Mahala's other parent," Rachel explains, "and she views it that way too. We really co-parent, although I definitely am the primary parent and have the final say. She does not beat down my authority, but if I'm unreasonable with Mahala — which I get sometimes — she will champion for her. So Mahala has somebody to go to when I'm crabby. I see that grandparents have a kind of love of children that is . . . freer. My mother just doesn't have as many issues around what Mahala does as I do as her parent."

By the time the fires died down between my mother and me, she had arrived at an unprecedented tolerance for chaos and developed a lively relationship with Elias. And I, with a therapist's wise guidance, had undergone the healing of a lifetime. Despite the fact that living in my parents' house as an adult with a child was one of the harder things I have done in my life, there were some undeniable bonuses. The chance to see the source of some of my own parenting practices had given me perspective on how I was raising Elias. And I began to understand how, for a child, a parent can be an overwhelmingly powerful force. Even when I didn't agree with my mother, I could find myself, before I knew it, marching off to do something she suggested. I got a chance to know my mother more deeply as a person. And the experience was probably the closest I could come to parenting with an actively involved partner. I could assume a level of shared commitment and willingness one might usually expect only from a child's other parent.

One afternoon during a break from my work, my mother and I stood talking in the kitchen, waiting for the teakettle to boil. Realizing how extraordinarily helpful she had been during the past months, I blurted out, "You're almost like . . . like . . . a husband!"

"I'm *better* than a husband!" she said, laughing. "I cook, I wash clothes, I'm a taxi driver, I do childcare. . . ." Actually she was being the "wife" every parent needs. As we stood there, talking over the stove, I realized how far we had come.

In her book *Just Friends: The Role of Friendship in Our Lives,* Lillian Rubin writes: "Partly because kin relationships have demonstrated their capacity to survive the storms of family life, partly just because we exist in the world as members of the same family, we experience these relationships with a sense of permanence that none other can match. Consequently, we have a greater sense of entitlement with kin than with friend, a greater sense of security, even in the face of behaviors that we know to be unacceptable anywhere else."[8] As parents raising children alone, however, we may have to reach beyond these assumptions and find with friends the kind of acceptance and participation in our lives that we often assume only with kin.

All of our relationships shift when we parent alone. We have far less time and more demands, and our lives are centered around our children. Whereas we might grow closer to those blood relations we can count upon, we might also drift away from friends who have begun to recognize that single parents have little casual time and that to be a friend to them simply requires, to some degree, entering their lives in a supportive role. As we proceed through life, friendships change to support new identities. So too we may look to new, child-oriented friends to be around. But because longevity and constancy, as Lillian Rubin points out, are basic qualities of *family*, those old friends who come along with us on our journey, themselves changing with us and our children, are real treasures.

◆ MORE PRECIOUS THAN GOLD

For those who do not have supportive relatives, friends become that much more vital. "I am blessed, I guess you might say, by having a very distant family," Maggie says with a note of irony, referring to how little pleased her family was at her choice to adopt. That attitude on the part of her family has, in fact, helped her to bond with her adopted daughter on the grounds of shared experience. "I think that my very long-standing, dear friends who have embraced Tessa are one of the assets I have for a child like this who has been rejected by her own blood family. I can tell her with real conviction, 'Your family is really made up of the friends who know you and love you for who you are. It is not necessarily your relatives.' Our friends are our 'aunts' and 'uncles.' It's our *friends* who are our extended family."

For Marge this was also true. Although her attempt to be officially disowned by her family wasn't realized, Marge was clear that she and her daughter didn't belong to them. But that didn't mean they were bereft of what Marge considered family support. "We have always had close friends in our lives in one way or another. Without them it would have been not just harder to raise Taylor as a single mother, it would have been intolerable," Marge says.

With Taylor graduating and moving back East for college, the major portion of Marge's task is almost over. The change is exciting but of course very hard for her; worry is etched into her face as we talk. "Always on days like this when I'd be tearing my hair out about something and need somebody to understand, my friends have been there. And they have also been available for Taylor as adult friends."

For Marge, sharing the parenting of her daughter with others felt like the natural thing to do. "I didn't feel possessive about parenting in the way some people do," she explains. "For one thing, by nature I'm just somebody who prefers to work in partnerships. Some people like to do things on their own, I like working with others. On the negative side, though, I felt inadequate to do a good job as a mother, and so I was open to somebody else being a part of this. The ways in which I did feel good about myself as a mother were more there when I didn't have to do everything myself all the time."

When Taylor was a year old, Marge gave up the struggle of living with her child's father and set out to find a place to live with one of her close friends. What would transpire in this particular relationship points out not only the benefits but also perhaps the basic fear we face when we reach out to friends as family. Luna had been Marge's friend for several years by the time Taylor was born. "Luna immediately made a commitment to having regular times every week when she would take care of Taylor so that I could go to work or whatever. To her, children and childrearing were really important. She was a primary school teacher and was very involved with children."

When the two of them decided to rent a place together, Luna became even more like a co-parent. "We weren't lovers, but in some ways our relationship was like a familial couple, because we had this life of children together through my daughter," says Marge. "Luna was like a partner in a lot of ways. I talked with her a lot about parenting issues. In some ways I saw her as having more authority as a mother than I did, even though she wasn't biologically a mother."

During the year and a half they lived together, Marge's skill and confidence as a mother grew. Despite the fact that Luna was providing relief from the day-to-day stresses of raising Taylor, Marge decided she was ready to tackle the task on her own. "I was becoming more aware of the fact that part of me felt that I *had* to live with other people because I couldn't manage this on my own. I see now that I was still dealing with my emancipation from my own parents and the extreme dependence they had fostered in me and my siblings. So when I could prove to myself that I could live on my own and support my child, it gave me a sense of strength about myself that I needed to develop.

"But it was a hard decision to make, and it resulted in a real separation and alienation between me and Luna. For me to make that decision emphasized the fact that, despite everything, Taylor was *my* child. That was really hard for Luna. So she kind of withdrew from our lives after that. She continued off and on relating to Taylor, but it wasn't ever the same."

Bonds with friends can feel and, in fact, be more precarious than those with kin. Lillian Rubin writes: "Friends *choose* to do what kin are *obliged* to do. . . . It is this very quality of friendship that is at once so powerfully seductive and so anxiety-provoking, indeed that is both its strength and its weakness. . . . If we can be chosen, we can also be *un*chosen."[9]

In some situations, everyone involved can end up feeling unchosen. "I felt particularly bad because of Taylor," adds Marge. "Luna had been like a mother to her." Our children hope for and expect continuity, and family, almost by definition, implies that. But our friendships can change as we change.

Endings are inherent in all families, as in life. But our children develop healthy responses to inevitable endings by learning to trust the constancy of love in their early years. Fortunately for Taylor, there were others, even though Luna was gone. "Another friend, Annie, has always been there for Taylor and me," Marge continues. "She's still like Taylor's aunt. If I was at work and Taylor was sick, she'd go pick her up from school. Sometimes she'd take her for an afternoon or an evening. We'd go camping together, do things with other kids. She'd help me plan parties for her. And I could talk to her about parenting things too. It wasn't boring to her. Her presence in our life meant that we weren't completely isolated living alone.

"Living on our own *was* hard, in fact. On the day-to-day level *I* did everything now. I always felt tired and like I could barely do the survival things. So I would lose patience and not feel very kind. But at least with Annie in our lives, it wasn't just Taylor and me in the world — ever. She was willing to take on that kind of responsibility, which is very rare. Annie was one of a handful. A lot of people who don't have children can't really participate in that part of your life, they don't feel attracted to it, and they don't understand it. But Annie did."

Before Taylor left for college, Marge arranged a farewell ceremony for her to say good-bye to "all her mothers," the women "Taylor has known and trusted for years. I always made clear to Taylor that they were there in her life for her. Through her teen years, for instance, when she felt she just really couldn't talk with me, she always had these other people. If she had a problem, she could talk with these women, and they would not tell me what she'd said. If I was worried, I could call Annie or Louise and ask if she'd been in touch with them. 'Yes, she is,' they'd say, 'and yes, she is having a hard time, but it's not anything you have to be concerned about.' Can you imagine the relief that is? I didn't have to know the details if I could just know that she was all right. That was one thing I was very careful to do — make sure that there has always been parenting available to her even if she couldn't get it from me."

From the moment my son was born into a circle of smiling friends at the home of his first godparents, he and I have been sustained by an extended family of both kith and kin, those we have lived with and others nearby or far away. Anna and Paul gave my newborn and me an idyllic month in their cottage in the woods. For several months after that, housemates took over my cooking and shopping duties. Sypko and Carolyn, a married couple without children, had established themselves as the "Godparent Institute" before Elias was born. During his first year, they brought weekly meals that always ended with one of them doing the dishes while the other took him upstairs for a bath — and they didn't just seat him in the tub, they climbed right in with him! As Elias has grown, Sypko has taken him on journeys by train and by imagination, offered male guidance on questions about anatomy, and stayed in touch over distances by phone calls and a stream of postcards and letters.

Nearly every friend I've known became more deeply involved once I had a child. At a time when I could scarcely plan the next hour, Elias's other godparents set up a college trust fund for him. He received so many hand-me-downs and gifts of clothing that until he was five he scarcely needed any new clothes. In addition to his own grandparents, he has many co-mothers, several godparents, a "non-grandfather," and a number of "uncles." Emotionally and financially, our friends have rained blessings. I may lament that our culture as a whole does not value children, but certainly these women and men have treated Elias like a national treasure.

From my perspective as a single parent, at times it seems like a one-way street, from them to us, and I rue having apparently so little to give back. But there is greatness in the hearts of those who value children. They recognize how much they receive in return — the opportunity to touch the renewing and magical world of childhood, as well as a chance to very directly influence the future. It takes very little to make a big difference, for anything done for a child is significant.

◆ MODELS AND MENTORS

"Probably one of my biggest fears," admits Rick, who has raised his two daughters and a son since they were toddlers, "was wondering if I had too many male influences in my kids' lives, especially for the girls. But I'm lucky in that I know a lot of nice women — not physical relationships but really good friends who I've kept in touch with through the years, and they have been positive role models. One of my daughters got a summer job working for one woman who is a friend of mine, and I was really happy about that. It gave her a connection with that woman. But I never made a point of asking any of them to *try* to be around the kids."

Many single parents agree about the importance of having special adult friends in their children's lives, but many also feel afraid to impose on others. For the sake of our children — and indeed also for those who discover the gift of getting to know a child — we need to ask. Like Marge, we need to work to ensure that there are always others available to give what we can't.

"Mia hasn't seen her own dad since she was nine months old," says Tammy, "and I know that she's lacking the male in her life. Any time there is a man around who I know and who she somewhat trusts, she is very clingy with him, wants a lot of attention from him, wants to play tag, hits him to initiate interaction. She really has a need for that."

When Tammy left her hometown to go to graduate school, Mia's needs became especially clear. Friends and family were "back there. I have an old friend back home who has always done things with

Mia, and whenever we go back, he still does, like taking her to buy Mother's Day gifts for me," says Tammy. "I have thought about asking him, when we move back there after I graudate, if he will take on that role in a special way. Also, now that my mom is recently remarried, Mia's new stepgrandfather is another man in her life there who adores her and does things with her. Living here while I'm in school, I take her along to group gatherings with friends from class, and some of those men are wonderful and understanding and pay tons of attention to her. But it's a need I am very aware of and I don't know what I would do if I didn't know these good men I can trust with her."

Girls and boys growing up in single-parent families need both women and men in their lives. When we don't have trusted friends or family to play these roles, it can be very hard to know where to turn. It is generally easier to find women interested in forming significant friendships with children than it is to find such men — not only because men in our culture have not been encouraged to involve themselves with children, but also because they are stymied at this point by circumstances. "There is such a mania of fear about molesting and child abuse that a lot of men feel discouraged from even trying to enter the lives of children," says Gordon Clay, director of the National Men's Resource Center.[10] Thus at a time when we especially need good men in our children's lives, we are paralyzed by a fear which, while not unfounded, is far too generalized. Mentoring programs, surrogate-grandparent programs, and organizations like Big Brothers/Big Sisters of America are places to find men and women who are interested in the welfare of children and can be trusted. The substantial screening process to become a Big Brother, for instance, can take months, and it includes a home visit, psychological tests, a check of police records, and extensive references.

However, what makes for a good match in any of these programs depends upon a variety of circumstances. Jill's son, Nicholas, who is now eighteen and just going off to college, had two Big Brothers before one came along who was "a perfect match." The first man "sort of faded away," explains Jill, who has raised her son alone since he was three years old and she became a widow. "I think that particular man didn't really know how to relate to a young child, and Nicholas was only five when he started." The second man got married, and when his wife had twins, he simply couldn't find the time to continue his relationship with Nicholas. But Ken, the Big Brother who has been in Nicholas's life for the past eight years, has been just right.

"I don't look at Ken as a replacement for a father," comments Nicholas. "But this is the closest thing to a father I can have. He is a friend who I am close to, an adult friend."

Ken, who is sitting next to Nicholas on the couch as we talk, explains, "I was married and divorced and had no children, and I was missing that. I had dated a woman who had kids and I enjoyed being with them. So when that broke up, I knew I wanted to have someone younger in my life to do things with, to teach, to kind of be a surrogate parent to in some way. Nicholas was the first person the organization matched me with, and it worked out really well. As we got to know each other, we found out how similar our interests were. We've gone camping together a lot, done computers, music . . ."

"I feel fortunate to have this relationship which involves a lot of my interests," Nicholas adds. "I suppose that's the way a relationship with a father should be — revolving around mutual interests — although I don't think it is that way for a lot of kids. I think I'm especially lucky because this has been such a positive experience for me with Ken. And besides that, my relationship with my mother is also a positive experience. A lot of people don't have relationships that good even when they have two parents!"

Nicholas's positive relationship with his mother is due in part to Ken. "When Ken first came into our lives, Nicholas was nine years old and very dependent on me," comments Jill from the opposite side of the room. "He was kind of clingy and fearful of losing me or of being away from me for too long. He had this very strong female influence with me, and it wasn't balanced. There were things I'd become concerned about. When he was little he wanted to do everything like me. He wanted to shave his legs, for instance." Jill laughs. "Little boys want to do what their parents do, but there was no male parent to show him what men do. We had friends and neighbors, but none of them were part of the day-to-day household. I thought, 'He needs a male role model. I can't be that for him. I simply can't.'

"It relieved me to have Ken come into his life. There was a sense that finally something I couldn't give Nicholas was being taken care of, and that was so wonderful. I felt, 'Whew, he's getting that at last!' I could see the change in Nicholas from being clingy and fearful to little by little becoming more independent." Nodding to this smiling stranger who became such a significant part of her son's family, Jill says, "That was a direct result of some of the things he did with you, Ken. Going on extended trips with you, going out into nature — those things really changed him."

"I think it's true that before I met Ken, my world was a smaller one, I was more dependent on my mother," Nicholas says. "Mom and I have a very strong connection, in some sense maybe too strong. We still need to be detached, and my moving now three thousand miles away to go to college is part of that. But I do think Ken helped me with that — getting away for periods of time with someone who was a real good influence. There weren't that many men around when I was growing up, and being with him introduced me to a new realm. I think it had a balancing effect.

"I think parents *have* to hang on, to a certain extent," Nicholas adds, smiling over at his mother, "in order to give their kids a sense of security, but I think for my mom and me, we felt we've got to hold on to each other because there was nothing else out there. This was *it*."

"The fact that I could trust Ken did mean I could let go a little more," Jill says. "Ken was always true to his word. And a big thing was that this was *their* relationship. It wasn't something I was personally involved in myself. That was freeing. I didn't have to be part of it."

"When you're with somebody who has a different life, you start to learn from that," Nicholas goes on. "Before Ken, whenever I wanted to talk with someone, it was my mom I'd go to. And sometimes she didn't have the time or the energy. I think being a single parent probably created for my mom an overwhelming feeling of a lot of stuff to do. So realizing that there was someone else out there for me to talk to was great. It wasn't like Ken and I were sitting down and talking about problems; it was more subtle. It was just being around someone different and in a different world."

It was a men's world, and even though they didn't discuss much of what it meant to be a man, some aspects of what that might be naturally came up in their friendship. One simple part of it was a certain kind of physical roughhousing that single parents say both their boys and girls sometimes look to men for. "Nicholas just seemed to have a physical need to do that," explains Jill. "He'd push against me, butt into me, and I just couldn't take it. But he and Ken could get into that. Think of all these young kids who have to face that resistance from their mothers. Where do they go?"

The San Francisco Bay chapter of Big Brothers/Big Sisters reported that in 1991 they had five hundred boys on their waiting list with no available sponsors. (On the other hand, two hundred Big Sisters were waiting to be matched to girls.) One of the greatest social revolutions we might hope for would be the large-scale involvement of men in the lives of children. There are far too few Kens. Perhaps those men who have recognized and grieved their own losses will reach out to fill the void for the next generation. Robert Bly has been known to suggest to men who have asked for scholarships to his workshops that they cover their price of admission in a different way. "Go find a young man, write to him or see him once a month, let him know you hold him in your heart," he tells them. Lamenting the fact that many young men do not know a single older man, Bly enjoins men "to recognize that they have some substance that younger men need in their lives."[11] So too do girls need women in their lives, and as many cultures have recognized, this "substance," which is essential for maturity, is often best given by adults other than a child's parents.

Ken did take his Little Brother to a sweat lodge with his men's group, an event which Nicholas says "sticks out as one of the highlights of my life." In that situation, "we talked a lot about what it is to be a man in today's society," Ken relates. "It seems to be an elusive quality, especially when masculinity is still defined as being independent and we want to know how to bond. But outside of that situation, he and I haven't talked about what it is to be a man. Yet it's part of our relationship." In the end, Ken feels that the essence of what he has conveyed to Nicholas is "an interest in and approach to life. I think it's important that a young man see life from many points of view, as he might were he in a large extended family. I don't think a father in a nuclear family could give a son everything either. That richness has to come from a variety of sources. But you have to make a conscious decision that you want your children to have that in their lives."

Just as building a network of support for ourselves takes focused effort, so too does engaging others to be models and mentors for our children. There may be false starts, as Jill and Nicholas encountered when they first sought a Big Brother. As Marc Freedman, author of

The Kindness of Strangers: Reflections on the Mentoring Movement, writes, "It is imperative to recognize the risks inherent in engineering relationships."[12] We don't want to set up hope only to lead to disappointment. While a degree of commitment and constancy is imperative in befriending children, different people may be willing to take on relationships that vary in terms of time and depth. We can plant the seed with many "aunts" and "uncles" to give our children the opportunity to see life "from many points of view," in Ken's words.

To ease our reticence to ask friends or family to fulfill this role, it is important to recognize that this request is also a gift. The majority of adults in our society live in such a way that they rarely encounter children, and then perhaps mostly in contexts which reinforce the belief that children are a bother, disruptive, even to be feared.

The tragedy is that the renewing impulse of life that children have represented and the perspective they offer through fresh eyes are often not recognized or welcomed. Because a task far too great for one person has been left in the hands primarily of mothers, we have ended up with the attitude revealed in a survey conducted by Ann Landers in 1975. When she asked her readers whether, if they could do it over, they would have children again, 70 percent answered no.[13]

Perhaps the issue is not so much whether children need fathers in their lives but rather whether fathers, and adults in general, need children in theirs. To relate to a child is to recognize what it is to be an adult. To take on responsibility for a child is an avenue to genuine maturity, an opportunity to attain what Erik Erikson called the "generative" phase, the crowning step in human development — passing on what we know to those who follow.[14]

When adults give time and attention to children, they are preparing those children to do the same when they mature, preparing them for the kind of satisfaction that an engaged life brings. Perhaps one day, adults in our culture will vie to have a special relationship with children other than their own, bringing balance back into the role of parenthood and extended family into the lives of many.

◆ FAMILY AS COMMUNITY

Extended family — or intentional community, as she now frames it — has become a primary interest for Lisa, the single mother of a school-aged boy. Raising her son alone is precisely what motivated her to move on from her profession as a nurse and into a master's program in sociology, where she is writing her thesis on structuring alternative communities. Ten years ago, when this all started, Lisa was a new mother and simply scrambling for a place to live.

When her baby's father made it clear, while she was still pregnant, that he didn't want a screaming infant in his apartment, Lisa found an affordable place to rent with several friends in a big house near the ocean. Two of them were a couple with their own baby, and the others were comfortable with children. "It was a beautiful cooperative household," Lisa remembers. Faced with an unexpected recuperation period after a caesarean delivery, she applied for AFDC and set to being a mother. Lisa was actually grateful for the opportunity this provided to have some time with her baby. One day when Ivan was just a few months old, a notice arrived that the owners wanted the house back. "You've been great tenants," the letter read, "but we need it for something else."

Lisa now faced finding housing with a baby in a West Coast oceanside town that commanded unusually high rents. "I could *not* find a place to live. When landlords found out I was a single mother on welfare, they didn't want to rent to me. It was impossible." Renting with friends had made costs affordable, but no one she knew wanted to share, or even to put them up until she found a place. "I knew a zillion people in town, but none of them wanted to live with a baby. Zilch! Either they were single or their own kids were older."

Lisa's search for immediate housing took precedence over that futile hunt for a home. She and baby Ivan ended up living in her van for a while. "For a few nights we were actually parked out on the street. Then for a few weeks a friend let us park in his driveway." Another friend and her new husband invited them to use the rooms of her children, who had gone to spend the summer with their father. After that, Lisa housesat for a friend who had gone out of town for a few months. "While I was in that place, I got sick for four or five days with a horrible flu. I remember one day when I was practically hallucinating from the fever and someone I didn't even know very well had stopped by. I asked if he would agree to take my child if I died. He was kind and didn't make fun of me. He just assured me that I wasn't going to die. But it showed me how strange it was to be that helpless and alone."

Soon after, the couple with the baby who had been her housemates at the ocean found a new place to live and invited Lisa and Ivan to join them again. "I realized it was my saving grace to be able to move in with other people with a baby. First of all, they understood my situation. And second, the kids could play together. During that time of moving around, I realized that it was almost more stressful to live with others and have a baby if they don't have kids than it is to live alone. When you have a child, you have to tolerate a level of mess and noise that childless people just aren't used to." Lisa set to pulling her life together, looking for a job, organizing her home.

"Shortly after I moved in, I went to place an ad in a newspaper with free classifieds to sell a piece of baby equipment I no longer needed," Lisa relates. "I felt very inspired by the fact that this newspaper provided free advertising. While I was filling out the form, I kept thinking about how hard it had been to find someplace to live. I started wondering about all the other single parents out there who might be experiencing the same thing. I knew I couldn't be the only one. In fact, I had a sense that I was part of a growing army of single parents who couldn't find housing.

"I've always had an interest in social action, and I had this vague thought that there is power in numbers, although I had no particular plan. So I did this strange thing on the spur of the moment: I put an ad in the free classifieds saying, 'Single Parents Unite! Call this number (mine) for free housing information.' Then I went home, hoping someone would call soon to buy the bassinet.

"The phone started ringing off the hook. There were single parents who had just been evicted, crying on the phone, asking 'What can I do?' The welfare office called — 'Can we send you people?' A housing agency that matched senior citizens with tenants called. They mostly had single parents coming to be matched and no one wanted to live with them. Someone called from the tenants' union. So many people called asking when the next meeting would be held that I decided we'd better have one."

A friend offered to lend the offices of her birth center, and about thirty people showed up for that first meeting, mostly women. Lisa had arranged to have someone babysit in the next room, "and we spent the evening introducing ourselves. Each person told their story. We had a whole spectrum of people. Some were on welfare, and some were professional women. A surprising number had been women who had been fairly comfortable until they got divorced, and they were finding themselves a few years down the line with no money left from their settlement and no adequate profession. There they were, trapped in a situation for which they hadn't made provisions. That's all we got done that evening, because people just broke down and started crying each time they talked. It was so moving. I thought, 'My God, yes, I'm not the only one.'"

The next week someone called who wanted to interview Lisa for his research on homelessness. "He said, 'I hear you have this agency that helps people find housing.' When I explained the story to him, he told me he was being funded by someone concerned about the homeless, 'and I bet she'd be interested in this.' The minute he said those words, I knew that it was going to happen."

Two weeks later Lisa found herself sitting in a lovely French restaurant with only a table draped in white linen between her and a bona fide philanthropist. The woman had asked to see a proposal. "I had never seen a proposal before in my life!" says Lisa. "The guy who interviewed me had coached me on how to itemize potential expenses and suggested I ask for the same amount of funding he had received — $10,000 for six months.

"When lunch was over, the woman said, 'Well, do you have anything for me?' My hands were shaking like a leaf, so I managed to push the proposal across the table without it getting messy. She glanced at my figures, smiled, and said, 'Consider it done.' It was like a miracle. Here I am on welfare, and then this . . . I thought, 'My God, my whole life has changed with that sentence.' I felt like I needed to go scream in joy somewhere."

Lisa's life did change. For the next two years, often with her son by her side, she organized and ran an agency that grew into a significant community of support for single parents. "We had two running ads in the classifieds. One said, 'If you have a place to share with a single parent, call us.' The other said that we could help single parents find housing. Some who called in were single parents who owned homes and wanted to rent out a room. Sometimes they had trouble renting due to the same prejudice against living with kids. Sometimes they thought they could benefit from living with someone who could do childcare or trades. Some who met here even ended up buying or renting places together.

"We continued with weekly meetings. It made sense to begin by having everyone interested get together. And sure enough, that in itself was helpful. Even if people didn't end up housing together, they were at least meeting people in the same situation. They could talk, exchange addresses, trade babysitting. We had a community!

"We had counseling classes for free with babysitting provided and support groups. Eventually we added a babysitting co-op. Everyone who joined got a certain number of coupons and a list of people in the co-op. One coupon was worth a half hour of childcare. It was a good way to keep track of exchange hours.

"For a while we had funding for a very nice office downtown, so every Friday night the office was open for single parents to drop off their kids and go out. Two parents would be on duty, and the kids would put out their sleeping bags, play games, eat, and go to sleep."

This supportive community continued for about five more years after Lisa left it to work on her sociology degree. By this time she had learned something about what it takes for people to live together successfully. "While there's an advantage for single parents in living with other people with kids, I found there can also be disadvantages," Lisa comments. "Now that Ivan is older, it's an obvious advantage for us. But when he was younger, it actually turned out to be twice the amount of noise and twice the chaos. The kids did sort of amuse each other, but they'd end up biting each other and fighting over the same toy. On the other hand, the parents could really help each other. One person could go to the store and leave the other with the kids, for instance."

Sharing housing requires cooperative skills and methods of organization that very little in our educational system or even our lives has prepared us for. Rugged individualism and independence are still held up as models of maturity. The structures of our housing — single-family dwellings and "apart"-ments — sustain the image that adults live in separate family units. However, as the recent census revealed, both for economic reasons and to fulfill a need for community, various forms of shared housing are increasing rapidly, from living with relatives to sharing with friends. For single parents clearly there are major advantages.

Sociologists at Stanford report that the presence of additional adults in single-parent households positively affects the behavior of adolescents and reduces delinquency. Children who have too much autonomy too young are the ones who tend to have low grades in school or express deviant behavior. When another adult is present in the household, the single parent has emotional support, someone to discuss decisions with, and another presence at home for the child.[15]

When we live with others, our children not only get to know other adults, they also get to witness adults interacting in potentially healthy, respectful ways. This is something often missing for children in our culture, as they move between their classrooms and homes with little clue as to how adults manage in relation to each other.

For Cath and Danielle, extending their family by inviting in another single parent ended up providing something essential for everyone — at least for a while. "Danielle and I had been talking about what kind of family we are when it's basically just the two of us. She had often said that her *family* was with her dad and her stepbrothers while her *home* was with me. She had been begging me to have another child or to adopt a sibling for her. Then she started talking about wanting a baby herself. Well, I'm forty-three, and she's twelve. One night I went to sleep thinking, 'This is a disaster. I am too old to have a baby, and Danielle is too young. I'm worried, but how to solve this situation?' I had read an article in the newspaper about unwed mothers finishing high school with babies, and I thought, 'That's what we need.' I woke up the next morning and called a friend who works as a counselor with young women. She said, 'My niece!' Four hours later, Joy and her baby were here.

"It actually was great for quite a while and gave us all something we needed. For Danielle especially, having a baby around and someone pretty close to her age to talk to was wonderful. But after about a year, Joy and I both felt it was time for a change. This sounds so ludicrous, but food and the different diets we had was a major problem. Joy and the baby ate entirely processed foods, and drank soda pop in the morning, which was appalling to me. And I felt uncomfortable eating seaweed and mangos in my own kitchen because that freaked *her* out."

The intricacies of blending lifestyles is one of the hardest aspects of working out shared living arrangements in a pluralistic culture like ours. In the mid-1980s, Pam LaCoe, who was newly divorced and on her own with two children, got together with some of her friends in Boston to start a nonprofit organization called Homehold Single Parent Resource. "The ultimate goal was to create housing for single moms," explains Pam, "and the interim goal was to be a referral center to facilitate shared housing." The group soon found that dealing with zoning ordinances and city laws on occupancy was only half the challenge. The other half involved the endless specifics of shared daily life — whether smoking would be allowed indoors, how to share a kitchen when diets were different, whether pets were welcome, differences in disciplining children, and so on. Despite these hurdles, a number of women found shared housing that proved to be supportive for their families. "For me," comments Pam in retrospect, "one of the most significant parts of the process was the sense of empowerment we all felt — that we were able to address these issues and do something creative about our needs." It is no small task.

I set out to interview a household of three single mothers I had heard about who in a large urban area had created what sounded to me like an ideal shared living arrangement. While their children were very young, each arranged an afternoon off work every week to pick up the three children and care for them at home. The children had known each other since birth, and this promised to be a tight family.

When a number of my questions were answered by an uneasy silence or nervous chuckles, I slowly began to realize that this group, despite having been together for nearly a decade, simply had not developed some of the basic skills needed to build a cohesive household. Among these are systems for house maintenance, schedules for house meetings, agreements on priorities, respect for private time as well as acknowledging the need for shared time, the ability to make and keep agreements, tolerance of differences, and the willingness to communicate openly. It was obvious that the housemates were basically kind to one another, but it seemed as if some of the best parts of living together were inaccessible to them, primarily owing to lack of the kind of structure *any* group needs in order to function.

One woman confessed that she longed for a family feeling in the group and wanted to do things together, but all agreed that that would not be possible unless some underlying contentions were addressed. For a while they had, in fact, seen a counselor together, but they had stopped when they could no longer afford it.

Despite their differences, these three single mothers all agreed that they wanted to continue on together, at least for the foreseeable future. "It's really good for the kids to have each other," one of them said. "And for our sakes too. The fact that our children have others to relate to besides their mother makes it much easier on each mother, it takes the pressure off. Logistically, the childcare works out so well. And besides, we all have relationships with all of them."

The glass wall between them that these three women have come to live with is built, one of them surmised, of "fear and lack of time to deal with the problems. And a lot of what is lacking is also just know-how."

"But we actually get along better than some of the two-parent families we know!" another added. "We're more philosophically aligned, and we're not having screaming fights in front of the kids. We have more free time as parents, and our kids have each other." Judging by the levity coming from the kitchen as the three children, two nine-year-olds and a seven-year-old, got themselves a bedtime snack, the children did indeed find security and pleasure in their little tribe.

When I asked these mothers before leaving if they would recommend shared housing, two responded that they would, "with certain upgrades." The third clarified an upgrade they all nodded vigorously at — for each parent-and-child pair to have its own kitchen, its own space, and more privacy.

Having extended family or community made up of individual homes close together has been a successful living model for millennia. This is exactly what Lisa found when she returned to school and moved into university housing for graduate students with families. "The ideal way to live as a single parent is to have your own dwelling — your own bathroom, kitchen, living room. To have your own front door and have it open up on this big green area with all the other doors of people with kids opening onto it. Our children could all play together, and you'd just have to look out the window to see them. I could sit inside and study or work on my thesis and hear Ivan playing outside or know he was next door."

As Lisa points out, graduate student housing is often built this way, which is one of the reasons she has encouraged single parents to return to school while their children are young. "You have a community with similar values. You've got your privacy so you can keep your sanity, and you have people next door you can share babysitting with. And the kids all have each other. They can go in and out of each other's homes and have a lot of safe freedom."

When Lisa graduated, she and her son spent two summers visiting intentional communities, mostly in rural environments, and eventually chose one to settle in. It is estimated that there are now three to four hundred intentional communities across the country, where members share social, political, and economic values and live with the kind of daily connection that many in our culture now only dream about. Intentional communities require a tremendous commitment of time and energy — perhaps more than many single parents can make — if they are to function effectively. But for some of the single parents I spoke with, such communities have proven to be the extended family they were looking for.

New modes of community living are springing up around the world. Cohousing, which is based on a model of shared housing that started in Denmark, has over seventy groups across the United States. For Jennifer, a single mother with a nine-year-old son, to live in a cohousing community is the dream she is working toward. For the last two years, she has been meeting with a group of individuals, both married and single, with and without children, who are together custom-designing the physical and social structures that will be their version of the cohousing model. Jennifer brings to the group the particular skills she is learning as a landscape architecture student at the University of California. But she hastens to point out that everyone becomes familiar with every aspect of the project during the long and intensive planning phase.

While styles and arrangements of cohousing projects can vary from converted warehouses to suburban spreads built from the ground up, the basic schema common to all of them includes private living units for individual households and shared structures such as a community kitchen, gardens, laundry, and workshop or office spaces. What the shared areas are arise from the unique needs and desires of each cohousing group. As Jennifer describes the cohousing model, "It's like a condominium owned and developed by the people involved, but the difference is that everyone knows each other, creates and manages it together, and forms an active community."

For the first three years of her son's life, Jennifer was married and living in the the homemaker/breadwinner model of family. "I was living the American dream — and I hated it!" she says. "I was isolated, home alone, going crazy in a suburb outside of Boston. It was a lovely, large home, a beautiful place, it was safe to leave bikes on the front lawn. I remember thinking, 'Is this all there is? Is this what we are supposed to be doing with our lives?'"

In researching the cohousing model for her master's thesis, Jennifer has found that a lot of people, no matter what their circumstances, have been asking the same question. "Everybody I interviewed is interested in cohousing because they want community. That is the number-one reason people are working so hard and waiting so long for these things to happen. It takes years to design and build these structures, and it's an enormous commitment. But we're doing it because we really believe that community is the most important thing."

The structure that Jennifer is helping to design will consist of twenty-seven units and a large common house. The group projects that half of those units will have children, so the common house and yard will include facilities for them, including a room for teenagers. As a single parent Jennifer looks forward to "the support system and other children around. You don't have to put them in a car to get them to play with other kids. There is spontaneity of kids going out the door to play. Matt will have other role models. He'll see other parents and children as they live together. And he'll see men, and have a chance to do things with them that I wouldn't do with him.

"Equally important is the chance to spend time with other adults you enjoy. And," says Jennifer, smiling, "for single parents to be able to come home and have a cooked meal ready every night is like having a spouse who does that for you if you're the breadwinner. And once a month, you get together with two other people and take your turn doing the meal."

That new households require new housing is being recognized by single parents like Lisa, Pam, and Jennifer who have worked to develop new models. Enlightened city governments are also recognizing the benefits of community housing for single-parent families. Warren Village, built in 1974 in Denver, Colorado, was the first housing development for low-income single parents that was designed to encourage community. On-site childcare facilities as well as on-site counseling, job training, and educational services are part of the project. A survey of single parents who used the supportive environment of Warren Village to meet their personal goals reveals how successful it has been: "While 47 percent of residents were employed at the time of entrance, 94 percent were employed two years after they left Warren Village. Even more striking is the finding that while 65 percent were receiving public assistance at the time of enrollment, only 6 percent were doing so two years after leaving the program."[16]

Boulder and Loveland, also in Colorado, followed suit, establishing attractive housing complexes that include on-site childcare, playgrounds, community centers, and training rooms. Projects in other cities have improved on the model by creating a mix of families, including both married couples and single people of all ages. Not only do such models give a new face to housing projects, they contribute models of success that point to the value of community housing designs for others as well.

Perhaps most of us are not going to make the radical shifts in our lives that some of these single parents made, but what they have found in various ways shows that creative solutions to our needs and challenges do exist. What we need, as do all parents, is emotional and physical support in parenting. Our children need "significant others." Families need community. The idea of family is indeed breaking open in our society, and as single parents we are a part of a pioneering effort.

"I meet some very wealthy women at my job at a nearby resort," comments Lisa. "One of them has a husband who is a very well known artist, and they have a couple of kids. This woman, with all the money they have, spends her whole life driving the kids around on the freeways from one lesson to another, from the private school to the private pool. That's her life. I compare myself to her. With all the money and beauty and advantages they have, my life here in this loosely organized, somewhat funky alternative community where Ivan has lots of playmates and a great little school makes more sense to me in terms of being a mother. It works better than what she's doing. She says herself, 'It's crazy. I don't like living this way. We don't have any neighbors with kids.'

"It's amusing to me," continues Lisa, "that we still have this old model stuck in our heads — even when it doesn't work. Part of what we have to get over is this idea that these other ways of raising our children are not the right way. In fact, the whole society still holds that idea, and that's why it hasn't adjusted to the reality as they have in other countries. There are so many gaps that could be filled so easily if we just brought ourselves up to the present time and faced the facts: This is what is going on. This is what our families are like now. It could be so much easier if some adjustments were made in our housing in particular. Families just have to live next to each other. Community is the secret. If we had community, we'd all be okay. Single parenting wouldn't be so stressful."

There are many ways of creating community and extending our

families. As Carolyn Shaffer and Kristin Anundsen write in *Creating Community Anywhere,* "You don't have to uproot yourself or your family and move to the country to experience the kind of mutual support and connection people often associate with small-town life. . . . You can begin to create satisfying community wherever you live and work."[17]

We create it through support groups, through our schools, churches, and neighborhoods, through childcare cooperatives and daycare centers, and by living with and near others who embrace our children as "family." The choices we make to define our own lives turn the wheel of change. What we as single parents are looking for in raising our children, others also are looking for. As we create it, we will find it. M. Scott Peck, author of *The Different Drum: Community-Making and Peace,* writes: "The gem of community is so exquisitely beautiful it may seem unreal to you, like a dream you once had when you were a child, so beautiful it may seem unattainable. . . . The problem is that the lack of community is so much the norm in our society, one without experience would be tempted to think, How could we possibly get there from here? It *is* possible. . . . To the uninitiated eye it would seem impossible for a stone ever to become a gem."[18]

While it may be difficult for us to learn the new skills needed to form community or to live in new kinds of families, by working to do so we are introducing our children to a reality that will enrich their lives. Needing others is not a weakness, it's wisdom.

Epilogue

The claims that the difficult work of love makes upon our
development are greater than life, and we, as beginners, are
not equal to them. But if we nevertheless endure and take
this love upon us as burden and apprenticeship . . . then a
small advance and a lightening will perhaps be perceptible
to those who come long after us. That would be much.

—Rainer Maria Rilke

"MY CHILD IS THE one who taught me what it is to love,"
Laurinda repeats. She leans into the same couch where she and her
son sat together one evening a year before and told me their story.
This time she sits alone, the afternoon sun lighting her face as she
talks. "But one of the greatest lessons actually happened *after* he left
home, when he was seventeen and moved to the other side of the
country. Not that it isn't excruciating for all parents who love their
children to see them leave, but for a single parent who has a deep
bond and connection like Eric and I did, it was letting go of the
primary relationship of my life."

Despite the sometimes overwhelming struggles, despite the round-
the-clock responsibility we face in raising children alone, when the
day arrives and they leave home, it is an ending that severs the threads
that have woven us together in so many unique ways, bonds that have
defined our own identity.

Those I spoke with describe this ending in the most wrenching and
dramatic terms. Julian groans still to remember the birth pangs that
led to Diego's departure. Angie admits that despite her preparations
and anticipating the freedom of her new life, "China's departure left
a huge void. I hadn't expected it to be so painful. I think for a single

356

parent it is very similar to the death of a mate, of a partner." Reaching for the terms to describe what she calls "a bigger ending than I ever experienced in my life," Jane Anne laments an absence for which "there is not even an afterimage. If I were still with Jonah's father, we would keep that memory alive between us every day when we'd talk about him. Somehow what made up Jonah, that DNA, would still be in the room. But this is like an amputation."

For Laurinda it was the same. "I panicked, not just for a few hours but for twenty-four hours a day for months on end. I didn't know what to do to handle it. One night I was watching a television program about social injustice, and I thought, 'Those people went through *that,* and I think *this* is hard.'" Viktor Frankl writes, "Suffering completely fills the human soul and conscious mind, no matter whether the suffering is great or little."[1] Laurinda's pain could not be diminished through comparison or denial, only by facing it. "I knew that I had to find a way through," she says. "I knew I had to walk through something, although I didn't know what it was." Laurinda booked a passage to the Himalayas, choosing "the longest and hardest trek they had available."

After two weeks of mounting higher and higher — in snow, freezing temperatures, and thinning air — Laurinda felt "like I was in hell. At the end of one day they told us that the next morning we were going to head up along a precarious ledge toward the highest point we had been so far. There was no already developed course; we would be finding our way. And if it were a clear day, they told us, we would see a magnificent sight. Because I had been having such a difficult time, they gave me the rare opportunity to turn back if I wanted. The leader of the party had gotten sick and needed to head down before the others. I had that one night to decide whether I would go with him or continue on.

"I passed the night terrified and so cold that I couldn't sleep. When they got us up at four A.M., I noticed the wide band of blisters on my hand that erupts when I am extremely anxious. But I knew what I was going to do. The truth of the matter was that the decision had already been made long before. There was only one way, and that was to go on."

How many of us, during the course of our days and hours as single parents, have not experienced that feeling? What do we do when we feel as if we can't take any more, when we feel that we can't go on?

We take more. We go on. Knowing that there is only one way to go, we endure, carving out a path along the way.

As I listened to the stories of single mothers and fathers, I began to see single parents as heroes, undertaking a monumental task. For an individual to face adversity for the sake of someone or something beyond herself or himself has been described in many cultures as the "hero's journey." The classical hero, facing a personal challenge that reflects a greater social issue, intentionally or of necessity sets out to discover what will set things right again.

In the process, we question deeply whether we are indeed up to the task, and daily we undergo trials that force us to renew over and over our will to succeed. We find or are granted the allies we need along the way, in friends and in a deepened faith. We discover our limitations, and we discover strengths we might never have imagined. By surpassing our own limits for the sake of others, we are ourselves transformed.

We may start out as naïve or self-centered, disappointed or angry single parents, but in time something happens. If we face the task and prove ourselves worthy of it, we find ourselves becoming strong, honest, reliable, resourceful, dedicated human beings. As we face the worst of ourselves along with the best, we turn the apparent liabilities of our lives into avenues of creativity and adventure, and we discover something that answers not only our own needs but the needs of others as well — the need for community and extended family, for treasuring our children, for reaching beyond ourselves.

"In my twenties, before I became a father," Denny remembers, "I was a very self-absorbed person. I think I must have explored self-indulgence about as far as anybody could take it! What got thrown into sharp relief for me as a single father — and of course every mother knows this too — is that it isn't always a lot of fun to take care of kids. It's a lot of giving and giving and giving. When I pick my kids up, there's no woman to do seventy percent of it or, as is more likely in the typical marriage, ninety percent of it. When my boys are with me, I do one hundred percent of the giving.

"But as the weeks and months and years have gone by, I have begun to realize something. I *like* this. It has given me an anchor and a focus. I think when you have a child, something happens to you that is beyond words, if you allow it. Even though I spent a lot more time reading pop psychology self-help books in the name of personal growth before I had kids, I think my spiritual life is infinitely richer now because of being with them. It's understanding sacrifice, not in some dark, self-negating sense but in a deeply enriching way."

"It always shocks me when people say, 'Oh, what a courageous, noble thing you are doing to raise this child alone," says Ruth. "When they say that, I think, 'Evita?! This is a noble, courageous act? This kid has given me more than anybody I have ever met in my life.'"

Many have echoed Ruth's protests, calling their experience as single parents "the best decision I ever made in my life" or "the most important thing that has ever happened to me." Some of that feeling arises simply because, as Michelle puts it, "The best part of single parenting is parenting." Alan comments, "It's not for everybody, but if someone asked, 'Would you rather be a single parent or not have children at all?' at different times I might have given different answers, but in the long run my answer would be, 'Yes, I still would do it.' Children are just that wonderful to be around."

It's not only the opportunity to know children that wins the acknowledgments. "Single parenting is the one thing that most changed my life and got me on a different course," Tammy attests. "Having Mia and raising her alone has forced me to take a look at myself, to buckle down and make some difficult decisions." More than one I spoke with said it: "Parenting alone has saved my life."

Children are our renewing hope for the future and our motivation to make it better. Just as our dedication to them leads us to our own maturity, so too as our nation increasingly recognizes the need to care for the children — not just for gain but for their inherent value — it is slowly moving from being a very young country toward its maturity.

One third of our nation's households are carrying the future of our country for the other two thirds.[2] As all other major industrial democracies have acknowledged, the task of raising families must be supported by the entire society. Either we care for the future or we have none.

Creative solutions are appearing in communities around the country: new designs in housing, innovative childcare alternatives, the elderly joining in mentoring programs, men reaching out to children, support groups of many forms. Successful business policies are encouraging flextime, on-site care, extended and paid parental leave for both mothers *and* fathers. Many are striving to enact social policies that will do what all sustainable societies of the earth have done: care for the children.

Whether or not such policies will endure and expand depends upon a broader change in society, however. Rather than focusing debate on the *structure* of family, it is our nation's attitude toward children and families in general that needs to be scrutinized. The attitude that those who take care of children — from childcare workers and welfare recipients to fathers who take parental leave — are "doing nothing" with their lives must be radically reconsidered. The idea that men who conceive children have less responsibility for them than the mother who carries them should be de-legitimated by social consequences. The belief that children are a burden to business, government, and society needs to be replaced by the conviction that the welfare of children is one of their main purposes.

As Tammy, whose graduate work has focused on social policy, puts it, "We really need to start changing our values. We need to value daycare teachers, social workers, mothers and fathers. Instead of coming up with good preventive policies — like helping parents in stress, creating good family-based childcare, workable housing — we've been focusing on cleaning up the mess. Look at the high percentage of criminals in prisons right now who were abused children. Why are we so willing to put money into killing them rather than into creating support systems for families?"

If we want the families in our society to work, we have to recognize that our children belong to everyone and that they are our future. Among social creatures, it is not tooth-and-claw competition that ensures survival but rather cooperation. The turning is long and slow, and our own choices are part of it.

"We started walking," says Laurinda, continuing her story. "I was the first one behind the head sherpa because I was the slowest in the group. At times we were wading through snow up to our chests and following narrow ledges. But for the first time I was really there, rather than back in Berkeley arguing with my lover or my roommate or fleeing that tremendous loneliness that had set in when Eric left.

"I was trudging along from one step to the next, and then all of a sudden there it was — not just the earth but the entire world. Twenty peaks over twenty thousand feet high were rising toward Macalou at twenty-four thousand. The air was utterly clear and silent. Flooding into my mind came the 'Hallelujah Chorus.' A voice inside me kept saying over and over, 'Oh ye of little faith . . .' And in the midst of that, I saw how my life is just a speck in all of this. And how wondrous, not diminishing, that I belonged to something bigger — and that I wasn't in charge of it. I knew in an instant that the only way I could have gotten there was to have climbed it, step by step."

Laurinda also knew that it was all the trauma and struggle of those years raising her son on her own that enabled her to hear what those twenty mountain peaks disclosed as they mounted, row upon row, toward the heights. "All those little ways of growing in ordinary daily life had set the groundwork for this more dramatic shift in my perception. And Eric's leaving pushed me even more. It pushed me to see that I didn't have control over him, this person I was most connected to and who seemingly represented everything I had done right or wrong, good or bad. It pushed me to a recognition about life itself — that I don't have any control over any of it altogether. All the books and formulas in the world aren't going to let me know what the outcome is going to be."

We passionately hope for a positive future for our children, yet we do not know what it will be for them. But it is in responding creatively and effectively to the lives we have right now that we not only change ourselves and our world but give our children models of possibility. "I went down that mountain understanding that all I could do was live life as it is presented to me and respond to that," says Laurinda, "rather than regretting what I don't have or what hasn't happened."

The previous year, when Eric sat facing his mother, it was her rigorous commitment to personal growth that he acknowledged as "extremely important to me in terms of seeing life as open and full of possibilities." And it was Laurinda "dragging me along as she changed, rebuilding trust and communication between us when it broke down, bringing me back to life when I didn't want to feel anything," that gave Eric the model to accept what his own life has been as a child of divorced parents and to move on, saying, "It's all right, I can do something with my life now, I'm a whole person with what I did get."

"Not only has my son been my greatest teacher of love," Laurinda concludes, "but also my greatest teacher of letting go. I remember a phrase I read once a long time ago: 'We are only on loan to each other.' That attachment to children that is so real for any parent is accentuated for single parents because, in many ways, our children are our whole life. Loving them enough to let them go, to accept that we only had them on loan, is one of the hardest parts."

There will always be children. But how men and women will sustain them is changing along with everything else. Clearly whether we care for our children or not cannot depend upon the status of partnership between parents. Of course two *good* parents are valuable for children, whether they live together or apart. Children need as many positive, kind, and committed adults in their lives as possible, both women and men. Jean Liedloff, the psychologist and author of *The Continuum Concept,* maintains that "one person who really loves them and makes them feel worthy and welcome — that's all children need to turn out fine."[3] And with many more, they turn out full and brilliant and alive in love.

During the course of my writing this book, Elias wrote one himself — a sheaf of papers stapled together, every page meticulously covered with squiggles. To his delight, he finished well before I did. "It takes a good deal of pencil to write a book!" he exclaimed, invoking Owl from *Winnie-the-Pooh.*[4] The topic of his manuscript? How to raise children better. I admit I was relieved to hear that his suggestions didn't rub salt into my particular shortcomings. Rather, he included ideas about "driving cars less, so that children can breathe fresher air, reading them books, and keeping them happy."

While waiting for *my* book to be finished, Elias has grown from baby to boy. For both of us the project has been much like trying to swim the English Channel together while I attempt to make a running commentary on our progress. It has meant fielding much of the instability and frustration that often mark the days of single-parent families while at the same time trying to create something focused.

The real dramas have been relieved by the little comedies that are the precious gifts of children. It has meant having an office floor strewn with tiny trucks and cars, the edgings of computer paper wound like snakes around chair and table legs, a file cabinet covered with magnetic alphabets, and plastic serpents coiled in my desk drawers. It has meant walking into my office to retrieve a newspaper article for a reference and finding it cut into many tiny newspapers for Elias's stuffed Piglet to read. It has meant saying no even when I wanted to say yes. But it has also meant having a computer surrounded by playdough people to keep me company — and to remind me that I am loved by a child.

Despite the fact that Elias has had to sacrifice many hours to "the book," he has also learned that life is much bigger than just our little world together and that it is possible to overcome obstacles to create a new dream. And he has managed, despite my crust of barriers, to introduce me to the basic lessons.

"Everything in the world is magical," Elias said one evening before sleeping, "because the world turns by making magic. But guess what?"

"What?" I asked.

"Love is the most magical of all."

Notes

Statistical Abstracts and Current Population Reports, compiled by the U.S. Bureau of the Census, are published by the Government Printing Office, Washington, D.C.

PROLOGUE

1. *Statistical Abstracts of the U.S.: 1992,* Table 89, p. C3.
2. Current Population Reports, Series P-20, No. 458, Table H, p. 11. No. 461, Table F, p. 8.
3. Urie Bronfenbrenner, "The Disturbing Changes in the American Family," *Search* 2 (no. 1, Fall 1976, State University of New York, Albany, NY): 4–10. Quoted in Antoinette Bosco, *A Parent Alone* (West Mystic, CT: Twenty-third Publications, 1978), p. 72.
4. Jerry Gerber, Janet Wolff, Walter Klores, and Gene Brown, *Lifetrends: The Future of Baby Boomers and Other Aging Americans* (New York: Macmillan, 1989), p. 28.
5. Sylvia Ann Hewlett, *When the Bough Breaks: The Cost of Neglecting Our Children* (New York: Basic Books/HarperCollins, 1991), p. 12.
6. Jenny Teichman, *Illegitimacy: An Examination of Bastardy* (Ithaca, NY: Cornell University Press, 1982), p. 119.
7. Conversation in October 1993 with Roger Toogood, executive director of the Children's Home Society in Minneapolis.
8. Rickie Solinger, *Wake Up Little Susie: Single Pregnancy and Race Before Roe v. Wade* (New York: Routledge, 1992).
9. Based on the responses of state departments of vital statistics to

a questionnaire I sent out in September 1993; also Harry D. Krause, *Illegitimacy: Law and Social Policy* (New York: Bobbs-Merrill, 1971); and Jenny Teichman, op. cit.

10. Current Population Reports, Series P-20, No. 458, Table A, p. 2.

11. Paul C. Glick, "Children of Divorced Parents in Demographic Perspective," in *Journal of Social Issues* 35: 170–181. Quoted in Sanford M. Dornbusch and Kathryn D. Gray, "Single Parent Families," in *Feminism, Children, and the New Families,* ed. Sanford M. Dornbusch and Myra H. Strober (New York: Guilford Press, 1988), p. 275.

   Arthur J. Norton and Paul C. Glick, "One Parent Families: A Social and Economic Profile," in *Family Relations* 35 (January 1986): 9–17, as reported in Current Population Reports, Special Studies, Series P-23, No. 162, p. 5: "An estimated 60 percent of children born this year will spend some portion of their childhood in a one-parent situation."

12. Stephanie Coontz, *The Way We Never Were: American Families and the Nostalgia Trap* (New York: Basic Books/HarperCollins, 1992), p. 2.

CHAPTER 1. BY CHANCE OR BY CHOICE
Becoming a Single Parent

1. Current Population Reports, Series P-20, No. 458, Table H, p. 11.

2. Frank F. Furstenberg, Jr., and Kathleen Mullan Harris, "The Disappearing American Father? Divorce and the Waning Significance of Biological Parenthood," draft, Department of Sociology, University of Pennsylvania, March 1990, p. 4. Quoted in Sylvia Ann Hewlett, *When the Bough Breaks: The Cost of Neglecting Our Children* (New York: Basic Books/HarperCollins, 1991), p. 12.

3. Current Population Reports, Series P-20, No. 458, Table H, p. 11.

4. Geoffrey L. Greif, "Mothers Without Custody: Life in the 1990's," *The Single Parent* 34 (no. 4, July/August 1991): 12, says that 30–45 percent of noncustodial mothers "are noncustodial because they do not have the same financial resources as the fathers." See also Geoffrey L. Greif and Mary S. Pabst,

Mothers Without Custody (Lexington, MA: Lexington Books/
D. C. Heath, 1988).

Harriet Edwards in her book on the same subject found a
much higher percentage — 75 of the 100 noncustodial mothers
she interviewed gave up custody for financial reasons. Harriet
Edwards, *How Could You? Mothers Without Custody of Their
Children* (Freedom, CA: Crossing Press, 1989).

Phyllis Chesler points out that good but financially poor
mothers can in fact lose their children in court to wealthy and
even abusive fathers. "Seventy percent of my 'good enough'
mothers lost custody of their children," p. xiv. Phyllis Chesler,
Mothers on Trial (New York: McGraw-Hill, 1986).

5. Greif, "Mothers Without Custody," p. 12.
6. Current Population Reports, Series P-20, No. 458, p. 11, text.
7. Stephanie Coontz, *The Way We Never Were: American Families
   and the Nostalgia Trap* (New York: Basic Books/HarperCollins,
   1992). "The rate of divorce tripled between 1960 and 1982,
   then leveled off at a point where 50 percent of first marriages,
   and 60 percent of second ones, are likely to end in divorce
   within forty years," p. 3.
8. *Statistical Abstracts of the U.S.: 1992,* Tables 82 and 89, p. C3.
9. Based on a report by Amara Bachu, "Fertility of American
   Women: June 1992," Current Population Reports, Series P-20,
   No. 470. "[The report] examined women between the ages
   of 18 and 44 who had never married. By 1992, 24 percent
   of them had become mothers, up from 15 percent a decade
   earlier. For women who had attended at least a year of college,
   the rate rose to 11.3 percent, from 5.5 percent in 1982. For
   White women, the rate rose to 15 percent, from 7 percent. For
   women with professional or managerial jobs, it rose to 8.3
   percent, from 3.1." Jason DeParle, "Census Reports a Sharp
   Increase Among Never-Married Mothers: Puncturing Stereotypes of Out-of-Wedlock Births," *New York Times,* July 14,
   1993, pp. A1, A9.
10. Henry A. Walker, "Black-White Differences in Marriage and
    Family Patterns," in *Feminism, Children, and the New Families,*
    ed. Sanford M. Dornbusch and Myra H. Strober (New York:
    Guilford Press, 1988), p. 110; and Coontz, *The Way We Never
    Were,* Chapter 10, "Pregnant Girls, Wilding Boys, Crack Babies,

and the Underclass: The Myth of the Black Family Collapse,"
pp. 232–254.

11. Current Population Reports, Series P-20, No. 458, p. 9.

12. Coontz, *The Way We Never Were,* p. 234; Walker, "Black-White Differences in Marriage and Family Patterns," pp. 94, 95, 99.

13. Current Population Reports, Series P-20, No. 461, Table D, p. 6.

14. Coontz, *The Way We Never Were,* p. 248.

15. Marian Wright Edelman, *The Measure of Our Success* (New York: HarperCollins, 1992), pp. 25, 23.

16. The Mother-Infants Care Education program (MICE), begun in 1974, serves almost all schools in Minneapolis, Minnesota. In 1992, when Dawanna was part of it, nineteen unmarried teen parents were enrolled, including two fathers. The program is limited to thirty-three months of participation, after which it helps the parent find daycare in the community. Susan Ryan-Nelson, coordinator of the program at South High School, reports a 50 percent dropout rate. "Kids have changed since 1977," she observes. "They're not doing as well. While they're not as likely to be put down in class for being in the MICE program, they also have more of an attitude that society owes them something. Their families are falling apart, extended family is breaking down. Society isn't helping adults or kids, and the sense of a viable future is missing for these kids." (Conversation, February 18, 1992.)

17. *Statistical Abstracts of the U.S.: 1992,* Table 89, p. C3.

CHAPTER 2. VICTIM OR VICTOR
Embracing the Challenge

1. Josephine Curto, *How to Become a Single Parent* (Englewood Cliffs, NJ: Prentice-Hall, 1983), p. 172; and Julie Perone, Ph.D. diss., Department of Psychology, University of Maryland, 1988.

2. Richard Kalish, *Death, Grief, and Caring Relationships* (Monterey, CA: Brooks/Cole, 1981), p. 184.

3. Robert S. Weiss, *Going It Alone* (New York: Basic Books, 1979).

4. Kalish, p. 183 ff.

CHAPTER 3. DO SINGLE PARENTS TRY HARDER?
Perfection and Guilt

1. Carin Rubenstein, "Guilty or Not Guilty," *Working Mother,* May 1991, p. 56.
2. Liv Ullmann, *Changing* (New York: Knopf, 1977).
3. Michael Stevenson quoted by Mitzi Foster in *Ball State University News* (Muncie, IN), February 11, 1991.
4. Sanford M. Dornbusch and Kathryn D. Gray, "Single Parent Families," in *Feminism, Children, and the New Families,* ed. Sanford M. Dornbusch and Myra H. Strober (New York: Guilford Press, 1988), p. 288.
5. Ibid., p. 291.
6. Stephanie Coontz, interviewed by Peggy Taylor, "The Way We Never Were," *New Age Journal* (September/October 1992): 64.
7. Robert S. Weiss, *Going It Alone* (New York: Basic Books, 1979).
8. Thomas D. Yawkey, "Imaginativeness in Preschoolers and Single Parent Families," *Journal of Creative Behavior* 19 (no. 1): 55–66.
9. Jeanne E. Jenkins, "Creativity: Its Relationship to Single Parent Family Structure." Presented at Annual Conference of Eastern Education Research Association, Department of Education, Cornell University, Ithaca, NY.
10. Margarita Elena Brenes, Nancy Eisenberg, and Gerald C. Helmstadter, "Sex Role Development of Preschoolers from Two-Parent and One-Parent Families," in *Merrill-Palmer Quarterly* 31 (no. 1, January 1985): 35, 43, 44.
11. Rie Bosman and Wiepke Louwes, "School Careers of Children from One-Parent and Two-Parent Families," *Netherlands Journal of Sociology* 63 (1988): 122. Cited in Stephanie Coontz, *The Way We Never Were: American Families and the Nostalgia Trap* (New York: Basic Books/HarperCollins, 1992), p. 223.
12. Conversation, August 1991.
13. Peter L. Benson and Eugene C. Roehlkepartain, *Youth in Single-Parent Families: Risk and Resiliency* (Minneapolis, MN: Search Institute, 1993), p. 9, and Figure 5, pp. 19–20.
14. Ibid., Figure 5.
15. Judith S. Wallerstein and Barbara Blakeslee, *Second Chances:*

Men, Women and Children a Decade After Divorce (New York: Ticknor & Fields, 1989), p. 7. Quoted in Benson and Roehlkepartain, *Youth in Single-Parent Families,* p. 9.

16. Benson and Roehlkepartain, *Youth in Single-Parent Families,* p. 4.
17. Example of a standard misconception: "Not race, not income, but family structure offers the best forecast of which children become criminals." Steve Berg, "Valuing the Family: A Perspective," *Star Tribune* (Minneapolis/St. Paul), June 6, 1993.
18. Henry A. Walker, "Black-White Differences in Marriage and Family Patterns," in Dornbusch and Strober, *Feminism, Children, and the New Families,* p. 110.
19. Jane E. Brody, "Problems of Children: A New Look at Divorce," *New York Times,* June 7, 1991, p. B1.
20. J. Eccles, S. G. Timmer, and K. O'Brien, *Time, Good, and Well Being* (Ann Arbor, MI: Institute for Social Research, 1985), quoted in David Elkind, *Miseducation: Preschoolers at Risk* (New York: Knopf, 1987), p. 24.

CHAPTER 4. FROM THE BOTTOM UP
The Imperative to Grow

1. Robert Bly, "A Little Book on the Human Shadow" (manuscript), 1988, p. 14.
2. Rainer Maria Rilke, *Letters to a Young Poet* (New York: Random House, 1986), p. 101.

CHAPTER 5. A SINGLE PARENT IS ALSO A PERSON
Nurturing Ourselves

1. Edward T. Hall, *The Silent Language* (New York: Doubleday, 1959), p. 152.
2. Joseph Chilton Pearce, "Journey to the Heart," lecture series, March 18, 1989, Auburn, CA. (Audiotapes produced by Enhanced Audio Systems, Emeryville, CA, 1989.)
3. Anne C. Roark, "How Watching TV Numbs the Mind," *San Francisco Chronicle,* April 30, 1990.
4. David Elkind, *The Hurried Child: Growing Up Too Fast Too Soon* (Reading, MA: Addison-Wesley, 1988).

CHAPTER 6. SINGLE PARENT/DOUBLE PARENT
Being One and Doing All

1. Margarita Elena Brenes, Nancy Eisenberg, and Gerald C. Helmstadter, "Sex Role Development of Preschoolers from Two-Parent and One-Parent Families," in *Merrill-Palmer Quarterly* 31 (no. 1, January 1985): 42. They also point out that "the development of gender identity follows a similar pattern for all children, regardless of sex and type of family."
2. Marilyn J. Freimuth and Gail A. Hornstein, "A Critical Examination of the Concept of Gender," in *Sex Roles* 8 (no. 5, 1982): 520.
3. Ibid., p. 523.
4. Ibid., p. 525.
5. Ibid., pp. 529 and 525.
6. Barbara J. Risman, "Intimate Relationships from a Microstructural Perspective: Men Who Mother," *Gender & Society* 1 (no. 1, March 1987): 6–32.
7. Diane Ehrensaft, *Parenting Together* (New York: Free Press/ Macmillan, 1987), pp. 97–99.
8. Christine Gorman, "Sizing Up the Sexes," *Time,* January 20, 1992, pp. 42–51.
9. Ehrensaft, *Parenting Together,* p. 94.
10. Robert Bly, *Iron John* (Reading, MA: Addison-Wesley, 1990), p. 234.
11. Brenes, Eisenberg, and Helmstadter, "Sex Role Development of Preschoolers from Two-Parent and One-Parent Families," pp. 43–44.

CHAPTER 7. WALKING THE BOTTOM LINE
Finances and Treasures

1. Stephanie Coontz, "Two Parents Aren't Always Better," *Oakland Tribune,* October 17, 1992, p. D-6.
2. Current Population Reports, Series P-60, No. 180, p. x: "Families maintained by women with no spouse present experienced declines in real median family income between 1990 and 1991 much higher than the decline experienced by married-couple families." No. 181, p. viii: "The increase in the number of poor families with a female householder accounted for 64.1 (+/– 4.6)

percent of the net increase in poor families between 1990 and 1991."

3. Tamar Lewin, "Rise in Single Parenthood Is Reshaping U.S.," second article in series, "The Good Mother," *New York Times,* October 5, 1992, pp. A1, A16.

4. Malcolm Gladwell, "Dad's Influence on Families Questioned," *San Francisco Chronicle,* September 29, 1992, p. D4.

5. Carol Kleiman, "Pay Gap Narrowing — at a Penny a Year," *San Francisco Examiner,* September 24, 1989, p. D-3; and Sylvia Nasar, "Women Gained Ground in '80's, Research Finds," *Star Tribune* (Minneapolis/St. Paul), November 8, 1992, p. 1-J.

6. U.S. Bureau of the Census, *Money Income of Households, Families, and Persons in the U.S., 1991,* Table 18: "Presence of Related Children Under 18 — Families by Total Money Income, 1991."

7. Lenore J. Weitzman, "Women and Children Last: The Social and Economic Consequences of Divorce Law Reform," in *Feminism, Children, and the New Families,* ed. Sanford M. Dornbusch and Myra H. Strober (New York: Guilford Press, 1988), p. 233.

8. Sylvia Ann Hewlett, *A Lesser Life: The Myth of Women's Liberation in America* (New York: William Morrow, 1986), pp. 51–69.

9. Geoffrey Greif, "Mothers Without Custody: Life in the 1990's," *The Single Parent* 34 (no. 4, July/August 1991): 12–13; Geoffrey L. Greif and Mary S. Pabst, *Mothers Without Custody* (Lexington, MA: Lexington Books/D. C. Heath, 1988); Phyllis Chesler, *Mothers on Trial* (New York: McGraw-Hill, 1986); Harriet Edwards, *How Could You? Mothers Without Custody of Their Children* (Freedom, CA: Crossing Press, 1989).

10. U.S. Department of Agriculture, Agricultural Research Service, Family Economics Research Group, 1992, *Expenditures on a Child by Families, 1991,* p. 12: "The example assumes a child is born in 1991, reaching age 17 in the year 2008, and the average annual inflation rate over this time is 6 percent." In 1991 dollar values, the amount would be between $89,580 and $175,380.

11. Ibid., p. 9, and Tables F and G on pp. 20–21.

12. As quoted in Weitzman, "Women and Children Last," p. 229.

13. Ibid., pp. 229–230. "It is very rare for any court to order more than 25% of a man's income in child support or more than 32% of a man's income in combined child support and alimony. Even though judges say that their typical award is closer to one half of the husband's income, the data from our analysis of court dockets and our interviews with divorced persons shows that the real proportion is quite different. Instead of a 50-50 division of the husband's income, the typical award is one third for the wife and two children to two thirds for the husband."

14. Bruce Low, "Child Support That Really Is," *Mothering* 42 (Winter 1987): 99.

15. Conversation, August 11, 1993.

16. Based on data from the 1993 Annual Minnesota Child Support Enforcement Report and Kids Count Minnesota.

17. *Statistical Abstracts of the U.S.: 1992*, Table 596, p. 372.

18. Ruth Sidel, "What Is to Be Done? Lessons from Sweden," pp. 180–181. In booklet reprinted from Sidel, *Women and Children Last: The Plight of Poor Women in Affluent America* (New York: Viking, 1986).

19. *Statistical Abstracts of the U.S.: 1992*, p. 457.

20. Sheila B. Kamerman, "Child Care Policies and Programs: An International Overview," *Journal of Social Issues* 47 (no. 2, 1991): 179–196; and "Europe's Answers for a Thorny Problem," special to *New York Times*, February 15, 1993, p. A7; and Amy Kaplan, "An Overview of Explicit European and American Family Policy," *Mothering* 59 (Spring 1991): 111.

21. Roger Cohen, "Europe's Recession Prompts New Look at Welfare Costs," *New York Times*, August 9, 1993, pp. A1, A6.

22. Current Population Reports, Series P-20, No. 458, p. 1.

23. Committee for Economic Development, *Children in Need: Investment Strategies for the Educationally Disadvantaged* (New York: CED, 1987), p. 3. Quoted in Sylvia Ann Hewlett, *When the Bough Breaks: The Cost of Neglecting Our Children* (New York: Basic Books/HarperCollins, 1991), p. 239; also David Peterson, "State Number One in Inmate Spending," *Star Tribune* (Minneapolis/St. Paul), July 30, 1992, p. 1A.

24. Data from House Ways and Means Committee, printed in *New York Times*, July 5, 1992, p. 16; also Jason DeParle, "Talk of

Cutting Welfare Rolls Sounds Good but Progress Is Far from Sure," *New York Times,* October 17, 1992, p. 9.

25. For fiscal year 1992, average number of monthly recipients was 13,625,342. Office of Family Assistance, Division of Program Evaluation, AFDC Information and Measurement Branch.

26. Erik Eckholm, "Solutions on Welfare: They All Cost Money," *New York Times,* July 26, 1992, p. A12. From series, "Rethinking Welfare," Part Six.

27. 1991 Green Book Overview of Entitlement Programs, WMCP 102-9, Table 24, AFDC Characteristics, 1969–88, pp. 579–580; and *New York Times,* July 5, 1992; and Peter T. Kilborn, "Lives of Unexpected Poverty in Center of a Land of Plenty," *New York Times,* July 8, 1992, p. A1. From series, "Rethinking Welfare," Part Three.

28. From a nationwide *New York Times*/CBS News poll conducted May 6–8, 1992. Referred to in Robin Toner, "New Politics of Welfare Focuses on Its Flaws," *New York Times,* July 5, 1992, p. A1. From series, "Rethinking Welfare," Part One.

29. Ibid., p. A16.

30. From the general guidelines for AFDC recipients in Hennepin County, Minnesota.

31. Report by Carlos Bonilla, Employment Policies Institute, 1992. Cited in Jonathan Marshall, "Many on Welfare Can't Afford Jobs," *San Francisco Chronicle,* May 9, 1992, p. A2.

32. Robert Rector on "All Things Considered," Anthony Brooks reporting; host, Lynn Neary; executive producer, Ellen Weiss. National Public Radio, September 2, 1992.

33. 1992 State Expenditure Report, National Association of State Budget Officers, April 1993. Of all states, California spends the highest percentage of its state source revenue on AFDC — 5.65 percent.

34. Steve Hagy, U.S. Office of Budget and Management.

35. Irwin Garfinkel on "All Things Considered," September 2, 1992. Verified in phone conversation with Garfinkel, October 5, 1993.

36. Department of Defense, Comptroller's Office, August 1993.

37. Jason DeParle, "Clinton Aides See Problem with Vow to Limit Welfare," *New York Times,* June 21, 1993, pp. A1, A9.

38. From David T. Ellwood, Harvard University, in Erik Eckholm, "Solutions on Welfare: They All Cost Money."

Another study further elucidates this issue: "In a longitudinal study that followed families over a 10-year period and recorded their welfare status, the typical single-parent household received aid for about 2 years, left the welfare rolls, and returned later in the period during another period of deprivation. Only 700,000 female-headed families in the United States were continuously on welfare for the entire period." Sanford M. Dornbusch and Kathryn D. Gray, "Single Parent Families," p. 279.

CHAPTER 8. WORKING AROUND OUR CHILDREN
Care and Childcare

1. U.S. Department of Labor, Bureau of Labor Statistics, March 1993; 26.5 percent of all working mothers are single parents.
2. Mary Ellen Schoonmaker, "The Baby Bind: Can Journalists Be Mothers?" *Columbia Journalism Review* 34 (March/April 1989): 35.
3. From report entitled *Children 1990: A Report Card, Briefing Book and Action Primer,* Children's Defense Fund. Reported in *Mothering* 57 (October/November/December 1990), p. 84.
4. Sheila B. Kamerman, "Child Care Policies and Programs: An International Overview," in *Journal of Social Issues* 47 (no. 2, 1991): Table 2, p. 188.
5. Sheila B. Kamerman and Alfred Kahn, "Family Policy: Has the United States Learned from Europe?" *Policy Studies Review* 8 (no. 3, Spring 1989): 581–598.
6. Amy Kaplan, "An Overview of Explicit European and American Family Policy," *Mothering* 59 (Spring 1991): 111; Ruth Sidel, "What Is to Be Done? Lessons from Sweden," pp. 180–181. In booklet reprinted from Sidel, *Women and Children Last: The Plight of Poor Women in Affluent America* (New York: Viking, 1986).
7. Kamerman, "Child Care Policies and Programs," p. 188.
8. Roger Cohen, "Europe's Recession Prompts New Look at Welfare Costs," *New York Times,* August 9, 1993, p. A6.
9. Stuart Oskamp, "The Editor's Page," *Journal of Social Issues* 47 (no. 2, 1991).
10. U.S. Department of Labor, Bureau of Labor Statistics, April 20, 1993. Table 4: "Families with Children Under 18 Years Old by the Employment Status of Parent(s) and Type of Family."

11. Catherine E. Ross, results of survey of 1,000 families, reported in *Star Tribune* (Minneapolis/St. Paul), February 23, 1993, p. 1C.

12. Jay Belsky and David Eggebeen, "Early and Extensive Maternal Employment and Young Children's Socioemotional Development: Children of the National Longitudinal Survey of Youth," *Journal of Marriage and the Family* 53 (November 1991): 1083.

13. Martha Zaslow, "Variation in Child Care Quality and Its Implications for Children," *Journal of Social Issues* 47 (1991): 126.

14. Ibid., pp. 130–131.

15. Alice Sterling Honig, "Quality Infant/Toddler Caregiving: Are There Magic Recipes?" *Young Children* (May 1989): 4.

16. Dorothy Conniff, "Day Care: A Grand and Troubling Social Experiment," *The Progressive* (November 1988). Reprinted in *Utne Reader* 57 (May/June 1993): 67.

17. Martha Zaslow, "Variation in Child Care Quality and Its Implications for Children," p. 132.

18. U.S. Department of Labor, Bureau of Labor Statistics, March 1992.

19. Barbara Willer et al., *The Demand and Supply of Child Care in 1990* (Washington, D.C.: National Association for the Education of Young Children, 1991).

20. Stephanie Coontz, *The Way We Never Were: American Families and the Nostalgia Trap* (New York: Basic Books/HarperCollins, 1992), p. 218.

21. Vivian Cadden, "Living on Luck," *Working Mother* (January 1993): 48.

22. Tamar Lewin, "Many Moms Can't Afford Their Jobs," *New York Times*, April 21, 1991, p. E18.

23. John H. Cushman, Jr., "Green Card Remains an Elusive Goal," *New York Times*, February 4, 1993, p. B6.

24. Conversation with Ruth Matson, founder of Chicken Soup and administrator of Sick Kid Kare in Minneapolis, August 15, 1993.

25. Robert Pear, "Clinton Nominees Will Be Screened for Illegal Hiring," *New York Times*, February 9, 1993, pp. A1 and A12.

26. Amitai Etzioni, "Children of the Universe: Good Parenting Benefits the Community as Well as the Kids," *The Spirit of Community: Rights, Responsibilities, and the Communitarian*

Agenda (New York: Crown, 1993). Reprinted in *Utne Reader* 57 (May/June 1993): 54.

27. Conniff, "Day Care."

28. Karen Skold, "The Interest of Feminism and Children in Child Care," in *Feminism, Children, and the New Families,* ed. Sanford M. Dornbusch and Myra H. Strober (New York: Guilford Press, 1988), p. 124.

29. Etzioni, "Children of the Universe," p. 54.

30. Eileen Ogintz, "How Can We Keep Good Caregivers?" *Working Mother* (August 1993): 48. Statistics from Child Care Action Campaign, 330 Seventh Avenue, 17th Floor, New York, NY 10001.

31. Willer et al., *The Demand and Supply of Child Care in 1990,* p. 9.

32. Because there is a stigma attached to leaving children alone, and also fear of danger, many parents don't report the practice. Some children are left in the care of siblings and, depending upon the age of the oldest child, there is not a standard cut-off point as to when this essentially constitutes self-care on the part of all children involved. Sandra Hoffers of the Urban Institute estimated that in 1990 there were 3.4 million children between the ages of five and twelve and 71,000 under five who were home alone while parents were working. The National Research Council in *Who Cares for America's Children?* (National Academy Press, 1990) estimated that the number could be as high as 15 million. In 1982 the Department of Labor placed "the number of children 10 years of age and under who care for themselves when not in school at 7 million" (Bryan E. Robinson, Bobbie H. Rowland, Mick Coleman, *Latchkey Kids: Unlocking Doors for Children and Their Families* [Lexington, MA: D. C. Heath, 1986]). According to the Bureau of Labor Statistics, in 1993, 62.2 percent of all children did not have a parent who stayed at home rather than participating in the workforce.

33. U.S. Department of Labor, Bureau of Labor Statistics, *News,* April 20, 1993, Table A: 52.9 percent of employed women have children under six; 61 percent have children under eighteen.

34. Peter L. Benson and Eugene C. Roehlkepartain, *Youth in Single-Parent Families: Risk and Resiliency* (Minneapolis, MN: Search Institute, 1993), p. 18, Figure 4. This study was based on one

that looked at the lives of 47,000 students in grades six through twelve in twenty-five states. Of the total number, 8,266 lived in single-parent families owing to divorce.

35. Ibid.
36. Etzioni, "Children of the Universe," p. 59.
37. Coontz, *The Way We Never Were,* pp. 220–221.
38. Kurt Chandler, "Video Witness: Child-Care Center Tries Surveillance," *Star Tribune* (Minneapolis/St. Paul), May 17, 1993, pp. 1A, 5A.
39. Milton Moskowitz and Carol Townsend, "100 Best Companies for Working Mothers," *Working Mother* (October 1992): 33–90; also *Working Mother* (October 1993): 28–69; and Robert Levering and Milton Moskowitz, *The 100 Best Companies to Work for in America* (New York: Doubleday, 1993).
40. Joseph Chilton Pearce, "Journey to the Heart," lecture series, March 18, 1989, Auburn, CA. (Audiotapes produced by Enhanced Audio Systems, Emeryville, CA, 1989.)

CHAPTER 9. WHEN OUR CHILDREN ARE OUR FRIENDS
Love and Limits

1. Janet L. Surrey, "Self-in-Relation: A Theory of Women's Development," talk presented at the Stone Center Colloquium Series, Wellesley College, November 1983.
2. David Elkind, *The Hurried Child: Growing Up Too Fast Too Soon* (Reading, MA: Addison-Wesley, 1988), p. 138.
3. Arlene Skolnick, *Embattled Paradise: The American Family in an Age of Uncertainty* (New York: Basic Books/HarperCollins, 1991), p. 224.
4. Sanford M. Dornbusch and Kathryn D. Gray, "Single Parent Families," in *Feminism, Children, and the New Families,* ed. Sanford M. Dornbusch and Myra H. Strober (New York: Guilford Press, 1988), p. 289–294.
5. Ibid., p. 287.
6. Germaine Greer, *The Madwoman's Underclothes* (New York: Atlantic Monthly Press, 1986), p. 13.

CHAPTER 10. DILEMMAS OF THE HEART
Dating and Seeking a Partner

1. David Elkind, *The Hurried Child: Growing Up Too Fast Too Soon* (Reading, MA: Addison-Wesley, 1988), p. 139.
2. Current Population Reports, Series P-23, No. 162, p. 27.

CHAPTER 12. NO ONE CAN BE A SINGLE PARENT
Extending the Family

1. Current Population Reports, Series P-20, No. 467.
2. Katherine Boo, "The Return of the Extended Family," *Washington Monthly* (April 1992), reprinted in *Utne Reader* (July/August 1992): 91.
3. Jerry Gerber, Janet Wolff, Walter Klores, and Gene Brown, *Lifetrends: The Future of Baby Boomers and Other Aging Americans* (New York: Macmillan, 1989), p. 65: "Programs to foster shared housing have increased by 800% since 1981."
4. Lillian B. Rubin, *Just Friends: The Role of Friendship in Our Lives* (New York: Harper & Row, 1985), p. 16.
5. Carolyn R. Shaffer and Kristin Anundsen, *Creating Community Anywhere: Finding Support and Connection in a Fragmented World* (Tarcher/Perigee, 1993), pp. 54–55: "When Massachusetts Mutual Life Insurance Company polled Americans on their views about the family in 1989, almost three-quarters chose as a definition of family 'a group of people who love and care for each other.' Less than a quarter chose the standard legal definition: 'a group of people related by blood, marriage or adoption.'"
6. Stephanie Coontz, "The Way We Never Were," *New Age Journal* (September/October 1992): 144.
7. Current Population Reports, Series P-20, No. 461, p. 8.
8. Rubin, *Just Friends*, p. 20.
9. Ibid., pp. 22–23.
10. Phone conversation, October 1993.
11. Robert Bly, personal notes from lectures.
12. Marc Freedman, *The Kindness of Strangers: Reflections on the Mentoring Movement*, a report sponsored by Public/Private Ventures, Philadelphia, PA, 1991. Subsequently published as a

book under the same title by Jossey-Bass/Macmillan, New York, 1993.

13. Ann Landers, Creators Syndicate. The question "If you had it to do over again, would you have children?" was published in her column for November 3, 1975; results were reported on January 23, 1976.

14. Erik Erikson, *Childhood and Society* (New York: Norton, 1964), p. 267.

15. Stanford M. Dornbusch and Kathryn D. Gray, "Single Parent Families," in *Feminism, Children, and the New Families,* ed. Sanford M. Dornbusch and Myra H. Strober (New York: Guilford Press, 1988), pp. 285–288.

16. Karen A. Franck and Sherry Ahrentzen, *New Households, New Housing* (New York: Van Nostrand Reinhold, 1989), p. 150.

17. Shaffer and Anundsen, *Creating Community Anywhere,* p. xiii.

18. M. Scott Peck, *The Different Drum: Community-Making and Peace* (New York: Simon & Schuster, 1987), p. 60.

EPILOGUE

1. Viktor Frankl, *Man's Search for Meaning* (New York: Simon & Schuster, 1984), p. 55.

2. Current Population Reports, Series P-20, No. 458, p. 1.

3. Personal conversation.

4. A. A. Milne, "Eeyore Has a Birthday," *Winnie the Pooh* (New York: Dell, 1988), p. 83. Owl says: "Well, *actually,* of course, I'm saying, 'A Very Happy Birthday with love from Pooh.' Naturally it takes a good deal of pencil to say a long thing like that."

Resources

Additional reading and resources for each chapter are listed first; general resources on single parenting follow. A number of the books noted here were recommended by single parents interviewed for this book.

CHAPTER 1. BY CHANCE OR BY CHOICE
Becoming a Single Parent

Adoption

Adoption: A Handful of Hope, Suzanne Arms (Berkeley, CA: Celestial Arts, 1990). A compassionate view of the emotional aspects of adoption for everyone involved, with a focus on open adoption.

The Adoption Resource Book (3d. ed.), Lois Gilman (New York: HarperCollins, 1992).

Are Those Kids Yours? American Families with Children Adopted from Other Countries, Cheri Register (New York: Free Press/Macmillan, 1991).

The Handbook for Single Adoptive Parents, Hope Marindin, ed. Published by the Committee for Single Adoptive Parents, P.O. Box 15084, Chevy Chase, MD 20825.

Raising Adopted Children: A Manual for Adoptive Parents, Lois Ruskai Melina (New York: HarperCollins, 1986). Includes consideration of unique issues faced by single parents.

"Single Adoptive Parents and Post-Placement Issues." Lecture by Betsy Burch and Jerri Jenista, Audiotape #5J91. Produced by

Adoptive Families of America, Inc., 3333 Highway 100 North, Minneapolis, MN 55422.

FOR CHILDREN

Being Adopted, Maxine Rosenberg (New York: Lothrop, Lee & Shepard, 1984). Ages 7–9.

The Boy Who Wanted a Family, Shirley Gordon (New York: Harper-Collins, 1982). Ages 9–13.

Growing Up Adopted, Maxine Rosenberg (New York: Bradbury Press, 1989). Ages 8–10.

How It Feels to Be Adopted, Jill Krementz (New York: Knopf, 1992). Ages 9 and up.

A Mother for Choco, Keiko Kasza (New York: G. P. Putnam's Sons, 1992). Picture book. Ages 3–8.

Why Was I Adopted? The Facts of Adoption with Love and Illustrations, Carol Livingston and Arthur Robins (New York: Carol Publishing Group, 1978). Ages 4–10.

ORGANIZATIONS

Adoptive Families of America, Inc.
3333 Highway 100 North
Minneapolis, MN 55422
(612) 535-4829
Provides information on support groups and agencies open to single parents, free information packet. Publishes *Ours: The Magazine of Adoptive Families,* which includes many articles on single parents.

Committee for Single Adoptive Parents
P.O. Box 15084
Chevy Chase, MD 20825
(202) 966-6367
Provides source list and supportive information specifically geared to singles seeking to adopt nationally and internationally. Publishes *Handbook for Single Adoptive Parents.*

Families Adopting in Response (FAIR)
P.O. Box 51436
Palo Alto, CA 94306
Provides support for parents of special-needs, transracial, and transcultural adoptive children.

The International Soundex Reunion Registry (ISRR)
P.O. Box 2312
Carson City, NV 89702
Facilitates reunion between birth parents and adopted children as well as between siblings.

Single Parents Adopting Children Everywhere (SPACE)
6 Sunshine Avenue
Natick, MA 01760
(508) 655-5426

Single Parents With Adopted Kids (SWAK)
4108 Washington Road #101
Kenosha, WI 53144
(414) 654-0629

Death

Being a Widow, Lynn Caine (New York: Arbor House, 1988).
The Courage to Grieve, Judy Tatelbaum (New York: Harper & Row, 1984).
On Death and Dying, Elisabeth Kübler-Ross (New York: Macmillan, 1989).

FOR CHILDREN

Everett Anderson's Good-bye, Lucille Clifton (New York: Holt, 1983). An African-American boy loses his father. Ages 4–12.
How It Feels When a Parent Dies, Jill Krementz (New York: Knopf, 1981). Ages 12–18.
Learning to Say Good-bye: When a Parent Dies, Eda LeShan (New York: Macmillan, 1976). Ages 12–18.
A Quilt for Elizabeth, Benette W. Tiffault (Omaha, NE: Centering Corp., 1992). Picture book. Ages 4–12.
When My Mommy Died: A Child's View of Death, Janice Hammond (Flint, MI: Cranbrook Publishing, 1980). Also by Hammond, *When My Dad Died* (1981). Picture books. Ages 3–10.

ORGANIZATIONS

Fernside: A Center for Grieving Children
P. O. Box 8944
Cincinnati, OH 45208
(513) 321-0282
For a small donation, information packet on how to talk to your child about death and loss.

THEOS
11609 Frankstown Road
Pittsburgh, PA 15235
(412) 471-7779

Widowed Persons Service
AARP
1901 K Street, N.W.
Washington, D.C. 20049
(202) 872-4700
Information on nationwide support groups, some for widowed single parents.

Divorce

How to Forgive Your Ex-husband and Get On with Your Life, Marcia Hootman and Patt Perkins (New York: Warner, 1985).
Mothers and Divorce: Legal, Economic, and Social Dilemmas, Terry Arendell (Berkeley: University of California Press, 1986).
Second Chances, Judith S. Wallerstein and Sandra Blakeslee (New York: Ticknor & Fields, 1989).
Surviving the Breakup: How Children and Parents Cope with Divorce, Judith S. Wallerstein and Joan Berlin Kelly (New York: Basic, 1980).

FOR CHILDREN

Always, Always, Crescent Dragonwagon (New York: Macmillan, 1984). Picture book. Ages 7–9.
Dinosaur's Divorce: A Guide for Changing Families, Laurene Krasny Brown and Marc Brown (Boston: Little, Brown, 1986). Picture book. Ages 4–10.
The Divorce Workbook: A Guide for Kids and Families, Sally B. Ives,

David Fassler, and Michelle Lash (Burlington, VT: Waterfront Books, 1990). Workbook format. Ages 4–12.

How It Feels When Parents Divorce, Jill Krementz (New York: Knopf, 1984). Ages 12–18.

The Kids Book of Divorce: By, For, and About Kids, The Unit at the Fayerweather Street School, Eric Rofes, ed. (New York: Vintage, 1982). Ages 10–14.

What's Going to Happen to Me: When Parents Separate or Divorce, Eda LeShan (New York: Aladdin/Macmillan, 1978). Ages 10+.

"Beyond Divorce: A Game for Kids in Changing Families," developed by Sam Braun, M.D. and Sylvia Skinner, ACSW. For ages 8 and up. Order from Waterfront Books, 85 Crescent Road, Burlington, VT 05401. (802) 658-7477.

Donor Insemination

Having Your Baby by Donor Insemination, Elizabeth Noble (Boston: Houghton Mifflin, 1987).

CHAPTER 2. VICTIM OR VICTOR
Embracing the Challenge

Necessary Losses: The Loves, Illusions, Dependencies, and Impossible Expectations That All of Us Have to Give Up in Order to Grow, Judith Viorst (New York: Ballantine, 1986).

Rituals for Our Times: Celebrating, Healing and Changing Our Lives and Our Relationships, Evan Imba-Black and Janine Roberts (New York: HarperCollins, 1992).

Total Visualization: Using All Five Senses, William Fezler (New York: Prentice-Hall, 1989).

Transitions: Making Sense of Life's Changes, William Bridges (Reading, MA: Addison-Wesley, 1980).

When Bad Things Happen to Good People, Harold S. Kushner (New York: Avon, 1980).

CHAPTER 3. DO SINGLE PARENTS TRY HARDER?
Perfection and Guilt

Adult Children Raising Children: Sparing Your Child from Co-Dependency Without Being Perfect Yourself, Randy Colton Rolfe (Deerfield Beach, FL: Health Communications, 1990).

Co-Dependent No More: How to Stop Controlling Others and Start Caring for Yourself, Melody Beattie (New York: Harper & Row/Hazelden, 1987).

The Dance of Anger: A Woman's Guide to Changing the Patterns of Intimate Relationships, Harriet Goldhor Lerner (New York: Harper & Row, 1985).

A Good Enough Parent, Bruno Bettelheim (New York: Random House, 1987).

If Only I Were a Better Mother: Using the Anger, Fear, Despair, and Guilt that Every Mother Feels at Some Time as a Pathway to Emotional Balance and Spiritual Growth, Melissa Gayle West (Walpole, N.H.: Stillpoint Publishing, 1992).

The Myth of the Bad Mother: The Emotional Realities of Mothering, Jane Swigart (New York: Doubleday, 1991).

The Two-Parent Family Is Not the Best, June Stephenson (Napa, CA: Diemer, Smith Publishing Co., 1991).

What Did I Do Wrong? Mothers, Children, Guilt, Lynn Caine (New York: Arbor House, 1985).

FOR CHILDREN

Perfectionism: What's Bad About Being Too Good?, Miriam Adderholdt-Elliott (Minneapolis: Free Spirit Publishing, 1987). Ages 13 and up.

No One Is Perfect, Karen Erickson and Maureen Roffey (Viking/Kestrel, 1987). Picture book. Ages 3–7. Features child and father.

ORGANIZATIONS

Al-Anon/Alateen Family Group Headquarters
P.O. Box 862
Midtown Station
New York, NY 10018
(800) 344-2666
(212) 302-7240

Childhelp/I.O.F. Forester's National Child Abuse Hotline
(800) 4-A-CHILD (422-4453)
TDD (800) 2-A-CHILD
For both children and adults; 24-hour crisis, information, and referral number. Trained counselors (with master's degree or higher).

Parents Anonymous
National Office
2230 Hawthorne Blvd.
Suite 208
Torrance, CA 90505
(800) 421-0353
(800) 352-0386 (in California)

CHAPTER 4. FROM THE BOTTOM UP
The Imperative to Grow

Growing Up Again: Parenting Ourselves, Parenting Our Children, Jean Illsley Clarke and Connie Dawson (New York: HarperCollins/Hazelden, 1989).

Healing the Child Within, Charles L. Whitfield (Deerfield Beach, FL: Health Communications, 1989).

Healthy Parenting: How Your Upbringing Influences the Way You Raise Your Children, and What You Can Do to Make It Better for Them, Janet G. Woititz (New York: Simon & Schuster, 1992).

Homecoming: Reclaiming and Championing Your Inner Child, John Bradshaw (New York: Bantam, 1990).

Man's Search for Meaning, Viktor Frankl (New York: Simon & Schuster, 1984).

Passion to Heal: The Ultimate Guide to Your Healing Journey, Echo Bodine (Mill Valley, CA: Nataraj, 1993).

The Road Less Traveled: A New Psychology of Love, Traditional Values, and Spiritual Growth, M. Scott Peck (New York: Simon & Schuster, 1984).

Self-Esteem: A Family Affair, Jean Illsley Clarke (San Francisco: Harper & Row, 1978).

When Your Child Drives You Crazy, Eda LeShan (New York: St. Martin's, 1985).

The Winning Family: Increasing Self-Esteem in Your Children and Yourself, Louise Hart (Berkeley, CA: Celestial Arts, 1993).

ORGANIZATIONS

Family Service America
44 E. 23rd Street
New York, NY 10010
(212) 674-6100
Has agencies nationwide offering counseling services on a sliding fee
scale.

Personal Counselors
719 Second Avenue North
Seattle, WA 98109
(206) 284-0311
Home office of the Re-evaluation Counseling movement, popularly
known as "co-counseling." Publishes *Present Time* quarterly, listing
people and teachers who are involved nationally and internationally.

CHAPTER 5. A SINGLE PARENT IS ALSO A PERSON
Nurturing Ourselves

At a Journal Workshop (rev. ed.), Ira Progoff (Los Angeles: J. P.
Tarcher, 1992).
*When Food Is Love: Exploring the Relationship Between Eating and
Intimacy,* Geneen Roth (New York: Penguin, 1992).
*The Woman's Comfort Book: A Self-Nurturing Guide for Restoring
Balance in Your Life,* Jennifer Louden (New York: Harper San
Francisco, 1992).

Support Networks

A Circle of Men, Bill Kauth (New York: St. Martin's, 1992). A
step-by-step manual for starting a men's support group, finding
new members, and fostering honesty and communication.
Mothers Club: Nurturing the Nurturers, Katie Williams Hoepke (Ark
Press, P.O. Box 50083, Palo Alto, CA 94303). Manual on how
to organize extensive social support in your community; 86
pages; $13.25.
Self-Help for Single Mothers: A Model Peer-Support Program, Deborah Lee (Support Group Training Project, 484 Lake Park Avenue,
#105, Oakland, CA 94610; (510) 482-4171). This report also

delineates what it takes to establish and conduct successful support groups.

The Self-Help Sourcebook: Finding and Forming Mutual Aid Self-Help Groups, compiled and edited by Barbara J. White and Edward J. Madara (Denville, NJ: American Self-Help Clearinghouse, 1992).

ORGANIZATIONS

To find local support groups and/or further information on how to start and maintain them, contact the single parents' organizations listed in the General Resources section, or call the following:

United Way, First Call for Help
Contact your local office for referrals to numerous support services.

Family Resource Coalition
200 South Michigan Avenue
Suite 1520
Chicago, IL 60604
(312) 341-0900
For free materials and information about family support programs in your community.

CHAPTER 6. SINGLE PARENT/DOUBLE PARENT
Being One and Doing All

The Chalice and the Blade: Our History, Our Future, Riane Eisler (San Francisco: Harper & Row, 1987).
FatherLove: What We Need, What We Seek, What We Must Create, Richard Louv (New York: Pocket, 1993).
Fathers and Babies: How Babies Grow and What They Need from You from Birth to Eighteen Months, Gene Marzollo (New York: HarperCollins, 1993).
Fathers, Sons, and Daughters: Exploring Fatherhood, Renewing the Bond, ed. Charles Scull (Los Angeles: J. P. Tarcher, 1992). Contributors include Robert Bly, Bill Cosby, Jack Kornfield, Linda Leonard, Marion Woodman.
How to Father a Successful Daughter, Nicky Marone (New York: McGraw-Hill, 1988).

In a Different Voice: Psychological Theory and Women's Development, Carol Gilligan (Cambridge, MA: Harvard University Press, 1982).

Mothers and Daughters: Loving and Letting Go, Evelyn Bassoff (New York: Penguin, 1988).

Mothers and Sons, Carol Klein (Boston: Houghton Mifflin, 1984).

The Nurturing Father: Journey Toward the Complete Man, Kyle Pruett (New York: Warner, 1987).

Parenting Together, Diane Ehrensaft (New York: Free Press/Macmillan, 1987).

Raising a Daughter: Parents and the Awakening of a Healthy Woman, Jeanne Elium and Don Elium (Berkeley, CA: Celestial Arts, 1994).

Raising a Son: Parents and the Making of a Healthy Man, Don Elium and Jeanne Elium (Hillsboro, OR: Beyond Words Publishing, 1992).

Recreating Motherhood: Ideology and Technology in a Patriarchal Society, Barbara Katz Rothman (New York: Norton, 1989).

The Reproduction of Mothering: Psychoanalysis and the Sociology of Gender, Nancy Chodorow (Berkeley: University of California Press, 1978).

The Wounded Woman: Healing the Father-Daughter Relationship, Linda Leonard (Athens, OH: Swallow Press, 1982).

Puberty issues

Girltalk: All the Stuff Your Sister Never Told You, Carol Weston (New York: HarperCollins, 1992). Gordon Clay of the National Men's Resource Center suggests this as "a great book for dads to read and then give to their daughters."

What's Happening to Me? A Guide to Puberty, Peter Mayle and Arthur Robins (New York: Carol Publishing Group, 1989). Ages 9–12.

The What's Happening to My Body? Book for Girls: A Growing Up Guide for Parents and Daughters, Lynda Madaras (New York: Newmarket Press, 1987). Also *The What's Happening to My Body? Book for Boys* (Madaras, 1988). Ages 9–16.

CHAPTER 7. WALKING THE BOTTOM LINE
Finances and Treasures

How to Turn Your Money Life Around: The Money Book for Women, Ruth Hayden (Deerfield Beach, FL: Health Communications, 1992).

Lives on the Edge: Single Mothers and Their Children in the Other America, Valerie Polakow (Chicago: University of Chicago Press, 1993).

When the Bough Breaks: The Cost of Neglecting Our Children, Sylvia Ann Hewlett (New York: Basic, 1991).

ORGANIZATIONS

Displaced Homemakers Network
755 8th Street N.W.
Washington, D.C. 20001
(202) 347-0522

Parent Action
B & O Building
2 North Charles Street
Baltimore, MD 21201
(410) 752-1790
Parent advocacy group in public policy.

Welfare Mothers Voice
4504 N. 47th Street
Milwaukee, WI 53218
(414) 444-0220
$15 subscription.

CHAPTER 8. WORKING AROUND OUR CHILDREN
Care and Childcare

Daycare (rev. ed.), Alison Clarke-Stewart (Cambridge, MA: Harvard University Press, 1993).

Growing a Business, Raising a Family, Jan Fletcher, ed. (Astoria, OR: Next Step Publishing, 1988).

The Handbook for Latchkey Children and Their Parents, Lynette and
Thomas Long (New York: Arbor House, 1983).

Immaculate Deception 2: Birth and Beyond, Suzanne Arms (Berkeley,
CA: Celestial Arts, 1993).

*Nannies, Au Pairs, Mothers' Helpers — Caregivers: The Complete
Guide to Home Child Care,* Lin Yeiser (New York: Random
House, 1987).

The 100 Best Companies to Work For in America, Robert Levering
and Milton Moskowitz (New York: Doubleday, 1993).

Working Parent, Happy Child, Caryle Waller Krueger (Nashville,
TN: Abingdon Press, 1990).

"100 Best Companies for Working Mothers," Milton Moskowitz and
Carol Townsend, Annual Surveys in *Working Mother* magazine.

ABUSE ISSUES

Please Tell! A Child's Story About Sexual Abuse, Jessie (Center City,
MN: Hazelden Foundation, 1991). Ages 4–10.

Protect Your Child from Sexual Abuse: A Parent's Guide, Janie Hart-
Rossi (Seattle, WA: Parenting Press, 1984). Accompanies *It's My
Body,* Lory Freeman (Parenting Press, 1982). Ages 3–7.

ORGANIZATIONS

Child Care Action Campaign
330 Seventh Avenue, 17th Floor
New York, NY 10001-5010
(212) 239-0138

Child Care Aware
National Association of Child Care Resource and Referral Agencies
(Funded by Dayton-Hudson)
(800) 424-2246
For resources and help in seeking quality childcare in your commu-
nity.

Children's Defense Fund
25 E Street N.W.
Washington, D.C. 20001

The Fatherhood Project
c/o The Families and Work Institute

330 - 7th Avenue, 14th Floor
New York, NY 10001
(212) 268-4846

School-Age Child Care Project
Center for Research on Women
Wellesley College
Wellesley, MA 02181
(617) 283-2547
Write for information and resources, indicating specific interests.

Telephone reassurance lines for latchkey children exist in many cities nationwide. These are often staffed by senior citizens. To find them in your community, call your local United Way, the school system, the Department of Human Services, or your local Area Agency on Aging. Grandma Please, a highly successful and well-organized program, provides comprehensive information on how to replicate the model in your own community. Write to them at 4520 North Beacon Street, Chicago, IL 60640; (312) 561-3500. The local hotline is (312) 271-0000.

CHAPTER 9. WHEN OUR CHILDREN ARE OUR FRIENDS
Love and Limits

The Continuum Concept: Allowing Human Nature to Work Successfully (rev. ed.), Jean Liedloff (Reading, MA: Addison-Wesley, 1985).
The Family Bed, Tine Thevenin (Wayne, NJ: Avery Publishing Group, 1987).
For Your Own Good: Hidden Cruelty in Child-Rearing and the Roots of Violence, Alice Miller (New York: Farrar, Straus and Giroux, 1984).
401 Ways to Get Your Kids to Work at Home, Bonnie Runyan McCullough and Susan Walker Monson (New York: St. Martin's, 1981).
Healthy Sleep Habits, Happy Child, Marc Weissbluth (New York: Ballantine, 1987).
How to Talk So Kids Will Listen and Listen So Kids Will Talk, Adele Faber and Elaine Mazlish (New York: Avon, 1982). Also *Siblings Without Rivalry* (Avon, 1988).

The Intimate Circle: The Sexual Dynamics of the Family, Miriam and Otto Ehrenberg (New York: Simon & Schuster, 1988).

The Magical Child: Rediscovering Nature's Plan for Our Children, Joseph Chilton Pearce (New York: Bantam, 1980). Also "Joseph Chilton Pearce's Complete Guide to Understanding Childhood," a set of four audiotapes, with Phylicia Rashad. Enhanced Audio Systems, (800) 321-3279.

The One Minute Mother: The Quickest Way for You to Help Your Children Learn to Like Themselves and Want to Behave Themselves, Spencer Johnson & Co. (New York: Morrow, 1983). Also *The One Minute Father.*

Organize Your Family! Simple Routines for You and Your Kids, Ronni Eisenberg with Kate Kelly (New York: Hyperion, 1993).

The Parent Handbook, A Systematic Training for Effective Parenting (STEP), Don Dinkmeyer and Gary McKay (Circle Pines, MN: The American Guidance Service, 1982). AGS publishes a series of workbooks for enhancing parenting skills.

P.E.T.: Parent Effectiveness Training, Thomas Gordon (New York: Penguin, 1970); Effectiveness Training, 531 Stevens Avenue, Solana Beach, CA 92075; (619) 481-8121.

Positive Discipline, Jane Nelsen (New York: Ballantine, 1987).

Questions from Dad: A Very Cool Way to Communicate with Kids, Dwight Twilley (Boston: Charles Tuttle, 1994).

Raising a Daughter: Parents and the Awakening of a Healthy Woman, Jeanne Elium and Don Elium (Berkeley, CA: Celestial Arts, 1994).

Raising a Son: Parents and the Making of a Healthy Man, Don Elium and Jeanne Elium (Hillsboro, OR: Beyond Words Publishing, 1992).

Raising Self-Reliant Children in a Self-Indulgent World, H. Stephen Glenn and Jane Nelson (Rocklin, CA: Prima Publishing and Communications, 1989).

Stop Struggling with Your Child, Evonne Weinhaus and Karen Friedman (New York: HarperCollins, 1991). Also *Stop Struggling with Your Teen.*

Whole Child/Whole Parent, Polly Berrien Berends (New York: Harper & Row, 1987).

Your Child's Self-Esteem: Step-by-Step Guidelines for Raising Responsible, Productive, Happy Children, Dorothy Corkille Briggs (New York: Dolphin/Doubleday, 1975).

FOR CHILDREN

Bringing Up Parents: The Teenager's Handbook, Alex J. Packer (Minneapolis, MN: Free Spirit Publishing, 1992).
Communication, Aliki (New York: Greenwillow, 1993).

CHAPTER 10. DILEMMAS OF THE HEART
Dating and Seeking a Partner

Genderspeak, Suzette Haden Elgin (New York: Wiley, 1993).
Journey of the Heart: Intimate Relationship and the Path of Love, John Welwood (New York: HarperCollins, 1991).
Keeping the Love You Find: A Guide for Singles, Harville Hendrix (New York: Simon & Schuster, 1992).
Making It as Stepparents: New Roles/New Rules, Claire Berman (New York: Harper & Row, 1986).
Women's Reality: An Emerging Female, Anne Wilson Schaef (New York: Harper Paperbacks, 1991).
Why Men Are the Way They Are, Warren Farrell (New York: McGraw-Hill, 1986).
You Just Don't Understand: Women and Men in Conversation, Deborah Tannen (New York: Ballantine, 1990).

FOR CHILDREN

Changing Families: A Guide for Kids and Grown-Ups, David Fassler, Michelle Lash, and Sally B. Ives (Burlington, VT: Waterfront Books, 1988). Workbook format. Ages 4–12.
My Mother's Getting Married, Joan Drescher (New York: Dial/Pied Piper Books, 1986). Picture book.
My Real Family: A Child's Book About Living in a Step-Family, Doris Sanford (Sisters, OR: Questar Publishers, 1993). Picture book.

ORGANIZATION

Stepfamily Association of America
215 Centennial Mall South
Suite 212
Lincoln, NE 68508
(402) 477-7837

CHAPTER 11. THERE IS ALWAYS AN OTHER
Talking To and About the Other Parent

Families Apart: Ten Keys to Successful Co-Parenting, Melinda Blau (New York: G. P. Putnam's Sons, 1994).

Getting to Yes, Roger Fisher and William Ury (Boston: Houghton Mifflin, 1981).

Getting Together, Roger Fisher and Scott Brown (New York: Penguin, 1988).

Mom's House, Dad's House: Making Shared Custody Work, Isolina Ricci (New York: Collier, 1980).

People Skills: How to Assert Yourself, Listen to Others, and Resolve Conflict, Robert Bolton (New York: Simon & Schuster, 1986).

Resolving Conflicts: With Others and Within Yourself, Gini Graham Scott (Oakland, CA: New Harbinger Publications, 1990).

The newsletters and magazines for single parents listed in the General Resources section address issues of co-parenting and how to talk to children about their other parent. Many of the books listed for Chapter 1 for divorced, separated, and bereaved families also cover these subjects. For a discussion of various scenarios for those who chose single parenthood, see Jane Mattes, *Single Mothers by Choice* (New York: Times Books, 1994).

FOR CHILDREN

At Daddy's on Saturdays, Linda Walvoord Girard (Morton Grove, IL: Albert Whitman & Company, 1987). Picture book.

Do I Have a Daddy?, Jeanne Warren Lindsay (Buena Park, CA: Morning Glory Press, 1982). This illustrated book for young children addresses the questions of the child of an unmarried mother. The author's note to parents is the best part of the book, with examples of how to talk with a child in several different circumstances.

My Mother's House, My Father's House, C. B. Christiansen (New York: Viking, 1990).

ORGANIZATIONS

Children's Rights Council
220 I Street N.E., #230
Washington, D.C. 20002
(202) 547-6227

Communications Options Training Programs
398 - 61st Street
Oakland, CA 94618
(510) 655-2126

The Joint Custody Association
10606 Wilkins Avenue
Los Angeles, CA 90024
(213) 475-5352

CHAPTER 12. NO ONE CAN BE A SINGLE PARENT
Extending the Family

Communities

Cohousing: A Contemporary Approach to Housing Ourselves (2d ed.), Kathryn McCamant, Charles Durrett, and Ellen Hertzman (Berkeley, CA: Ten Speed Press, 1993).

Collaborative Communities: Cohousing, Central Living, and Other Forms of New Housing, Dorit Fromm (New York: Van Nostrand Reinhold, 1991).

Communities: Journal of Cooperative Living, c/o Sandhill Farm, Route 1, Box 155-M, Rutledge, MO 63563.

Creating Community Anywhere: Finding Support and Connection in a Fragmented World, Carolyn R. Shaffer and Kristin Anundsen (New York: Tarcher/Perigee, 1993).

The Different Drum: Community-Making and Peace, M. Scott Peck (New York: Simon & Schuster, 1987).

Families We Choose: Lesbians, Gays, Kinship, Kath Weston (New York: Columbia University Press, 1991).

"Follow the Dirt Road," video on alternative intentional communities, by Monique Gauthier, 1325 West 27th St., #306, Minneapolis, MN 55408; (612) 872-8338.

Intentional Communities: A Guide to Cooperative Living, 1993. Fellowship for Intentional Community, Betty Didcoct, P.O. Box 814, Langley, WA 98260.

New Households, New Housing, Karen Franck and Sherry Ahrentzen, eds. (New York: Van Nostrand Reinhold, 1989).

Rebuilding Community in America: Housing for Ecological Living, Personal Empowerment, and the New Extended Family, Ken Norwood and Kathleen Smith (Berkeley, CA: Shared Living Resource Center, 1994).

ORGANIZATIONS

The Cohousing Company
1250 Addison, Suite 113
Berkeley, CA 94702
(510) 549-9980

Cooperative Resources and Services Project
3551 Whitehouse Place
Los Angeles, CA 90004
(213) 738-1254

Shared Living Resource Center
2375 Shattuck Avenue
Berkeley, CA 94704
(510) 548-6608
Provides counseling, workshops, and resources on shared living and community-building skills; also community housing designs.

Mentoring

The Kindness of Strangers: Adult Mentors, Urban Youth, and the New Voluntarism, Marc Freedman (New York: Jossey-Bass/Macmillan, 1993). Focuses on the experience of mentors and young people. Includes suggestions on how mentors can be most effective.

ORGANIZATIONS

Big Brothers/Big Sisters of America
230 N. 13th Street
Philadelphia, PA 19107
(215) 567-7000
Local offices often have information on other mentoring programs as well.

International Youth Council
c/o Parents Without Partners
7910 Woodmont Avenue, Suite 1000
Bethesda, MD 20814
(800) 638-8078

National Media Outreach Center
4802 Fifth Avenue
Pittsburgh, PA 15213
(412) 622-1491
Free materials on mentoring.

National Rainbow Coalition
1700 K Street N.W.
Washington, D.C. 20006
(202) 728-1180
National program for African-American youth, 8–18 years old.

One to One
2801 M Street N.W.
Washington, D.C. 20007
(202) 338-3844
Information for adults interested in being mentors; programs established in Atlanta, Boston, Detroit, Long Island, Los Angeles, Newark, New York City, Omaha, Philadelphia, and Richmond.

United Way, First Call for Help lists mentoring programs. Call your local office for referrals.

Childhood's Future: Listening to the American Family, Richard Louv
(Boston: Houghton Mifflin, 1990).
You and Your Grown-Up Child: Nurturing a Better Relationship,
Howard M. Halpern (New York: Simon & Schuster, 1992).

GENERAL RESOURCES

Organizations

National Men's Resource Center
P.O. Box 800-PR
San Anselmo, CA 94979
(415) 453-2389
Excellent resource for fathering and men's issues: books, support
groups across the nation, newsletters and periodicals, father-daughter
rites of passage.

National Organization of Single Mothers
P.O. Box 68
Midland, NC 28107-0068
(704) 888-5063
Ample how-to information for single mothers (and mothering fathers) with emphasis on connecting individuals with local self-help
and support groups. Publishes *Single Mother* magazine.

Parents Without Partners
401 North Michigan Ave.
Chicago, IL 60611
(312) 644-6610
Local chapters across the nation for support and social activities with
emerging focus on public policy issues. *Single Parent* magazine comes
with membership. International Youth Council focuses on support
and activities for teens in single-parent families.

Single Mothers by Choice (SMC)
P.O. Box 1642
Gracie Square Station
New York, NY 10028
(212) 988-0993
Provides newsletter, support, and resources for women who choose
to be single parents. Support groups in many states and Canada
emphasize positive aspects of parenting alone; some local groups also
welcome single fathers.

Single Parent Resource Center
141 West 28th St., Suite 302
New York, NY 10001
(212) 947-0221
Referrals to services and support groups for single parents across the
nation; information and materials, including self-help group-develop-
ment manual.

OTHER RELEVANT ORGANIZATIONS

Gay and Lesbian Parents Coalition, International (GLPCI)
Box 50360
Washington, D.C. 20091
(202) 583-8029
GLPCI also sponsors a newsletter and group called COLAGE, Children
of Lesbians and Gays Everywhere.

Mothers Without Custody
P.O. Box 27418
Houston, TX 77227
(800) 457-6962

Books

One on the Seesaw: The Ups and Downs of a Single-Parent Family,
    Carol Lynn Pearson (New York: Random House, 1988).
Operating Instructions: A Journal of My Son's First Year, Anne La-
    mott (New York: Pantheon, 1993).
Single Fathers, Geoffrey L. Greif (Lexington, MA: Lexington Books-
    D. C. Heath, 1985).

The Single Fathers' Handbook: A Guide for Separated and Divorced Fathers, Richard Gatley and David Koulack (New York: Anchor/Doubleday, 1979). Out of print but available through public libraries.

The Single Mother's Book: A Practical Guide to Managing Your Children, Career, Home, Finances, and Everything Else, Joan Anderson (Atlanta: Peachtree Publishers, 1990).

Single Mothers by Choice, Jane Mattes (New York: Times Books, 1994). Written by a therapist and single mother, this is a how-to book for those considering and those who have already chosen single motherhood; focus on emotional ramifications.

Solo Parenting: Your Essential Guide, Kathleen McCoy (New York: Penguin, 1987).

Successful Single Parenting: A Practical Guide, Anne Wayman (Deephaven, MN: Meadowbrook, 1987).

ALSO OF INTEREST

Different and Wonderful: Raising Black Children in a Race-Conscious Society, Darlene Powell Hopson and Derek S. Hopson (New York: Simon & Schuster, 1992). Also valuable for anyone parenting transracial and transnational children.

Mothers Without Custody, Geoffrey Greif and Mary S. Pabst (Lexington, MA: Lexington Books/D. C. Heath, 1988).

Wake Up Little Susie: Single Pregnancy and Race Before Roe vs. Wade, Rickie Solinger (New York: Routledge, 1992).

The Way We Never Were: American Families and the Nostalgia Trap, Stephanie Coontz (New York: Basic, 1992).

Books for Children

A Chair for My Mother, Vera Williams (New York: Morrow, 1988). Also by Vera Williams, *Something Special for Me* (New York: Morrow, 1986). Illustrated; multicultural children with single mothers.

Families, Meredith Tax (Boston: Little, Brown, 1981). Illustrated.

Families Are Different, Nina Pellegrini (New York: Holiday House, 1991). Illustrated.

How to Live with a Single Parent, Sara Gilbert (New York: Lothrop, Lee & Shepard, 1982). Ages 9 and up.

How Would You Feel If Your Dad Was Gay?, Ann Heron and

Meredith Maran (Boston: MA: Alyson Publications, 1991). Ages 6–12.

The Kids' Book About Single-Parent Families, Paul Dolmetsch and Alexa Shik (New York: Doubleday, 1985). Ages 10–14.

Living with a Single Parent, Maxine B. Rosenberg (New York: Bradbury Press, 1992). Ages 8–12.

My Kind of Family: A Book for Kids in Single-Parent Homes, Michele Lash, Sally Ives Loughridge, and David Fassler (Burlington, VT: Waterfront Books, 1990). Workbook format.

Some of these and many other books "to help children [and parents] deal with life's challenges" are available from:

Waterfront Books for Kids and Parents
85 Crescent Road
Burlington, VT 05401-4126
(800) 639-6063

For an extensive selection on all parenting issues:
Imprints
Newsletter/Catalog of the Birth & Life Bookstore
7001 Alonzo Ave. N.W.
P.O. Box 70625
Seattle, WA 98107-0625
(800) 736-0631

Periodicals

Full-Time Dads
The Journal for Caring Fathers
P.O. Box 577
Cumberland, ME 04021
(207) 829-5260
Includes many articles for single fathers and resources for support.

Single Mother
(Publication of the National Organization of Single Mothers)
P.O. Box 68
Midland, NC 28107-0068
Call (704) 888-KIDS for free back issue.

Single Mothers by Choice
(Newsletter of the national organization)
P.O. Box 1642, Gracie Square Station
New York, NY 10028
(212) 988-0993

The Single Parent
(Journal of Parents Without Partners)
401 North Michigan Ave.
Chicago, IL 60611
(312) 644-6610

OTHER RELEVANT PERIODICALS

Biracial Child
P.O. Box 12048
Atlanta, GA 30355-2048
(404) 364-9690

Mothering
P.O. Box 1690
Santa Fe, NM 87504
(505) 984-8116

Working Mother
230 Park Ave.
New York, NY 10169
Subscriptions: Customer Service Manager
P.O. Box 5239
Harlan, IA 51593-0739